FOR THE COMMON GOOD AND THEIR OWN WELL-BEING

For the Common Good and Their Own Well-Being

SOCIAL ESTATES IN IMPERIAL RUSSIA

Alison K. Smith

UNIVERSITY PRESS

Oxford University Press is a department of the University of Oxford. It furthers
the University's objective of excellence in research, scholarship, and education
by publishing worldwide. Oxford is a registered trade mark of Oxford University
Press in the UK and certain other countries.

Published in the United States of America by Oxford University Press
198 Madison Avenue, New York, NY 10016, United States of America.

Library of Congress Cataloging-in-Publication Data
Smith, Alison Karen.
For the common good and their own well-being: social estates in Imperial Russia /
Alison K. Smith.   pages cm.   Includes bibliographical references and index.
ISBN 978-0-19-997817-5 (hardcover : alkaline paper); 978-0-19-093962-5 (paperback : alkaline paper)
1. Estates (Social orders)—Russia—History— 18th century.   2. Estates (Social orders)—Russia—History—
19th century.   3. Peasants—Russia—History.   4. Community life—Russia—History.   5. Group
identity—Russia—History.   6. Taxation—Social aspects—Russia—History.   7. Russia—Social
life and customs—1533-1917.   8. Russia—Social conditions—18th century.   9. Russia—Social
conditions—1801-1917.   10. Russia—Social policy.   I. Title.   HN523.S59 2015
306.094709033—dc23
2014016790

Contents

Preface and Acknowledgments

I did not expect to write a book about the institution of *soslovie* in imperial Russia. In May 1998, I traveled to Kazan' to do dissertation research at the National Archive of the Republic of Tatarstan. While I was there, I ordered files from the Kazan' city artisan's society, hoping to find information about bakers and others engaged in the food trades. Instead, I found requests by individuals to leave the society and to take on new *soslovie* identities. My interest was piqued, and I kept at the back of my mind that there might be more interesting materials to do with social mobility in local archives.

Then, half a decade later, I found myself thinking about a second major research project at nearly the same time that it was announced that the Russian State Historical Archive (RGIA) would be closing for an unspecified amount of time. I remembered my experience in Kazan', and started planning a project that would focus on regional and local archives. I initially conceptualized the project as a study of social mobility in imperial Russia, and I thought it would be a quick project, gathering the few records I might find in some number of local archives.

On my very first trip to start archival research on the project, however, I found so much more. On that trip, in 2007, I worked in local archives in Moscow, St. Petersburg, Tver', Riazan', and Saratov. I found not the tens or hundreds of cases I thought might be there but, instead, thousands upon thousands of them. And I found that they were about much more than I had initially expected. The detail in some records brought the individual lives of the little people of the past to vivid life. And, too, rather than being simply a way to trace patterns of social mobility, the individual cases brought out the meaning of *soslovie* more broadly. By finding the moments when people changed their status, I also found what they meant by those statuses.

Fortunately, I was also able to return to Russia for several more trips. These later trips gave me the opportunity to travel to another local archive, in Iaroslavl', and also to move out beyond the bounds of the current Russian state. I traveled to Riga and Vilnius, in part to try to follow up on one particular story (the story of émigré fugitives who returned to Russia), and in part to see how far the issues I had seen elsewhere in the empire traveled.

Even more important, these later trips occurred after RGIA had reopened. There, in the records of imperial ministries, I found yet more visions of what *soslovie* meant, both to individuals and to government institutions. Virtually every file I ordered contained some new vision of what *soslovie* meant, and I quickly realized that the story I had to tell was not just one of social mobility; it had much broader import. Although the idea of movement is still a theme throughout this book, it has grown to be about that larger system of *soslovie*, the system that gave status and opportunities, but that restricted mobility and set the boundaries of every individual imperial life.

In the course of researching and writing this book, I have accrued many debts, fortunately ones of friendship and aid rather than those of soul taxes and other duties that plagued so many of those I have written about in these pages. First, I received funding to carry out research for this project from the Summer Research Lab at the University of Illinois, Urbana-Champaign; from the International Research and Exchange Board; from the University of Toronto through its Connaught fund; and from the Social Sciences and Humanities Research Council of Canada. Given the archive-heavy nature of this project, this funding has been absolutely necessary for carrying out its research.

While in Russia, I worked at a number of archives and libraries, and must give thanks to all their staff. They include: in Moscow, the Russian State Archive of Ancient Acts, the Central Historical Archive of Moscow, the Russian State Library and its Manuscript Division, and the State Public Historical Library of Russia (whose cinnamon pastries fueled much of my work); in St. Petersburg, the Russian State Historical Archive, the Central State Historical Archive of St. Petersburg, and the Russian National Library; in Tver', the State Archive of Tver' Region; in Saratov, the State Archive of Saratov Region; in Riazan', the State Archive of Riazan' Region; in Iaroslavl', the State Archive of Iaroslavl' Region; in Riga the Latvian State Historical Archive; and in Vilnius the Lithuanian State Historical Archive. I should also give special thanks to the Russian National Library for its project of digitizing the *Complete Collection of the Laws of the Russian Empire*, giving wide access to this boundless source of information on imperial Russia. I must also thank Emma Antselevich for her friendship and enthusiasm.

I have presented parts of this book at a long series of workshops and conferences, and feedback from audiences and commenters has helped it develop. These include the Russian History Workshop at the University of Chicago; the Pogrankom held at Carleton University; meetings of AAASS/ASEEES in Philadelphia, Washington, D.C., and New Orleans; the conference Europe in Upheaval: The Era of the Napoleonic Wars, in Espoo, Finland; at the European Social Science History Conference, Lisbon; at the Women's History Network Conference, Oxford; at the conference Mass Sources for the Study of the Social and Economic History of Russia, Moscow; at the Midwest Russian History Workshop in Madison and Evanston; and in talks at the University of California, Riverside, the University of California, Berkeley, and at the University of Rochester. This is an incomplete list of those whose questions and comments have been helpful as I have presented and discussed this work, and my apologies go to anyone I may have omitted: Sergei Antonov, Kate Pickering Antonova, John Bushnell, Prachi Desphande, Sheila Fitzpatrick, Victoria Frede, Boris Gorshkov, Richard Hellie, Elizabeth Jones, Aleksandr Kaplunovskii, Matthew Lenoe, Andrei Markevich, Alexander Martin, David McDonald, Tracy McDonald, Harsha Ram, David Ransel, John Randolph, Alison Rowley, Christine Ruane, David Schimmelpenninck, Mark Steinberg, Charles Steinwedel, Thaddeus Sunseri, Kiril Tomoff, Galina Ulianova, Christine Worobec.

Just before I started real work on this project I moved to the University of Toronto. Teaching here has led to work with inspiring colleagues and students. Colleagues, including especially Lynne Viola, Doris Bergen, Donna Tussing Orwin, Heidi Bohaker, and Carol Chin, have let me talk through ideas and given sensible advice. Leo Livak told me I wouldn't be able to understand *soslovie* until looked at Chekhov, and I thank him for that. Alex Rowlson gave me research assistance. Students in one graduate class asked probing questions about *soslovie* exactly when I was first trying to articulate the book's overall approach to the subject—I have to especially thank Sarah Rutley, Roxane Samson-Paquet, and Francesca Silano. A student-organized reading group also gave me feedback on the introduction—thanks to Anka Hajkova, Lilia Topouzova, Seth Bernstein, Vojin Majstorovic, Kristina Pauksens, Zbigniew Wojnowski. Thanks also go to Sonya Tycko, Rebecca Hecht, and Nancy Toff at Oxford University Press for seeing me through the process of finishing the book, and to the reviewers for the press, whose generous comments helped make the final book better.

Final thanks should go to my parents, Rosemary and David Smith, to my sister and brother-in-law, Amy and Matt McGowen, and to my niece and nephew, Megan and Ben McGowan, who are about as old as this manuscript now is, and who are far more fun than any two such small people have any right to be.

FOR THE COMMON GOOD AND THEIR OWN WELL-BEING

Introduction

BY THE END of the nineteenth century, Moscow had become a city where the drama of late imperial Russia's modernization played out at virtually every level of society, on virtually every street. The city had already experienced significant change over the past century, as its streets were lighted and cleaned, as its populations swelled in numbers and shifted in composition, and as local governance was reformed again and again. Now in the second half of the century, Moscow's merchants were leaving behind the supposed "dark kingdom" of their past and becoming the philanthropists and collectors who would transform the city's cultural world. Even its streets took on a new mien, as advertising came to adorn many facades, promising a new, modern, and outward-looking world. At the same time, huge influxes of peasant workers dwarfed similar movement from earlier years, altering the world of Moscow's geographical and social fringes, and re-traditionalizing the city, to the consternation of some observers.[1] The city was expanding and changing, becoming at once more ordered and more unruly, more modern and more archaic.

The persistence of *sosloviia*—of official social estates or statuses, usually based on birth, that defined individual rights and duties vis-à-vis the state and other subjects of the tsar—into this period encapsulated many of these opposites. Although *soslovie* membership meant different things at different times, it consistently defined the kind of taxes one paid, the kind of duties one owed the state, the kind of legal process one was entitled to, and the economic and educational opportunities available to one. It also consistently meant ascription not simply into a broad category or status but also into a specific, local society (*obshchestvo*) associated with a town, a village, or a province. Although they clearly still existed, at the end of the nineteenth century these identities had been often understood as obsolescent, if not totally obsolete relics from earlier times. By 1909 the legal scholar N. M. Korkunov could even claim that "it is not unusual to meet a man who does not himself know to which *soslovie* he belongs."[2]

Despite this, *soslovie* identity still mattered—to individual subjects of the Russian empire, to local administrations, and to the imperial state based in St. Petersburg. Even through the late nineteenth century, and, indeed, through the early twentieth century as well, many individuals sought to alter their *soslovie* identity by leaving behind the *soslovie* of their birth and by entering a new one. That process involved literal ascription onto the membership rolls of a specific local society. And the whole concept was governed by rules put forward by St. Petersburg, as it consistently demanded that all subjects have an official place within the larger society.

Nowhere was that confluence of continued relevance and perceived obsolescence more visible than in Moscow. Like today, Moscow's unofficial population crowded its streets far beyond its official numbers, but those official numbers—in particular, those who were formally registered as *meshchane*, or lower-ranking townspeople, not merchants—were still enormous. Their numbers were far too large to consider or administer as a single whole, and so Moscow's townsperson society was subdivided into a number of separate groups. This was normal practice; according to a mid-century journalist, in "heavily populated cities," *soslovie*-based societies were usually divided by "police districts."[3] In Moscow, however, a different system ruled. Moscow's townsperson (and merchant) society was divided, not according to the police districts that governed most town functions, but instead by *sloboda*, an earlier division by, roughly, suburb or neighborhood, that most accounts claimed had disappeared early in the eighteenth century.[4] In pre-Petrine Russia, this term had been associated with specific populations linked to particular places, particular economic activities, or particular services to the state.[5] Because these suburbs had implications similar to those of *soslovie* (regulating taxes and other duties), it was perhaps natural that the term persisted in connection to these newer categories. Even so, the continued use of the term emphasized the perceived archaic nature of *soslovie* in a world increasingly influenced by other social divisions, be they class, religion, or ethnicity.

The shifts in just one year, in just one *soslovie*, in just one suburb of Moscow, demonstrate the many ways that individuals could govern their own *soslovie* identities. In 1870, 136 individual heads of household (94 men and 42 women) were entered onto the rolls of the *meshchanin* (townsperson) society of Sretenskaia neighborhood.[6] Most of them (76 percent) brought with them family members, so the actual number of new townspeople entering the society in that year was far higher. In one way, this was an unusual year: 58 of the men came from military backgrounds, mostly soldiers freed from service as part of the run-up to the major army reform that would take place four years later.[7] Although this influx was something singular, it represents a much longer history of groups, sometimes large ones, who had to choose a new *soslovie* when their old one disappeared or was taken from them. At various points during the eighteenth and nineteenth centuries, those included large groups like manumitted serfs during the time of serfdom or smaller ones like fugitives who were granted amnesty.[8]

More than a third of the new townspeople were peasants by birth. They were just a few of the thousands of migrant peasants who flooded the capital each year, and they represent the most familiar variation of a story of social mobility: rural–urban mobility.[9] Theirs is a particular version of that mobility, however. In contrast to the idea of those who were still both peasant and worker, or "*muzhik* and Muscovite," these peasants by birth chose to fix their status and their place of residence in the town. They were thus legally removed from their status and place of origin, and were now full members of the town society in which they lived. Of course, they might still hold on to rural connections of family and even of work patterns, but their formal status now placed them firmly in Moscow.

A smaller number of the new townspeople came from other town *sosloviia*, usually merchants demoted to the status of townsperson. They, in contrast to the peasants, reflected a kind of downward social mobility, as the movement from merchant to townsperson was a clear sign of social (and financial) failure. Merchants were classified among those with certain privileges that townspeople lacked; losing that status was a demotion, one that had long been feared by many merchants. This kind of movement also reflected another persistent trope of *sosloviia*: that in some cases, they were governed by rules that removed individual agency from mobility. Status as a merchant depended on financial well-being; those who failed were demoted not by choice, but by law.

A final group of new townspeople were those with no prior *soslovie* identity at all. Registering the unregistered had been a goal of central mandates from the early eighteenth century, and had by this point created a society in which nearly everyone had an official place, even if they sometimes preferred to ignore it.[10] In this Moscow group, the few remaining unregistered were all young, ranging in age from seven to twenty-three, and had all been born into a certain social limbo, either because their fathers had status that could not be inherited or because their birth was illegitimate. Their entry onto the rolls of the townsperson society gave them an official place within Russia's *soslovie* society. Among them was a seven-year-old girl named Elena Sergeevna Tolstaia, who appears in the record books as "a foundling of unknown parentage living as a ward of Count Tolstoy." She was registered as a member of the society of townspeople in 1870, and remained there until her marriage in 1893. In reality, Elena Sergeevna was the illegitimate child of Count Lev Tolstoy's sister Mariia, born of her mother's affair with a foreign nobleman.[11] Despite her noble parentage, Elena Sergeevna had no official place in Russian society because she could not inherit that nobility from either her mother or her foreign father. As a result, she, like the other illegitimate children from far less exalted families, had to find an official place as a simple townswoman.

As these cases demonstrate, looking at the choices that individuals made about their own *soslovie* identity (or, in the case of children like Elena Sergeeva, the choices people made for them), at the local authorities who accepted or rejected them, and at the laws that constricted those choices illuminates the structures of imperial Russia's society of social estates. It does so in two ways. First, individual choices to change *soslovie* reflect not only experiences of social mobility in imperial Russia but also the changing value of *soslovie* identities.[12] Second, the legislation and administration of the process of changing *soslovie* provide a unique vision of the interrelationship of the many different elements of the larger society.[13] As laws described the process of changing *soslovie*, they also defined the boundaries of individual *sosloviia*.[14]

These two themes play out on three levels at which the institution of *soslovie* had meaning. The first level is the central, imperial state of the tsars, the ministries, and other administrative bodies in the capitals. Over and over, from early in the eighteenth century through to the First World War itself, these organs of the imperial state variously developed, changed, or reaffirmed the notion that *soslovie* administration and membership was and should be part of the larger Russian social world. The consistency of central interest in the institution of *soslovie* does not mean a consistency in practice, of course. From at least the early eighteenth century, the central administration had been conflicted in its relationship with the institution of *soslovie* because of its mixed desires for stability and mobility. On the one hand, central authorities wanted the imperial population to stay fixed, so resources could be extracted and stability ensured. On the other, territorial acquisition and the changing economic world demanded mobility, as new places and new industries needed bodies to settle or staff them. Over and over through the imperial period, central decisions dealt with this conflict by allowing certain bureaucratic means of mobility, either temporarily through passports or more permanently through changing *soslovie* membership.[15] But despite moments, particularly in the post-Reform period, when one ministry or another challenged the entire institution of *soslovie*, never did the central state as a whole ever come close to eliminating this form of social structure. The state maintained the *soslovie* system in part out of a desire to protect noble privilege, but also out of an inability to conceptualize what rural and urban society might be like without their networks of separate *soslovie* societies.

At the second level were many local authorities based in towns and villages, as well as intermediaries at the provincial level, whose interests and actions were based in their own understandings of *sosloviia*. *Soslovie* identities were just as much geographical identities as they were social ones. An individual's membership in a *soslovie* was based not simply on the larger social category of peasant, merchant, or noble, but equally on the specific place in which that individual membership was located. A generic Ivan Ivanov was not simply a generic peasant; he was a peasant from a particular township (*volost'*) and village (or, in an earlier era, belonging to a particular owner). A generic Anna Pavlova was not simply a townswoman; she was a townswoman from a particular town. And they were not simply "from" these places, but also members of the societies—*obshchestva*—of these towns or villages, listed in registry books or on tax rolls, written in and out at birth, marriage, imprisonment, or by petition. As a result, local authorities in towns and provinces became central to the regulation and administration of *sosloviia* and of *soslovie* membership, as it was they who had authority over freeing their members or accepting new ones. Their concerns changed through the imperial period, as did their duties and their role in the governance of society at large, but they remained an active part of the imperial social world even past the end of the Romanov dynasty.

At the third level were the individuals who possessed and who tried to change *soslovie* identities. They were those who found value not simply in moving to a new place temporarily, or even semi-permanently, on passports. Instead, they were those who desired to find an official position in their new environs by formally joining a local *soslovie* society. As such, their petitions are examples of a kind of official social mobility that was widespread throughout the Empire, and throughout the imperial period. Mobility of various kinds, both official and unofficial, was prevalent in imperial Russia. Wanderers and vagrants were perpetual problems in the eyes of the central state, even if passports allowed for official mobility, as well. But the individuals who petitioned were looking not to wander, but to transform their station in life. They were the many individual Russians and non-Russians, both male and female, who took advantage of the central state's decisions allowing for movement between *sosloviia*. Their experiences highlight not only the patterns of social mobility in eighteenth- and nineteenth-century Russia, but also the changing nature of *soslovie* membership and identity themselves.

Any historian of *soslovie* has first of all to grapple with the word itself. Foreigners translate the term, most often using estate, *état*, or *Stand*, but also trying on caste or class. Alternatively, they translate the single word into a phrase that tries to explain the complexity of the concept: *sosloviia* become legal social categories, or legal social statuses. These issues of translation are compounded by a second problem that affects scholars both Russian and Western: the word *soslovie* was not used consistently even in imperial Russia. It could be used to describe all sorts of social groups—"the *soslovie* of boxers," "the excellent *soslovie* of women, "the *soslovie* of those who are able to read."[16] Other general terms were at times used interchanably with the term *soslovie* itself—most commonly *sostoianie* (condition) but at various points also *chin* (rank), *klass* (class), or *zvanie* (calling).[17] Even the *Digest of the Laws*, which in principle brought order to early nineteenth-century legal usage, went back and forth in its usage of *soslovie* and *sostoianiia*.[18]

In this book, therefore, *soslovie* will be used throughout to refer to the social categories that governed the rights and duties of individual Russians (and non-Russians), into which most subjects were born, but which could also be changed by extraordinary act or by bureaucratic procedure. This usage is slightly anachronistic for the earlier parts of the eighteenth century, but at least by the Legislative Commission convened by Catherine the Great in 1767 the term was in regular use, as delegates to the commission often used the term in their discussions of noble, or merchant, or other group privileges.[19] In part, this is meant to emphasize that while the concept of *soslovie* overlaps with other forms of social organization (be they class, caste, or estate), it was also unique to Russia. Moreover, it reflects the standard use of the term in much of the historiography—and the fact that, as Michael Confino put it, "although not well defined and not entirely clear, the term 'soslovie' is too well established in the historians' vocabulary to be abandoned at this late date."[20]

Perhaps because the word *soslovie* represents a concept that is notorious for its fluidity, its uncertainty, and its resistance to neat categorization, much of the historical debate over the essential composition and meaning of *sosloviia* in imperial Russian history has focused on big, broad questions. Were *sosloviia* "true" estates—"true" meaning an ideal from Western Europe involving self-consciousness and corporate rights—or something different?[21] When were they firmly established?[22] Were they rigidly defined, or amorphous and unbounded?[23] Had they lost all meaning by the time the revolutions of the early twentieth century swept them away, or had they continued to hold sway through the end of the imperial period?[24] These macro questions lead to disagreement among historians, in part because they tend to look primarily at their own specific set of sources or cases in trying to examine a large concept that encompassed such a wide range of legally, socially, and culturally distinct categories.[25] Those specific cases, drawn from specific groups, perhaps necessarily lead to different conclusions when historians seek to extrapolate larger concepts, or to identify systems or paradigms from them.

One problem has been the desire to find a single meaning for *soslovie*—even if a meaning that changed over time. But, really, *soslovie* perhaps not always, but for much of the imperial era, had at least two meanings at the same time. One was the often changing meaning of some sort of larger social group, whether that group was a "true estate" or something else. This is where the term begins to enter high-level legal debates, and to confound the best efforts of historians to describe and analyze it.[26] At the same time, however, *soslovie* was also something much more specific. A *soslovie*, or perhaps more correctly, a *soslovie* society (*soslovnoe obshchestvo*) was something that not only defined individuals in terms of their rights and privileges but also located them in a specific place.[27] And this was true beyond those subject to the soul tax—the peasants and the townspeople who paid their dues to the state communally. Descriptions of the corporate organization of Russia's nobles, for example, often focus on the fact that that organization was exclusively local.[28] Nobles were juridically—and often both socially and culturally, as well—just as geographically bound as others in imperial society.[29]

Focusing on this second meaning, of course, runs the risk of reinforcing the stereotype of the overweening autocratic state that differed from the later Soviet state only in the thoroughness of its control over its population.[30] This is the idea forcefully argued by opponents of the autocratic regime. In the 1850s, Count Gurowski argued that the generally held belief that Russia was a land of nobles and a mass of those who were either "a serf or a slave" was false. Instead, he believed, nobles, too, "join with the other classes in ragging along the iron yoke. The Czar is, in principle, an absolute unaccountable master, as well over the person of a nobleman, as over that of a burgher, a peasant, or a serf."[31]

Certainly it is true that if one were to look only at the laws governing *soslovie*, and movement between them, that might be the impression. It may be true (and probably is true) that the imperial state generally lacked a specific desire to create *sosloviia* in the sense of overarching identities, but it certainly did have one consistent goal: to leave no subject uncategorized in a *soslovie* and unregistered in a specific society.[32] But to take the end result of the laws as indicating a controlled, frozen society would be a mistake. For one, the imperial state had a simultaneous interest in allowing mobility and flexibility, one reflected in policies regarding everything from passports that allowed temporary residency away from home to permanent internal migration.[33] In addition, even those laws that strove to fix the population into categories were not always put into practice in ways that emphasized control. Instead, actual practice shows well the many ways that individuals, and even local administrations, challenged that desire to register and control, at times to the point of forcing change on the imperial state. In the end, *sosloviia* were perhaps not mutually constituted by state and society, but were defined by each, in ways that variously worked together and worked against one another.

Individual *sosloviia* could be as challenging to define as the concept more broadly. One image of the state of *sosloviia* at the end of the imperial era, from Nikolai Rubakin's statistical description of the empire, includes seven separate categories: peasants,

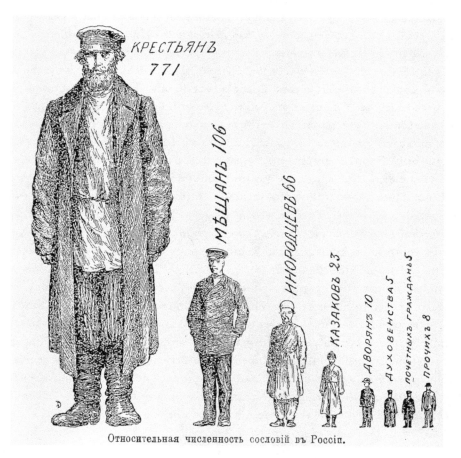

Comparative strength of *sosloviia* (official social statuses) in Russia [c. 1900]. Numbers are out of 1000. Captions from left to right are: peasants, townspeople (meshchane), non-Russians, Cossacks, nobles, priests, honored citizens, others. *N. A. Rubakin, Rossiia v tsifrakh* (St. Petersburg: Vestnik Znaniia, 1912), 53.

townspeople, aliens (*inorodtsy*), Cossacks, nobles, churchmen, and honored citizens, as well as a general "other." This listing reflects certain changes that had altered the *soslovie* structure of society by the early twentieth century. For one, peasants now were juridically a largely uniform group, while in the years of serfdom they had been divided into many separate statuses: serfs (owned by private individuals), court peasants (owned by members of the imperial family), church peasants (owned usually by an Orthodox monastery), or state peasants (owned by no person in particular, but still bound to a particular place of residence by tax and other duties). The last group sometimes went by other names; treasury (*kazennye*) peasants, for example, or economic peasants, which was the term given to former monastery peasants after church lands were seized by the state in the late eighteenth century. The transition from serfdom brought a new array of statuses, as peasants made their way through the various stages of the emancipation process. By 1912, despite the new economic divisions created by the Stolypin reforms, which altered the basis of peasant land tenure, and as a result the basis of peasant society, peasants had finally coalesced into a more unified group, in legal status, if not in occupation.[34]

Rubakin's array also shows major changes in the *soslovie* organization of residents of towns. He lists only *meshchane*, or townspeople narrowly defined—the lower ranking townspeople who historically made up the bulk of the official population of towns (that is, of those registered in towns, as opposed to peasants living there on passports)—and honored citizens, a status created in the 1830s to reward particular individual success. But merchants, who so heavily figured into laws regulating towns and their *sosloviia* in the eighteenth and nineteenth centuries, have melted into the general "other" category. This is a radical change from the way town statuses were discussed in earlier periods, when merchants were at the top of the town hierarchy; the *tsekhovye*, or artisans who belonged to a town's craft guilds, sat somewhere in the middle; and townspeople were numerically supreme, but for the most part simply members of the "forgotten *soslovie*."[35]

Two of the other small groups in Rubakin's array are nobles and those with church status (priests and other church servitors along with their families). These *sosloviia* were distinctly different from peasants and townspeople, in large part due to the provisions for movement into or out of them. While peasants and townspeople all moved back and forth between the two statuses (that is, peasants became townspeople and merchants, and townspeople became peasants) through legal process and petitions, the boundaries between noble or church status and the rest of society were differently porous. Excess churchmen could, and did, leave the church *soslovie* to enter other *sosloviia*.[36] Only rare individuals, however, entered church status, either through the priesthood or through monasteries. By the end of the eighteenth century, the priesthood had become a nearly closed estate, open only to sons of the church, while monasteries were seen as suitable only for the aged, for excess young women, or for young men deemed unlikely ever to marry. Although those restrictions opened up somewhat during the nineteenth century, and monasteries in particular saw a surge in enrollment, the priestly *soslovie* remained one more easily exited than entered.[37]

The status of noble was, in a way, the total opposite to the church *soslovie*: possible to enter, difficult to leave. Entry into the nobility was accomplished most famously through service to the state, and by consequent movement up the hierarchy of the Table of Ranks. According to its initial establishment by Peter the Great, if non-nobles reached the eighth rank (or the fourteenth rank in the military) of the Table, they also attained hereditary noble status.[38] This opportunity remained an important dream of social improvement well into the nineteenth century, only eventually eliminated during the reactionary reign of Alexander III (1881–1894). It suggested one possible path to nobility: through active and excellent service to the Russian state. And this path has implications for the system as a whole: access to the highest rung, the nobility, was based (in principle, at least) entirely on merit, earned or not. Either one's ancestry was glorious enough or one worked one's way up the bureaucratic (or military) hierarchy.

The very commonplaceness of the image of the impoverished Russian noble shows the way that nobility was not a *soslovie* to be exited, regardless of significant economic downward mobility. The Petrine emphasis on noble service to the state further developed the notion that nobility was hard to leave. When Peter III "emancipated" the nobility by eliminating their obligation to serve, he accompanied that act with a statement of the true and proper nature of Russia's nobles. Later laws also made moving out of the nobility into another social estate nearly impossible, because, as one put it, a noble's most important role was in "military service, in peacetime in administering civil justice, for which they should from youth prepare themselves in such and other knowledge," or possibly in agricultural management. Anything else was not a properly noble activity.[39] Even when nobles were eventually granted the right to engage in trade, something made possible only after trade had been declared an honorable occupation, it could only be an addition to one's essential noble status.[40] Leaving the nobility was, for the most part, unacceptable, and made possible only by petition to the highest authorities. Loss of noble status was instead a mark of the state's displeasure, as it served as a particularly harsh punishment for particularly egregious crimes.[41]

Rubakin's image of the empire's *soslovie* society is also explicitly imperial: he includes the many non-Russians and Cossacks who lived in areas around the core of old Russian settlement. This is a very modern image of *soslovie* as part of imperial schemes of control, and not simply of the Russian population. Of course, these were complicated statuses, as well; Cossacks had changed enormously from their earlier freebooting ways, now legally settled and ascribed into communities. Non-Russian nobles might be subsumed into the general category of nobility—assuming, of course, they could prove their nobility.[42] The more general category of *inorodtsy* itself encompassed many individual subsidiary groups, creating yet more uncertainty and complexity at the empire's borders.[43] Through much of the imperial era, indeed, the annexation of new lands went along with new legislation of their social order; as a result, imperial spaces were often reconceptualized and reorganized according to new official ideals.

A second image from Rubakin's statistical volume shows two major lacunae in the earlier image: its ostensible subject, professions, and women. Showing the population divided by the work they did, as opposed to the status they held, uncovered a more complicated world. Some of the figures map on to *soslovie* divisions rather neatly: the giant figures representing agricultural labor, for example, or the man and woman standing at a table, engaged in trade. But many of the others find no clear representation in the vision of the world according to *sosloviia*.

Some represented bygone *soslovie*. The small military figure would once have been part of essentially its own *soslovie* of those under military authority; the army reform, which replaced the older practice of drafting few individuals for long terms with the practice of universal service for short terms, had eliminated (or at least significantly altered) that category.[44] Earlier in the imperial era, not only were soldiers taken away from their status of origin but their sons inherited military status as well. That began to change in the middle of the nineteenth century. Retired soldiers were allowed to take on new statuses, and as of 1856, their sons could also leave military status.[45]

Others belonged to newly forming groups that had not yet found their place either alongside or inside the *soslovie* system—members of professions or classes based on

The professional composition of the Russian population. Comparative strength of professions. The horizontal tag reads agricultural activities; the vertical tags from left to right read: state and social service; military; professions tied to societal needs; private service (servants); living on the state's or their own means; mining; working at industry and crafts; transportation; trade; others. *N. A. Rubakin, Rossiia v tsifrakh (St. Petersburg: Vestnik Znaniia, 1912), 97.*

alternative, and often individual as opposed to communal, definitions of social status.[46] The second largest group comprised those engaged in manufacturing; this was a tricky group for the state, the workers who by 1912 had become either a political force, or the object of a political force, but one without clear status.[47] Several of the others represent professions, the other major new force in late imperial politics. While they represented distinct economic statuses, in other ways these two groups were only loosely defined, standing in, in some ways, for *soslovie* identities, but not necessarily entirely replacing them.[48]

Women also appear in this image, working in agriculture, in trade, in service, in factories, and in professions, and contrary to their exclusion from the earlier image. Women are rarely considered in the context of *sosloviia*, perhaps because so many of the duties and privileges associated with individual *sosloviia* accrue primarily to men.[49] But in reality, women had *soslovie* status, and often chose to alter that status.[50] Their practices evolved over time. Through much of the eighteenth century there was little call to register or list women, so their place was uncertain. But by the early nineteenth century, they were definite members of *soslovie* societies, with certain rights and duties of their own—not the same as men, but still integral to discussions and conceptions of the role of *soslovie* in state structures and in the everyday lives of individuals.

Rubakin's images were structured on purely demographic grounds and focused on a particular time, and therefore lack any sense of the organization or structure of *soslovie*. But two other ways of thinking about *sosloviia* help to conceive of them in terms of a structure that gave shape to imperial society. The most recognized version of the structure of imperial Russian society is a four-part division of categories, developed in the *Digest of the Laws;* according to this version there were "four main kinds of people": the nobility, the clergy, "town residents," and "rural residents."[51] These separate categories implied a clear hierarchy, with nobles at the top and peasants (and particularly serfs) at the bottom. It also strove to give order to the *soslovie* system as it subsumed most of the many possible statuses into the four overarching groups, despite significant differences of status, of duties, and of privileges, within each.[52]

Others came up with simpler, binary classifications. K. I. Arsen'ev, an early nineteenth-century statistician, described an empire divided into "productive" and the "non-productive" populations.[53] More often, however, commentators saw the division in starker terms of the privileged and the unprivileged—or of the "free" and the "obligated," as one delegate to the Legislative Commission put it.[54] For some, this meant the stark divide between a Westernized elite and its far more numerous traditional opposite. When viewed as such a display of culture, however, this was a difficult division to map exactly on to *soslovie*, for it could be blurred by those who acted and lived outside the norms of their official status, as so many clearly did. A basic division that aligned more clearly with official status distinctions was between the soul-tax paying and those free of that obligation.[55] This distinction retained its potency even after the end of the soul tax; one late imperial legal scholar explicitly linked the concepts of privilege and non-privilege to these rights: the former were "free from taxes and corporal punishment," while the latter were "not freed."[56] Another commented that the latter were "subject to the strict disciplinary power of *soslovie* societies," a fact that made their lack of privilege persist even after the abolition of certain state obligations.[57] This distinction cut not just betwen but even within the categories established in the *Digest of the Laws*.

Investigating *soslovie* means tackling all these many sources of complexity, from the definition of *soslovie* itself, to categorizing those *soslovie* into understandable groupings, to thinking about how those understandings changed over time. The choice of sources can both obscure and illuminate these complexities. A particular difficulty has long been the need or decision to rely on laws as major sources. Of course, laws are central to the understanding of these concepts, as they were, after all, at base legally defined social categories.[58] However, examining laws alone, without attention to the ways in which those laws were interpreted and used, ignores the ways that local authorities and, indeed, individuals negotiated these concepts.

At the same time, the greatest difficulty in constructing a coherent narrative of the ways in which *soslovie* mobility developed over two centuries is the fact that the archival files that record that movement are at once overwhelmingly vast in number and frustratingly incomplete in coverage and content. Aside from the hundreds of central state files that record policy discussions, thousands—if not tens or even hundreds of thousands—of files record the individual cases of those who petitioned one administrative body or another to exit or enter a society. On the one hand, the records are so numerous that poring through them becomes a daunting task for any individual researcher. On the other, each of these individual files may be little more than a page or two, perhaps a petition and a decree, giving scant information about the people who actually made changes. Or, alternatively, they may be single files that record all movement for a single year or for a single region over a longer period of time. Furthermore, even taken en masse, all these individual files do not necessarily add up to a coherent story. Not every society kept careful records, and even where the files were originally complete, fires, mold, or other problems have destroyed some of the written record, leaving gaps of years between clumps of records. Even those files that remain often tell incomplete stories or simply provide a glimpse of a person or a family at one particular moment.

This book begins with an examination of the many meanings of *sosloviia*—as obligation, as opportunity, as belonging, and as hierarchy—as they are reflected in individual decisions to change status, and in the legal and administrative structures that allowed them to do so, as well as with a brief overview of the patterns of mobility through the long nineteenth century. Over the following five chapters, the evolution of *sosloviia* from the early eighteenth through the early twentieth century is traced, proceeding largely chronologically but with alternation between a focus on the central state and one on local authorities and individuals. It concludes with a chapter that examines several longer life stories, and therefore examines the ways that *sosloviia* and decisions to change *sosloviia* affected individual lives.

In the end, looking at not just the laws but also the way they were used by individuals to change their lives, and the way they were administered by local authorities with interests sometimes at odds with those of the central state, creates a different image of how conceptions of *sosloviia* changed over the imperial era. It shows first that the conflicting interests of the central state left options for individuals and local societies to push forward their own interests. And it also shows that conflict between those individuals and local societies at times allowed central authorities to develop further their own control over their populations. Thus, *sosloviia* become not just institutions created by the state, and not just meaningless labels, but something much more vital, evolutionary, and perhaps at times even revolutionary.

I

The Meaning of *Soslovie*

IN THE MID-1850S, the young Nikolai Chukmaldin decided to take formal legal steps to change his *soslovie*. A state peasant by birth, Chukmaldin wanted to enter the townsperson society of Tiumen', the Siberian town in which he had lived for several years. He soon discovered that what was in principle a simple bureaucratic act was in reality anything but:

> To do this required a freeing agreement from the village, an acceptance agreement from the townsperson society, and confirmation of it all by the local Treasury Office. What a huge and demeaning fuss it cost us to receive the freeing agreement from the village society, I remember even now with bitterness. My father offered the village all our allotment (pastures, meadows, forests) for this agreement, and beyond that 100 rubles cash, but nothing helped. The society refused to let me go. But when several of the bloodsuckers were given gifts, when five buckets of vodka and several pounds of nuts were given to the society, the freeing agreement was compiled right away. And my god, what scenes of drunkenness and riot did that gift of vodka bring out in the tavern! The tavern stood just about across from the building of the township [authorities]; sharing out the vodka and nuts took up the whole length of the street. I remember the horror of my father, who used neither beer nor spirits, when he saw these off-putting scenes, saying "only Satan came up with vodka." To get the acceptance agreement from the society of townspeople cost less work and money, although even there much depended on the town bloodsuckers. After these agreements, I had to go to the Tobol'sk Treasury Office, where, thanks to the influence of the late N. A. Triufin, very quickly everything turned out well. I returned to Tiumen' already the son of a townsman's family.[1]

By the time Chukmaldin sought to change his *soslovie* membership, the process of doing so had been more or less bureaucratized by decades of legislative and administrative acts, a fact that ought to have made it straightforward.² And yet, as his account clearly shows, the process could be so stressful that Chukmaldin remembered it years later as a source of significant personal and familial trauma.

As Chukmaldin's memoirs suggest, in many ways, even the regulations that allowed individuals to change their *soslovie* served above all to impede such change. The legal structures that governed the process of changing *soslovie* or changing society were complicated by any measure. Standards and protocols shifted as local societies and central authorities came into conflict, and individuals who wanted to alter their social position had to negotiate not only their place in the world of *soslovie* but also the bureaucratic structures of the empire. Once the process became bureaucratized, in principle to change *soslovie* required only acquiring and registering specific documents. That process, however, could pose significant challenges, due in large part to the interactions between individual Russians and local societies and the conflicts that arose as both acted out of self-interest. As a result, in the descriptions of individuals who made such changes, the process comes across as anything from relatively straightforward to something that caused a crisis of belief in the very institution of *sosloviia*.³

Despite these systemic constraints, changing *soslovie* was not only an option on paper but one that many individuals decided to pursue. Given the constraints that greeted those seeking to change their official estate, it is unsurprising that a significant degree of social mobility in imperial Russia took place outside the official state structure of *soslovie*. For one, there was the option of living outside the law, either risking life without documents or living on falsified or purchased ones.⁴ In addition, the longstanding practice of *otkhod*, of peasants leaving their villages for part, or even much, of the year to work in towns, provided yet more opportunities for a variety of geographic and social mobility.⁵ Certainly the number of those who changed their status compared to those who simply moved to new places, particularly towns, while living on passports was very low.⁶ Even so, and although many were content with their lives partly in town, partly in the village, others decided that such divided lives were unacceptable.⁷ As a result, they were willing to confront the various layers of bureaucracy because of some perceived need that outweighed the alternative, of staying a serf, a state peasant, a mere lower townsperson.

Few of the many archival sources left behind by the process actually address the question of why individuals sought to change their official status. Petitions to change *soslovie* are at once incredibly detailed—listing places of origin, new addresses, professions, family members, and sometimes even physical descriptions of individuals making these changes—but also frustratingly opaque as to the specific reasons that motivated those who submitted them.⁸ The document may show that a given peasant petitioner already lived in a particular region of Moscow and traded in a particular good, but not why that situation had become untenable enough to warrant a petition to leave peasant status. Or it may give a reason, but a reason so general as to give no real insight into the issues that individuals faced within the social structure of the empire. Vasilii Karpov, for one, wrote only that "various circumstances" compelled him to change his status, while Nikolai Dmitriev was even terser, stating only that he "did not wish to be in this *soslovie*."[9] These reasons are barely reasons at all.

Even if few petitioners spoke to their motivations, some did; their stories, along with memoir accounts like Chukmaldin's, help to uncover the meaning of *soslovie* membership in the everyday lives of individuals. The laws that enabled this kind of movement also help fill in the gaps between archival sources and memoirs. They reflect most of all the imperial state's desire for people to live according to their official categories, and to be sure that it knew its people, in a way, but they also defined the outlines of what *soslovie* membership meant: what it brought people as opportunities and what it demanded of them as duties. These official images of what *soslovie* membership meant intersected with individual interpretations of their own status. Thus, the motivations of individuals, whether visible through their own writings or through the laws that governed their status, provide a sense of the meaning of *soslovie* as part of real life and not just as a distant principle of imperial order. After all, why go through a "huge and demeaning fuss" to change status if that status did not have meaning on the ground?

Moreover, bringing these various sources together helps remedy a persistent tendency to ignore the fact that women possessed and negotiated *soslovie* identities. In part, this tendency reflects a disjuncture in official attitudes toward women and *soslovie* from the early eighteenth century onward. On the one hand, women had official places in society, and could be fugitives or vagrants or runaways, just as much as men could be.[10] And yet, at the same time, women were initially left out of the process of counting the population in the semi-regular revisions of the census rolls. It was not until the third census was announced in 1761 that women were to be counted during the census revision, and not until 1781 that official census forms included spaces to indicate women's names.[11] Likely as a result, during most of the eighteenth century, women virtually never sought to change their own status—only two of 357 records from that period involve women seeking to change their own legal status—while starting at the turn of the century they became much more prevalent among petitioners.[12]

Soslovie meant different things to different individuals and different parts of the state apparatus. It had real association with specific ways of life, by affecting individuals' obligations to their local societies and the central state, the obligations those institutions owed their individual members, and both economic rights and educational opportunities. It also had more abstract meanings. *Soslovie* had implications for a whole way of life into which individuals fit or did not fit. And, too, *sosloviia* were tied to notions of social hierarchy, from low to high and from unfree to free. Taken together, these many ways of understanding *sosloviia* helped impel thousands upon thousands of individuals to change their status during two centuries of imperial rule.

SOSLOVIE AS OBLIGATION

Soslovie membership, at least for those in the "unprivileged" masses, was perhaps above all associated with the concept of obligation. When an individual was placed on the membership rolls of a particular town or village society, he (or occasionally she) was bound to that society through the need to provide taxes and other duties. At the same time, however, that society was obligated to supply its members with certain social services. These obligations could easily become motivating forces behind individual decisions to change status. Some believed their obligations to be too great, and they sought to leave a status to free themselves from them. Others wished to take advantage of the social services provided by particular societies. In both cases, *soslovie* was above all understood as a network of obligations between members of a society, between societies and their members, and between individuals and the imperial state.

The obligations of membership in a particular *soslovie* society were in large part enforced by documents. For many members of Russian society, movement around the empire was, in principle at least, made possible only through possession of a passport that linked an individual to his or her place of registry. Such documents were mentioned in the *Ulozhenie* (Law Code) of 1649, but they gained new importance in the early eighteenth century, in large part due to Peter the Great's institution of the tax census. Peasants came to need passports to travel even locally, within their district; as printing capabilities expanded through the middle of the eighteenth century, more of the population was required to carry passports for travel. While the fact that laws continued to restate the need to carry printed official passports suggests that many did not, the idea that membership involved documents was well established by the beginning of the nineteenth century.[13] It only grew during that century; by mid-century the *Digest of the Laws* could state in no uncertain terms that "no one may go away from their place of permanent residence without a lawful document or passport," and that "each status has its own particular documents or passports set by law."[14]

Furthermore, passports were only one of a number of different documents that governed and ensured proper registration, as a mid-nineteenth-century writer on Moscow's townsperson society described. He listed the multiple kinds of documents local townspeople might need in order to live according to the law: "A [Moscow] townsperson wishing to live in any [other] town of Russia should have a passport (*plakatnyi passport*); one living only in Moscow should have a so-called residence ticket (*zhiloi bilet*); one wishing to leave Moscow should have an exit ticket (*vyezdnoi bilet*) or a short-term passport; one living in the province should have a so-called ticket for the province (*bilet na guberniiu*)."[15] Nor were these documents necessarily simple to obtain. A townsman wishing to obtain a passport was to submit an application to the local *soslovie* authority. That authority then carried out an inquiry. It looked into whether the applicant had any debts or was under any legal restrictions. And it obtained additional paperwork from the applicant: a sworn statement that he did not belong to any dangerous sects, and a statement that neither he nor any member of his family owned any real estate in Moscow. After all this, the applicant could appear in person to pay his fee and receive his passport. It then had to be brought to yet another office for proper registry. It was possible to send someone else, with power of attorney, to handle the transaction. Those living elsewhere could send money through the post, and would receive their passports through the police network.[16]

So integral were documents to the fact of membership in a particular *soslovie* society that access to them could itself motivate individuals to change their official status. Many petitioners argued that they wished to change their *soslovie* membership in order to gain easier access to proper documents. Ivan Zavertkin, a serf belonging to Count Sheremetev, had long lived away from his village of legal registration. In 1830, he petitioned his owner for freedom because "I do not have enough money to go [home] every year to get [my passport]."[17] Through the rest of the nineteenth century, and even into the early twentieth century, petitioners repeated much the same idea. Being required to return to their places of formal registry only to get the documents they needed to live elsewhere was a burden. They hoped that registry in a new society was the solution.[18]

The state also came to recognize the important role documents and access to them played in the everyday meaning of *sosloviia*. In March 1819, the Senate heard a report from the St. Petersburg Treasury Department, in which it asked for permission to receive petitions from townswomen from other towns who wished to change their registration to the capital. This was significant because, in 1800, Emperor Paul had restricted the right of state peasant women to enter town societies and that had been interpreted as a general ban on women's mobility. Now, though, the Treasury Department argued that such petitions should be allowed because, although women could in principle live in the capital on passports, in practice the resulting need to travel sometimes great distances in order to renew those passports had created real hardship for many. The Senate agreed with this proposal, and agreed to allow townswomen to register formally in new towns.[19] Later, in 1831, a year before the ban on state peasant women moving into town societies was finally ended, it was weakened by a law that drew on the importance of documents. This law gave the Ministry of Finance authority to allow the registration of state peasant women, both "widows and the unmarried," into towns if they, "living in them for their constant trade, do not find it convenient to return to their prior place of residence to get passports."[20]

The imperial state was so convinced of the importance of documents in part because it saw them as a way to be sure it could mobilize its population to fulfill its obligations. Before the army reform of 1874, military service loomed as a dreaded obligation of membership in certain *sosloviia*, and this was perhaps the most important motivation to change status or society. When Peter the Great instituted a regular standing army staffed with soldiers serving for life, he also set up a system that continually drained able-bodied men from the countryside and the lower ranks of town populations. Between 1705 and 1825 alone, ninety levies gathered more than 2 million peasants and townsmen for the army.[21] Being sent off as a soldier effectively removed peasants and townsmen from their homes and families. As a result, even after the length of service demanded was reduced, being sent as a soldier continued to be a fate to be feared and, if possible, avoided. Over time, regularized systems (often called line systems) developed in villages to make the process of choosing draftees more orderly, and terms of service eased slightly; even so, levies could cause significant conflict within villages, and tales abound of peasants running away or self-mutilating in order to avoid military service, or otherwise working their local system to get themselves removed from draft rolls.[22] Such fears were also common among the townspeople, with the result that many townspeople with draft-eligible sons formed "a stratum of 'fictional' third-guild merchants" who falsified their financial status until their sons were free from the threat of the draft.[23]

Nikolai Chukmaldin expressed in particularly vivid ways the effect that the threat of being sent as a soldier had on him and his family. His family was a prosperous one in their state peasant village. Both parents were artisans, and although they themselves were illiterate, they made sure their son learned to read; as a result, he was able to bring additional income into the family by working as a scribe. However, despite the family's economic success within their peasant community while possessing peasant status, they still sought both a geographic and a social change for Nikolai. Their reason was simple and direct:

> despite such an improvement in our peasant well-being, an approaching internal worm of family disaster tormented us every minute. The fact of the matter was that two brothers of my father, Kornil and Nikifor, who lived in their own households, were for purposes of the registry books listed in one family under one number with us. Uncle Kornil had two sons, but both had physical disabilities, and my other uncle Nikifor had one son, but he was underage. As I approached adulthood, in our single registered family there would be six full workers, from whom there would immediately be demanded an army recruit. And I, the only son of my parents, would have to go off as a soldier on behalf of my uncles and their sons.[24]

According to Chukmaldin's memoir, it was the fear of army life alone that pushed his family to seek a new *soslovie* membership for their son. And once he had finally made the move to townsman, Nikolai Chukmaldin celebrated his release from the peasant community chiefly because he saw it as freedom from army life: "we finally breathed free of the sword of Damocles hanging above us. I will never forget the great happiness of my mother and father, when they knew that their son would no longer be taken as a soldier." However, according to his memoir, he soon realized that to be certain of avoiding military service he had to make yet another move: from townsman to merchant, because only merchants were not subject to the draft. Thanks to family connections, he was soon able to do so, and to guarantee a life free of, as he put it, "the red cap."[25]

Chukmaldin's vivid account is echoed by a whole series of other references to the threat of military service. According to his memoir, the fear of military service hung over the early years of the townsman (and eventual artist) Aleksandr Stupin.[26] Many of the laws that governed movement between *sosloviia* societies not only emphasized military service as a major feature of *soslovie* membership, but even suggested that so many men—in one case, particularly townsmen—were trying to change their *soslovie* membership when they were subject to military service that laws had to be put into place to stop them.[27] The fear of military service clearly also pushed some men to run away from their home societies without formal release; when such runaways were granted amnesty to return, and the threat of military service was removed, they often returned home.[28] Although petitioners were generally much more circumspect in their writing, some petitions, when combined with their investigation, also hint at the role military service played in inducing some to seek changes in their status. In 1867, the Riazan' townsman Nikolai Polovin, for example, petitioned for freedom on very vague grounds—that he had "a wish to leave the Riazan' society of townspeople [and to join] some other kind of tax-paying *soslovie*." The reason for this unspecific wish may explain why the townsperson society refused to free him: he was in line for military service.[29]

Other obligations of various sorts, be they taxes, rents, or service to the state or community, were also part of the concept of *soslovie*. From the time of Peter the Great until the end of the nineteenth century, the soul tax was the most elemental of *soslovie* obligations. Peasants, townsmen, and artisans owed the soul tax; merchants, priests, and nobles did not. Even in the empire's borderlands, social division was reflected in different kinds of monetary or other obligations to the state. As a result, for much of the imperial era, the greatest division between categories of *sosloviia* was the distinction between those who owed the soul tax and those who did not. Only several decades after emancipation was the soul tax finally abolished, replaced by indirect taxes and eventually a general income tax.[30] Even then, however, a difference remained between those who had paid the soul tax and those who had not, and moving between those statuses still involved being subject to or free from a series of "natural obligations" that one historian has described as "heavy [and] socially demeaning."[31]

In addition to the soul tax, all peasants owed some sort of dues to their owner or to the state. State peasants owed *obrok*—quitrent—that was centrally levied and paid to state coffers. Peter initially set their quitrent at 40 kopeks per soul, and by 1783 it had risen to 3 rubles. In 1798 the state divided the provinces of the empire into four categories, ranking them by economic status. Peasants living in economically more prosperous provinces were assessed higher quitrent rates than those living in less economically prosperous provinces (according to the initial law, the rates ranged from 5 rubles to 3½ rubles per soul). Given changes in the buying power of the ruble, state peasant dues increased through the mid-nineteenth century, but not as quickly as those of private serfs.[32] Private serfs also owed dues to their owners, but their dues were far less predictable. Owners collected labor dues (*barshchina*), quitrent, or a combination of the two from their serfs, and had the freedom to demand whatever level of dues they desired. Emperor Paul famously limited the amount of labor dues a landowner could demand to three days a week, but the rates of quitrent were consistently levied at the whim of owners.[33]

Because the monetary demands that owners placed on serfs were more erratic than those placed on state peasants, serfs in particular seem to have found dues to be reason to ask for the freedom to take on a new *soslovie* identity. Owners could suddenly demand not just slightly increased dues from their serfs but also sometimes significantly higher ones. Such, claimed Savva Dmitriev, was the case in his home village. According to Dmitriev, he had been forced to think of freedom when his owner died in the early 1820s and custody of his village changed. The old owner's daughter inherited, and her husband clearly saw the village as a source of quick money. He first announced to the villagers that because he needed cash immediately, if they were to collect 200,000 rubles right away, they would be freed from quitrent for ten years. When the peasants were unable to come up with such a sum, the new owners mortgaged the estate and forced the peasants to pay interest on the mortgage (30,000 rubles a year) on top of their previous quitrent dues (20,000 a year). Dmitriev found this new arrangement outrageous.[34] As he saw it, it made more rational sense to pull together an extraordinary amount of money for the purpose of purchasing his freedom rather than to solidify his owner's control over him. Nor was he alone; Leontii Travin similarly reacted to newly increased quitrent demands occasioned by his owner's second marriage by stepping up his campaign for freedom.[35]

Even when an owner's demands were reasonable, how they were assessed within the village could be a problem. Serfs who had done well enough to find themselves thinking of changing estates were often hit with a heavier tax and quitrent rate. Nikolai Shipov, for example, remembered just such a situation in his native serf Vyezdnoe, a village about 80 kilometers south of Nizhnii Novgorod. His father kept up a significant trade in livestock, enough so that he made yearly trips to far-off provinces to buy stock. As a result, he owed disproportionate quitrent to his owner, a member of the Saltykov family. According to Shipov, Saltykov demanded quitrent of 110 rubles per soul per year. However, because Shipov's family had amassed significant wealth, and continued to succeed economically, their village apportioned them a disproportionate share of quitrent dues. Although the household consisted of only a few souls, it paid more than 5,000 rubles each year because of its relative wealth.[36] Shipov saw this as unfair, and a motive to escape his serf status.

Unlike other forces at play in understanding *soslovie*, the concept of obligation was explicitly gendered in a way that particularly affected practices of mobility. Because women owed neither recruit duties nor the soul tax, village or town societies had less interest in restricting their mobility, and they were more willing to give up female members than male members. That is, the barriers to movement for women were lower than those for men because the legal obligations that tied them to particular *soslovie* societies were fewer. Particularly in the later imperial era, women had an additional advantage over men: while men had to receive formal acceptance in order to join a new *soslovie*

society, women, at least those without male dependents, were freed from that obligation. They could register essentially at will—although they still had to pay some fees, the
bureaucratic hurdles to new registration were fewer.[37] On balance, other than the period
in the early nineteenth century when state peasant women were restricted from moving
between *soslovie* societies, these administrative decisions meant that women who governed their own lives (a small minority) were freer to move than men.

Military service, taxes, and rents were obligations of individuals to their state, their
communities, or their owners, but the obligations of those communities to their members were also important to the concept of *soslovie*. Over the course of the nineteenth
century, *soslovie* societies, particularly in towns, became increasingly responsible for the
health and welfare of their members.[38] As a result, this shift created an impetus for some
individuals to seek formal membership in the society of the towns in which they lived.
Certainly according to almost any account, pre-Revolutionary Russia was short on public aid. Private charitable institutions did play important roles during the nineteenth
century, but they were nowhere near able to aid all those who might need help.[39] Much
of the aid that existed was organized on basis of *soslovie* and membership.

In principle, at least, town and state peasant populations were served via the Offices of
Public Care founded by Catherine the Great; these offices had responsibility for providing a wide range of public services, including schools, charitable institutions, and medical
oversight, and they were explicitly meant to operate on a local level. In addition, town
soslovie societies often ran their own more or less *soslovie*-specific charitable institutions
meant to aid their members.[40] During the nineteenth century, those institutions grew
and developed, even as other sources of public aid from private charitable institutions
developed in concert with them.[41] In addition, other *soslovie*-specific groups found themselves burdened at times with care for their members; diocese and parish authorities, for
one, found themselves troubled by welfare provisions for members of the church status.[42]

These various regulations meant that, already by 1857, the *Digest of the Laws* could
list a whole series of obligations that town and village authorities owed their official
inhabitants. They were not only to ensure public order among their population; they
were also to make sure that "poor and indigent people do not wander and beg in the lowest manner for charity," that those able to work did do, and that the "aged and infirm"
were supported by their relatives. If there were no relatives to watch over those unable
to support themselves, then they were to be sent to almshouses, hospitals, and "other
charitable institutions run by those *sosloviia* and societies."[43] This was a clear statement
of the importance of *soslovie* societies in supporting their members—but one that barely
hinted at the role that such obligations played in everyday life.

In his memoir of leaving the Moscow townsperson society, Aleksandr Miliukov
described in passing some of the many kinds of services the town supplied its population. When he went to request a document that would allow him to leave the society in
order to attend school, he saw a whole series of other petitioners seeking aid. One "bent,
grey haired old man, with head strongly shaking and bony hands" had long been seeking

a place in a Moscow almshouse (*bogodel'nia*), but was again told that "all the almshouses are full to the brim." A woman sought aid for her and her two daughters. Others found their demands either quickly dealt with or, more often, quickly dismissed.[44] The society was a source of services, even if it did not always fulfill all its members' needs.

These sorts of practical, pragmatic services played a role in individual choices to change estate. In the eighteenth and early nineteenth centuries, a more normal path for the aged and infirm was to seek permission to enter a monastery. In 1749, Mikhailo Moskolev claimed that after a life of good service as a Kursk merchant, now, in his "aged and childless" position, and due to the "deathly illnesses that have afflicted me more than once," he wished to exit his position and enter a nearby monastery. In his case, the merchant society agreed to bear his dues and allowed him to leave.[45] Similar cases appeared in many regions, at least through the early decades of the nineteenth century, but they largely disappeared later in the nineteenth century.[46] This may in part reflect a shift in monasteries themselves; while many came to run separate charitable institutions in this period, the revival of monasticism in the era meant they more and more brought in younger men with a vocation, not older ones seeking charity.[47]

Instead, from the middle of the nineteenth century onward, particularly for those seeking to enter town societies, local public aid was a clear draw. Some petitioners outright stated that they needed to change their registration in order to receive documents that would allow access to public aid. The townswoman and widow Liubov' Kondrashenko, for one, wished to move her registry from Smolensk to St. Petersburg, where she lived, in large part to find aid for her "wretched crippled daughter."[48] And other documents show that individuals sought entrance into societies explicitly to make use of their social services.[49]

Moreover, both according to their own petitions and according to local *soslovie* authorities, women were particularly drawn to town societies in part because of their social services. As one writer put it, in towns at least, "more than half of the money for welfare and medical care is spent on women."[50] Although he did not link this expense to women choosing to enter town estates, other town societies certainly did in their correspondence with central authorities.[51] The process of registration could be actively useful for new members, and women were both aware of that fact and able to take advantage of it.

SOSLOVIE AS OPPORTUNITY

The meaning of *soslovie* was bound up not only with obligation but also with opportunity. Much of the legislation governing *soslovie* focused on specific elements of rights to engage in different kinds of trade or ply different crafts, to own different kinds of property, or to attain different levels of education.[52] Not only were these issues a major focus of the laws, but also they were interpreted by individual Russians as central to the meaning of *soslovie*. During the Legislative Commission of Catherine the Great, when representatives of Russia's many social groups were called together to discuss her proposed new code of laws, conversation bogged down over the the intersection of specific economic rights of particular *sosloviia* and larger societal goals.[53] During the next century and a half, despite occasional efforts to free up the empire's economic system by removing *soslovie*-based restrictions on economic activities, the reality of *sosloviia* continually stymied such plans. Nearly throughout the imperial era, *soslovie* membership affected individual opportunities in ways that not only defined the meaning of *sosloviia* but also impelled individuals to alter their particular status.

Above all, laws defined who had the right to engage in various trades or occupations. Throughout the eighteenth century, laws urged registry in towns as a prerequisite for full trading rights, while they also consistently protected the right of peasants to trade in their own products.[54] The Charter to the Towns formalized the economic options available to different categories of townspeople, using strict *soslovie*-based distinctions to allocate kinds of trade. Merchants had the right to trade in all sorts of goods and in all sorts of places; the three guilds had slightly different levels of trade associated with them (the second guild was "not only allowed, but also encouraged to engage in any kind of trade inside the Empire, and to transport goods by water and by dry land to towns and fairs"; the first guild could additionally trade outside the empire, and the third guild was limited to "minor" trade and to their home towns and surrounding regions), but all were differentiated from members of other estates.[55]

Later laws refined or complicated this system in ways that at times lessened incentive to change *soslovie* and at others increased that incentive. In 1798 and 1799, Paul greatly expanded the rights of peasants to trade in the capitals by allowing them to open regular shops in which—with the payment of a fee—they could sell not only their own products but even imported goods like sugar, tea, and coffee. Furthermore, another statute allowed peasants to open general stores (*melochnye lavki*), "due to the circumstance that has come to light, that the local merchantry is itself not occupied with trade in various absolutely necessary minor products."[56]

But these expanded rights did not last. In the very early nineteenth century, concerns arose over peasants living and working on the margins of the law by paying sometimes exorbitant fees to "borrow" a townsperson's trading rights.[57] In 1824, another set of supplementary laws set out slightly altered economic opportunities for members of town estates, including lists of wares that could be sold by members of the different statuses (for example, only those having attained merchant status could engage in beer brewing). In 1826, a law set out detailed lists of the wares that could be sold by peasants who had purchased the right to trade in towns; despite the earlier law that had given them expanded rights to trade virtually on the same level as merchants and townspeople, peasant trade was now significantly more controlled than that of members of town estates.[58]

The Great Reforms brought with them expanded economic opportunities and a leveling of *sosloviia* distinctions, but that leveling was only partial and some distinctions remained. In towns, the removal in the 1860s of *soslovie*-based restrictions on rights to trade made merchants feel strongly that the privileges of their status were under attack by outsiders gaining new opportunities.[59] But in the post-emancipation village, access to land became increasingly associated with *soslovie*. Lands initially allotted to peasants could not be alienated from that association.[60] So, as residents of towns saw less need to change their official status, those wishing to engage in agriculture—in certain areas, at least—might need to do so.

These economic distinctions appeared—if at times only by implication—as motivating factors in individual decisions to change *soslovie*.[61] In the mid-eighteenth century, Leontii Travin wanted to speculate in land, but was held back by his serf status. According to his memoir, he faced the choice of being unable to buy the land he wanted because he lacked the proper status or of having to buy it through intermediaries, the latter a possibility he described as "mixed with the danger of losing it all together."[62] He further directly linked his decision to seek his freedom and to join a town estate to this realization. At nearly the same time, the monastery peasant Aleksandr Berezin was making a similar transition. He began his life in trade in Petersburg; his merchant employer there set him up in a dry goods shop, initially for a salary and later for a percentage of the profits. After several years in this position, Berezin purchased his freedom in order to become a sole proprietor of his own shop. Upon receiving his freedom, he purchased a house in St. Petersburg (for 800 rubles), started a brewery, and registered in the city's merchant estate.[63]

Similar motivations appear in petitions submitted by those wishing to alter their status—and were given both as reasons to leave a former status and to gain a new one. Many were somewhat vague in their statements. In the 1850s, Vasil'i Korobov wished to register as merchant in Riazan' in order "to strengthen" his trade, which "demanded" such a move, while Agaf Suslov believed that changing his *soslovie* would allow him "to widen the circle of my mercantile activities."[64] Nor were explicit economic opportunities the only reason given by petitioners. One Sheremetev serf, Parfen Balandin, petitioned for freedom on the grounds that, although he was already a successful trader in Moscow, by "becoming a free [*svobodnyi*] person and registering in the merchant status" he would "strengthen others' confidence in [him]."[65]

Others were more specific about the benefits they might gain. Egor' Vasil'ev (sometimes Bykov), who petitioned to change his status from church peasant to Kursk townsman in 1726, stated that one reason for his change was to gain access to markets in "Ukrainian [Little Russian] towns."[66] Two serfs who ran a soap manufacturer petitioned for their freedom on the grounds that they had "the opportunity to increase their capital by means of credit, and lacked only the status to do so."[67] Another pair of serfs, the brothers Mikhailo and Aleksei Morozov, were even more specific about the reasons for requesting their freedom to register as merchants: "the ability to further develop mercantile trade and credit is now located more with the class of free people—merchants."[68]

Even when economic factors did not play a direct role in prompting movement, they still affected conceptions of *soslovie*. The serf Vasilii Barkov and his family were freed somewhat unexpectedly in their owner's will and immediately had to decide on what their next status would be. While often families moved from one *soslovie* society to another as a single household, in Barkov's case the different generations joined different *soslovie* societies in different towns, reflecting their different economic preferences.[69] Something somewhat similar came up in Chukmaldin's description of his life. Even though Chukmaldin's decision to leave his state peasant estate was primarily driven by his desire to avoid military service, his decision to join the Tiumen' society of townspeople, and later its merchant estate, was also clearly linked to economic opportunities. Before taking these steps, Chukmaldin had worked in the city, initially at the leather factory run by a relative, and then was buying and selling in his aunt's shop in the town's merchant arcade for several years. His clear talent for trade, in particular, also served as a positive reason to join the society of townspeople, and then eventually the merchant estate.[70]

Even in less narrative sources, economic opportunities were an apparent influence on individual decisions, but their exact role is harder to determine. The records of some town societies show well that many of those who sought to become members were already actively engaged in local trade. New Moscow merchants during the nineteenth century had established businesses and traded in all sorts of goods, from firearms and photographic materials, to pomades and candles, to wooden dishes. Many either manufactured or traded in cloth, while some traded in foodstuffs or ran taverns. A few worked as stewards or overseers.[71] All had clearly prospered without having the official status of Moscow merchant—and yet all apparently found it advantageous now to take on that new status.

Soslovie—particularly its sense of belonging to a specific society—could also affect marriage opportunities. Finding a suitable marriage partner could be a challenge for members of almost any estate. Small communities in particular might have difficulty supplying all their members with eligible marriage partners, so a certain amount of boundary crossing helped solve such dilemmas. No group, however, had as many possible limitations imposed on their marriage patterns as serfs had. In principle, at least, serf-owners had the right to control their serfs' marriages, and while they did not always, they could exert this right in part by allowing or refusing to allow movement across the social boundary of a single estate.[72] This seems to have played at least some role in the story of Nikolai Shipov. Shipov came from a well-to-do serf family, one respected enough outside his village that merchants wanted to marry their daughters into the family. However, although according to Shipov "every one of the Arzamas merchants would gladly have given me their daughter with a big dowry and money," such a marriage, advantageous as it might be, was impossible while he remained a serf. Shipov's owner would allow no such marriages, and Shipov was forced to marry a fellow serf. Shipov was lucky that his home village, Vyezdno, was a large one and that as a result there were three possible brides, "daughters of wealthy peasants," when time came for him to marry.[73]

Marriage could, but did not necessarily, transform social status.[74] According to the laws, men shared their higher status with the women they married, but women could not do the same (nor could they lose status through marriage; however, their children would follow their husbands' lower status). But this unequal status could lead a man to petition to change his *soslovie* to something more fitting his wife's status (and marital economy). Il'ia Svin'in, a peasant from Usolskii district, petitioned to be accepted by the Sol'vychegodsk merchants in part because he had "married the late Sol'vychegodsk merchant Petr Kostromin's daughter, the widow Anna Petrova, with an understanding with her mother, the widow of the above mentioned Petr Ivanov, Natal'ia Semenova, that I would live with them in the town and be the master of her whole estate and affairs."[75]

Even more than economic opportunity or marriage, access to education was an opportunity that could be truly transformative. Education was the promise of future advancement, an idea that grew during the nineteenth century as subsequent waves of educational reform linked completing various levels of study to attaining certain statuses.[76] It became the gateway to an individual status based on personal worth and achievement, not on birth and social ties—in 1837, Nicholas I even lamented the tendency of certain members of "the lower *soslovie*," to believe that education could "pull them out of the *soslovie* to which they belonged, [could] free them from their social and *soslovie* obligations."[77] Even memoirists who were unable to attain their goals of formal education often highlighted their extensive reading, or other proofs of their intellectual development; one such former serf even explicitly linked his inability to gain a formal education to his serf status, and bemoaned this as part of Russia's overall backwardness.[78] For him, as for many others, *soslovie* was explicitly linked with education—or, more properly, with being kept from a proper education.[79]

Among the most vivid accounts of the way that a desire for education motivated individual change is that of Aleksandr Nikitenko, the famed serf turned government censor. He described his early aptitude for learning, something encouraged by his father, himself an educated serf, as the family moved from village to village in service of their owner. Eventually he attended a pre-secondary school in Voronezh, one from which many students went on to further schooling. His teachers considered young Nikitenko among the most promising students at the school, but because of his serf status, he was not able to continue his studies. As a result, as a fourteen-year-old, Nikitenko found himself working as a teacher in Ostrogozhsk, a position he described as "simply improbable."[80]

Nikitenko was not content, and continued to dream of furthering his education. He wrote to his owner, the young Count Sheremetev, asking for his freedom, but was rebuffed. Then, in the early 1820s, he and his friends founded a bible society in Ostrogozhsk, a fact that suddenly drew him into a different world. The then minister of religion and education, Prince Golitsyn, read one of Nikitenko's papers written for the society and was so impressed he decided to intervene on behalf of the young serf. Faced with a serf who had already received a better education than he had, and thanks in large part to Golitsyn's (and others') efforts, Sheremetev was convinced to free Nikitenko. Nikitenko's reaction was a recognition that his life had been transformed: he described himself as "reborn to a new life!"[81]

The way that education could radically alter individual status is apparent, though somewhat hidden, in the archival accounts. The files of Moscow's townsperson society include records of those who were released from the society. Most left to join other town statuses—usually merchant, occasionally honored citizen—but a substantial group left due to their educational attainments. The fates of four such men show well the many ways that education could be transformative.[82] In 1890, Aleksandr Shchukarev left the society formally after completing a degree at Moscow University. He stayed on to complete a doctoral dissertation, and then moved to Khar'kov to take a position as professor at the technological institute. He went on to create a "thinking machine" credited with advancing early computing technologies.[83] In 1903, Timofei Kasatkin was also released from the society upon completion of a law degree, in his case at Tomsk University. He went into civil service and reached the rank of collegiate assessor before retiring to take religious orders. He was confirmed as a deacon in 1910, a priest in 1912, and was still serving as a priest in Barnaul in 1921, after which his fate is uncertain.[84]

Finally, two brothers—Vladimir and Grigorii Lobachev—went on to radically different futures in the early twentieth century. Vladimir, the older, left the society in 1913, as a graduate of Moscow's Higher Technical School. From 1914 almost until his death in 1955, he worked as an engineer for Moscow's anti-fire services, planning and building the city's water supply for fighting fires. His brother Grigorii left the society in 1915, after graduating from the Musical-Dramatical School of the Moscow Philharmonic Society. After the revolution, he worked for the music department of Proletkul't, and went on to become a composer. Although he wrote a number of operas and other pieces, he was better known for his songs, often on political themes.[85] Education had transformed both their lives, but in radically different ways.

Perhaps because education was recognized as truly transformative, it could also spark dissent within individual families. When Aleksandr Miliukov sought the opportunity to leave his townsperson society to gain additional education, it brought him into conflict with his father. To his father, literacy was enough, and his son ought to start working. To the son, however, education promised a way out of the more stilted environment of his life as a townsman.[86] Much later, one of Nikolai Rubakin's correspondents wrote about just such a conflict. The author, Ivan Klimov, by birth a peasant, by occupation a carter, described his family drama: "but unfortunately I have been positively forbidden to read books by my parents... due to their opinion that to read books is too dangerous a habit for a future peasant.... [H]ow could I be satisfied with such a life[?] [I]s my love for learning somehow unnatural?"[87]

SOSLOVIE AS BELONGING

Klimov's cry from the heart brings up another way *soslovie* had meaning: it could imply a culture, an occupation, a place or role in which one belonged. *Soslovie* had very specific associations with obligations and opportunities, but it also had a more general meaning linked to an abstract sense of belonging to a particular status or a particular community. Some believed that there were, simply put, different norms of behavior for different *sosloviia*. As an amateur ethnographer put it in a report to the Imperial Russian Geographical Society in 1853:

> Every state *soslovie* of people has its own way of life, belonging only to it. A way of life is the necessary condition that places a known class of people into a delineated circle or sphere, native to it alone…. In this way there is a way of life of the upper nobility, of the merchantry, of the townspeople, of the simple, country people, and even a soldiers' way of life,—and all these circles, or classes of people, are sharply divided by their conditions of life. It is necessary that every member of a given status master and fulfill in reality the conditions of his rank without fail. Thus, if a peasant by spirit, disposition, action, and way of life does not correspond to the conditions of his peasant status, then he is no longer a common man, not a peasant, not a member of his *soslovie*.[88]

Some later reader of these musings found them objectionable enough to cross them out, perhaps because they lacked the scientific rigor expected by the society. Even so, the idea that *soslovie* implied a certain way of life was certainly a common one. It could suggest the existence of a whole peasant or townsperson or merchant or noble culture, or it could be more narrowly conceptualized as implying a natural or proper occupation for those who possessed it.

This sense of *soslovie* as belonging could be either general or specific. On the one hand, it meant fitting in with the norms of the cultural and economic behavior associated with a particular status. In this way, it meant fulfilling the duties and taking advantage of the opportunities allotted to the status of peasant, townsman, or merchant, and of living a life appropriate to that status—or of seeking a status that actually did fit one's way of life. But the idea of belonging had a second meaning, as well, one based in the idea that *soslovie* membership was geographically specific. Individuals could feel that they did not fit in their specific community, not just in their larger status—and those feelings could impel individuals to seek a radical change that would sever their ties with that old community. It might also be reflected in a more positive force that sought membership in a community, as a means of moving away from the uncertain, marginal, even liminal status of migrant to establish a firmer sense of belonging in a specific place.[89]

In petitions to change *soslovie*, a lack of aptitude or fit frequently appeared as a major, if not the major, reason an official change of *soslovie* was requested. *Soslovie* was supposed to define occupation, but not all members of a given *soslovie* actually fit those definitions, and some used that lack of fit as a reason for change. Many petitioners focused above all on why their personal economic (or other) behavior meant they were unsuited to their *soslovie* of origin. Some were vague in their rationale; they reported that they no longer wished to be members of particular societies and live in particular places "due to the kind of my occupation," or due to "changed circumstances."[90] Such petitioners in essence argued that lack of fit was a real reason to alter *soslovie,* even if they had no specific lack of fit to report. Others, though, were more specific.

Individuals legally classified as peasants often described themselves as simply not peasants in reality because they did not fit the economic definition of peasant as one defined by agricultural occupation. During the eighteenth century, such petitioners often described lives completely separate from agricultural pursuits. In some cases, they noted that they lacked a land allotment; one went further and said that he was "not used to agriculture." In all cases, they touted this lack of aptitude for the economic identity associated with their official *soslovie* as reason why they wished to enter a town *soslovie* society.[91] Throughout the nineteenth century, too, similar phrases appeared in peasant petitions. Peasants by legal status commonly reported that they neither owned property in the village nor engaged in agriculture as reasons they should be allowed to change that status.[92]

There were many other variations on this idea. Townspeople claimed to lack both property and trade, and thus desired to leave their towns and their status; artisans, too, might mention that their actual occupation was not that of their registry.[93] In one case from 1762, the widow of an artisan pushed this to perhaps an extreme degree. She argued that her eight-year-old son lacked all abilities in her late husband's craft, and that he should thus be allowed to register as a merchant in their hometown of Cheboksary. Her rationale was that her son's uncle was a merchant and could properly train him in his business.[94] Similarly, Cossacks by definition fought, and so a Cossack who could not fight due to ill health or injury could argue that he did not fit his *soslovie.* Indeed, some petitioned to leave their Cossack status on the grounds that they were unable to fulfill their proper role as fighting men. Matvei Zdornov, for one, provided evidence that he had an "internal incurable illness" that kept him from fighting, evidence that served as reason for him to leave his Cossack status and become a merchant in Saratov.[95]

Similarly, those seeking to move out of church status usually commented that they were unable to fulfill the duties associated with their *soslovie.* One petitioner reported that he wished to change his status, and gave as a reason his inability to read: "because I am illiterate I cannot find a position in the church and remain idle."[96] Another churchman, the deacon Mikhail Smirnov, claimed to be no longer able to fulfill his duties due to a fall and a blow to the head that left his hands with a permanent tremor. He asked permission to join Moscow's merchant society.[97] Throughout the nineteenth century, too, a sense of oneself as not fitting one's official *soslovie* continued to drive change. According to Laurie Manchester, priests' sons who formally left the clerical estate did so for a number of reasons, including "the chasm between clerical reality and ideals ... and the lack of a clerical calling."[98]

Just as some individuals petitioned to change their *soslovie* on the grounds that they did not fit their old status, others petitioned on the grounds that they did fit the *soslovie* society they sought to enter. Among this group were those who already lived virtually as if they were members of the new society, and were asking simply for that status to be confirmed. Others thought of it as a desire to be a resident of a new place or a member of a new society.

Many drew on their long residence in a place as reason for registration there, in a way giving the abstract notion of fit a basis in reality. In 1798, Dmitrii Pelevin, a court peasant from Vologda province, noted that, in part because of his village's proximity to Vologda itself, he had "since childhood" lived in the town "learning metalwork" and now wished to regularize that position.[99] In the late 1850s, the Riazan' townsman Il'ia Utkin used a similar rationale for why he should be registered as a state peasant in the village of Popodin'a. He had lived in the village for sixteen years and had there not only a house but livestock and a kitchen garden as well. He worked as a blacksmith, and he also rented and farmed land.[100] There were many similar cases of townspeople living in villages and of peasants living in towns, all seeking to regularize what was already a fact of life.[101]

These claims were perhaps more formulaic than anything else, as they were essentially stating something that guarantors often were called to attest to; but at least sometimes, they seemed to be aiming at a different, more abstract sense of "fit." In essence, such petitions emphasized the idea that there were particular ways of life associated with particular statuses—that *soslovie* implied culture. In 1798, a petition from two court peasant brothers brought up just this point; not only did they note that they had since childhood lived in St. Petersburg, working on passports for various merchants and traders, but also they had "gotten into the habit of this way of life."[102] Grigorii Titov drew on the idea of work, rather than long residence, in his petition to enter the Moscow merchantry; he noted that he had "an inclination for mercantile trade."[103]

In some ways, these descriptions of fitting into a particular society were also ways of emphasizing a petitioner's prosperity and ability to thrive. In 1767, three Cheboksary artisans, Kozma Kurtybyshev, Mikhailo Afanas'ev, and Andrei Ivanov, all petitioned to be accepted as merchants in the town. The three men had been registered as craftsmen during the last census, each with a different specialty (leatherwork, hat making, and metalwork, respectively). But each had since moved on in life. Kurtybyshev had built a tannery and now traded as far as Astrakhan'; Afanas'ev and Ivanov now traded at markets in all sorts of goods, including "copper and cast-iron cauldrons, silk and cotton and silk and cotton brocades and all sorts of ribbons, beads and copper and tin crosses."[104] Because of their success—something confirmed by the list of property submitted with the petition, and which described in great detail not only the real estate owned by each but the specific wares currently on hand in their warehouses—all three now wished formally to become merchants.

In addition, women argued that they fit better in the societies they sought to enter, whether through long residence or through active participation in economic activities. In 1815, the economic peasant widow Anis'ia Fedotova asked to register as a Moscow townswoman on the grounds that she had long lived there, that all her near relatives had registered there, and because she and her daughter both engaged in trade in the town.[105] Her petition was refused because it fell during the period when state peasant women were not allowed to register on their own as members of town societies, but it nonethe-less speaks to the demands and interests of women. In 1866, the Cossack widow Mariia Simashkina requested registration as a Taganrog townswoman largely on the grounds of her "permanent residence" there. As she put it, that residence made it "useful" for her to change her registration.[106] Some even looked for other kinds of movement. In 1857, Tat'iana Balantsova, a freed serf with an illegitimate son, requested entry into the Riazan' *meshchanin* society. Two years later, she petitioned again, now requesting regis-try as a third guild merchant in a petition she signed herself.[107]

Particularly in memoirs, the idea of belonging was often tied more to a specific com-munity than to a larger social identity. These ties could make it difficult for people to leave their status of origin. Much of the literature that discusses peasant migration to towns in the late imperial era emphasizes the strong ties that bound those peasants to their homes. Wives, families, and property all served as links not simply to a geo-graphical space but also to their *soslovie* society of origin.[108] Even some individuals who eventually changed their estate experienced feelings of dislocation, sometimes severe.[109] Aleksandr Berezin, the son of a monastery peasant, eventually became a high-ranking St. Petersburg merchant. And yet, he described his initial move from his village as some-thing traumatic. As he put it, he was "forced by poverty" to leave the "bosom of his fam-ily." Despite his eventual success, his first experience with mobility was unsought and unwanted.[110] Nikolai Chukmaldin was similarly initially unhappy with his transition from the village to town life. He actively disliked many things about his village well before he finally faced its leaders to ask for his freedom. But when, as a sixteen-year-old, he moved to nearby Tiumen' to work in a relative's leather factory, he felt extreme dis-location and unhappiness, to the point that he ran back to the village. He was lucky; his family had enough connections that he could find different work that better suited him.[111] Others, however, had no such ability to navigate between places and positions.

On the other hand, the sense of a lack of fit could easily be transformed into some-thing stronger: active dissatisfaction or even anger with not just a status that kept one from certain opportunities but also a specific community. Whatever the dreams of certain Slavophiles, peasant villages were hardly idyllic and free of conflict. Peasants could be fractious, argumentative, and even litigious in their interactions in the village. Questions of property led peasants to seek legal redress even before the eighteenth cen-tury; discord in the serf villages both large and small often meant that owners had to take action to safeguard the social order; and by the late imperial era, it has been argued, peasants took full advantage of local judicial institutions once they had access to them.[112] Anything from petty jealousy to significant conflict could affect peasant lives, either as instigators or as victims.

A number of former peasants particularly noted this aspect of village life in their memoirs. They did not necessarily directly link specific problems in their villages to their desires to leave them, but clearly many had been significantly affected by this kind of bad behavior. In Leontii Travin's account of his early life, he described a village filled with enemies, jealousy, people "lacking good conscience," and even "evil"—certainly one with which he very consciously wanted to cut ties. He particularly blamed some of the village overseers sent by his owner, "the count," including the "Frenchman Devals, who darkened the light which we enjoyed, and covered the whole estate with the gloom of misfortunes, for the description of which there is not enough time."[113] Travin was not alone; Shipov, too, claimed to have been robbed and generally ill-used by his fellow serfs after his wealthy father's death, and Nikitenko's memoirs are filled with similar descriptions of enemies in the village. Although he primarily blamed various Sheremetevs for moving his family around their many villages, he also described some of these actions as motivated by peasant complaints and evildoing—his father's work as an agent of the Sheremetevs frequently put him at odds with the local peasants he was supposed to govern.[114]

The bitterness on display in these accounts seems to have something in common with more general trends in the literary production of Russia's lower classes. The worker poetry of the early twentieth century, for example, was "saturated with a rich vocabulary of personal affliction," from sadness through misery to tears and pain.[115] And, too, it is a reminder of the fact that *soslovie* identities were above all local. In these cases, peasants were pushed less by the fact of their peasant status and more from the traumas of their specific villages. That is, for all that some of their problems could be blamed on their serf or peasant status as a whole, the particular degree of bitterness felt by these men was about a specific community, as well.

Women faced an additional problem of fit within some particular societies. Some sources suggest that women deemed to be burdens or disruptive may well have been pushed out of their native communities. Unattached women, childless or not, aged or young, were often seen as social (and moral) disruptors. Unmarried mothers and aged women without family support were possible financial burdens. The never married were morally suspect. These fears were, according to some historians, real ones for peasant villages, which in other contexts were so happy to rid themselves of the problem of unattached women that they might allow them to leave without paying normal discharge fees.[116] Single women were, at base, often outsiders in their village communities, and thus more likely to be forced into "marginal" positions—or even out completely.[117]

Archival evidence supports this interpretation. Women (by definition single, or they would be registered under their husband's name) accounted for only 5.3 percent of new merchants in Moscow between 1860 and 1888, but 47.2 percent of new townspeople in one Moscow district between 1859 and 1896. That meant that the women were far more prevalent among the poorer townspeople. Moreover, all of the new merchant women listed as heads of household were widows with adult sons and, often, those sons' families as well. In other words, relatively prosperous widowed mothers were acting not on their own but rather as the common bond between brothers sharing resources to qualify as merchants.[118] Among the new townswomen, however, only 33 percent of women entered with family members—the remainder entered the society alone, without support. Furthermore, unlike the new merchant women who had adult sons, the new townswomen had children whose average age was only eleven—and 32 percent of them were mothers to illegitimate children. Both were likely indicators of the more marginal status of such women in their native societies.

SOSLOVIE AS HIERARCHY

The idea of *soslovie* was tightly bound with the notion of social hierarchy. There was, simply, a general and persistent belief that *sosloviia* were arrayed in a hierarchy, with some distinctly higher and others distinctly lower. Marriage laws put this clearly, describing the ways that "higher status" was or was not shared with spouses and children. Furthermore, these gradations of status were not simply the large ones between nobles and everyone else; they extended to the generally lower soul-tax paying strata of society. Townspeople were higher than peasants, and state peasants were higher than serfs. These distinctions persisted as well—even the final edition of the *Digest of the Laws* used the same language of high and low that the very first one had.[119]

Furthermore, these gradations of status were at times literally displayed on the body. Peter the Great's demand that nobles and others of privileged status shave their beards physically marked them as separate from their subordinates.[120] In addition, *soslovie*-based distinctions in the application of corporal punishment further served to emphasize distinctions between high and low. Catherine the Great freed Russia's nobles from flogging, and her successors freed additional social groups later in the nineteenth century. Thus, being marked as subject to the knout (whip) was part, in a way, of peasant—or lowly—estate identity, just as freedom from such punishment emphasized the social hierarchy. For some state officials, too, the act of granting such privileges was explicitly linked to inculcating "a sense of dignity and self-worth."[121]

Similar concerns of status and honor were endemic to the *soslovie* system, dating back even before it was well established. Prior to Peter the Great, the system of *mestnichestvo*, in particular, made minute gradations of rank an obsession for Moscow's elite. But this concern with rank resonated through the Muscovite social hierarchy; as Nancy Shields Kollman notes, "no matter how lowly in the social hierarchy, Muscovites objected if their social rank were insulted."[122] Later, too, those of non-elite status were deeply concerned with questions of honor and status. A description of local conflict in an eighteenth-century town found many instances of insults to honor, and many similar cases were brought to township courts in the early twentieth century.[123]

Peter's reforms of recruiting and taxation may have emphasized this idea of hierarchy. Not every imperial subject owed the soul tax or was subject to the draft, as members of the nobility and clergy were exempt from such obligations from the start, and merchants came to owe taxes levied on a different basis (by capital).[124] In addition, those who did owe the soul tax were increasingly seen as a single undifferentiated mass, as when the new legislation eliminated slaves as a category and instead conflated them with taxpaying peasants, thus emphasizing the lower status of taxpayers.[125] In this way, Peter's reforms created two large social groups: the burdened soul-tax paying, and the privileged exempt—and with this created a real incentive for individuals to move from one group to the other.

This concern with hierarchy helped affirm and reaffirm the power of *soslovie* for individuals. Such a belief in social hierarchies and mobility lay behind Aleksandr Stupin's desire to leave the society of townspeople, for example. According to his account, he by rights belonged to a much more august estate: the nobility. His mother's father, he said, had been a governor in Kostroma and her uncle "a general in the navy." But Stupin himself had been handed over to an Arzamas townsman, Vasilii Stupin, before his mother's early death, and was from the age of three registered as a townsman. His tale, with its nonsensical titles, seems suspect—more the dreams of an artist (he later became one) with social aspirations than reality. Nonetheless, there is a ring of truth to those social aspirations, particularly in the appearance of his sister who, "being raised in the noble home of G. Annenkova, and either from her own pride or from love for me could not stand my town status, and relentlessly urged me to exit it into a bureaucratic order." Thanks to her efforts, supplemented by a letter from her protector (and a golden ring as additional security), Stupin was made an undersecretary and, thanks to the Table of Ranks, was given a new status.[126]

In addition, these notions of social hierarchies often mapped onto geographical hierarchies. One such hierarchy was a basic distinction between town and countryside. Townspeople believed themselves to be of higher status than their peasant fellows.[127] In his memoir, Ioann Belliustin described this as a particular problem for some priests. According to him, priests in small towns were in many ways worse off than their country fellows. Peasants believed their priests were of higher status than they, but the same was not true in towns. There, merchants, and even petty townspeople, believed that they enjoyed higher status than their priests.[128] For many, the town itself was a draw, not simply the means to a better salary. L. B. Genkin, describing the pre-emancipation serfs of the Central Industrial Region near Moscow, claimed that "it is possible to say, with good reason, that a piece of dry bread in the city seemed to the migrant peasant more delicious than a rich pie in the country."[129]

A second geographical distinction also implied status: towns were of high status, but the capitals—Moscow and St. Petersburg—were the highest of all. Chukmaldin, for one, found the apex of his career not the moment when he became a Siberian merchant but when he moved on and joined the Moscow merchant society. Nearly a century earlier, Ivan Tolchenov made a similar move, from Tver to Moscow, and also saw it as a move up in the world—even as it went with a move down from merchant to mere townsman.[130] The capitals were often seen as the apex of the social hierarchy in a way that blurred the value of *soslovie* status.

In some memoirs, authors described their desire to change *soslovie* as based in a desire to better their own, abject position. In many cases, these writers described moments of a sudden, shocking realization that they were of low status. For some, it was nearly an epiphany that brought them face to face with their place in society and prompted them to seek change. After Savva Dmitriev's owner suddenly raised quitrent rates, Dmitriev had just such an experience. For him, it was not purely a matter of finances; the increased quitrent rates were of course an economic hardship, but Dmitriev felt something else. According to his memoir, "at that moment for the first time in my life I felt the bitterness of my enserfed condition! Right then into my naive mind for the first time came the terrible question 'What are we?' "[131] Aleksandr Berezin remembered a similar crisis; he, a monastery peasant, suddenly found himself wondering at age eight, "For what reason did my mother bear me?" Although he initially tied this concern to his religious belief, he also soon actively pursued a path toward social advancement that simultaneously frightened and elated him.[132]

For serfs in particular this generalized recognition of a desire for escape could easily be transformed into a basic desire for freedom for freedom's sake.[133] This sort of idea runs through the tale of Aleksandr Nikitenko, whose long siege of his Sheremetev owner owed something to his desire for an abstract freedom. As he put it, "passionate urges for freedom, for knowledge, for a broader experience sometimes overwhelmed me to the point of physical pain."[134] Even after the end of serfdom, the idea of freedom continued to play a role in individual conceptions of social status. Certain post-emancipation statuses were interpreted as freer than others. Peasant life was still a place seen as constricted in social mores and possibilities for advancement. Movement to the towns was both an escape and a goal. And even into the early twentieth century, such desires for mobility and escape featured heavily in the imaginative world of Russia's proletarian writers and thinkers.[135]

A desire for freedom occasionally went along with a desire to escape totally from the world of *soslovie*, but it more often co-existed with the recognition that having a place, even a low one, was better than being without formal status. At times, this understanding was something entirely practical. Mar'ia Efimova, for one, a serf freed by legal judgment, felt herself in legal limbo as she waited for the Smolensk Treasury Department to register her as a Gzhatsk townswoman, which left her "without the necessary documents."[136] Her desire for a formal place in the Gzhatsk town society was forced upon her by law, but it also meant she would have a place.

At the same time, the power of specific *soslovie* identities may have been fading by the end of the imperial era. Certainly that has been the interpretation of some commentators, who argue that the rapid social change after the emancipation took place beyond the bounds of *soslovie* rather than within it—for them, *soslovie* is thus interpreted as less relevant to modernizing lives, a static force now overcome by other identities.[137] Nevertheless, the persistent practice of changing *soslovie* even during the late imperial era demonstrates the continuing power of *soslovie*, whether as hierarchy, as belonging, or as a source of opportunity and obligation.

TABLE 1.1

Number of new Moscow merchants by decade

	Total	Average per year	Percent change from previous decade
1795	790		
1810s	297	30	
1820s	326	33	9.8
1830s	261	26	-19.9
1840s	242	24	-7.3
1850s	308	31	27.3
1860s	240	24	-22.1
1870s	200	20	-16.7
1880–1888	159	18	-11.7

Source: TsIAM f. 397, op. 1, d. 121; f. 2, op. 1; f. 2, op. 3; f. 3, op. 1.

CHANGING *SOSLOVIE*

In addition to those records that mention the reasons individuals wanted to change their official status, there are thousands upon thousands more records that note only the bare facts of such changes. The records are scattered across many archives, in the files of different *soslovie* administrations and central authorities, and further complicated by different practices of record-keeping at different times and in different places. Despite these limitations, the records add weight to the idea that, despite the significant limitations on mobility faced by subjects of the imperial state, many did manage to alter their official status. And they help outline the contours of that practice of mobility as it changed over nearly two centuries.

Moscow's merchant society brought in hundreds of new members during the late eighteenth and nineteenth centuries. The most distinctive change in the patterns of movement into Moscow's merchant *soslovie* was one of sheer numbers: in this time period, there was a clear decline in the rate of movement into the society, even given the possibility of changes in record-keeping practice. In 1795, 790 new merchants (plus their families) entered the society; in no single year in the nineteenth century did anywhere near that number of merchants join. That earlier year coincided with the fifth revision of the census (1795–1796), the first time the tax rolls had been cleaned up since the Charter to the Towns had been promulgated a decade earlier. The particularly large numbers of new merchants—indeed, the Senate was so concerned about excessive movement into

TABLE 1.2

Percent of new Moscow merchants by *soslovie*

	1795 (N = 790)	1810–1860 (N = 1,458)	1861–1888 (N = 575)
Peasants (all)	81.4	73.7	70.1
Town *sosloviia*	14.3	20.8	22.4
Church	1.9	0.2	0.0
Non-Russians	0.5	1.2	0.7
Military	0.6	1.1	5.7
None	0.0	1.4	0.0
Other	1.3	1.6	1.0

Source: *TsIAM f. 397, op. 1, d. 121; f. 2, op. 1; f. 2, op. 3; f. 3, op. 1.*

merchant status that it placed a moratorium on such movement in the middle of the year—almost certainly reflect that event.[138] During the nineteenth century more broadly, the rate of movement into the society generally declined, likely reflecting increased economic opportunities for those outside the status of merchant. Only in the 1820s (after the disruption of the Napoleonic wars, and when changes in the regulation of the merchant guilds slightly opened up the status) and in the 1850s (when two census revisions allowed for greater mobility) was that larger downward trend disrupted.

The social origins of the new merchants varied widely, from peasants and serfs, to retired soldiers and non-Russians, to a youth "found at a tavern not knowing his parentage," taken in by a merchant.[139] Despite this variety, the records from the end of the eighteenth century through the end of the nineteenth century show some significant continuities in the social make-up of new merchants because two groups consistently dominated. Throughout this era, by far the majority of those entering merchant societies were of peasant background, whether serf or non-serf, although the proportion of peasants among the new merchants did decrease slightly over the course of the century. Furthermore, consistently, a significant minority of cases came from those of other town origins, and their numbers grew throughout the nineteenth century.

This overall pattern, however, masks a number of differences. For one, the general consistency in rates of people of town status among the new merchants masks one anomalous decade: the 1820s, when people with town status made up an unusually high proportion (37.4 percent) of those seeking entry into the society. Nearly all of that increased mobility occurred in a single year: 1825. This was the year following a series of reforms that restructured the rules for merchant status, including an easing of the movement of townspeople into the higher town status.[140] Although the bulk of the resulting mobility occurred immediately, it also kept rates of intra-town mobility higher for the rest of the decade, as well.

The overarching sameness in these patterns of mobility also masks a significant change in the composition of the new merchants of peasant origin. During the eighteenth century, that larger peasant group had been dominated by non-serf peasants.[141] The pattern held true through the beginning of the nineteenth century, but soon thereafter that relationship reversed itself, and freed serfs came to outnumber non-serf peasants by a significant margin. The initial shift likely reflects significant new restrictions placed on non-serf peasant mobility at the end of the eighteenth and beginning of the nineteenth centuries.[142] However, its persistence past the time when those restrictions had been either relaxed or abolished is harder to explain. It could, on the one hand, reflect a habit of manumission on the part of the Russia's serf-owners.[143] Or, it could reflect the more significant strictures placed on mobility by communal village administrations. A serf had only to convince his owner to free him; a state peasant, however, had to convince his whole community.

One other small group saw significant change from the end of the eighteenth century to the post-Reform era. Petitioners with military background—that is, retired soldiers, soldiers' sons, or soldiers' wives or widows—increased markedly both in number and in proportion within the overall array of new merchants. They were barely present at the end of the eighteenth century, and grew in number and proportion only slightly in the early parts of the nineteenth century. After 1860, however, their numbers increased

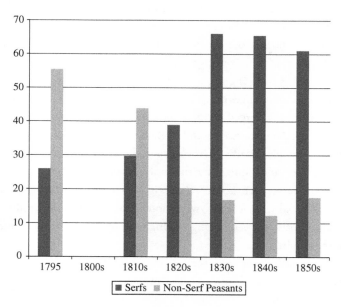

Percent of serf and non-serf peasants among all peasants entering the Moscow merchant society, 1795–1860. *TsIAM f. 397, op. 1, d. 121; f. 2, op. 1; f. 2, op. 3; f. 3, op. 1*

TABLE 1.3

Percent of new provincial merchants by *soslovie*, 1804–1913		
	Pre-Reform (N = 301)	Post-Reform (N = 61)
All Peasants	8.6	8.2
Serfs	3.3	
Other Peasants	5.3	
Town *sosloviia*	87.4	88.5
Church	0.3	0.0
None	0.3	1.6
Other	3.3	1.6

Source: GAIaO f. 79, op. 1; f. 100, op. 4; f. 501, op. 1;
GARO f. 4, op. 100; f. 49, op. 1; GASO f. 2, op. 1; f. 3, op. 1;
f. 28, op. 1–2; f. 94, op. 1; GATO f. 21, op. 1.

more significantly. This may reflect the failure of the imperial state to meet the needs of its former soldiers; although it began to grant pensions to retired soldiers at the end of the eighteenth century, it was not able to support them as their numbers grew during the nineteenth century.[144] The more significant growth in the later nineteenth century also reflects increased opportunities to move, as the Army Reform altered the basis of military service. When able to change their status, some soldiers clearly did.

Merchant societies in the provinces had rather different sources of new members. The decline in overall numbers from the first to the second half of the nineteenth century may simply reflect a quirk of recording practice, but the drop is severe enough to suggest that merchant status was losing some of its attractiveness in the provinces. But while that change agrees with changes in Moscow, patterns of the *soslovie* origins of new merchants in the provinces diverged strongly. While Moscow's new merchants were above all peasants by origin, new merchants in Iaroslavl', Riazan', Saratov, and Tver' were overwhelmingly townspeople already. This held true in both the pre- and post-Reform world, and among both men and women. Furthermore, while former serfs came to dominate the larger group of peasants turned merchants in Moscow, that pattern did not hold true in the provinces. Freed serfs, it seems, were more inclined to register in Moscow than in a provincial town, perhaps recognizing the higher status of Moscow within the social hierarchy of the empire.

Although Moscow's merchant society received many new members, an early nineteenth-century statistical guide to the city showed an even bigger transformation in its social composition from the late eighteenth to the mid-nineteenth century. According to the guide, the number of merchants in the town had increased from 11,900 at the end of the eighteenth century to 17,800 at the end of the 1830s. Over the same time

TABLE 1.4

Percent of petitioners to become Moscow townspeople by
soslovie and gender, 1813–1817

	Men (N = 853)	Women (N = 1,048)
Serfs	84.2	94.8
Non-serf peasants	1.3	1.2
Town *sosloviia*	5.6	1.7
Church	5.7	0.4
Military	0.9	0.9
Non-Russian	0.4	0.2
None	1.1	0.6
Other	0.8	0.2

Source: *TsIAM f. 32, op. 9, op. 12.*

span, however, the number of townspeople and artisans had increased far more dramatically. While only 9,100 of the lower ranking town residents had been registered in the late eighteenth century, four decades later their number had climbed to 75,300—more than eight times their earlier number.[145]

At least in the early nineteenth century, this increase in numbers was accounted for, above all, by freed serfs. From 1813 to 1817, nearly two thousand individuals petitioned to enter Moscow's society of townspeople. They came from a wide range of *soslovie* backgrounds, but by far the majority were freed serfs. This marks the beginning of a stronger differentiation between *meshchane* and merchants. Serfs were growing in prominence among those entering Moscow's merchant society, but in this same decade they were still outnumbered by non-serf peasants. That was obviously no longer true among the townspeople. Instead, it appears to foreshadow comments made later about changes in the capital's society of townspeople—home, it came to be said, to more and more freed serfs.[146]

During and after the Great Reforms, the situation in Moscow changed. Now, while peasants still accounted for the majority of new townspeople in Moscow, their numbers were much reduced. Among men, the numbers had actually fallen even more steeply, largely reflecting new groups, particularly retired soldiers, that began to appear in greater numbers. Furthermore, this period saw a resurgence of the registry of those who had no prior *soslovie* status, ranging from illegitimate children, to wards of the foundling home, to the children of men with only personal, not hereditary, statuses.

Such new members were so prominent in the St. Petersburg society of townspeople that they totally upended the pattern of social mobility there, particularly among women. Among women who entered the society in 1849, while a solid majority (55.3 percent)

TABLE 1.5

Percent of new Moscow and St. Petersburg townspeople by *soslovie* and gender,
c. 1859–1899*

| | Moscow | | St. Petersburg | |
	Men (N = 346)	Women (N = 307)	Men (N = 636)	Women (N = 1,159)
All peasants	40.5	66.1	39.9	17.1
Town *sosloviia*	6.6	5.5	38.4	3.1
Church	0.9	0.0	0.3	0.0
Military	33.8	15.3	5.5	7.8
None	10.1	12.4	14.2	71.5
Other	8.1	0.7	1.7	0.5

* Moscow townspeople entering only Sretenskaia suburb, 1859–1896;

St. Petersburg townspeople entering the town society as a whole in 1859, 1883, 1892, and 1899.

Source: TsIAM f. 5, op. 1, dd. 209–13; TsGIASPb f. 222, op. 1, d. 360–61, 421–22, 506–507, 1108.

came from peasant backgrounds, a significant minority (36.3 percent) were wards of the
Imperial St. Petersburg Foundling Home.[147] Later in the nineteenth century, people
without prior status became even more prominent among those who entered the society.
They accounted for 71.5 percent of all new townswomen; even discounting the hundreds
of wards, those with no status accounted for nearly 30 percent of all women.

St. Petersburg and Moscow diverged in other ways. Far more men of town status, especially merchants, entered St. Petersburg's society of townspeople in the late nineteenth
century, reflecting either differences in record-keeping practices (i.e., that such changes
in status were kept in different record books in Moscow) or greater financial instability
in the northern capital. In addition, St. Petersburg had far fewer new male members from
the military, but more new female members. The former likely reflects the fact that the St.
Petersburg sample does not include the years immediately surrounding the Army Reform,
when so many former soldiers entered Moscow's society of townspeople. The latter, however, is in keeping with years of records on town populations in St. Petersburg, which was
always home to larger numbers of both men and women associated with the military.

In the provinces, different patterns again emerged. The major difference is the lack of
large numbers (although the persistence of small numbers) of those without prior status.
As in the capitals (at least before the appearance of wards), however, women were particularly likely to come from peasant origins and, in the pre-Reform era, from serfdom.
Men often did come from peasant origins, particularly after the reforms, but also from a
wider variety of backgrounds. In the provinces before the reforms, men from church and
military backgrounds were common; after the reforms, men from other town societies

TABLE 1.6

Percent of new provincial townspeople by *soslovie* and gender, 1801–1917

	Men		Women	
	Pre-Reform (N = 643)	Post-Reform (N = 252)	Pre-Reform (N = 219)	Post-Reform (N = 108)
All Peasants	44.3	63.5	81.3	76.9
Serfs	18.8		64.8	
Others	25.5		16.4	
Town *sosloviia*	2.6	2.4	0.5	7.4
Church	23.5	2.4	3.2	2.8
Military	13.2	7.1	3.7	8.3
None	4.2	4.8	0.9	2.8
Other	10.9	4.8	10.5	1.9

Source: *GAIaO f. 79, op. 1; f. 100, op. 4, 8; f. 501, op. 1; GARO f. 4, op. 77, 100; f. 49, op. 1; GASO f. 2, op. 1; f. 3, op. 1; f. 15, op. 1; f. 28, op. 1–2; f. 94, op. 1; GATO f. 21, op. 1.*

more frequently came to join local townspeople societies. A focused look at one town, Saratov, shows something rather different. In several individual years, the social origins of those who joined the Saratov townspeople society varied widely. In 1858, 898 men joined the society. Just under half of them (47.9 percent) came from peasant, mostly serf, backgrounds. Nearly as many had military status (44.8 percent); a small number had other town status (3.9 percent); and the remaining few came from statuses ranging from postal workers to "a prisoner taking part in the defense of Sevastopol'" (and apparently winning his freedom by that act).[148] A decade and a half later, however, the situation was very different. In 1872, 584 men joined the society. In this case, the vast majority of them—85.8 percent—came from military statuses, while only very small numbers came from peasant or town societies (4.1 and 5.3 percent, respectively).[149]

Archival records also show quite clearly that townspeople themselves were likely to change their status. In part this movement reflects the statutory changes required by Catherine the Great's Charter to the Towns. According to that document, merchants and townspeople were defined most of all by financial status; if a merchant had a business failure, he could well find himself demoted to the status of townsperson. Among the Moscow merchants who changed *soslovie* between 1810 and 1888, more than half moved down into the townsperson or artisan societies. The next largest group of merchants sought in some ways the opposite kind of mobility: 12 percent became honored citizens, a status created in 1832 to provide a means of fixing privileged status.

TABLE 1.7

Percent of those leaving Moscow merchant society by merchant
status and destination, 1810–1888

	Merchants (N = 153)	Relatives (N = 272)
Townspeople and artisans	52.9	15.8
Honored Citizens	11.8	0.4
Education	3.9	32.4
Professions	5.2	10.3
Bureaucracy	8.5	9.9
Arts	3.3	4.0
Military	2.0	7.0
Church	7.2	9.6
Peasants	0.7	0.4
Unknown	4.6	10.3

Source: TsIAM f. 2, op. 1; f. 2, op. 3; f. 3, op. 1.

At the same time, these Moscow records show a rather different kind of mobility among merchant relatives. Because merchant status was not exactly hereditary—the head of a merchant household alone was the merchant, while others had the status of merchant's sons, grandsons, or brothers—those relatives were listed separately in the archival records. And these figures show a very different pattern of mobility. If merchants stayed within town societies, their relatives gained release in many different ways. The single largest group of these were merchants' relatives (usually sons and grandsons) who were released to pursue their education; taken together, nearly as many moved into some sort of other work—in the bureaucracy, in the arts, in the professions, or in the military.

Townspeople from the capitals also changed their *soslovie*. Except for Moscow at the start of the nineteenth century, when nearly half of those who changed status sought to enter monasteries, most of their movement occurred within towns themselves. These were townspeople most often becoming merchants, and occasionally finding access even into other town ranks of artisan or (very rarely) honored citizen. Others moved into professions, entered state service, or were released from their society for educational purposes. And particularly in the later imperial era, some also became peasants. No townspeople at the start of the century made that move, but in the later nineteenth century, the second largest group of Moscow townspeople left the town for the village. In the post-serfdom world, apparently, the village had become a place that could also attract new residents, not only push its own residents away.

TABLE 1.8

Percent of those leaving Moscow and St. Petersburg townsperson societies by destination*

	Moscow		St. Petersburg
	1813–1817 (N = 129)	1856–1915 (N = 93)	1854–1861 (N = 440)
Peasant		11.8	2.3
Town	15.5	68.8	78.4
Church	48.8	2.2	0.5
Professions/Service	13.2	9.7	12.0
Education		6.5	6.8
Unknown	22.5	1.1	

* Moscow-wide numbers in 1813–1817; only Sretenskaia suburb for 1856–1915; St. Petersburg-wide numbers for 1854–1856, 1861.

Source: *TsIAM f. 5, op. 1, dd. 209–13; f. 32, op. 9, 12; TsGIASPb f. 222, op. 1, dd. 23, 106–107.*

Personal decisions to change *soslovie* could be based on many different desires—for escape, for community, for economic opportunity—reflecting both the power of legal standards and the power of more abstract identities. These decisions show well that, fairly consistently throughout the imperial era, for many Russians *soslovie* membership retained its power even in the face of alternative identities and new economic and social opportunities in the "modern" world. Its importance changed along with rationales for changing status, but it never disappeared, and it always prompted some individuals to interact with what could seem a terrible burden of bureaucracy.

Not only did *soslovie* matter, but the process of moving between *soslovie* could be the source of immense personal satisfaction. The former serf Nikitenko ended his memoir with the following lines, expressing his reaction to receiving his freedom, and therefore suddenly becoming able to purse the educational goals (and movement upwards in society) that he had long desired: "I refuse to speak of what I endured and experienced during those first minutes of deep, tremendous joy.... Praise be to the All Mighty and eternal thanks to those who helped me be restored to a new life!"[150] That new life was the goal of these petitions: not simply new work, but also a new life, in a new place, with a new social identity.

These many individual decisions took place within an official *soslovie* structure, one that was constantly adapting to the actions of both the central imperial state and local *soslovie* authorities. Individuals were at times constricted in their desires by the force of law. But at the same time, individual desires, brought to the attention of local authorities, and later to central ones, often forced change upon them. As individuals sought to change their status, officials came to decide on whether their desires should be allowed. As a result, the interplay between individual desire and the interests of both local societies and the central state created an ever-shifting landscape of regulation of the process of social mobility.

2

Legal Standards and Administrative Reality

LOCAL INTERESTS AND CENTRAL IDEALS IN THE

EIGHTEENTH CENTURY

IN 1726, A man named Egor Vasil'ev (sometimes also known by the family name Bykov) submitted a petition to the Kursk Magistracy. Magistracies were responsible for adjudicating many elements of the everyday life of townspeople, and in particular were responsible for deciding who was a true member of the local town community. Vasil'ev/Bykov was by origin a church peasant from Kostroma province, but according to his statement, he had lived in Kursk working as a trader and as a carpenter for some thirty years. Because he had been absent from his home village for so long, he had not been counted during the first census of the population that went along with Peter the Great's introduction of the soul tax two years before. He was, therefore, petitioning to be counted in his current home of Kursk, and in so doing to take on a new status, that of townsman.[1]

For Vasil'ev/Bykov, gaining this official status was both a formalization of what he believed he already was and a way of fixing himself in a particular place. The Magistracy drew on legal precedent dating back to the mid-seventeenth century, but based its decision on several recent decrees that it read as allowing such formalization. It decided to accept Vasil'ev/Bykov as a townsperson if he provided proof of his economic status. Although Vasil'ev/Bykov delivered an attestation that stated that he had sufficient trade and capital to prosper as a merchant, he failed to complete his registration. As a result, a year later he fell into trouble near Kiev, when local authorities questioned who he was and whether he had the right to be there.[2] Without formal registration, he had no real answers for their questions.

The eighteenth century was a time of extraordinary transition for Russia. Beginning with Peter the Great and his radical reforms to elite culture and public administration, developing through the waves of reforms and counter-reforms of his successors, and culminating in the reign of Catherine the Great, virtually all subjects of the Russian Empire saw their relationships with both the state and their fellow subjects altered. Nobles found themselves pulled into a new culture, first bound to service, then freed from it and allowed to develop as something akin to landed gentry. While serfs were increasingly separated from direct contact with the state by the growing authority of their noble owners, they were also burdened with new demands for taxes and military service, as were the many peasants on state or monastery lands. Residents of towns, too, were alternately protected and alarmed by imperial decrees supporting trade or altering their own social statuses.

The governance of *sosloviia* was at the center of many of these changes. For one, many of the changes of the eighteenth century applied to specific *sosloviia*, not to all of Russian society. More specifically, however, laws that regulated who belonged to which status and how individuals could go about changing that status were integral to defining what *soslovie* meant. They drew the lines between different statuses, but also, in allowing for those lines to be crossed, more fully developed a conception of what possession of a status implied. While many historians have dated the "full" institution of *soslovie* to the reign of Catherine the Great,[3] well before that time laws had delineated a concept of *soslovie* as something linked broadly to occupation and duty and also to membership in a specific local society. That idea of membership had many implications for how *soslovie* grew and developed, and for how both individuals and local authorities understood their relationship.

Furthermore, by looking not only at central decrees that set up regulations for *sosloviia* but also at the ways those decrees were interpreted by local authorities, two things become apparent. First, by the late eighteenth century, two legal principles defining what *soslovie* meant—belonging to a society and owing duties—had been well developed in laws regulating mobility, even as those laws continually came up against problems based in shifting social categories. Second, the laws promulgated by the state to govern estate mobility reflected an essential conflict in central state desires. The laws most often focused on ensuring social stability, ensuring tax revenues, and ensuring military recruits, all goals made easier by restricting mobility. At the same time, the eighteenth century was an era of expanding borders and changing economic demands, an era that demanded at least some degree of social mobility. As a result, for much of this time laws struck an uneasy balance between these two demands, a delicate balance that individuals and localities could exploit.[4]

FIXING AND FREEING: CONFLICTING STATE AIMS IN EIGHTEENTH-CENTURY LAWS

During the eighteenth century, a whole series of regulations—mostly Senate decisions, but also imperial manifestos and administrative ukases, or decrees—came to govern the process of changing *soslovie*. Most of these regulations were at base efforts to ensure that everyone possible was registered as accurately as possible on the tax rolls, and thus that the state would receive the maximum benefit from its population. As such, the rules were in many ways an effort to reduce the number of "free people," or of *raznochintsy*, and instead to be sure that as many subjects as possible were easily identifiable and, more important, taxable.[5] Although the laws from this period were sometimes conflicting, two main principles began to emerge by the final third of the century. First, individuals needed documentary evidence that they were free and capable of making such moves. Second, such moves should lead to no losses in taxes or duties to the state or to local authorities.

In many ways, the process of constructing imperial Russia's *soslovie* structures began with the codification of Muscovite laws in the middle of the seventeenth century. By the seventeenth century, social categories among the elite had splintered into many separate and evolving statuses based variously on service or geography.[6] The multitude of "lower" orders, however, were far less distinct; until the sixteenth century, there was simply a "homogenous tax-paying mass, consisting of town and village inhabitants," and only then did differences, largely based on the development of serfdom and slavery, begin to develop within that "mass."[7]

Out of this confusion came the *Ulozhenie* (Law Code) of 1649, initiating a period during which laws began to define and redefine social categories, and also to classify individuals according to those categories.[8] In particular, the *Ulozhenie* finalized the process of enserfment and bound other parts of society (townspeople, in particular) into an ever more rigid structure. Although there were certain large distinctions of status, most Muscovite subjects belonged less to a particular social group than to a particular place—peasants to their villages, townspeople to their towns.[9] Furthermore, by most accounts, the *Ulozhenie*, perhaps because it so focused on fixing people in place, left little room for mobility.[10]

Several reforms by Peter the Great altered the approach to classifying and regulating the population of the Russian Empire while maintaining the importance of that process of fixing the population in place. From early in his reign, Peter tried various methods of increasing the size of his army and of state revenues; eventually, he settled on regular recruitment levies to collect soldiers and the soul tax as a new way to improve state finances and fund his wars.[11] These reforms had larger consequences for Russia's social structures. To create tax rolls that would enable the state to collect its proper due in money and recruits, Peter instituted a semi-regular census of the population—a "revision," as it was called—the first of which was carried out in 1722–1723 and found 5.5 million souls subject to the tax.[12] These rolls were drawn up by the localities, and the act of recording the local populations gave a new language of belonging to the communities. Individuals were now "written in" or "written out" (or sometimes "counted in" or "counted out") of communities in a literal statement of membership. The rolls drawn up in one revision would regulate taxpaying and military obligations until the next revision; therefore, the central state and local communities were placed somewhat at odds, as the state wished not to undercount and local communities wished not to overcount. Moreover, because taxes were paid communally, local societies had an incentive to keep their members at home or risk losing a taxpayer whose name could not be struck off their lists until some future point in time.

The result of these laws was, according to one mid-nineteenth-century official historian, the end of a longer process. I. P. Rukovskii, writing for an official "commission to examine the system of taxes and duties," believed that Peter's soul tax, and particularly the headcount that went with it, "finished off the process… of tying the tax-paying population to their places of residence." Furthermore, he noted the importance of the Petrine innovations in the development of the idea of collective responsibility—the famous *krugovaia poruka*—in Russian social structures and particularly its effect on mobility. Now, he wrote, the combined forces of communal responsibility and the census "produced a new constraint on tax-paying people when they move from their *soslovie*; to be exact, in consequence of collective responsibility it was established, that a person both when leaving a society, and when entering one, must ask for the permission of the societies."[13] Rukovskii, however, was speaking more from his nineteenth-century perspective than from eighteenth-century legal practice; in reality, it took decades to establish those documentary requirements and to create a real system of *soslovie* mobility for the empire.

Throughout the eighteenth century, laws continued to fix people to locations as best as possible by tracking down fugitives and, through laws about the tax rolls, by emphasizing the importance of registration. Laws on fugitives focused on two basic commands: first, that fugitive peasants or townspeople be returned to their place of origin; and second, that those who gave refuge to fugitives should be punished.[14] Many of these fugitive laws suggest that the interests of the state were above all financial; one law noted that fugitive townspeople who were found and returned to their place of registry were still liable for the taxes and duties they had missed during their absence.[15]

Revisions of the tax rolls were also occasions to emphasize social stability. First, they were opportunities to address changes in terminology or categorization since the previous census, and thus to redefine social categories more firmly.[16] In addition, the ukases announcing new census revisions emphasized the importance of registry, and those providing additional instructions exhorted local authorities to find and record all unregistered people. Instructions were in principle clear: any newcomers were to be interrogated to find out whether they were truly not registered or instead were hidden fugitives.[17] And yet, each revision was accompanied by scores of additional laws addressing the many complications that arose when the supposedly simple count was imposed on a society that was neither static nor simple. These laws also had a real effect on registry. Records from local magistracies show surges in petitions to change status around the times of the second revision (announced 1743, carried out 1743–1745) and particularly the third revision (announced 1761, carried out 1762–1764).[18]

Even as legislation sought to fix individuals in social categories and particular places, larger demands, particularly those of the empire, made some degree of controlled mobility desirable. The *Ulozhenie* had earlier recognized this need, as it set border regions as places outside the bounds of "normal" life and law.[19] Furthermore, peasants had long moved to towns in large numbers, and the state found itself interested in regularizing that process. Peasants had so persistently moved to towns that earlier efforts to restrict those movements had ended in failure.[20] But also, the imperial state recognized that it needed towns, and towns needed people. As a result, monarchs beginning with Peter the Great tried to attract new town residents and create a thriving commercial culture. What started with Peter's founding and forced construction (both physically and socially) of St. Petersburg culminated in many ways with the actions of Catherine the Great, who made cities a major focus of her regime, founding new ones out of whole cloth or out of rural settlements.[21]

In addition, lands newly annexed or newly secured needed to be populated in order to bring benefits and stability to the imperial state. In large part, unofficial (i.e., extralegal) or temporary (via passports) mobility supplied those new settlers for the new societies. But at the same time, the imperial state faced a dilemma, as it feared both the emptiness of the new territories and the emptiness that might result in the older territories after an extensive outmigration.[22] This conflict, between the desire to keep subjects in their place so as to ensure the economic health of existing communities and the desire to expand and develop the interests of the imperial state, became the major source of legal contradictions in the adjudication of estate mobility during the eighteenth century.

As a result of these opposing forces, many laws were passed to balance a restrictive notion of status with allowances for movement. Both these elements were present in Peter's establishment of the Table of Ranks. This piece of legislation not only created a formal hierarchy of positions within the civil, court, and military services but also set out rules that governed and restricted those who possessed noble status, By granting non-nobles the right to gain nobility and privilege through service, however, it also allowed a degree of social mobility meant to bring benefit to the state.[23]

A second Petrine innovation went even further, creating not just a chance for a kind of social mobility, or at least of social redefinition, but also an apparent demand for it. In 1722, Peter founded a new institution, the *tsekhi*, or craft guilds, and a new social category to go with them, the *tsekhovye*, or artisans. In principle, the guilds were to promote crafts and manufacturing, a goal that had appeared in various earlier laws. Peter's instructions to the new Main Magistracy included, for example, an exhortation to increase trade and manufacture in Russian towns.[24] The guilds would aid in this process by organizing crafts and by setting into place an official apprenticeship system. Practically, though, this caused certain problems. In a series of statutes, all those who wished to continue to practice a craft of some kind were now instructed to register in a guild or else give up their craft. At the same time, restrictions were placed on who could register: serfs, in particular, had to have freedom to do so.[25] This was a dilemma for both individuals who might find themselves instructed to do something forbidden and local institutions that adjudicated such measures, charged as they were with encouraging the growth of crafts. Although in principle the initial law founding the craft guilds gave clear guidelines, those guidelines were in practice contradictory; perhaps as a result, the craft guilds were slow to develop and to attract members.[26]

Other laws that allowed for mobility between statuses similarly juggled opposing instincts of stability and mobility in ways that could be contradictory. Initially, most laws gave too much credence to the second desire of the imperial state—to allow mobility that would develop the economic health of the state—and failed to address the first desire, which was to keep people registered in particular places. Indeed, these laws seem in some cases simply to have ignored the larger body of laws that sought to reduce flight and impel social stability, a development all the more surprising given the many early eighteenth-century laws stating, for example, that regardless of the state's need for soldiers, serfs and other unfree people were not permitted to run away to join the army.[27]

Early in the reign of Peter the Great, several laws dealt with the legal standing of peasants who wished to trade in towns by encouraging mobility. The first law proposed that peasants wanting to trade in Moscow should register there, a second law extended the demand for registry to all towns, and a third law stated that those who did not wish to register as merchants were henceforth forbidden to engage in mercantile activities.[28] One nineteenth-century historian interpreted these laws as a sign that Petrine desires for increased industry and trade had "compelled the state to break the bounds of serfdom."[29] Certainly they emphasized mobility over stability, as long as that mobility reflected actual occupation and brought benefit to the state.

Both of these concerns continued to appear in laws emphasizing mobility. A flurry of laws promulgated in the last several years of Peter's reign focused on the question of trade in towns and on the need to ensure that those engaging in trade were properly registered. The rationale behind these laws was twofold: first, as in the earlier laws, individuals ought to be registered according to their actual occupation; and second, towns ought to receive appropriate taxes from those who lived in them.[30] In 1747, the Senate made it clear that potential new merchants had to prove their worth with actual, written evidence of their financial status.[31] This decision—like the earlier Petrine ones—sought to supply towns with capable, prosperous merchants, above all, whatever their original social status.

All these laws ignored one aspect of Russian social structure: that not all those seeking to become merchants were free to do so.[32] It was not until 1762, during the brief reign of Peter III, that another Senate decree fixed that loophole by forbidding the registration of peasants as merchants without attestations of freedom from their previous societies. This law set up two major features of virtually all future laws dealing with the matter of changing estate. First, like the 1747 Senate decision, it emphasized the importance of written documentation. This time, however, it emphasized the importance of documentation of freedom. Serfs had to acquire and present a letter of manumission from their owners; monastery, state, or court peasants had to acquire and present a similar document that formally stated they were free to register elsewhere, from either their communities or their communal authorities. Second, the law reiterated a basic duty of most peasants: to pay taxes and dues. Specifically, freed peasants had to make arrangements (or have arrangements made for them) to continue to pay dues at their former place of residence. In other words, the former villages or former owners could not be stuck with the tax bills of their freed peasants.[33]

Although this law might have set a precedent for future mobility, it took a series of separate laws to spread its provisions, with necessary adjustments, to other parts of imperial society. In part, this stream of separate laws reflected the difficult concept of precedent—or, perhaps more accurately, the official lack of such a concept—in Russian legal structures. Autocratic rule demanded that local authorities not try to interpret the law but, rather, simply apply it.[34] Even more, the many laws reflected the time period— the eighteenth century was when new social categories were developing, while older, pre-Petrine ones still held on, as well. Each new category had to be treated distinctly, as procedures meant for one legally defined group could not necessarily be applied to another.

In 1777, the Senate again addressed policy regarding peasants seeking to register as merchants. Because of some intervening laws addressing other social groups, which could have been interpreted as replacing the earlier decision, and because the Senate believed that a larger change was coming (presumably the Charter to the Towns, then less than a decade away), the Senate considered banning all such moves. But because there had been no laws repealing the 1762 decision, it decided instead to lay out clear principles for future movement. First, the Senate decision stated that "it is not forbidden for peasants to enter the merchant estate, as long as they pay taxes as merchants do, by percentage and guild; and in addition… the normal taxes enforced by previous laws in that place from which they came." In other words, peasants who entered merchant societies carried a double tax burden for the foreseeable future. Second, as earlier decisions had stated, the new merchants had to have written proof of their freedom. Third, should a new statute be passed, all the new merchants had to abide by its rules or return to their status of origin.[35] By this point, those standards were well on their way to general usage. In a 1770 decision, the Holy Synod had used much the same rationale when it concluded that all peasants and merchants seeking to enter monasteries had to present written permission to leave their previous status, and they had to provide evidence that someone would keep paying their dues in their old places of residence.[36]

In this period of uncertain and shifting legal standards, individuals seeking to change their status along as yet unlegislated paths often found themselves at the mercy of central institutions that at times did not dare to build on precedent. In practice, this meant that local or central authorities could refuse to approve movement between categories if that movement had not already been specifically addressed by the laws. In 1782, the Senate did just that in the case of Peter Ivanov, an economic (or former monastery) peasant from Pskov province who had petitioned to enter the society of townspeople of nearby Novgorod. In practice that meant that Ivanov lacked the capital to qualify as a merchant, but he wanted nonetheless to join a town society. Petr Ivanov had fulfilled all the duties required of one seeking to change his status: his village had given him permission to leave with his three underage sons, on the grounds that he had no debts and was not next in line to be given by the village as an army recruit. However, the local authorities were uncertain how to proceed because "there [was] no prescription that allows a peasant to register as a [simple] townsman, and it is only allowed to enter the merchant estate." In this case, the Senate decided that the case ought not serve as a precedent for future mobility. Because there was no existing law covering such mobility, it decided that such movement was therefore unlawful, and it furthermore concluded "let the Pskov and Novgorod Local Authorities know, that the first did not have the right to free the peasant and the latter to accept [him]."[37]

This decision was surprising because at that time there existed precedent for one kind of peasant—freed serfs—to enter societies of townspeople. In a 1775 imperial manifesto celebrating the end of her first war with the Ottoman Empire, Catherine the Great waived many taxes and gave various other amnesties to her subjects. At the end of a long list of items, she did two things. First, she declared that "all those manumitted by their owners" were not allowed to re-enter serfdom, but instead were to "declare what sort of Our service they wish to enter, either into the townsperson or merchant status." Second, she formally defined what "townspeople" were: those registered as members of a town society who did not have more than 500 rubles in capital, and thus who could not be classified as merchants.[38] Taken in tandem with the preceding point, and with another point in the manifesto—which granted the "mercy" of being exempt from the soul tax to merchants—this manifesto instead seemed to emphasize the importance of specific *soslovie* identity, which in towns, at least, had implications both financial and social.

In other cases, however, individuals trying to move along as yet unregulated social paths led to decisions that established new laws that would henceforth cover more and more of the population—and more and more different kinds of mobility. A series of laws considered the case of "excess" sons of priests or church servitors who lacked the education to serve as priests or deacons, but who were still classified as churchmen because of their birth. Initially, Empress Anna ruled that all such men ought to be taken into the military. Then, in 1737, she modified this earlier rule: those excess churchmen who wished to avoid the army could buy themselves out of such service; if they then studied enough, they could qualify as church (which required study in grammar, rhetoric, and philosophy) or state (with arithmetic and geometry, too) servitors. If they were still not inclined to study, they could register as merchants in towns.[39] This was social mobility by legislative fiat, with state interests (more soldiers, more educated public servants, more merchants) at its core, not practical concerns like taxes or documentation.

Two later Senate decisions brought the rulings for churchmen more in line with other laws on mobility. In 1745, the Senate made it clear that new merchants from any status, including churchmen, paid taxes like their fellows.[40] Finally, in 1775, the Senate considered the case of several excess churchmen who had been registered as merchants in the town of Balakhna. In this case, the fact that none of them had official documents stating the freedom to do so, either from the Synod itself or from their local authorities, was raised as an issue. Because the men were "unneeded" by the church, the Synod gave an opinion that they should be retroactively freed, and thus allowed to stay in their new merchant positions, essentially complying with earlier statutes. In the future, however, all such excess churchmen should gain documentation of freedom from the Synod before seeking entry into a new status.[41]

In the decades leading up to Catherine's Charters to the Nobility and to the Towns there was no consistent legal structure in place to deal with the many permutations of evidence and individuals that might arise in a case involving changing estate. Laws existed in contradiction with one another in large part because the central government had sometimes contradictory interests. Although there were basic principles of documentation and duty that echoed throughout the legal record, the exact kinds of evidence and the exact statement of duties were unclear. As a result, even efforts by central legal institutions—the Senate and the Main Magistracy, and sometimes emperors or empresses themselves—to clarify how to deal with these contradictions could easily lead to yet more layers of complications. Decision after decision might have reinforced the idea that evidence was needed to prove freedom or that an individual was financially secure and willing and able to fulfill their allotted duties, but new cases could always bring in new classifications of people or new kinds of evidence that made decision making more an art than a science.

MAGISTRACIES AND THEIR DOCUMENTS

In the eighteenth century, most cases of individuals seeking to change their *soslovie* were handled by local legal institutions—town or provincial magistracies; these authorities found themselves in the tricky position of having to interpret supposedly incontrovertible autocratic law. In so doing, they were at times overwhelmed by the responsibility of evaluating individual cases (which meant evaluating individual lives), of representing local interests (as most members of the magistracy were locals), and of respecting central imperial interests (as the institution of the magistracy was supposed to be the face of the central government in the towns).

Before Catherine's Charters established more regular administration organized on *soslovie* lines, magistracies were among the most important local institutions. Their responsibilities for keeping order in towns came to include watching over the membership of town societies and regulating movement between places and between social statuses. Magistracies were supposed to decide whether individuals were legal residents of their towns or not, to send away those who were illegally resident there, and to register formally as townspeople or merchants all those who qualified. They were, in essence, the adjudicators of town populations, with full responsibility for ensuring that the right people were registered in the right town societies.[42]

After Peter's death, the role of the magistracy fluctuated; sometimes it was more responsive to central concerns, sometimes to those of local *soslovie* societies. In principle, at least, the magistracies continued to serve the interests of both local societies and central authority. Some historians argue for a strong interpretation of the magistracies as representatives of central authority.[43] But the archival files suggest something very different: magistracies were just as likely to consider local needs as central precedent. The documents they collected to make their decisions fulfilled the demands of the central state, but the decisions they made were often far more uncertain, and far more likely to fulfill local demands.

Even as the laws on *sosloviia* changed, the basic documents likely to appear in a given magistracy's files remained relatively constant through much of the eighteenth century. Magistracies received petitions, and then followed up on them, amassing supporting documents from both local and distant sources. Transcripts of the magistracies' decisions then followed, often including the legal reasoning behind their decisions, as well as specific provisions that might follow a given individual's change in status. The files end with documents reflecting the outcome of the magistracies' decisions. But while the consistency of these categories of documents—petitions, supporting documents, decisions, and outcomes—demonstrate a certain administrative uniformity in many regions of Russia and through much of the eighteenth century, there were nonetheless significant variations that reflected the changing legal basis for administering and altering *soslovie*, as well as regional peculiarities in social organization and legal thinking.

Cases began when an individual petitioned to change his[44] status, and as a result, the first document in most files is a petition addressed to the magistracy of the region in which the petitioner wished to register. In some cases the initiating document came from a relative (usually a parent petitioning on behalf of a child) or from some other administrative body (though in that case, the report usually included note of a petition that other body had received), but most came from those wishing to change their status themselves. Written on official stamped paper, they generally follow a fairly rigid pattern. Most open with a third-person statement of petition, which includes a lengthy phrase indicating the legal social position of the petitioner, always in a particular order: place of origin, including either town or district and village; status of origin, including ownership (or former ownership) in the case of serfs and monastery or church peasants; and name. This order translates awkwardly: for example, "petitions from Khotmyshkii district, Terebrenoe village, [belonging to] *odnodvorets* Timofei Iakovlev Kurilov, the manumitted household serf Larion Mikhailov Zukov."[45] This statement set up the formal nature of the petitions and indicated both a way of addressing petitions and a way of presenting one's legal identity, including status and geographical descriptors, that would hold fast until the end of the Russian Empire.

Petitions are most varied in their narrative accounts of individual desires, but even these descriptions often follow a basic script. After the third-person opening, the petitions usually switch into first-person narratives in which petitioners plead their case. Zukov's case shows the basic parts of most petitions:

> On January 14 of this year 1771, my above named owner freed me with my wife Matrena Stepanova and with my young children, my son Andrei and daughter Aksinia, who are one and a half year old (my son) and four years old (my daughter); for this I was given by the Kursk Department of Serf Affairs a manumission document which I herewith supply.
>
> And today I myself, by the authority of Your Imperial Majesty's decrees, and with the above named manumission document and due to my commercial trade, wish to be in the Kursk merchantry, and I will pay taxes and other government dues both with the Kursk merchants and in the Khotmyshskii Chancellery (where I currently am listed in the soul tax registers) without any arrears, and I can provide trustworthy guarantors of that.[46]

Zukov covered all the main points that were likely to appear in petitions from those seeking to change their estate. First, he described his family because, although petitions came from individuals, those individuals often brought their families along into their new status. In this case, Zukov was somewhat unusual in that he gave detailed information about his wife and daughter, as well as his son; because the soul tax and recruit duties were levied on men alone, often only sons or other male relatives appeared in the records. Second, he stated the documentary evidence he could supply to show that he was free to join a new estate: a statement of emancipation that had been properly registered with the authorities by his owner. Third, Zukov stated the place and *soslovie* he wished to join, and described briefly why he wished to make that change (in this case, because he had trade). Fourth, he made mention that his request was in accordance with the laws of the land. Fifth, Zukov promised to uphold his legal obligations to his old and new societies, showing that he would act in accordance with the laws. Sixth, and finally, Zukov stated that he was able to provide guarantors to prove that he was worth accepting into a new *soslovie*.

Not every petitioner touched on all of these six points, but every petition did address most of them. They all stated their basis for change, where they wished to go, and why they were free (or ought to be free, in a few cases) to make the change they desired, and virtually all mentioned at least the male family members who were included in their request. These statements had to be made because their contents—essentially, evidence of freedom from a former *soslovie* and desire and ability to join a new *soslovie*—were in many ways the legal underpinnings of individual cases. Of course, these were also the elements of petitions that showed the most variety because they were the most personal, while the statement of the legal basis on which a petition drew, the obligations of the petitioner, and the guarantors were often pro forma passages made simply because they were part of the process. But even so, the "personal" elements of petitions could be incredibly impersonal, as in Zukov's statement that he had vaguely defined "commercial trade."

Although the reasons given for changing status were rarely explored in much detail, giving them an abstract, universal quality, the apparently stock phrases about laws, obligations, and guarantors, could show some significant differences. While Zukov's petition simply noted that his request was in keeping with the laws, others went further and cited specific laws relevant to their cases. Petitioners who were seeking to make a change in their social standing under the auspices of a specific law, as in the case of returned runaway serfs given amnesty by an imperial manifesto, were almost certain to cite that law in their petitions.[47] On the other hand, when it came to mention of obligations, Zukov's petition was perhaps a bit more detailed than the norm; most simply said they would "pay all their dues and do all their service without fail," rather than mentioning anything as specific as their dues in their former place of residence.

Petitioners who were asking for special treatment—usually because they lacked full freedom from their home societies—tended to give more detailed accounts of their lives, as if to justify to magistracies why they deserved special consideration. For example, the Nerekhta townsmen Dmitri and Kozma Ikonopistsov first petitioned to enter the Iaroslavl' craft society in 1762, using only their passports as evidence of freedom. Both men (at the time 22 and 20 years old) had been born in Iaroslavl', where their father had long lived, married to a Iaroslavl' native. Although registered on the Nerekhta tax rolls, since that was their father's place of origin, the younger Ikonopistsovs had "no acquaintances or relatives or a house" in that town, and instead had even already fulfilled service obligations for the local society in Iaroslavl'. Their decision to petition to register formally as Iaroslavl' citizens was certainly a result of a recent realization that their paper registration still mattered: in 1759, Nerekhta had demanded that their father enter the military on behalf of the town. Initially the Iaroslavl' Magistracy decided to accept the men, but in this case the Main Magistracy intervened, noting that Nerekhta had not freed the men. After several years of inaction, the men petitioned again, with the same request and same documents. This time the Iaroslavl' Magistracy simply registered them and neglected to inform the Main Magistracy of its actions.[48]

Most of the material in archival files consists of documents gathered by the magistracies to support or supplement the claims made in the petitions that began them. In principle, the most important supporting document was a copy (or in some cases, an original) of the papers that gave a petitioner the right to register in a new estate.[49] This would prove his freedom, and usually also confirmed the family members included in the petitioner's claim. In some cases, such evidence was supplemented by inquiries made by the magistracy to officials in a given petitioner's home district, asking for confirmation that the petitioner was free to make a change. Really, though, petitioners should have presented the magistracy with appropriate documentation for their claims, as the

Pereslavl' Zalesskii Magistracy wrote to the Rostov Magistracy. In that case, Rostov had written to Pereslavl' Zalesskii inquiring after the status of several petitioners seeking to enter Rostov's merchantry. The Pereslavl' Zalesskii Magistracy wrote back testily: because the petitioners had presented legal documents, "the Pereslavl' Magistracy should not be troubled with such matters, and in the future do not present such affairs to us."[50] In other words, documents were by definition proof and should be taken as answers, not the beginning of new questions.

Only slightly less important were documents attesting to the petitioner's trade and economic standing. These were statements that petitioners engaged in trade, had property, paid their taxes, and were law-abiding, all signed by guarantors from the place in which the petitioner wished to register; in Zukov's file, two such statements appear, one from professional and one from personal acquaintances.[51] In the case of those seeking to enter a craft guild, these statements were usually supplemented or replaced by a statement from the head of the relevant guild, confirming that the petitioner had the skills necessary to ply his trade.

These were important documents, and magistracies appear to have taken the need to check on petitioners' stories seriously. In 1746, the Orel Magistracy received reports from the local craft and trade elders that often supported petitioners (12 cases in one file), but also rejected some claims based on lack of trade, lack of residence in the town, or problems with their manumission documents. The merchant elder even reported that one petitioner, the deacon's son Timofei Epifanov, "had no wares and is not likely to pay his dues and is not worthy of being added to the rolls of the Orel merchantry."[52] In most cases, guarantors either in these documents or in supplementary ones also promised to take financial responsibility for the petitioner should he fall behind on tax payments for some time.[53] Then, these documents were in some cases confirmed by a statement from the local town authorities to the magistracy agreeing to accept the petitioner into their ranks.[54]

The documents supporting the petitioner were often followed by documents supporting the magistracy's decision. Zukov's file was somewhat unusual, in that the Kursk Magistracy included only a copy of the letter it wrote to Zukov's home district chancellery reporting that it had confirmed Zukov's change in status.[55] In most cases, magistracies collected more documents to inform their deliberations, even if they rarely discussed the exact reasoning behind their final decisions. In particular, they collected documents that addressed one of the stock phrases in Zukov's petition: that his request was in accordance with "the power of Your Imperial Majesty's ukases." Most files included sometimes lengthy extracts (*vypiski*) from relevant laws, written out and included as the basis for decision making. The laws were simply listed, not compared or discussed. Still, their very presence became the rationale for many decisions, as a stock phrase in magistracies' decisions was that they were "according to the ukases of" and then a list of dates. Even into the 1780s, most lists began with the *Ulozhenie*, and included many references to Petrine decisions; after 1775, virtually all cited Catherine's Manifesto of that year. In a few cases (and usually in cases in which magistracies were pushing at the limits of the law) magistracies cited specific laws as reasons for specific parts of their decisions, but more often a simple list preceded a simple outcome: register, or, more rarely, do not register the petitioner into his new *soslovie*.

The final documents in most files were those that put the magistracies' decisions into practice. These often included letters from the magistracy to other authorities who needed to know about the decision—usually those responsible for the tax rolls of a petitioner's place of origin. These were for the most part purely informative reports, but occasionally further administrative directions appeared as well. In 1746, the Saratov Magistracy found itself in correspondence with the Chancellery of the General Revision, part of the administration of the governor of Astrakhan', over the registry of several landless peasants in the Saratov merchantry. In this case, it was the magistracy that was told specifically what to do: "and when the registry book of the Saratov merchants is composed, write [them] down in it from the landless peasants, and soul tax monies, until the future [revision] make arrangements for Ivan to pay them as he paid with the landless peasants for the last revision."[36]

Also part of this final accounting were documents that told petitioners of the end result of ther petitions. In many cases, files included a document from the petitioner himself confirming his new position or recognizing the failure of his petition. Petitioners like Zukov swore oaths, with attestations by others, that they would uphold the responsibilities of their new positions.[57] In some cases, additional oaths were demanded; around 1780, the Moscow Magistracy demanded a sworn oath of loyalty to Catherine II and her son Paul from newly made merchants.[58] Even those whose petitions were not granted could be brought in to the magistracy to have the decisions read out and then sign a document stating they had received notice of the decisions.[59]

MAGISTRACIES AND THEIR DECISIONS

In principle, magistracies simply applied laws based strictly on the supporting documents, but in practice, particularly given the complications and contradictions of eighteenth-century laws, their decisions were not always consistent. While many decisions certainly followed the laws as best they could, leading to the simple registration of a petitioner in a new estate, in other cases magistracies acted contrary to some laws, whether willfully, out of lack of knowledge, or in response to local or even national concerns. In many cases these latter decisions simply went into effect, but in others, either higher administrative organs or individuals involved in the cases challenged the magistracies. Furthermore, perhaps because magistracies were known to act against the law, individuals sometimes challenged apparently valid decisions, uncovering in the process either their own lack of knowledge of the laws or the fraud perpetrated by individuals and administrative bodies across the empire.

A particular issue that complicates investigating eighteenth-century legal practices is one of sources: the *Complete Collection of the Laws* is, in fact, incomplete. For one,

Nicholas I controlled and restricted access to the files of certain institutions.[60] But also, the compilers had to choose which of the many decisions by central administrative and judicial organs really counted as laws. As Speranskii, the head of the commission charged with compiling the collection, noted in his introduction to the project, "all particular, all personal, all temporary and incidental matters are excluded," on the grounds that they were specific legal decisions that failed to have the force of general law.[61] This was, however, an imperfect system. A look at the actual administrative practices of local legal institutions during the eighteenth century shows that at times they considered as binding decisions that appear nowhere in the *Complete Collection*. In particular, local magistracies—local judicial authorities that extended the judgment of the central authorities into towns and provinces—often used decisions by the Main Magistracy—a central judicial body, but one barely represented in the *Complete Collection*—as precedent for their judgments. This fact means that relying solely on the published sources provides a somewhat skewed vision of actual legal practice in place under the authority of magistracies during much of the eighteenth century.

Because the system of census revisions was just beginning, throughout the eighteenth century the magistracies frequently decided cases involving people who were not yet registered on the tax rolls of a particular community. These were people who had slipped through the system and were not tied to any particular place or legal status—not officially "people of various ranks," at least by title, but they were assorted other people who did not yet have a place. Some were peasant or townsmen's sons born between censuses, who often lived away from the village or town of their father's registry. In 1741, just before the second census revision, several peasant and town sons who claimed never to have been registered in their home villages or towns entered the Astrakhan' merchantry. Born after the first census, they had all moved to Astrakhan' as children, after the deaths of their fathers, and had lived there as if registered. Now they wanted their lives to be made official.[62] In 1762, during the third revision, the soldier's son Sidor Emel'ianov petitioned for entrance to the Kursk craft guilds on the basis of not being registered. As he put it, "I am registered nowhere because I am sixteen years old and so I was not skipped." In other words, he was not unregistered because of a mistake or because of unlawful acts, but simply because he had not yet been born when the last rolls were drawn up.[63]

Other petitioners who were categorized as unregistered found themselves in that position due to administrative or other shenanigans. When the church peasant Egor Bykov petitioned to enter the Kursk merchant estate around 1727, he claimed to have been working in Ukrainian towns as a carpenter for much of his life, and thus to have missed the first census. Although he described himself as a peasant from Kostroma district, he nonetheless used his unregistered status as reason to grant his entry into another estate.[64] Nikolai Chelobitchikov had even less reason to be unregistered in the Briansk merchant estate. His mother, Anna Maksimova, petitioned on his behalf in 1771 to explain. Anna was widowed while pregnant with Nikolai; then, "when the third revision happened I was sick, and due to my lack of knowledge I didn't end up counted anywhere"—and neither did her son.[65] And even more complicated was the case of Fedor Petrov. His father was born a state peasant, but was taken into the Moscow hat-making guild, a special guild set up under the jurisdiction of the military to make uniform hats during the reign of Peter the Great. In 1722, Fedor's father had petitioned to be released from the guild to his home village, on the grounds that "due to agedness and illness [he could] not work at any kind of labor." At that time, both the father and Fedor's younger brother Dmitrii ("born without an arm") entered the charity house, and Fedor was supposed to be entered back onto the rolls of the village—but due to administrative oversight, he never was, and instead remained unregistered.[66]

Of course, the supposedly unregistered sometimes turned out not to be so. In 1722, Ipat and Filip Zabelin were entered on the rolls as Moscow townsmen as part of the first census, on the grounds that they were not associated with any particular other place. However, in the 1730s, their registration in Moscow was revoked when the truth of their story came out. The brothers were born into the family of a church peasant who died just after the turn of the century. At that time, both boys, then aged ten and nine, moved to Moscow to live with relatives. Each started to trade in the cloth markets, and by 1722 they had settled firmly into the city and its merchant life. But the tie with their home village turned out never to have been properly severed; both were still listed as belonging to their original village, and were forced to return there, at least legally. Only in 1738 did Filip petition to enter the Moscow merchant estate under proper circumstances.[67]

The Iaroslavl' Magistracy found itself similarly misled several decades later. Andrei Esipov petitioned to enter the town's merchantry in 1744. He claimed, first, that he had been born after the last census, and was thus not registered and free to enter the tax rolls of whichever estate he wished; and second, that he had a passport to learn to trade in Iaroslavl'. Furthermore, he noted, his brother still lived in his home village and could pay any dues that might accrue to him in his absence. These were clearly contradictory claims, for if he was not registered on his village's tax rolls, he would not need a brother to pay his dues. Furthermore, individuals received passports from authorities in whichever locality they were registered; the unregistered, in principle at least, had no local authority to supply them with such documents. Nonetheless, the Iaroslavl' Magistracy accepted his petition. Almost ten years later, Esipov's owner, the widowed noblewoman Maria Sokovnina, petitioned the Main Magistracy to complain. According to her account, Esipov was and always had been her property. When he ran away, he took 3,500 rubles of her money with him, and he left his fellow serfs to pay his taxes, "due to which her peasants suffer not a little difficulty." Sokovnina had since heard that Esipov was living in Iaroslavl', "calling himself a merchant… and why I do not know."[68]

Even if individuals themselves were not registered in the tax rolls, their registration in a new place could pose problems for a magistracy. In 1780, Mikhail and Maksim Gonin claimed they were the unregistered sons of a now dead Petrovsk farming soldier, Semen Gonin, who had lived for years in Saratov and married there; now the two sons (aged

14 and 10) were either studying bootmaking or about to apprentice in bootmaking. On that basis, they petitioned to enter the Saratov craft guild, promising in the process that they were not fugitives. However, the Petrovsk Provincial Chancellery sent a report to the Saratov Magistracy that challenged this position. Semen and his son Egor "Gunin and not Gonin" had indeed been registered in the third revision in Petrovsk. Semen then received a passport to live "in various towns" and had been in that position for fifteen years, but in all that time he failed to pay any of his dues. As a result, his society had been forced to pay a total of 60 rubles on his behalf, which had caused "not a little loss and ruin." As a result, a local official had requested that the Petrovsk Provincial Chancellery seek out the two underaged boys, Mikhail and Maksim, to make them pay for their father and older brother.[69]

Given the complexity of the laws, some magistracies decided their best option was not to make a decision themselves but, rather, to refer to higher authorities for permission. In 1764—just as laws were beginning to better clarify the process of changing estate, but when numerous laws could still be considered—the Rostov Magistracy essentially abdicated responsibility for making several decisions, referring instead to the Main Magistracy for guidance. One case was unusual; it dealt with several falconers from Pereslavl' Zalesskii, members of a small separate legal group with particular duties to the imperial hunt. These falconers wished to enter the Rostov merchantry, but the Rostov officials were uncertain whether such specialized individuals were allowed to do so. The Main Magistracy allowed the registry, but with a particular note that the falconers had to keep up their duties to the hunt.[70] The falconers were a bit of a tricky case, but that same year Rostov also turned to the Main Magistracy for the seemingly straightforward case of several Rostov artisans (brickmakers by registration) who wished to enter the merchant rolls due to their trade in flour. They had manumission from their craft society, as well as attestations of trade and capital, which meant that their cases were simple. However, the Rostov Magistracy refused to decide, and instead sent a long report to the Main Magistracy requesting its decision. The Main Magistracy confirmed that the men should be allowed to change their affiliation.[71]

Not every turn to higher authorities ended positively. Also in 1764, a group of *odno-dvortsy* had petitioned the Kadoma Magistracy for entrance into the local merchantry. Kadoma wrote to the Main Magistracy, but in this case, the Main Magistracy disallowed the petition for two reasons: first, the various individuals did not possess enough capital to qualify as merchants; and second, the laws then active did not include the category of *odnodvorets* among those allowed to enter the merchant estate.[72] Even later, when the laws became clearer, local authorities continued to seek permission from higher authorities to make changes that were poorly indicated by the laws. In 1779, the Dmitriev Magistracy turned to the Astrakhan' Provincial Magistracy for help deciding the case of a Ukrainian who wished to join the local merchants. Both the Dmitriev and Astrakhan' officials thought the man should be allowed to register in the district, the latter using as its basis a recent law that said no undue restrictions should be placed on those seeking to enter the merchantry. However, the Astrakhan' Provincial Magistracy wrote to the Astrakhan' governor's office for clarification and permission, and there its plans hit a roadblock. The governor clarified the law for the magistracy: while it did state that no undue restrictions should be placed, it did not pave the way for individuals who were not free to register in new places. Therefore, because the Ukrainian lacked manumission from his village, he should not be allowed to register in the Dmitriev merchants.[73]

If these were cases in which magistracies acted seemingly in good faith, but were misled by false documents or claims, or recognized their inability to interpret the laws, in other cases they chose instead to violate the laws in order to change the status of those who had no right to do so. Before the 1762 Senatorial ukase that formally stated peasants had to show proof of their freedom before registering in towns as merchants, local magistracies had to evaluate two conflicting bodies of legislation in order to make their decisions.[74] On the one hand, there were the many laws punishing fugitives and demanding their return; on the other, there were laws demanding that those who had trading capital ought to register as merchants.[75] Peter the Great's law of 1722 establishing the craft guilds should have given magistracies a model; it noted that while peasants with manumission from their owners or overseers who wished to work as artisans ought to register formally as artisans, no fugitives should be accepted, whatever their skills.[76]

Despite these many legal precedents, some magistracies were likely to base their decisions on the laws that gave them greater latitude to increase the population (and tax rolls) of their own towns and regions, and to ignore laws about fugitives that would force them to deny petitioners their requests.[77] Even after 1762, and despite the fact that the Main Magistracy sent out a stream of ukases reminding its subject institutions about the rules, and particularly about their duty not to register fugitives,[78] some magistracies still continued to grant the requests of petitioners without full freedom from their old statuses, ignoring the fact that the law required freedom, and instead continuing to focus on the laws that emphasized mobility and trade. When the Selenginsk Magistracy accepted one petitioner into the local merchant society, it argued that they were right to do so based on his possession of capital—and totally ignored the fact that he lacked the proper freedom document that might make the registration proper.[79]

At times, magistracies directly noted that bringing in new members would be to the benefit of their localities or to the state as a whole, using the greater good as justification for acting according to the laws they chose. In 1722, a large group of runaway serfs (around 30) were brought into the Briansk merchantry despite their lack of official manumission. In its statement reporting its decision, the Briansk Magistracy noted that its town was severely under-populated—to the point that it had too few merchants to fill all the positions in local governance demanded by law. It simply needed more people.[80] A far grander claim, however, came from the Irkutsk Magistracy in 1780. It oversaw the petition of a Kiakhtin artisan who wanted to enter the Udinsk merchantry, but whose home society actively refused to release him based on his outstanding recruit duties and arrears. The Irkutsk Magistracy decided that the man ought to be registered as a merchant because that would create a greater societal good: "because in the craft guild he pays a flat rate of taxes, while if he registers as a merchant he will pay a percentage of his capital... consequently those taxes in comparison with the soul tax will bring an increase to state coffers... and therefore he should not be left in the guild."[81]

Elsewhere, individual magistracies accepted petitioners contrary to the law without reference to larger societal goals, but provided some alternative explanation of the reasoning behind their decisions.[82] In 1776, Ivan Suetin, a state peasant, petitioned to enter the Aleksin merchantry. He explicitly stated in his petition that he had asked for but had not received a manumission document from his home village. Despite this, the Aleksin Magistracy accepted his petition. They reasoned that because he had no outstanding dues (the magistracy had written to the relevant provincial chancellery to check), there was no logical reason for his home village not to have freed him. Therefore, the magistracy was fully within its rights to accept him, treating the case as it ought to have been had everyone acted in accordance with logic.[83] Of course, not only did the magistracy completely ignore the body of law that established incontrovertibly that individuals seeking to enter a new estate had to have freedom to do so, its logic regarding how localities ought to make their decisions was seriously flawed. The magistracy did check on whether Suetin had outstanding monetary dues, but failed to investigate his larger place within peasant society—most importantly, whether his family had outstanding recruit duties. In other cases, magistracies otherwise sought to stick as close as possible to the law (except the law regarding manumission) in their decisions, by explicitly noting petitioners' duties to continue to pay taxes in their old communities, as they would have to do were they registered legally, as well.[84]

The Aleksin Magistracy may have been keen to explain its reasoning because it made a regular habit of accepting people contrary to the laws. A whole series of state peasants entered the merchantry around this time, none with proper documents granting them manumission.[85] And the Aleksin Magistracy was not alone in its actions, as other magistracies also habitually accepted individuals contrary to the laws. At the same time as the Aleksin Magistracy was accepting petitioners wrongly, for example, the Orel and Cheboksary Magistracies also allowed townspeople and merchants from other towns to register formally in their town societies, based only on temporary passports as proof of their manumission.[86] While it is possible that they intended only to register the men as temporary merchants, which would give them certain trading rights in the town without altering their base registration, in at least one case it seems certain that the registration the magistracy intended was permanent. The Bolkhov townsman Aleksei Zhdanov had only a yearly passport as evidence of his manumission. But after the Orel Magistracy confirmed his registry as an Orel merchant and reported this fact to Bolkhov, the Bolkhov Magistracy wrote back to say they had removed Zhdanov from their rolls.[87]

Furthermore, a follow-up to one of the Aleksin cases made it clear that its magistracy saw the changes it ratified as permanent ones. After a series of state peasants were registered as Aleksin merchants, they complained that they were still tied to their former status. They petitioned the Aleksin Magistracy that, although they had been registered the year before and had kept up their duties to the Aleksin merchants, "now in October 1778, for unknown reasons we were called to a session of the Aleksin Lower Rural Court at which we were ordered to pay both soul tax and recruit dues at our old state black-smith village, which we refused to do." In response, the Aleksin Magistracy wrote to the Aleksin District Treasury office, asking it to remove the state peasants from the tax rolls of their village.[88] This was totally wrong from the point of view of the laws, both because it reaffirmed the permanency of this improper registration and because it sought to eliminate the double tax burden levied by the law.

Perhaps the most egregious cases of magistracies acting in contravention of the laws came from places in and beyond the Urals. Siberia had been a target of special legisla-tion since early in the eighteenth century, as the Senate released decrees specifically warning Siberian authorities not to act contrary to the laws on registry.[89] However, they clearly continued to do so. In the 1760s, the Cheliabinsk Magistracy attempted to register a whole series of people, including peasants from European Russia and townsmen from elsewhere in Siberia, none of whom had proper documentation. The Cheliabinsk Magistracy based its request on an earlier decree that had discussed the need to "increase" the population of merchants and townsmen in Orenburg, and used expired passports as supposed evidence of manumission. In this case, the Main Magistracy immediately told them not to do this and reversed the Cheliabinsk deci-sion.[90] However, that did not stop other Siberian magistracies from taking stands based on unusual legal reasoning.

At various points in the 1760s, Siberian magistracies made decisions that were based on logic, perhaps, but not on the law. In 1766, the Selenginsk Magistracy decided to solve a problem with a simple switch. It had been presented with a case of two local indi-viduals. One was a townsman, Petr Kovelin, twenty-one, literate in Russian, and able to speak Mongol, who wished above all to enter military service. The other was a Cossack named Ivan Reviakin, whose injuries and illnesses had made him unfit for service, but whose business sense had made him wealthy. He desired formal registration in the town in order to further his business interests. The magistracy made a very simple decision: let Kovelin serve, and let Reviakin enter the town and pay dues in Kovelin's place. A logical decision this certainly was, but it was based on sparse legal grounds.[91]

Similarly, in 1767, the Irkutsk Magistracy released a decree to its subject magistra-cies giving them permission to register people who ought not to have been registered. It stated: "people who have appeared here from various other towns with lapsed pass-ports and who, having turned out to be skipped in the current third revision and not registered in the soul tax register" should be allowed to register in Siberian towns.[92] On the one hand, this was simply a case of registering unregistered people, something that happened frequently during the eighteenth century; on the other hand, it meant that the idea that fugitives could always face capture and return to their place of origin, the standard that had finally closed the last loophole from serfdom in the *Ulozhenie,* was no longer valid for those who made it to Siberia.[93]

Yet another permutation of such alternative readings of the law appeared in Siberia a decade later. In 1780, the Sol'vychegodsk district state peasant Ivan Beloborodov petitioned to enter the Selenginsk craft society, based on a passport (which was almost, but not yet quite, expired). The Selenginsk craft alderman attested to his abilities and reported that the town's artisans agreed to accept Beloborodov. The Selenginsk Magistracy violated the law on freedom by agreeing to accept him, despite his lack of proper documents; it also added a clause to its decision that violated the rule on double taxation: "do not register him on the soul tax rolls until he is excluded from the peasants and rolls of his former residence so that he does not have to pay the double tax." Later that year it repeated the same conclusion in the case of two other state peasants.[94]

Of course, not every petition contrary to the law was accepted. In 1744, the Uglich townsman Semen Shetenev petitioned to enter the Iaroslavl' merchantry. In the petition, Shetenev described his long residence in Iaroslavl', which had led not only to work there but also a marriage and children. He noted that he had originally left Uglich due to "lack of means," and that if forced to return there his finances would be in such "disarray" that he would be unable to pay taxes. However, despite his argument that allowing his registry in Iaroslavl' would be to the greater good (through tax payments), the Uglich authorities not only refused to grant Shetenev manumission but also reported that he was a fugitive with significant tax arrears. The Iaroslavl' Magistracy followed the laws and did not accept him.[95] But despite this case, clearly magistracies were not always good at catching problems with petitioners or at making decisions that followed the bulk of the body of the law. And in some cases, those magistracies were caught out.

MAGISTRACIES CHALLENGED

Many improper registrations seem never to have been caught or challenged, but others certainly were. In a few cases, individuals higher up the ranks of the administration caught magistracies making decisions contrary to the laws—and in one case, even caught a case of out-and-out fraud. More often, magistracies were challenged by individuals or institutions—serf-owners, monasteries, or village authorities—petitioning to assert their own claims to authority over individuals. Even in these cases, however, questions of interpretation still emerged, as in some cases these noble (or other) petitioners were themselves writing from a shaky understanding of the legal structures that then ruled.

Given the number of cases in which magistracies made decisions contrary to the law, they were relatively rarely chastised by higher officials. Still, in a few cases other authorities intervened in the affairs of a local magistracy, forcing it to change. This became far more common during the reign of Catherine the Great, perhaps because the legislation became clearer at this time and the need for prospective registrants to provide documents became more absolute. Initially, when the state peasant Mikhailo Izosimin petitioned to enter the Sol'vychegodsk society of townspeople in January 1776, he was quickly accepted first by the town authorities and then by the magistracy—the entire case lasted less than a month. However, several months later, the local Provincial Chancellery, which had received notice of the decision, wrote to the magistracy with a corrective. Izosimin had no documents from his home community, which meant that he was not free to become a townsman. The chancellery chastised the magistracy for its incorrect decision, and demanded that Izosimin be returned to the tax rolls of his village.[96]

Elsewhere, too, provincial level offices or even central authorities might serve to catch lower-level wrong-doing. The Orel Magistracy in the mid-1770s was one of those that consistently registered individuals without proper manumission papers. But in 1778 it was caught out by a higher authority. The magistracy had registered a Kolomna economic peasant and family into the Orel merchant estate when it received an indignant message from the State College of the Economy, the department placed in charge of lands confiscated from monasteries a decade and a half before, as well as of the peasants living on those lands. The college was still in the process of deciding whether to free the family when it received notice that they had been registered in a new estate. Such a registration was completely unacceptable: "he, Il'in, with his children was accepted and registered into the merchantry by your magistracy without written agreement from this College, and so we are sending you this statement to say, that the College does not consider their registry as valid, and that this registry was done by your magistracy in contravention of a Senatorial Decree. We are sending the Main Magistracy a report about this matter." In return, the Main Magistracy wrote to Orel's superior magistracy, ordering it to investigate and to fine any wrongdoers in the Orel Magistracy.[97] Despite this moment of drama, the Main Magistracy's demands clearly did not alter normal practice in Orel; instead, the Orel Magistracy continued to register some petitioners without manumission papers.

Although it is hard to imagine that it was actually unique, the various magistracies' files show only one case of clear, out-and-out corruption. The matter was discovered in the investigation of the case of Gavril Stolarev, a fugitive serf from the Nizhnii Novgorod estate of P. A. Demidov who had been registered as a artisan in Dmitriev, a district town in Astrakhan' province. Demidov complained to his local authorities, and they—the Nizhnii Novgorod Provincial Chancellery—took up the case. The investigators discovered that after Stolarev ran away in 1755, he lived for some time in Saratov "without documents," and then in 1762 he moved to Dmitriev. There he worked for various merchants, always without documents, and eventually came to the attention of a petty clerk in the Dmitriev Magistracy, Fedot Kostromitenin. Kostromitenin asked Stolarev whether he wanted to register in the Dmitriev craft society in order to regularize his position. According to the report, "Stolarev told him that he was a fugitive" but that he would indeed like to register in the taxpaying population. The petty clerk, "having taken from him money—ten rubles" proceeded to get him registered as a master joiner in the craft society. Because this showed clear corruption, the Nizhnii Chancellery asked not only that Stolarev be returned to Demidov but that the clerk Kostromitenin be punished. In the end, he was fined but allowed to stay on the job.[98]

In some cases, higher authorities caught and punished local magistracies for acting in opposition to the laws, but in others those higher authorities themselves validated problematic decisions. Just before the 1762 law that linked documentation of manumission to registry in a new estate, the Main Magistracy itself reviewed several cases involving monastery and court peasants who wished to join the Moscow merchantry but who had only passports as evidence of freedom from their home villages. In both cases, the magistracy allowed their registry, although it did note that the men had to be sure to keep up their tax payments in their villages of origin. One of the cases involved the *iasak*-paying (a kind of tax or tribute in principle owed by some of the non-Russian population of the Empire) peasants Sergei Tikhanov and Afanasii Poliakov, who wished to register as Sviiazhsk merchants without possessing full freedom from their home communities. The Sviiazhsk Magistracy had agreed to their registry as long as they continued to pay taxes, and furthermore noted that at the next census revision the men should be removed from the rolls of their old villages and from that point on only be registered as merchants. The Main Magistrate approved the decision.[99]

The higher authorities were not infallible in other ways, either. In 1762, the monastery peasant Petr Poliakov petitioned to enter the Iaroslavl' merchantry. He had a letter from his monastery stating that the peasants of his village had agreed to free him, a promise from a brother back in that village to keep up payments on his behalf, and attestations that he possessed 500 rubles in capital and had experience in commerce. The Iaroslavl' Magistracy quickly signed off on this seemingly unproblematic registration; however, when it received the Iaroslavl' report of this affair, the Main Magistracy took issue with several points. According to the Main Magistracy, the Iaroslavl' Magistracy had decided improperly because, first, Poliakov did not say that he actually engaged in trade, only that he possessed capital; second, his manumission paper was from the hegumen of the monastery, not from the other peasants; and third, the decision did not mention keeping up payments in his previous place of residence. The Main Magistracy ended its response to Iaroslavl' with a withering critique: "the Iaroslavl Magistracy acted in opposition to the laws very improperly, and so in the future be more careful and do not make decisions that are so false and contrary to the laws, under threat of being fined according to the laws."

In this case, however, the Iaroslavl' Magistracy was quite certain that it had acted properly, and it responded to the Main Magistracy defending its position with a "Report on why we cannot act in accordance with the decree you sent." The magistracy noted that attestations of trade and capital were enough proof for registration, even if Poliakov had not mentioned everything in his petition. And it particularly took issue with the question of Poliakov's freedom. The Iaroslavl' Magistracy agreed that the letter he presented was "not from his brother peasants," but from the hegumen of the monastery. However, the letter clearly stated that it was written on behalf of the village peasants and elder. Furthermore, according to a Senate decree, such letters were valid proof of manumission for monastery peasants; but even had that decree not existed, the Iaroslavl' Magistracy had taken the step of writing to the monastery's Provincial Chancellery to confirm that the manumission was the desire of the entire village, not simply of the hegumen.[100]

Individuals who had claim (or who thought they had claim) to people who had changed (or who thought they had changed) also challenged the magistracies' decisions. Some of their petitions were relatively straightforward, or at least were quickly resolved. In 1747, Afanasii Goncharov petitioned for the recovery of a group of his runaway serfs, all of whom had been wrongly registered as Briansk merchants; the Main Magistracy and Senate between them quickly ordered the serfs be returned to Goncharov's estate.[101] Individual serf-owners were not the only petitioners; in 1756, the Rostov Borisoglebskii monastery petitioned the Main Magistracy to address a problem with a number of their fugitive serfs who had registered in the Moscow merchantry without permission from the monastery. In this case, they seemed not to have minded the registry as long as the serfs continued to pay taxes back in Rostov; however, once they stopped paying, the monastery petitioned, asking not for their return, but for the resumption of tax payments.[102]

Not all cases were as easily resolved. In 1768, two serf-owners from Kaluga province petitioned for the return of their fugitive serfs Leon, Vasili, and Ivan Poskrebukhin. They blamed the Orel Provincial Magistracy and "the whole Orel merchantry" for having accepted and registered the men. Their petition, however, remained unresolved, in large part because of administrative problems. The serf-owners petitioned in Kaluga, their home province, but getting Orel—which had, after all, been making a regular habit of registering those it should not—to pay proper attention to their claim was a challenge. Eventually, the Kaluga authorities demanded that the Orel Magistracy send a member of the local merchant society to Kaluga to testify. The merchant they chose, one Nakovalnin, failed to appear, and the case remained in limbo.[103]

Because these sorts of challenges often arose out of property or inheritance disputes, decisions could also be held up. In 1779, the registry of the freed household serf Stepan Kanakhovskii into the Belyi merchantry was challenged by the wife of his former owner. Kanakhovskii had been freed with his whole family, but his owner's wife claimed that his two daughters actually belonged to her, and thus could not be considered as part of the original emancipation. Their registration, according to her, was invalid.[104] The case dragged on and on, leaving Kanakhovskii without an official status for years.

Even after years in a new position, individuals who had wrongly registered could still be caught. That happened in the case of Nikifor Pavlov, who entered the rolls of the Orel merchants in 1723. Pavlov claimed in his initial petition to be a Kaluga townsman by registration, and to have long lived in Orel and been involved in the grain trade. Although he was registered as a merchant, even that original registry was suspect, as Pavlov did not provide notice of his manumission. Nonetheless, soon after his initial registry, several family members joined him in Orel, and two of his nephews eventually joined the merchantry, too. However, in 1745, the archimandrite of the Donskoi monastery in Iaroslavetskii district petitioned the Orel Magistracy, alleging a number of irregularities. First and foremost, Nikifor Pavlov had not been a Kaluga townsman, but a serf of the monastery. Second, Pavlov's family members were also serfs, and had been made merchants despite lacking capital or trade. And third, none of them had paid proper taxes back in the village for years, causing distress.

The case wound up in front of the Main Magistracy, which discovered a complicated story. Around 1704, Nikifor Pavlov's father had sent his son to Kaluga for schooling. Pavlov lived there for three years, studying "without any kind of written documentation" until his parents died. He then stayed in Kaluga without documents, first studying icon painting and then marrying a merchant's daughter. He became involved in the grain trade, and he and his wife had two children, both of whom died in childhood. Soon thereafter, Pavlov and his wife sold their house in Kaluga for 50 rubles and moved to Orel. Despite having no documents to his name, Pavlov registered in the Orel merchantry, and then lived there for "27 years and 6 months" before his registry was challenged. Based on this personal history, the Main Magistracy had, it believed, no choice but to conclude that the entire extended family did not belong in the Orel merchantry; instead, they ought to be sent back to their village of origin, and, moreover, punished for the crime of running away.[105]

Over and over during the eighteenth century, Russian emperors and empresses lamented the fact that their laws were frequent victims of local disregard, remaining unimplemented either through lack of knowledge or through flagrant dishonesty. Peter commented that they were "played with like cards," while his daughter Elizabeth bemoaned the "widespread internal enemies" who distorted the laws to their own ends.[106] This was, of course, a problem not just with the adjudication of social mobility but also with the legal system more generally. And yet these cases show well the ways in which these confusions played out on the local level.

Many of the cases show that individual magistracies were often quite willful in their actions. They were not necessarily actively engaging in graft or corruption (although certainly some did), but some clearly were actively and knowingly violating laws. Their confusion could be blamed at this point on the lack of clarity in the laws, cobbled as they were from a whole series of different ukases and manifestos, of reports from the autocrats themselves, from the Senate and from the Main Magistracy. Late in her reign, Elizabeth thought the solution for this disorder was more oversight by the Senate, a statement she made in no uncertain terms.[107] But soon, her (near) successor, Catherine the Great, would strive first to create a new law code for the entire empire, and when that effort failed, to regularize and systematize at least some elements of the legal structures of her state. And, in particular, she looked to regularizing the system of organizing her population in clearly defined social categories.

3

The Freedom to Choose and the Right to Refuse

IN DECEMBER 1815, a freed household serf named Vasilisa Vasil'eva submitted a short petition to the Moscow Magistracy. In it, she declared that she had been freed by her owner four years before, and that she now wished to register as a formal member of Moscow's society of townspeople. Along with her petition, she provided her official letter of manumission as proof that she was without formal status, and thus free to gain another one. The case was straightforward, and the magistracy was willing to approve her new registry. But then, barely a month later, she submitted a second petition, asking to have her letter of manumission returned to her because, as she put it, "I do not wish to be registered in this *soslovie* but wish to enter into a different status."[1] As a freed serf, Vasil'eva was under the compulsion to "choose a way of life," in order to find a specific place within Russia's system of *sosloviia*. Despite being compelled to choose, Vasil'eva's multiple petitions suggest that she understood her choice as a real one, with real implications for her eventual life.

The case of Vasil'eva highlights the major developments in the regulation of *sosloviia* in the late eighteenth and early nineteenth centuries. First, Catherine the Great attempted to bring order to the chaos of eighteenth-century laws through her Legislative Commission and then her Charters; that order, however, was limited by the very complexity of the current social system. As a result, at the same time and continuing through the reigns of Paul and Alexander I, the central imperial state consistently sought to control movement in ways that echoed, but at times also altered, eighteenth-century precedents. Furthermore, during this period the central state, with its desire to control the population via registry, came into conflict with local *soslovie* authorities, who desired not necessarily autonomy but at least control over local populations. This conflict developed most of all in early nineteenth-century debates over registering those like Vasil'eva, who had the "freedom to choose a way of life." In many ways, these debates revolved around a conflict between the center's desire to make actions mandatory and localities' or individuals' desire to retain agency—a conflict that remained not only unresolved but also embedded in certain statuses.

CATHERINE'S CHARTERS AND THE EFFORT TO ORGANIZE SOCIETY

By the reign of Catherine the Great, it had become obvious that the current legal system for allowing social mobility of a limited sort was insufficient to meet the needs of the imperial state and of local societies. Aside from actual cases adjudicated by local magistracies or sent on to the Main Magistracy or Senate for their decisions, concerns over registration and re-registration in various *sosloviia* came to the state's attention through delegates to the Legislative Commission, the great council called to debate a new law code for the empire. Those delegates, drawn from across the empire and representative of most of its social groups, largely failed to come to an agreement on the larger issues raised by Catherine, focused as they were on the privileges of their own statuses.[2] But in part due to their very interest in their own separate statuses, they found common ground in their understanding of *sosloviia*.

As the delegates understood them, *sosloviia* were not exactly the many statuses of the Muscovite state; instead, they were a newer form, created in part by eighteenth-century legislation and administrative practice. Furthermore, *sosloviia* were described in two major ways: as rooted in the essential nature of Russian (or, in one case, Ukrainian) society, and as ever evolving in the face of changing economic or other influences. Solutions to apparent disjunctures in the economic and social status of individuals— legally ascribed peasants who lived off trade, most often—focused on these two interpretations. Either peasants were supposed to be peasants, and thus return to agriculture, or the mutability of *soslovie* could allow those peasants to become something else—to become townsmen or merchants either individually or en masse.

When Catherine the Great sent out her *Nakaz*, the *Instructions* meant to guide her people in drawing up a new law code for the empire, she certainly intended to spark a discussion on social structures and the concept of *soslovie*.[3] The *Instructions*, after all, stated forthrightly that the proper division of her people was into multiple *soslovie*. And discussion at the commission did indeed focus on the privileges of *soslovie*. First, the delegates considered the question of noble privilege, and then they moved on to matters concerning the merchantry and its position.[4] The story usually told about the commission is that it failed in no small part because representatives of different *sosloviia* jealously guarded their own privileges and thus were unable to work together to create an actual law code. The delegates' own words certainly bear this out, as individuals directly addressed one another, arguing most often for the privileges of their own *sosloviia*. Nobles wanted freedom to trade but the exclusive right to own serfs; merchants sought to restrict the rights of all others (peasants, people of various ranks, nobles) to trade while asking for permission to purchase household serfs. With interests so basically at odds, the commission was, it seems, doomed to failure.

Despite this, because Catherine apparently used the debates to inform her later legislative efforts, the discussions of the Legislative Commission had significant implications for mobility between *sosloviia*. First, much of the discussion of merchant privilege, in particular, looked at one major question of social mobility: peasants and other non-merchants registering in town societies. Town delegates consistently demanded that all those who wished to trade in towns—mostly peasants and people of various ranks—join local merchant or craft societies.[5] A few demurred, suggesting that allowing peasants to join merchant societies might harm agriculture. The Vologda town delegate Andrei Blaznov claimed that peasants who wished to trade had, in fact, "forgotten the fear of God," and ought not be allowed to register.[6] One noble delegate, Vasilii Plokhovo of Dankov, even argued that although peasants should be allowed to register as merchants, that right should be limited to periods of up to ten years only. But this was an unpopular position for townspeople; the town delegate Egor Demidov immediately replied that any registry as a merchant had to be permanent.[7]

In addition, at least one noble delegate borrowed the rationale used by merchants to promote his own interests. A deputy from Siberia had noted that many local merchants engaged in agriculture and asked that this pursuit be formally allowed; Nikifor Tolmachev, a noble delegate from Liubim, retorted that agriculture was clearly the exclusive domain of agriculturists. By their own logic, if merchants wanted to farm, they ought to register as peasants.[8] What holds all these points together is their shared belief in the utility of *soslovie* registration to control and influence social and economic structures.

Second, these discussions demonstrated the failure of existing laws to create a clear system of *soslovie* membership and privilege. Like the magistracies that oversaw their interests, merchants often cited decrees and manifestos in abundance as they sought to prove that peasants and others were already forced to register in towns in order to trade.[9] These merchants claimed that laws clearly stated that trade was a privilege of their own *soslovie* that could be gained only by registry there, and no other means. Many of their opponents, however, found alternative sources of legal judgment that suggested the law was instead on their side, that various manifestos and decrees had allowed peasants and others to engage in trade since at least the reign of Peter the Great.

A third implication of the discussion at the commission—and one that was in many ways an outgrowth of the second—was that the question of social structure was particularly unclear on the borders (or former borders) of the empire. Many regions of the empire were at this point administered differently, sometimes to the delight, and sometimes to the dismay, of their inhabitants. Delegates from the Baltics and Kiev spoke strongly of the need to preserve the unique administration of their regions, an administration that owed much to ideas of town governance from places further west. Others recognized that their geographically distant location had either allowed for greater freedoms that they hoped would continue to be recognized, or had created unique social and economic circumstances that required separate standards.[10] But some, perhaps particularly those in former border regions that no longer were, found themselves hoping for more standardized regulation of the social order. Aleksei Pod"iachev, a delegate from Ufa, noted that his town was in just such a region: "there was a time long ago when Ufa's inhabitants were… due to their different faith and location on the border, administered by laws different from those from the interior of the state… [but] now these provinces have already become internal, and not border"—and those earlier, distinct laws no longer fit the economic life of the region's inhabitants.[11]

Finally, a fourth outcome of the commission with implications for *soslovie* in general and mobility in particular was the very fact that the discussions there most often served to reaffirm *soslovie*-based privileges. Membership in a particular *soslovie* was given so much weight in these discussions that those citizens of the empire who sought a different life for themselves were almost forced to think, at least in part, in terms of changing their *soslovie* membership. In other words, building up *soslovia* as uniquely privileged institutions helped create a greater impetus for social mobility, as more and more individuals found themselves in need of change.

Furthermore, some delegates explicitly noted that there was a hierarchy of social status implicit in the laws—but that hierarchy was not always clear. Stepan Skrynitsyn, a noble delegate from Kineshma, stated that there was at that point a significant disparity between tax regulations and the social hierarchy: "the merchant estate is more exalted and more respected than that of agriculturists," but actually paid less in taxes than did most peasants. In Skrynitsyn's view, this was "as if the merchants are lower than the peasants, and this brings the merchants no little shame."[12]

Based at least in part on these sources of information about the status of social mobility in the provinces, Catherine the Great created new laws that systematized and clarified not simply town organizations and administration but also the rules that regulated movement between estates. First, her 1775 Manifesto redefined the distinctions between town estates (merchants and townspeople) based on fiscal definitions, dealing with a problem in town organization that had been recognized by some delegates. Mikhail Shcherbatov, noble of Iaroslavl province, and a noted conservative commentator on the current state of Russia, had stated that

> the townsman is different from the merchant; for although every inhabitant of a town may call himself a townsman of it, that does not yet make up a *soslovie*. Therefore I consider it necessary that measures be taken to found one, and believe that such a *soslovie* should consist of those merchants who do not come up to the level of the three classes [of the merchants].[13]

This was, essentially, the goal of the 1775 Manifesto: to define the lower town status specifically as those townspeople with less capital than the lowest merchant—less than 500 rubles, in practice—in an effort to give specific form to the "lower" townspeople.

Between the 1775 Manifesto and the 1785 Charter to the Towns, several more statutes built on this initial intervention into the social structure of towns. In 1781, on the same day she announced a new census, Catherine released a personal decree that gave specific instructions for registering merchants and townspeople in St. Petersburg, as well as a more general statement on social mobility. Merchants and townspeople from other towns who lived in St. Petersburg and had valid passports were to register in the capital; those whose passports had expired had to go through, essentially, a background check in order to make their residence permanent. In addition, the statute reaffirmed that freed serfs and other peasants in towns were allowed to register as merchants or townspeople, depending on their economic standing and as long as they provided proper guarantors.[14] The rules on the census also reaffirmed these multiple ways of classifying town societies.[15] Later that year, the idea of double taxation was stated formally: peasants who had registered as townspeople were subject to tax on both their former and new statuses until they had been formally excluded from their place of origin at the drawing up of new tax rolls during a census.[16] But even then, the laws were not read as perfectly clear; it is in this period that a Senate decree also appeared stating that peasants were *not* allowed to enter societies of townspeople, although other decrees clearly stated the opposite, even describing the outcome of such registration.[17]

When Catherine released the Charter to the Towns in April 1785, at least some of these contradictions were replaced with a new set of regulations meant to streamline and organize the administration of the empire's towns. Nevertheless, the conflicting goals of the eighteenth-century imperial state continued to complicate matters and to make the outcomes of the Charter unclear and continuously debated.[18] In some ways, the Charter was an attempt to summarize decades of legislation. Many of the individual statutes that made up the Charter reiterated ideas that had been appearing in decrees for decades; for example, trade allotted to townspeople was limited to those formally registered as such and the double tax burden was reaffirmed.[19] In this way, the Charter suggested that a standard of practice had been established by prior legislation, and the Charter merely confirmed those standards.

At the same time, however, the Charter failed to standardize other aspects of the legislation of *sosloviia*. For one, it failed to establish consistent conventions for labeling the inhabitants of towns, even contradicting earlier practice. In her 1775 Manifesto, for example, Catherine had distinguished between townsperson proper (*meshchanin*) and merchant, but in the Charter she most often used the former term for all those registered in towns, whatever their specific status. This conflicting usage reappeared in the sections enumerating the various kinds of townspeople. The Charter listed six groups: property owners, merchants (literally, "those written down in the guilds, the first, the second, and the third"), members of the artisan's guilds, out-of-town or foreign "guests," "noted citizens" (those with particular abilities in the arts, in finance, or in local service), and petty townspeople.[20] But later in the Charter, Catherine addressed the "middle type" of town inhabitants, using the term for plain townspeople and now conflating these residents with property owners.[21] The Charter thus failed to legislate a standard terminology for town *sosloviia*.[22]

The seemingly neat list of categories also belied a confusion over who exactly counted as part of town society. In the first section of the Charter, Catherine addressed "those settling in towns," stating that such settlers were to swear allegiance to her Imperial Majesty and to accept the rights and duties of citizenship (*grazhdanstvo*) and membership in the *soslovie* of townspeople.[23] This suggested a kind of membership in an estate defined by rights and by conscious belonging. A later point similarly emphasized the role of choice in membership, as the first statute defining the status of townsperson stated simply "it is not forbidden for anyone to register in the society of a town."[24] The larger part of the Charter, however, described a rather different way of belonging to a town society: "If someone is not written into the residency books of a given town, then he not only does not belong to the citizenry of that town, but also does not enjoy the townsperson's benefits of that town."[25] Here, the status of townsperson depended purely on an individual's ascription, on his or her registry in the official town books.

The registry books were significant because they not only provided evidence of belonging but also required evidence. The Charter stated that all families who wished to be listed in the registry books—which, of course, they needed to be in order to enjoy the economic privileges of town life—had to show proof of their status; furthermore, it listed twenty-five specific kinds of evidence that could be used to prove town status, as well as a note that "any other proof" might, under the right circumstances, be considered valid. Local authorities were to examine such evidence carefully, and if at least two-thirds of the deputies did not believe that a family had sufficiently proved their town credentials, that family was not to be added to the books.[26] The Charter to the Nobility, released on the same day as the Charter to the Towns, set out similar lists of evidence required for nobles to be written into their district heraldry books as part as marking the nobility as a clearly defined estate.[27] Nor was this procedure simply a matter of finding evidence for more privileged groups, as Catherine's draft Charter on the peasantry made similar statements and would have required both formal bookkeeping and formal evidence of belonging for peasants, as well.[28]

According to a mid-nineteenth-century history of the Ministry of Internal Affairs, after Catherine's 1785 Charters to the Towns and to the Nobility, "nothing remained to be done" regarding the status of Russia's nobles, merchants, and townspeople.[29] To an extent, this was true. The Charters did, indeed, lay out clear guidelines as to what was appropriate for these statuses in terms of economic and political (or quasi-political) activities and strove to define who currently belonged in specific statuses by listing the evidentiary requirements for such registration. And, too, their provisions have often been taken as marks of a particularly important moment in the development of *sosloviia*—and, indeed, at times as the finalization of a process of creating *sosloviia*. The early Marxist historian N. A. Rozhkov, for one, suggested that the Charter to the Towns, in particular, with its listing of six types of townspeople, and its creation of an administrative body of six members (the *shestiglasnaia duma*, or six-person council) to represent them, was an example of the *soslovie* principle in action. As he put it, the reform not only organized the wider society according to specific categories but also, by establishing the representative body, it granted each of those separate categories—those separate *sosloviia*—"its own voice."[30]

At the same time, the question of movement between *sosloviia* remained vexing, a question that multiple offices of the imperial state would soon find themselves involved in investigating and attempting to answer. Eighteenth-century laws had succeeded in establishing certain general provisions for moving between estates. Freedom had to be proved, as did the ability to thrive in a new status (at least for merchants). The double tax burden that strove to ensure neither the state nor the locality suffered tax losses as a result of changing status was similarly well defined by the time of the Charter. So, despite continuing uncertainty about labels and categories, and despite the ease with which local authorities could interpret the existing laws in conflicting ways, there was established a regularized system of changing estates.

Still, there was "more to do," in contravention of the nineteenth-century statement. The majority of eighteenth-century laws focused in one way or another on mandatory registry: demands that those engaged in trade register properly, demands that censuses record all taxpayers. Peter the Great had begun this process with his tax censuses and their records, and it was in many ways perfected by the Charters to the Nobility and Towns, which stated that all subjects of the empire had to be recorded on some kind of official list. Now not only were peasants listed in their villages' soul-tax registers, but nobles were listed on their districts' heraldry lists, and merchants in their towns' residency books. This suggests, then, that this was the moment when all imperial subjects were truly locked into their positions through formal ascription in a particular society. The result could be read as a perfectly organized—even well-ordered—society. This perfect order, however, belied the urge to movement that underlay the system, and it came to require new ways of thinking about the realities of social mobility. Over the next decades, these new approaches to mobility came from the central state, from local authorities, and from individuals. The result was twofold: alternating emphases on restriction and freedom on the part of the imperial state and tension between the central state and local societies regarding the question of registration.

FROM RESTRICTIONS TO FREEDOMS

During the last decade of the eighteenth century and the first decades of the nineteenth century, two major strands appeared in legislation regarding movement between *soslovie*. By the time of Catherine's Charters, laws regulating movement between statuses had focused on three particular issues: maintaining tax revenues via the imposition of a double tax burden on those who moved; registering the unregistered; and providing valid documentation of freedom. Throughout the first decades of the nineteenth century, laws continued to restate and refine these tenets of mobility. First, the laws initially supported, and at times increased, eighteenth-century restrictions on mobility by reaffirming the double tax and at times increasing the requirements to receive official freedom. But then, in an abrupt change in the 1820s, many of these restrictions were reduced or eliminated in an effort to encourage urban growth.

At the turn of the century, a series of new laws restated the double tax burden placed on those who changed status, always in ways that strove to increase the state's revenues. Under Paul, the Senate addressed a complaint about this policy that had originated in the peasant communities left behind by members who had joined town societies. According to the Kaluga Treasury Department, many former state peasants were failing to pay taxes in their old status, causing problems for their old communities. The treasury requested not that the peasants who had moved be compelled to pay but, rather, that their names be stricken from the tax lists before the next census. The Senate refused this request on the grounds that the double tax duty was mandatory; instead, it required henceforth that all state peasants seeking exit from their present *soslovie* provide specific guarantors of their ability to pay future taxes. These guarantors would themselves be liable for any arrears, thus protecting those village communes from "extreme hardship."[31] A day later, another decree again emphasized the importance of tax income. In this law, the Senate addressed the tax position of the children of peasants who had registered in towns just after the last census, and who were thus obligated to pay the double tax. Even children born after that census, which meant that they had never been registered in peasant villages, were now subject to the double tax along with their fathers.[32]

Legislation emphasizing tax revenue continued throughout much of the reign of Alexander I, as well. In 1806, the Senate looked at the tax status of former townspeople who had moved into merchant societies in new towns, and it decided that they, like peasants, were subject to double taxes: they had to pay new merchant fees in their current towns and the soul tax in their former societies.[33] Two years later, a decree allowed movement into the merchant *soslovie* at any time of year, with the caveat that the timing of movement had important tax implications.[34] However often this provision was restated, it continued to create administrative questions, which provincial treasuries or other institutions frequently sent on to the Senate. The result was essentially always the same: double taxes were the rule.[35]

In part as a result of these rules, movement into town societies seems to have clustered around the times of census revisions. Perhaps worried that too many people were seeking to change their status during one such revision, it was during the fifth census revision (1795–1796) that the Senate demanded all changes in status be suspended until the revision was completed. Only then would peasants be allowed to join town estates—and would thus then also be subject to the double tax duty until the unscheduled next census.[36] This provision was restated during the sixth revision, as well.[37]

Despite these limitations, there was increased mobility around the time of census revisions, reflected in eighteenth-century records and continuing through the nineteenth century. In Moscow, for example, 790 new merchants were added to the town's society in 1795, despite the moratorium on such moves decreed halfway through that year.[38]

A longer look at movement into Moscow's merchant society from 1810 on also shows a rise in rates of movement that correspond to the censuses, particularly during the 1850s, when two separate revisions allowed societies to clear up long out-of-date tax rolls.

Also during these decades, laws continued to emphasize the importance of formal documentation of freedom for most who wished to change their *soslovie*. In 1800, Paul's Senate strongly criticized the Narva Magistracy for accepting into local societies "vagrants" without proper papers, as several of those vagrants turned out to be fugitives. It extended its criticism in a new decree restating the importance of documents.[39] Early in Alexander's reign, several statutes reiterated the need for churchmen to receive formal freedom from higher authorities in order to enter civil service or to gain a non-religious social status.[40]

In 1808, the Senate made another decision that emphasized the importance of formal freedom. A debate had arisen in Saratov province over the proper procedure to guide the movement within a single town of townspeople into the merchant estate. On the one hand, such movement was supposed to be nearly automatic, based purely, as Catherine's Charter had put it, on the amount of capital a townsman possessed. On the other hand, that "automatic" change belied the complex network of rights and responsibilities that were based on specific legal status. The Saratov case developed owing to several "large families" whose move into the merchant estate left their former fellow townspeople in "disarray" over their communal recruit duties.

The local authorities had tried to solve the problem by demanding monetary compensation for the townsperson society from any of its members who wished to move into the merchant estate while in line to provide a military recruit. The Senate, however, found such a method unacceptable, and instead ruled that in the future all townspeople who wished to follow the Charter to the Towns and move into the merchant estate had to provide proper attestations from their townsperson society stating that they were not subject to recruit duties in the immediate future, as well as evidence from actual trading merchants that they had both capital and the ability to engage in merchant-appropriate activities.[41]

During this time, as well, there were laws that specifically increased the restrictions placed on state peasants. Early in Paul's reign, the Senate insisted that state peasant societies consider not just taxes but also other duties—particularly military service—before freeing their members.[42] Not even a decade later, Alexander's Senate added yet another complication regarding freedom. The St. Petersburg Treasury Department had presented it with a problem: ought it recognize the freedom of a state peasant if the remaining peasants in his village would be unable to cultivate the lands he left behind? The Senate decided that even if the other peasants were willing to free one of their members, they could not do so if that freedom resulted in uncultivated lands.[43]

This proclamation was not without effect. At least some freedom documents in this period made explicit mention that state peasant lands would not go uncultivated.[44] On this basis, as well, and very late in his reign, Alexander released a personal decree in which he forbade state peasants in Kherson' Province from leaving their status, claiming that the region was already underpopulated and undercultivated.[45] These actions echo eighteenth century fears about emptiness and underpopulation, particularly in areas deemed somewhat insecure.

Throughout this period, the idea of a need for documentation of freedom was based on a particular understanding of the relationship of responsibility between *soslovie* societies and individuals. This point was made most clearly in a Senate decision from 1810. The issue at hand was whether merchants who wished to move to a new town were subject to the same laws requiring formal freedom as were peasants and townspeople. The legal record for those two latter groups was clear, but that for merchants was more confusing. The Charter to the Towns stated that merchants from other towns (*inogorodnye*) were "not forbidden" from settling in new places and registering to trade; a decision from 1808 had said that the statutory movement from guild to guild based on capital should be just that—statutory, not subject to the whims of the merchant society as a whole.

In the end, the Senate decided that the merchants ought to be allowed to register in new towns without formal freedom as long as they had passports. And the rationale for this was based in the different relationships that merchants, on the one hand, and townspeople and peasants (the soul-tax paying), on the other, had with their societies:

> merchants must pay [their dues] each by [themselves], without any responsibility on the side of the society for it; in contrast, townspeople and peasants are responsible for payments for all those who have left their society, until the [next] revision of the tax and recruit rolls; consequently merchants are not responsible for each other in paying dues, and do not have the right to allow, nor to forbid, their movement from one to another town.[46]

In other words, the need for freedom documents reflected the collective responsibility inherent in the societies of those subject to the soul tax.

At the same time, because *soslovie* had persistently been conceived of as an economic identity, the laws and high-level discussions also focused on aligning an individual's economic activities with his formal status of registration. In 1810, the Ministry of Internal Affairs proposed legislation that would formally grant townspeople the right to leave their town status and become peasants. This act had earlier been prohibited on the grounds that it might lead to a depopulation of the empire's towns. But recently a number of townspeople had petitioned for special permission to enter peasant societies on the grounds that their livelihoods were based on agriculture. Out of this, the ministry concluded that prohibiting such townspeople from engaging in peasant activities would likely lead them "into total idleness, and by that towns, instead of useful citizens, will be obligated to take care of people totally alien, and sometimes even dangerous, to it."[47] Hence, previously prohibited movement was now allowed on the grounds that not only would it align activity with registration but that without such alignment only idleness would ensue.

Similarly, throughout the early years of the nineteenth century, the laws continued to state firmly that registry in towns was meant for those actively engaged in trade, while registry in villages was for those actively engaged in agriculture.[48] This emphasized the idea that *soslovie* was intended to reflect actual occupation and residence, not simply status or registry. But these laws remained within a context that largely controlled and restricted the mobility that might otherwise allow such alignment of status and function. And this was a context in which the act of registering had not necessarily always been properly linked to actual life. In 1815, for example, the provincial administration of the empire's Lithuanian territories sent out decrees to all towns under its purview, noting that there had been a problem, particularly in Vil'na itself, of "residents of not just other towns, but even of other provinces, who have neither residence nor trade in the city" nonetheless successfully registering as local merchants. This was clearly unacceptable, as it damaged the status of the town and its merchant ranks by severing the link between registration and reality.[49]

Starting in the mid-1820s and culminating in the early 1830s, however, a series of laws began to reflect a new approach to the question of movement by easing the way for individuals of various statuses to enter town societies.[50] Even before this time, there had been moments when higher authorities chastised local ones for placing high barriers on mobility. For example, in 1814, the Senate warned the Tver' Treasury Department not to exceed the legal standards then in place by demanding extra proof of an individual's freedom, in part because it "served for nothing more than an unnecessary prolonging of the matter."[51] But for the most part, the rule had been to emphasize strictures and controls.

More consistent movement toward easing those restrictions began in 1824, the year of the Guild Reform, usually interpreted as a response to the increasingly straitened economic status of Russia's merchants.[52] Rather than addressing the rules governing trade in the towns, as in the Guild Reform, there was a series of other measures that attempted to bolster the ailing merchantry, not by protecting those already in it but by allowing more to enter it. In February of that year, the Senate stated several new rules for the statutory movement between townsperson and merchant. Earlier laws had demanded that townspeople present an official statement that they had no recruit obligations in the town, and they also had to provide guarantors to attest to their fitness as merchants. Now, the Senate eliminated both measures.[53] A few years later, another Senate decree tried to ease mobility by allowing individuals to submit their paperwork to the treasury of the province in which they wished to register rather than have to travel back to the one in which they were presently registered. The decree furthermore warned the treasuries to deal with such petitions "without the least delay."[54]

Reducing the barriers to freedom for potential new merchants was one step toward easing the merchants' economic situation; reducing their tax burden was the other. On July 3, 1824, the Committee of Ministers decided to ease the process of moving from one soul-tax paying status to another by removing the double tax requirement.[55] The rationale was twofold. Minister of Finance Kankrin argued for the change on the grounds that, first, eliminating the double tax would not have a significant negative effect on the empire's finances, as it only brought in 50,000 rubles each year; and, second, that it would have a positive effect on the well-being of towns.[56] Moreover, he argued that it was better for peasants to become "real city residents" than to pursue trade on the side.[57] The result was confirmation of the proposal to "abolish the payment [of taxes] by one person in two statuses or in two provinces," as well as wiping out all arrears in such payments.[58] This decision was limited to certain kinds of mobility, but nevertheless it set a new precedent for easing mobility where barriers had more often been erected.[59]

Finally, in 1832, Nicholas I released a new decree that regulated all movement into town societies. It was a different sort of decree, one that combined an effort at clarification with a clear vision of what the law was supposed to accomplish: "increasing the population in towns and building useful institutions, which make up the most important methods of bringing them [towns] into better condition."[60] Compared to past practice, this decree aimed to make entry into town societies easier. The double tax burden had already been eliminated but now opportunities for mobility were expanded for state peasants. They no longer had to prove that they were not engaged in agriculture and had long-established trade in towns; that they primarily lived in towns; or that their lands would not lie fallow if they received release. In addition, their villages were henceforth not able to refuse release of their members based on future service obligations (as long as recruit duties were taken care of by proper payments).[61]

THE FREEDOM TO CHOOSE AND THE RIGHT TO REFUSE

These laws of the 1820s and early 1830s spoke to a new concern—or perhaps, to the return of an old, Petrine one—for making towns prosperous and productive. Even the occasional laws that continued to restrict movement couched those restrictions in terms of protecting towns.[62] But Nicholas I's 1832 decree was particularly important, in that it marked the culmination of another strand in the development of legislating *sosloviia* and their boundaries. It stated that towns could not refuse to accept new townspeople unless there was a very clear reason to believe they were likely to disrupt the peace. In so doing, this decree directly addressed the other side of the mobility process: entry into a new society, rather than exit from an old one. Entry came to require formal acceptance, a development that arose as much out of custom from below as by statute from above. But at the same time as the central state was recognizing the right of *soslovie* societies to accept (or not) new members, it was also trying to force registration on unregistered individuals, a process that brought it into conflict with its provinces and towns.

During the eighteenth century, legislation regarding movement between *sosloviia* initially focused on ensuring that individuals were free to leave a society, not on whether they were welcome in a new one. Laws from early in the century demanded that all those who traded in a town ought to register there. They saw registration as a definite good, as in a 1723 decree that demanded unregistered people register in towns in order to ensure they paid local taxes.[63] The laws that developed in the second half of the century stressed the importance of documenting freedom to move in order to ensure that fugitives were not improperly registered. These laws were not particularly concerned with the health of the societies into which people moved; or, rather, they assumed that new members were generally good for societies.

Slowly, however, practice and legislation together served to create a process through which societies were granted not only the right to release their members but also to accept new ones. The clergy had successfully fought to close its ranks by the end of the century, limiting access to clerical status to those born within it, thus making it perhaps the most caste-like of Russia's *sosloviia*.[64] Increasingly, other societies began to do the same. Eighteenth-century laws that focused specifically on entry into the merchantry began now to emphasize that all who wished to register as merchants had to prove their ability to prosper in such status.[65] Individuals had to provide written evidence of their financial status and their good behavior, and magistracies took those pieces of evidence into account as they made their decisions.[66] This was, then, a kind of attention to the needs of the communities, as the end result was, in principle, to ensure that the societies would not be burdened with new members who could not fulfill their duties as merchants.

Although this development meant only that towns had the right to demand assurance that their new members could support themselves, in practice many *soslovie* societies acted as if they had broader rights to accept or refuse new members. The files of local magistracies show this in many ways. For one, the magistracies themselves used the language of "acceptance" in many of their decisions. But, more important, they reported on individual merchant or townsperson societies "accepting" (or not) petitioners. In legal decisions, phrases like "the merchantry wishes to accept them," or "the society of townspeople does not refuse to accept these petitioners," often appear.[67]

Some files contain formal statements of acceptance by societies that suggest those societies took the idea of acceptance very seriously. In 1757, a deacon's son presented a statement by the Suzdal' merchants along with his petition: "the undersigned people of the first, second, and third guilds, having been at a council of the commune [*mirskoi sovet*], with general agreement have declared [the petitioner] accepted."[68] Not only did townspeople themselves believe in their right to accept, at times magistracies even asked for formal statements of acceptance in order to bring a case to its proper conclusion. In 1778, the Sol'vychegodsk Magistracy formally asked the town elder whether the local merchants accepted a particular petitioner; within weeks, they had met and agreed that "we wish to accept him."[69]

These many statements of acceptance were, however, based almost entirely on custom, not on law. In fact, even as these practices had become common, the laws showed a strong stance in favor of new registry and against the idea that societies might refuse new members. A decree of 1747 affirmed the ideal of universal registry even as it noted that some town societies had refused to bring in the infirm and impoverished.[70] In 1786, an Imperial ukase began the process of extending the Charter to the Towns to the Baltics by stating that those wishing to enter the merchant or townsperson societies of the region should proceed according to the Charter "and Our other laws and ukases." But while the Charter had said nothing in particular about the idea of acceptance, this ukase included something new: "a town society may not refuse, if the applicant is of good and unsullied behavior, and has the qualities necessary for a townsman or a merchant."[71] This was nearly the first time a law described a town society as possessing a real voice in deciding who should be part of that society—but it did so for one region only and in the context of arguing for restrictions on that right.

Even as this decree placed limits on the idea of local control over membership, another promoted local control in at least one context. In 1785, the Senate addressed a question from the St. Petersburg Treasury Department—was it possible for freed household serfs to register as state peasants?—and in its answer it added yet another new layer to the discussion of how social mobility ought to be regulated. The Senate decided the case based on two major precedents. First, it noted that freed serfs were allowed to join town estates; therefore, mobility was possible. Furthermore, some freed household serfs might not want to join a town estate, instead preferring "to choose for themselves a rural way of life." Based on these considerations, the Senate decided that freed household serfs ought to be allowed to register where they wished. However, it also included a caveat: the freed serfs could only enter villages that did not suffer from limited land and resources—that is, they could cause no "distress to the existing residents" of their new village.[72]

This last point was something new. While earlier laws had insisted that would-be new merchants had to prove their fitness to prosper in their new status, this new law focused on the effect that new members could have on a specific society. Several years later, the Senate again addressed the question of the process by which foreigners and freed serfs could enter rural societies. A report from the St. Petersburg governor noted that there had been many irregularities in carrying out these sorts of changes in the recent past. Investigation of the matter brought in a new standard: in order to join a village society, an individual needed not just the absence of problems but also an actual document supplied by that society, and ratified by the local Lower Land Court, agreeing to accept him or her. The decision went on to say that this would prove there was "already agreement between both sides"—in other words, that the decision was a mutual one.[73]

Finally, in 1800, the Senate extended the idea of the right to accept or refuse new members to town societies. In a law that largely addressed the need to ensure tax revenues, the Senate agreed with a proposal that extrapolated from earlier laws requiring guarantors, as well as the earlier statement that peasant societies had the right to vet their new members. Most of the new law focused on guarantors; at its very end, however, the Senate declared "when someone receives from his original status freedom to register in the merchantry, the society of townspeople, or some other status, then [the administering authority] is obligated first of all to turn to that place, in which he wishes to register, and request agreement for that."[74] From this point, societies had the legal right to agree to accept new members.

At the same time as these laws developed the idea of localities having control over their memberships, another strand of legislation began to challenge that control: the idea that some individuals had the freedom—or eventually the duty—"to choose a way of life." This was part of a larger imperial goal of ensuring both that all members of Russian society had a defined place in that society and that that place was made official by formal registry. The census revisions were times when this goal was perhaps the most pronounced, as the unregistered became registered.[75] But many more specific laws also sought to ensure that the population be properly listed and registered.

Fairly clearly, this desire for registration emerged not only out of a desire to control the population but also out of a belief that registration was necessary to be a productive member of society. This belief was most clearly stated in a decree of Empress Anna, from 1738, but it would be repeated in various forms throughout the decades. Anna's decree demanded that "aged, infirm, or twice-married" churchmen who were suitable neither for service in the military nor for the church ought either to be registered in towns or sent to Siberia for settlement. This was a desire to ensure that these former churchmen be registered in new statuses. The rationale behind the demand, however, focused on what that registry would do. It was not, according to the decree, a concern for social control; instead, registry was necessary because "it is not possible to allow [people] to live in idleness, for according to scripture, idleness is the root of all evil."[76]

Anna's decree focused on one particular group and its particularities, but Catherine came to use much the same logic to create a new "freedom" for the unregistered—a freedom that was in practice a duty. In 1783, Catherine released a ukase in which she "presented to free people the freedom to choose a way of life." The idea was a simple one: the recent census had shown that there were unregistered, "free" (*vol'nye*) people: former churchmen, freed serfs, and various others. Now, Catherine was telling them they could not remain free, that they should instead choose a way of life (*izbrat' rod zhizni*)—whichever one "they themselves decide is best for the common good and their own well-being."[77] She also distinguished between different kinds of "unfreedom." Drawing on the 1775 Manifesto, in which she had stated that freed serfs could not re-enserf themselves, all "free" people were now to choose any way of life "other than serfdom."[78]

The phrase "choose a way of life" became shorthand for the demand that individuals register in a (usually taxpaying) society. Laws over the next several years and decades used the phrase in relation to different social categories and with increasing insistence that making this choice was mandatory. These laws emphasized that those with the freedom to choose had to do so in order to start fulfilling the duties associated with their new status.[79] The phrase began to appear more and more in decrees, starting at least as early as 1797 and becoming standard through the early parts of the nineteenth century.[80]

At the same time as laws began to refine the concept of the right to choose a way of life as a discrete, if transitory, social category, the phrase also began to appear in wider use. Individual petitioners used the phrase as part of their statements of who they were or what they wished to do, as in 1793, when Grigori Titov, the son of a deacon, petitioned to enter the Moscow merchant society, and used the phrase "I wish to choose a way of life" as part of his justification.[81] Official documents granting freedom to serfs or prisoners, or residency rights to unregistered people, began to include the phrase often, as in the case of Vasili Ivanov, the as yet unregistered son of a Ukrainian, with the additional note that such a decision should be made "without the least delay."[82]

Even more telling, the phrase started to appear in petitions by individuals already registered but seeking to change their registration. By 1814, a Moscow townsman requested freedom from his society "because I have no particular trade appropriate to this status, [and] I therefore wish to choose a different way of life for myself," wording that suggests this concept had become a more generally accepted way of talking about changing estate membership.[83] And, a few years later, when the illegitimate son of a household serf petitioned to enter the Moscow society of townspeople, the Moscow Treasury Department delayed his case on the grounds that he failed to provide evidence of the right to choose a way of life.[84]

Also during this period, it became clear that this "right" was actually a duty.[85] The choice of a way of life was meant to find "free" people a real place within the context of the imperial Russian ideal of registry tied to service. Therefore, these "freedoms" were really demands, part of the larger goal of avoiding vagrancy. The link was made explicit in a case brought to the attention of the Moscow Provincial Administration during the 1840s. Then, one Ivan Aleksandrov, a deacon freed from church status due to his "doubtful" behavior," had failed to choose a way of life. The provincial administration warned that if he failed to do so, he would be dealt with according to the laws governing vagrants.[86]

Failure to register promptly brought punishment. Already in the 1810s, local courts came to adjudicate punishments for those who had failed to fulfill their duty to choose a new way of life. The Moscow Lower Court investigated the case of Fedor Vasil'ev, a serf freed in 1806 with the duty to choose a new *soslovie*. In a way, he had chosen— apparently, he wanted to join the Moscow society of townspeople—but he had not yet finalized his choice owing to "not having money even to pay for the paper required for the registration, nor to pay the taxes appropriate to that *soslovie*," and as a result he was considered guilty of a crime.[87] Later, fines became the most common response to a failure to register in proper time. In 1856, for example, the freed household serf Efrosimiia Efimova (aged 75) was fined 90 kopeks for not choosing her way of life quickly enough.[88]

Just as Senate decrees had tied registry of the previously unregistered to revisions of the census during the eighteenth century, a Senate decree of 1815 specifically linked the choice of a way of life to those census revisions. It stated that all freed serfs, both those now living freed and those who would be freed in the future, should choose a way of life before the next revision of the census rolls following their manumission. All those freed before previous revision who had not yet chosen a way of life within a year were to be dealt with strictly: adults would be sent into the military or into exile, the children and adolescents to military schools.[89]

Clearly, these decrees were heard. Although the demands for prompt registration changed in their specifics over the next decades, the idea remained in force that everyone with the "freedom" to choose a way of life had to choose, and had to register, or face legal repercussions.[90] And census revisions were times when unusual numbers of individuals, particularly freed serfs, found their way into new societies. Records from Moscow make this clear. The number of male former serfs applying to enter the Moscow townspeople society spiked just after the 1815 Senate decree: 83 in 1814, 129 in 1815, 329 in 1816, and 297 in 1817. Later in the century, census revisions continued to bring spikes in new registries. Although a report from 1847 claimed that Moscow's townspeople society each year saw an "increase, in a rather large amount... first, from the movement of merchants into the townspeople society; second, from the registry of [former] serfs," the specific numbers it provided showed clearly that census revisions brought with them surges in registry.[91] Furthermore, those surges were of those with the right to choose a way of life (freed serfs) rather than those with no such compulsion to do so (merchants).

As the idea of mandatory registration developed, it led to growing tensions between local authorities and the central imperial state, and eventually to a confirmation of the idea that local societies had a certain, but limited, right to choose their own members. The basic problem was that, put bluntly, some of the people with the "right to choose a way of life" were far from the upstanding citizens a community might hope to attract. They were, for the most part, the unregistered—but in an increasingly registered society, that meant they had some peculiar, if not actively illegal, reason for being so. Furthermore, this problem affected towns, and particularly townsperson societies, most of all. Because anyone registering as a state peasant had to be guaranteed an allotment of land, even those in need of a new place could not automatically join such a society. As a result, the "choice" of a new way of life usually meant joining a townsperson society. Village societies might not have enough land, merchants had to have a certain amount of capital, and craftsmen needed a certain trade.[92] Societies of townspeople got the leftovers.

Soon after the idea that societies had the right to choose their members was formally stated in 1800, that right was limited with regard to those with the right to choose their way of life. A Senate decree from 1805 looked at two such categories: children of church servitors and former fugitives who had returned to Russia under an imperial amnesty. Because members of both groups currently lacked a place in the empire's social hierarchy (which meant they neither paid taxes nor had access to the economic rights associated with *soslovie*), they were obligated to register somewhere. Laws did say that local authorities had the right to accept new members, but in this case the Senate decided that that right could only be used in regard to peasants—that is, those already paying taxes and with a legal place. Those with the right to choose a way of life could be registered without formal acceptance.[93]

This decision set up a conflict between central state interests and those of localities, a conflict that continued through much of the rest of the century.[94] Over and over, local authorities tried to defend their right to choose their own members, with differing responses on the part of the central state. At times, such requests arose over individual problems. In the late 1820s, the Viatka Treasury Department was uncertain about how to proceed regarding the case of two men, Vasilii Dvinianikov and Vasilii Sveshnikov. Both men had moved from church status into the postal service. Their "drunkenness and bad behavior," however, got them removed from their positions. According to the law, anyone who failed to complete a full twenty-year term with the postal service was supposed to be returned to his *soslovie* of origin. In the case of Dvinianikov and Sveshnikov, however, that posed a problem, as their *soslovie* of origin was not a taxpaying one. Because of this, it was agreed that they should choose a new way of life as long as that choice got them on the tax rolls. But owing to their "drunkenness and bad behavior," no society wished to accept them.[95]

Individuals presented problems on a small scale, but some laws led to much more significant problems for societies. In one case, a Senate decree of 1808 examined the status of children of non-noble bureaucrats who were not registered on any tax rolls, but who were also "unfit" to become bureaucrats. The Senate decided that those who were fit for military service ought to serve. The remaining persons—those unsuited either to bureaucratic life or to military life, which presumably meant they were neither physically nor mentally strong (or that they were troublemakers)—were to be registered as townspeople or artisans or state or court peasants, as they wished.[96]

A stronger statement of the need for registration, whatever the desires of local communities, came at about the same time, in two laws about Roma. In 1809, as part of a general law on their condition, Alexander I stated that "those Gypsies who have no passports and are registered nowhere" should find themselves a place of ascription within a year or face prosecution according to the laws on vagrancy.[97] More than a year later, Alexander repeated the injunction to register, as many had failed to do so even in this longer period of time. And in this ukase, he brought up an issue that was at that point becoming significant more generally. He stated that "when ascribing Gypsies to towns[,] take care that their numbers do not overly burden towns, but also without demanding the agreement of town societies for such ascription."[98]

Eventually, the complaints of local authorities created changes in the regulations governing mandatory registry. Starting in the late reign of Catherine II, a series of manifestos had granted the right to choose a way of life to émigré fugitives if they repatriated themselves.[99] Fugitives, however, were by definition those who had fled their obligations to their communities—hardly a good recommendation to a new community. As a result, after one such manifesto from 1814, several towns found themselves coping with large numbers of people they did not necessarily want to accept, and wrote to central authorities for increased rights in relation to these possible troublemakers. In 1816, the military governor of Kherson province wrote to the Ministry of Police, noting first that Odessa had been overrun by hundreds of returning émigrés (with a resulting increase of "thievery and other crimes") and, further, that the town had no desire to accept these people as full members. Their status as fugitives made them seem dubious prospects at best from the point of view of a local society that would have to take responsibility for their future stability.[100]

Other communities were just as troubled by far fewer newcomers, with the result that the central state had to weigh the implications of such newcomers for town societies and their own rights. Later that year, officials from Taganrog made a similar complaint as that of the Kherson governor, though this matter concerned the disruption that a mere nine returnees could cause a smaller community.[101] The Taganrog *meshchanin* society asked whether they were obligated to accept the men—and if so, if they could immediately be sent into the army to fulfill part of the town's military obligations. The Committee of Ministers and Senate discussed the problem, and resolved in favor of the right of communities to choose their own members. Local town and village societies had to "voluntarily agree to accept" new members; those they did not want to accept could be sent into the military or registered in towns as "workers," which meant as individuals not part of the actual town society.[102] In other words, acceptance was again the rule for full membership in a *soslovie*, with this new category of worker as a catchall for those deemed truly dangerous to society.

This solution was only a temporary one, in part because it tried to solve the problem through an unworkable means—essentially by establishing a new category, without thought for how that category would fit imperial realities. A decade and a half later, a similar situation developed in the western provinces. In 1829, the Volyn' Provincial Administration wrote to the Ministry of Finance about a problem that had developed out of a recent demand that nobles prove their nobility in order to retain their status. A large number of people who had been classified as Polish nobles had been unable to find documents to prove their status, and they were thus in need of a new status. Most were petitioning to enter the local townsperson society; that society, however, "due to the fact that [the nobles] had not presented trustworthy guarantors for their payment of taxes and dues," did not agree to this. The ministry turned to the Senate for help in addressing the important question: "how should one deal with the registry on the tax rolls of such people, who, having been forced to choose a way of life, have expressed a wish to register in the place of their residence, on estates among the free people, or among the townspeople, but now are not accepted by landowners or townspeople societies?"[103]

In this case, the Ministry of Finance presented a particular argument. Current laws, in its interpretation, had formalized the principle of acceptance, but they all applied to those moving from one taxpaying status and society to another. The former nobles, however, had never been listed on tax rolls. In the ministry's interpretation, this meant that they did not need formal acceptance because automatic registry was in the interests both of the petitioners (who found a status), and the central state (who found new taxpayers). It was true, the ministry wrote, that in general it was important to preserve the right of societies to choose their members, as they did indeed have "responsibility for the payment of taxes and the fulfillment of duties for its members." However, not allowing these former nobles to join local townspeople societies would cause them "difficulties"; furthermore, it would cause "great losses to the treasury, for societies for the most part refuse to accept people simply because they are unknown to them, or because they are not of the economic standing that would allow them to promise completely the regular payment of taxes, but at the same time, these people would end up being left without registration on the tax rolls, and without a voice (*v bezglasnosti*)." To the ministry, which was responsible for the financial state of the empire, not of localities, this rationale seemed clear, and it concluded that "all those people who have been given the right to choose a way of life, and who wish to do it, and for the registry of whom there are no particular problems, register them according to their wish into the town or rural societies, only making sure that in the latter case there is not an insufficiency of land, without demanding the agreement of the societies."[104]

At about the same time, the Ministry of Finance began to suggest a new solution to the problem of finding places for everyone: the use of tax waivers (*l'goty*). At issue was that tension between the imperial desire to demand registration and the local desire to control membership. Initially, in 1828 the State Council proposed using waivers to help former serfs freed by judicial decision, who were likely to be "for the most part not well-off, and placed in a difficult position by the necessary costs of moving into a free condition." That is, such people "needed waivers from paying taxes" to help them settle in new positions.[105] This decision saw waivers as a solution for these individuals. Soon, though, local authorities would induce the central authorities to see waivers as a way of dealing with their demands, as well.

A series of local questions helped lead to this new solution to the tension between registry and control. In 1829, the Viatka Treasury Department asked the Senate for help in determining the proper procedure for those with the freedom to choose a way of life, given that a whole series of laws "clearly exposed the will of the High Government, that neither to town, nor to rural societies should those people who might burden them in regard to taxes and recruits be registered."[106] The Viatka Treasury wanted the Senate to decide in favor of local societies, but but found their hopes dashed. The Senate, in a series of decisions, instead affirmed a different principle: registration trumped local concerns, for lack of registration was worse than possibly burdening local societies with people who might fail to pay their taxes. The Senate seemed particularly swayed in its decision by the case of one Andrei Atskovskii, who had failed to choose a way of life because, he said, "he does not know any society, nor any landlord, from whom he could obtain a written agreement to accept him" and who, as a result, had fallen into vagrancy.[107] This fate seemed proof of the eighteenth-century notion that registration was necessary for a productive society.

As a result, here and in other cases, the Senate confirmed that those with the duty to choose a way of life—those without prior registration, in other words—could be registered in societies without formal agreement. In 1830, it heard a proposal from the Ministry of Finance that suggested freed serfs, wards of foundling homes who had come of age, and the illegitimate children of unregistered mothers, should all be allowed to register in societies without the agreement of those societies (those excluded from the postal service for bad behavior who could not gain agreement were to be sent into the military or set to factory work).[108]

Then, in 1832, the ministry again presented a proposal that refined its stance toward certain freed household and landless serfs. Past practice suggested that they were more or less like others who needed to "choose a way of life" and would be registered as townspeople in town societies that accepted them, or as "working people" if no society would. However, the Ministry of Finance now suggested that this was not a sufficient solution. In part to speed up the process of registration, they now suggested that a group of landless serfs currently in this position be registered in townspeople societies with a five-year waiver from paying taxes. The Senate agreed, and released a decree confirming this approach.[109]

At the end of that same year, Nicholas I's new statement of rules for joining town societies standardized both the idea of registry without acceptance and the use of tax waivers to ease that process. In the decree, the various kinds of "free" people were now able to join townspeople societies without the agreement of those societies, but with no taxes to pay or duties to fulfill—state or local—for two years. Following this, "for three years the town is not responsible for their taxes; the responsibility for paying them remains on them [the individuals]." After these three years, however, "these people are obligated to petition for the agreement of the society to ascribe them permanently, and only them will they have a vote (voice)."[110]

In principle, this solution offered the best of all possible worlds: everyone found a place to be productive, while towns were not burdened with responsibility for those with little responsibility of their own. It was not, of course, a perfect system. For one thing, as laws gave new groups the right to choose a way of life, towns and villages could feel besieged by influxes of unwanted new members.[111] But even more important, the proposed solution—waivers—often only postponed the problem. Eventually, permanent decisions had to be made.

At least in some places, local authorities took seriously their responsibility to control their membership at the end of the waiver period. Riazan' local authorities were particularly likely to differentiate between temporary registration with waivers and permanent registry that occurred only with formal acceptance after the waiver period. In a series of cases, both local Riazan' town officials and the provincial treasury department emphasized this difference, as well as the role that the town society played in moving individuals from one status to the other.[112] Although the freed serf Grigori Evlampiev had registered in Riazan' as a townsman and, indeed, claimed that status in his petitions, the town society refused to accept him permanently, with no explanation.[113] In another case, Grigor'i Ivanov, a Vladimir serf freed by judicial decision, had been registered in the

Riazan' society of townspeople in 1850, with five years' tax waivers. In 1854, the Riazan' Treasury asked that he be required to appear in person in Riazan' before he was "permanently registered" as a member of the society starting the following year. This request was complicated, though, owing to the fact that Ivanov then lived in Poland (with, as it happened, his former owner). After much correspondence with Polish and Russian officials, Ivanov was found, moved to Riazan', and was then formally accepted into the society as a full member.[114]

Elsewhere, troubles at the end of the waiver period led local authorities to propose yet other solutions. Riga found itself home to many former Polish nobles who had been registered as temporary townsmen with a three-year tax waiver. In 1840, the Livland governor sent a report to the Ministry of Finance describing the troubles this policy had caused. He noted that even before they had been stripped of their noble status, most of these "nobles" had actually been in "utter poverty," a position their demotion to taxed status did nothing to lessen. At the end of their three-year period, all were expected to approach the Riga society to request formal, permanent addition to the Riga tax rolls. The governor noted that at that point they faced two options: formal addition to the society or, for those not accepted, registry on the tax rolls but "without the responsibility of the town society"—in other words, outside the system of collective responsibility that helped keep the empire running. Furthermore, the governor noted, in their few years without collective responsibility, the 217 male souls so registered had already amassed arrears of 2,666 rubles. The governor's solution was, quite literally, to establish collective responsibility. He suggested that a particular Riga institution "with collective responsibility" be established to oversee these individuals—essentially a particular *soslovie* society of "former members of the Polish nobility." The Ministry of Finance found this proposal unworkable.[115]

Shortly before this, however, the Committee of Ministers had received imperial permission to release a statement that proposed something even more radical. In 1833, the taxpayers of Kursk had fallen so far into arrears that they faced a Senate investigation. It found that most of the arrears came from people who had been registered by the treasury department into the town society without the town's agreement—and furthermore that most of these people were merely names in a register, having "neither houses nor other property in the city of Kursk, having been absent for many years, [and] living who knows where." The Senator sent to investigate, E. I. Mechnikov, found it to be such a problem that he recommended local societies once again have power of approval over all new members. The proposal was presented to the Committee of Ministers, but it was rejected on the grounds that the demand would by necessity leave some undesirables without membership—and thus without restraint.[116]

The committee, did, however, agree to resurrect an earlier idea: all those registered in towns temporarily, who could not produce the guarantors necessary to gain formal acceptance at the end of their waiver period, would be considered "workers"—"that is, impose townsman's rates of taxes on them, subject each to personal responsibility according to the laws, in case of insufficient payment of dues."[117] This meant that only those who gained formal acceptance into the society were subject to—but also benefited from—collective responsibility for paying taxes. In the words of a later legal writer, these statutes together defined "working people" as "those ascribed into a townsperson society," but still with "their own personal responsibility for paying their townsman's taxes."[118]

This ending is an important one, for it gave new meaning to the idea of collective responsibility. In the past, collective responsibility had applied exclusively to those of lower status—those who were *not* the privileged, non-taxpaying few. Merchants escaped collective responsibility with their movement up from the society of townspeople. But now these new "workers" were judged to be not worthy of being part of collective responsibility, which meant that collective responsibility was itself something to be desired.

By the 1830s, a regularized system allowing social mobility had helped to define the outlines of Russia's system of *sosloviia*. It established that *soslovie* membership was based in localities, and that those localities had significant, but not total, control over that membership. It also affirmed that *soslovie* membership carried obligations to the state and to the locality, as well as for occupation, and that these were tightly linked. Furthermore, it implied that being fully part of a local community was a not only a duty but also a right that was not available to every individual. It had to be earned with good behavior and responsible actions. In so doing, the system reaffirmed the notion that *soslovie* was not just a label but was an integral part of Russian society.

Coming into the middle of the century, then, *soslovie* was still the dominant mode. The ministries of the imperial state used *soslovie* to help ensure that all Russian subjects had a proper place and occupation, for *soslovie* implied belonging and opportunity. Finding those places, however, could prove troublesome for some individuals, as they faced local authorities who had control over their lives. As some subjects sought to change their *soslovie*, they had to gain the approval of two such societies: the one they left, and the one they wished to join. That process highlighted another interpretation of *soslovie*, as the issue of obligation came to the forefront in local decisions.

4

Communities and Individuals

SOSLOVIE SOCIETIES AND THEIR MEMBERS

ALEKSANDR MILIUKOV SPENT his childhood largely unaware of the nature of imperial Russia's society of *sosloviia* until his desire for an education brought him face to face with the power his local society had over his life. Born in 1817, he was by registry a member of Moscow's townsperson society, but according to his memoirs he understood his life simply as Russian. For one, his extended family and circle of acquaintances crossed *soslovie* boundaries. His father worked for a cousin wealthy enough to own a factory in the southern suburbs of the great city; he remembered his childhood as filled with visits to the nearby Novodevichii Monastery and visits from its nuns to his home. His best friend in primary school was the son of the manager of a wealthy nobleman whose habits he also got to observe. And, too, the life he described was one filled with "all the old Russian habits," from painting Easter eggs to baking holiday pastries, and even to constructing ice slides for Carnival. The mixing of statuses combined with a life bounded by religious holidays seemed purely "old Russian" to Miliukov, as he recalled his past.[1]

Soon, though, the limits of his specific *soslovie* identity became clear. Miliukov describes himself as being consistently interested in school and learning; his mother began the process of teaching him to read, and soon had him reading Bible stories and Russian history, despite his own greater interest in then-current events. He began to attend primary school in Moscow, and his success led him to consider attending secondary school—something, however, that would move him beyond his place, both metaphorically and administratively. His father initially discouraged Aleksandr from going on for more schooling, believing that he should instead simply get down to work. But the family's patron (and relative) urged them instead to allow Aleksandr to go first to secondary school and then on to university. The patron's point of view won out.[2]

Almost immediately, however, it became clear that the act of crossing a boundary from unschooled boy to educated man would also require crossing a boundary based in *soslovie* membership. As soon as the decision was made to send Aleksandr to secondary school, his family started the process of gaining him the freeing agreement necessary for him to enroll. First, his father enlisted (and paid) an acquaintance to help procure the necessary document. But finally, it became necessary for Aleksandr and his father to visit the Moscow town administration to plead their case. For him it was "the day when my fate would be decided."[3] Would he receive freedom from the society and be allowed to study and take full part in the wider Russian world he had so frequently encountered, or would his request be rejected and he be confined to the narrower options of a mere townsman?

The two set off for the duma offices early in the day. The waiting room they entered was "remarkably dirty," and soon was filled with dozens of petitioners, from a "hump-backed grey old man" to a "young man with a red wide face." A few spoke in whispers to one another, but most worried in silence. Their first interaction with officialdom came when "suddenly from the side door a tall, thick-set bureaucrat appeared… glancing over the crowd, which had gotten up from their chairs at his entrance[;] he began to toss out 'calming' phrases on all sides, such as 'come again tomorrow! Try again in a month!'"[4] In short order, Miliukov saw some of the ways that townspeople and their society interacted. One old man was refused entrance to the almshouse on the grounds that it had no more room. A woman seeking aid for herself and her two daughters was sent off to wait in another line. A young man who wished to leave the society to enter a monastery was refused. When Miliukov and his father entered the hearing room, a large hall with a portrait of the emperor, an icon, and shelves filled with thick books, they were quickly told that the society was willing to free Miliukov—if his father could bring them 700 rubles.[5] Miliukov was left with a feeling that his society viewed him not as a person, but as an entry in an account book with only a fiscal value.

Miliukov later described the experience as recognizing the *soslovie* administration as the "terrible areopagus," the frightening, remote power with undue control over the lives of its members.[6] His interpretation was essentially correct. Although legislation regarding those with the freedom to choose a way of life had eroded some of their authority, local *soslovie* societies nonetheless continued to wield significant power over the process of official social mobility during the eighteenth and early nineteenth centuries. In the eighteenth century, this power over others' freedom was fully recognized while the power of their acceptance was less strong. Even so, many local societies acted as if they had full control over both sides in the process of changing *soslovie*. During the nineteenth century, except in certain cases, local societies had full legal authority to grant or deny both freedom and acceptance. And as both memoirs and archives suggest, they used this power to promote their interests against both the central state and their members. The interactions of the *soslovie* societies with their members and would-be members demonstrate the importance of soslovie not just as a system of control but as an interlocking network of interests, duties, and desires.

At the same time, in part because the *soslovie* system failed to reflect the full array of occupations and statuses plied and desired by Russia's subjects, the imperial state continued to regulate the concept of *soslovie* membership.[7] The uneasy relationship between merchant and townsperson societies was a consistent source of complications that challenged the concept of membership. Even more confusing, however, were the newer statuses based on specific individual achievement—the status of honored citizen and certain professional or quasi-professional positions—that placed individuals entirely outside the realm of collective responsibility and allowed them to interact with the imperial state directly. These few statuses were both created out of the *soslovie* system and placed in contrast to it, in ways that dramatically affected their future development.

LEAVING THE COMMUNITY: LOCAL AUTHORITIES VS. INDIVIDUALS

In Miliukov's story, the Moscow townsperson society took quite seriously its role in adjudicating social mobility, and archival records suggest much the same thing. A sampling of petitions from townspeople seeking to leave the society in the 1810s shows only one successful outcome in ten such petitions. The others were either left undecided or refused outright.[8] This pattern in Moscow is part of a larger world of *soslovie* governance during the eighteenth and early nineteenth centuries. At that time, local *soslovie* authorities and the imperial state alike viewed *soslovie* members primarily as taxpayers and potential soldiers. The laws that governed changing *soslovie* reinforced this view by placing particular emphasis on individual duty to society and state. As a result, from the eighteenth century through to the era of the Great Reforms, communities consistently evaluated their members' financial and service obligations above all other considerations when deciding whether to free them to enter other *sosloviia*. That did not mean these were the only issues; *soslovie* societies also worried about maintaining local order. Still, duties were the focus, and they compelled *soslovie* societies to demand sometimes seemingly exorbitant amounts in return for grants of freedom.

Laws on social mobility often emphasized taxes, and perhaps as a result *soslovie* societies were first of all concerned with whether those seeking freedom had been good taxpayers. Certainly if individuals owed back taxes their petitions requesting freedom could easily be held up by their local societies.[9] But also, local authorities saw requests for freedom as opportunities to force payment of outstanding duties and debts. The Riazan' townsman Iakov Sapchakov had arrears of 2 rubles, 28 kopeks in 1856 when he petitioned to exit into a state peasant society. His request was granted only "as long as he clears the arrears that accrued to him."[10] These financial efforts could even be extended to relatives of debtors. The Smolensk townsperson society refused to allow the widow Liubov Kondrashenko and her daughter to exit that society because her late husband had left behind debts. Only if she cleared those debts would she be allowed to leave.[11]

For the most part, if petitioners had no outstanding dues, or if they had clear plans to repay any arrears, the local authorities were willing to free them.[12] But during the period when the double tax burden was imposed on those who changed status, some local authorities were warier; after all, if such petitioners had failed so far to keep up with their dues, how was the society to collect future taxes once the petitioners were legally members of another *soslovie* society?[13] A history of arrears, even if cleared at the time of petition, did not incline societies to grant freedom. Furthermore, they were probably right to worry about this possible complication, as some individuals did fail to keep up their dues after their status was changed. The Vil'na townsman Sidor Kupriashkin, for one, fell into arrears in his dues to the town after he had moved into the status of a free agriculturist in 1839. In his case, the town kept after him, and it eventually got its money.[14] Generally, though, the townsperson and other societies certainly wished to avoid having to take such measures to keep their books in order.

These concerns were valid because the double tax burden kept the petitioner tied to his old society even after he had gained a new *soslovie* membership. That is, taxes created a bond that lasted until the next revision of the census. At times, the laws made this continued connection abundantly clear; those that allowed for mobility also demanded that petitioners provide guarantors who would ensure future payments of taxes in their status of origin.[15] Even after the abolition of the double tax burden, those who had moved could still find themselves required to make payments to their former societies. One law of 1826, for example, noted that all townspeople who had moved up into the merchantry were still liable for dues accruing to dead relatives left behind on the tax rolls of their former societies.[16]

Individual societies recognized this continued bond, and acted to preserve their own interests in the face of requests for freedom. Often, and following legal precedents, societies demanded money or guarantors from its members who wished to leave. In 1845, the Saratov society of townspeople initially refused to free Anna Uvarova and her family because her petition failed to mention that her family (which included two sons, and thus taxpayers) would keep up tax payments as needed after their exit from that society. Once the family swore an oath to keep up payments, the townspeople agreed to let them go.[17] A few years before that, the case of Semën Mokrusov, a state peasant petitioning to enter the Saratov society of townspeople, was held up in part due to irregularities in his arrangements to continue paying his state peasant duties after his registry in the new estate. Once those arrangements were made (and once he provided guarantors for his good behavior), Mokrusov was accepted.[18] At mid-century, the St. Petersburg craft society demanded that its members leave behind money to help cover future dues. Some members were required to pay only 15 rubles, but petitioners like Eduard Kolkovskii, who would leave behind an aged father, had to pay significantly more; the craft society demanded 100 rubles from Kolkovskii, to pay "not only taxes, but local fees, too."[19]

In other cases, societies might be loath to release their members because those who actively sought their freedom were likely to be particularly important to the economic health of that community. In other words, if the rich who could be relied on to fulfill their (and possibly others') duties exited, then the poor were left with increased burdens. Records from some serf villages give a sense of how these issues might have played out in peasant villages. When Count Sheremetev considered whether to grant a serf freedom, his estate management office consulted the serf's village about the effect that freedom might have on its economic position. In many cases, losing the serfs who actively sought their freedom would mean losing among the most economically successful members of a community—and that might leave a village unable to meet its rent (and, presumably, tax) obligations. Some of the serf industrialists from the then village of Ivanovo paid dues well beyond the amount that would normally accrue to their households, either because they were responsible for the dues of their workers or because the community allotted them more work-units because they were able to pay for them. After they were freed, the Ivanovo Estate Administration reported, losing those payments created problems for the rest of the society's peasants: "these 6,615 rubles fell on the poor peasants, who have been harshly punished for non-payment by the society, and they, finding themselves insolvent, and from time to time [with] arrears built up in their accounts,... fall into despair, and even into thievery and drunkenness."[20]

This kind of thinking was widespread. In the early 1860s, the Gorodok society of townspeople placed significant restrictions on granting freedom to one of its members. As it reported, the society as a whole owed more than 5,000 rubles in unpaid soul taxes, and "if the wealthy are freed from the society, then there will remain only the poor, who will not have the ability to cover these arrears." As a result, when one such wealthy townsman requested freedom, the society decided that it had to protect its own interests. Because the man in question, Ivan Potashko, had long lived in St. Petersburg, "he had never taken on local responsibilities on par with other members of the society, and never even fulfilled recruit duties, due to the fact that there was never anyone in his family liable for the draft, [the society] found it just that Potashko take on some of the society's burdens." Therefore, it had requested from him 26 rubles "to pay for the dead, the poor, the underaged orphans, and those completely destitute." Until he paid up, the society "did not consider it possible to free him." Potashko, of course, claimed that he was wealthy "only in their opinion, but not in reality."[21]

Local societies were just as concerned with the effect that losing a member might have on their ability to fulfill the military duties demanded by the state. Towns and villages were subject to irregular but frequent demands for new draftees, and they had to figure out as best they could how to fulfill those demands. In 1831, a formal "line system" (*ocherednaia sistema*) was instituted to bring order to the process, but before that military duties were somewhat more haphazardly handled.[22] Nonetheless, even before the formal system was established, some localities had started to view people as being in line for the next call for the draft; and because taking individuals into the military meant removing a taxpayer and a worker, the choice of who to send was one fraught with problems. The laws also recognized this fact, and so emphasized that men had to prove they were not in line for the draft if they were to be allowed to leave a society.[23] Therefore, if an individual had been identified as a likely candidate for the draft, his community was likely to want to keep him in reserve.

In 1780, military duties became a problem for Ivan Zhiriaev. Zhiriaev stood next in line for the Kiakhta craft society in the next draft (a fact that might have affected his decision to petition to enter the Udinsk merchantry). In his case, the local magistracy decided that this was not a valid reason to keep him, and it accepted his change of estate against the will of his society.[24] Something similar happened in 1777, when the economic peasant Ivan Vasil'ev, from Vladimir district, petitioned to enter the Moscow merchantry. His home village did not wish to release him "because from his father and two brothers and nephews[,] no one has been sent as a draftee." In other words, Vasil'ev's family was overdue when it came to sending soldiers to the draft, and the home village wanted to reserve the right to send Ivan. In this case, the College of the Economy intervened; they pointed out that although such a large family would indeed be subject to providing a soldier in a near future draft, the very fact that the family was so large meant that there were many other eligible men within it to draft. The college overrode the local decision and granted Vasil'ev his freedom.[25]

During the nineteenth century, unlike the matter of arrears, which could at times be forgiven by a quick payment, unfulfilled military duties on a family's part could be reason for a rather summary judgment against a petitioner. In 1854, the townsman Vasilii Korobov submitted a petition written, as he noted, by himself ("and it was not rewritten by anyone") in which he tried to prove that he was not subject to military duties because his family had provided a (purchased) draftee in 1830. But the rest of his detailed account of his family and trade went for naught, as the townspeople council quickly dismissed his case: that long-ago soldier no longer freed the family from its obligations. Instead, the council decided, "the family of the townsman Korobov should be in line to provide a recruit in the next draft." To add insult to injury, the Riazan' Town Duma resolved to collect 45 kopeks for the use of officially stamped paper from Korobov when he showed up to hear the result of his petition.[26] Riazan's Town Duma seemed particularly focused on the possibility of military duties; several years earlier, it had refused to release the townsman Tikhon Bobrov, owing to the "great size of his family."[27] Left unstated was the idea that such a large family would have to supply multiple soldiers for the draft.

Military duties were so absolute that even those with what seemed like iron-clad excuses could still be subject to them. In 1857, Ivan Ozeritskii sought freedom from the Riazan' society of townspeople. Although he was in principle subject to the draft in the near future, he gave as additional evidence a certificate signed by the senior Riazan district doctor that proved him to be unfit for military service: he had "near the ankle of his left leg a lymphatic tumor, due to which he cannot wear a leather boot and only with a soft boot can he walk with difficulty." However, laws governing recruitment said that individuals could not be excluded from draft lists due to illness, and as a result Ozeritskii's position could not be changed.[28] Perhaps because of their rarity, petitioners who were free of future military duties might be worthy of special notice. That happened in the case of Vasilii Orlov, a Saratov townsman petitioning to leave the town and enter a state peasant village. The society of townspeople agreed to free him in part because he owed no dues, but "even more because he is not on the draft list."[29]

A final worry for local societies was that of maintaining good order in the community. In some cases, this could lead to communities deciding to waive their interests in tax and recruit duties in order to free themselves of troublemakers. In several eighteenth-century cases, this clearly happened when local communities were willing to cover the future dues of members they wished to be free of. The Saratov merchant society agreed to use their own funds for Terentii Sokolov when he requested freedom to enter a monastery in order to rid themselves of responsibility for the man. He was first of all "already old," and furthermore, he was so badly behaved that he was considered "useless for the society."[30] In archival records, at least, this was a far less common thread than more tangible issues like taxes and other duties. But other sources suggest that local communities wished to rid themselves of responsibility for the aged and infirm. At the time of Catherine the Great's Legislative Commission, a number of peasant delegates specifically requested the right to exclude such individuals from the soul tax lists. While such requests were couched in terms of freeing communities from tax obligations that were difficult to meet, nobles and town delegates argued that this carried over to peasant societies wishing to be free from obligations to care for the infirm.[31]

In the end, local societies weighed these various factors and generally decided that demanding money was the surest way to ensure their interests were met. The amount of money demanded by local authorities varied, but generally it far exceeded a plain accounting for future soul taxes. In principle, though, it was this tax duty, plus other local duties, that entered into societies' calculations. Indeed, many case files include a list of the obligations that had to be met in order for individuals to be freed from their home communities. When the Tver' state peasant Kondratii Savel'ev wanted release from his home village, that village eventually produced a statement that "the commune frees him for registry in the *soslovie* of townspeople as a cooper; he has good behavior and standing, he owes no outstanding dues to the district, he has promised to pay all state taxes and local duties accruing to his household until the next revision of the census."[32] But this sort of list was only a starting point for negotiations; local societies often demanded far more.

The kinds of demands societies could exact from those who wished to leave were based in multiple sorts of accounting. Court peasants were subject to official statute, which set sums that applied to all those who wished to leave their societies to move to towns. At the end of the eighteenth century, the price for freedom for court peasants was set at 360 rubles per soul; in 1809, it was raised to 500 rubles. In 1812, the price went up to 1,000 rubles for those who wished to join the merchant estate and to 700 for those seeking to become townspeople. Then, in 1826, the Department of Court Lands decided that it was in the best interest of the tsar's family (and of peasant villages) to restrict mobility even further. To do so, it raised the price for freedom to 5,000 rubles for entry into a merchant society and 2,000 for registry as a townsman.[33] Here, demands were tied not to actual economic impact but instead to the larger interests of the Romanov family itself.

For most other cases, the exact sums demanded from those leaving their home societies were up for negotiation, and different communities came to different conclusions as they weighed individual obligations and community needs. At the most basic level, some communities simply wanted to receive enough money to cover the costs of losing one member. That was the story told by Aleksandr Berezin, the son of a monastery peasant, who remembered a simple but significant process of payment. In 1752 he paid his village commune 23 rubles in return for an attestation of freedom. This was not an insignificant sum; for the previous four years he had been earning a salary of 15 rubles a year while working for a Petersburg grain merchant.[34] But as far as the society knew, it would have to wait at least ten years to remove him from its tax rolls, and the soul tax was not the only duty Berezin had to pay From its point of view, the sum was based largely on his actual future obligations. Perhaps that is why Berezin did not recall this demand as being something particularly burdensome; it was a bump on the path to a new life, not a true obstacle.

Others remembered far greater exactions, and saw them as far more unreasonable. In his memoir, Aleksandr Miliukov recalled his townsperson society demanding 700 rubles for his freedom, a sum he and his family found unreasonable, particularly given that his father's yearly salary was only 600 rubles. Comparing this to Berezin's case, however, suggests that the "unreasonableness" was based on point of view rather than on real burden. Berezin had paid 23 rubles for his freedom, with a yearly salary of 15 rubles—more than half again his yearly salary. The fee to free Miliukov was only a bit more than 15 percent above his father's annual salary. It was a large sum, to be sure, but not an utterly unreasonable one.

Of course, the situations are not entirely comparable; Miliukov's father's salary supported his whole family while Berezin had fewer dependents. Miliukov would be studying, and not contributing to the family economy, while Berezin was looking at increased economic opportunities. And, too, the cost of living in nineteenth-century Moscow was likely higher than in an eighteenth-century peasant village. Still, given Berezin's case, the Moscow town elders were more modest in their demands than Berezin's village elders had been. That it was seen as a greater burden suggests not only differences in the two men's attitudes but also the complicated process of gaining freedom itself.

These were complex issues for local communities and individuals, but in many cases they were also of interest to higher authorities. As a result, petitioners could find themselves in an awkward position, as different levels of administrators fought over their cases. Much of the concern of higher authorities was based on the fact that, in principle at least, communities and their leaders or overseers were not supposed to place undue restrictions on members who sought to leave. In 1799, a set of instructions sent to overseers of court peasant villages made this clear, as it cited a recent law affirming that "court peasants, if they wish, may exit into the merchantry or the estate of townspeople." In particular, the instructions noted, while those seeking exit could be expected to pay for the privilege, that payment should not be excessive, and "if someone considers himself to be hurt in this situation, he may complain to the Department [of Court Possessions], and seek protection for himself in the beneficence of the Monarch Himself."[35] In practice, however, some communities made decisions that seemed as arbitrary as that of any serf-owner.[36]

At times, the decisions of local communities were simply opaque—there was no clear reason why they refused to allow someone to exit. In 1776, several state peasants seeking entrance into the Aleksin merchantry all claimed that, although they had no outstanding dues or duties and although they had promised to continue to pay their taxes, they had been stymied in their efforts to gain official freedom from their home villages. All used nearly the same language: "that document of freedom [which I requested] was not given for unknown reasons."[37] Even more confusing was the case of Vasilii Karpov, a Riazan' townsman who sought exit so as to enter a state peasant village. His fellow townspeople refused to free him despite the fact that he had no arrears and was not due to provide military service. There was a rationale, but one that made little sense to Karpov: the townspeople reported that because "where exactly this Karpov lives is not apparent from his petition," so they simply "could not free him."[38]

In other cases, the problems with a release had more to do with out-and-out corruption.[39] Such a case came to the attention of the Riazan' Court (*Nadvornyi sud*) in the 1840s. In 1842, nine members of the Riazhsk townsperson society submitted a complaint to the Riazan' Provincial Administration alleging that two of the society's members, Ivan Ponamarev and Andrei Fadeev, had been improperly freed in order to join the merchant estate. Both men were due to fulfill recruit duties for the town, and therefore, the petitioners claimed, the townspeople as a whole did not want to let them go. The head of the town, Ivan Kalashnikov, however, had ignored the will of the society and forced a few of its members to sign a document freeing the two men. Clearly, this was a contentious issue within the town, for later other townspeople submitted petitions disassociating themselves from both the original freeing document and also the later petition.

As more documents were collected, more evidence of corruption appeared. One townsman claimed that, at a meeting of the Riazhsk commune, Ponomarev had promised to pay the society 700 paper rubles in return for a document allowing him to leave. Another claimed that the town head had made a side deal with Ponomarev to collect half that amount personally. Ponomarev himself claimed never to have promised such payments. And yet others claimed not to have attended any meeting at all. In the end, although the court found irregularities in the original decision to free the men (for example, that only 31 of Riazhsk's 98 townsmen were involved in the decision, and only 13 had signed the freedom agreement), it found the original petition that brought the case to its attention even more troubling, because the townsmen who had submitted it had falsified signatures to make their case seem stronger. The ringleaders of that group were the ones who were punished (two days in jail) because of the falsification of signatures. Otherwise, the town was told to watch out, and to be sure that in the future all decisions be kept within the law and reflect the will of the majority.[40]

Because of these sorts of problems, higher authorities sometimes intervened on behalf of petitioners. In 1852, the Riazan' Provincial Treasury wrote to the Riazan' Town Administration on behalf of a local townsman, Mikhailo Pokrovskii, who had failed to receive permission to leave the society and join a state peasant village society. It specifically noted that "on the part of the Treasury there are no obstacles at all to this and the fact that there are a large number of singletons in your society cannot serve as an obstacle to his reregistry." In this case, the town had suggested that while Pokrovskii was not directly in line for recruit duties, because there were so many households consisting of single male souls, it wanted to hold on to a healthy family. But in light of the Provincial Treasury's letter, the townspeople agreed to free Pokrovskii as long as he paid certain outstanding dues.[41]

A few provincial treasuries went even further, taking on the role of eighteenth-century magistracies as the arbiters of justness. A provincial treasury might decide that the local society was simply wrong to refuse freedom to its petitioning members. These were cases in which there were no clear reasons to refuse a petition, as the petitioner had no outstanding dues or recruit obligations and was otherwise eligible for change. In one case, the Perm Treasury registered twelve townsmen and their families—a total of thirty-eight souls—as state peasants without the permission of their home society in Krasnoufimsk. The Krasnoufimsk townspeople complained about the decision, and the case went before the Senate for decision. Although it did not clarify exactly why, the Senate "found the action of the Treasury lawful."[42]

In other cases, local societies could be more reasonable about dues and duties than the higher state institutions. In 1866, the Cossack Mariia Simashkina petitioned the Ministry of Internal Affairs for help in resolving her case. She wanted to move with her family from her Cossack community into the Taganrog society of townspeople, and she had received the support of her local community. At a meeting of the district commune, her fellow Cossacks had agreed that, although in principle her family was still in line for recruit duties, owing to actual local conditions they were unlikely to be called up; as a result, the district commune saw "no impediments" to releasing her. However, the Poltava Office of State Domains, which had authority to check local decisions, disagreed and blocked her transfer. Upon appeal, the Poltava Governor and Ministry concluded that, because the local community agreed to free her, the decision of the Office of State Domains was invalid and Simashkina's transfer should be allowed.[43]

These were individual cases, but such local concerns could actually alter the legal structure of the *soslovie* system as a whole. In 1849, the State Council confirmed a proposal made by the Minister of State Domains that put forth the idea of "easing the movement of state peasants into the town *soslovie*." For the most part, the new laws restated the existing regulations guiding state peasant mobility and "eased" the process simply by laying out the rules more clearly. However, the law introduced one new element, as it took on the question of societal control over mobility. One clause of the law forcefully stated that "the village society does not have the right to refuse anyone a freeing agreement, if there are none of the aforesaid reasons preventing their movement into town status." Another clause extended similar language to gaining an acceptance agreement: "if the petitioner brings in a year's worth of dues in advance, then the [town] society does not have the right to refuse him its agreement of acceptance." In other words, while it did not negate the ability of local societies to govern their own membership, the new law reminded them that their rights were limited and, by implication, that individuals had rights to mobility, as well.[44]

GATEKEEPERS: ENTERING A NEW SOCIETY

According to some of the documentary evidence about the process, gaining admission into a new estate society was a far more straightforward process than gaining freedom. Nikolai Chukmaldin, who had to bribe his peasant society with vodka to gain his freedom, was more measured in his account of gaining acceptance: "to get the acceptance agreement from the society of the town cost less work and money, although even there much depended on the town bloodsuckers."[45] Local societies still had concerns, but the prospect of gaining a new tax-payer, should he turn out to be a reliable one, was easier to accept than the prospect of losing one.

The actual practices of the magistracies and local *soslovie* administrations governing such movements supports Chukmaldin's impression that entrance into a new society was easier than exit from an old one. The files of eighteenth-century magistracies show a high success rate: 95.5 percent of 265 total cases in which the outcome is recorded led to new registries. Furthermore, the refusals were most often based on the fact that a petitioner's paperwork was not in order, with problematic passports or lack of evidence of a trade in the town as the most frequent culprits.

At first glance, a small sampling of the several thousand cases brought to the attention of the Moscow Magistracy in the first decade of the nineteenth century suggests that things had changed from the eighteenth century. Based on the records, only sixteen of thirty-three petitions (48.5 percent) led to successful registry in the Moscow townsperson society. Seven cases had no outcome recorded, which almost certainly meant they did not lead to registry. Ten cases (30.3 percent) were wrapped up with notes stating formally that the individuals involved had not been registered.

These numbers, however, reflect multiple reasons the petitions failed, none of which were based in the local society's negative decision. Four of the petitioners were not registered because they failed to appear to finalize those registrations; in these cases, the Moscow society was willing to accept them, but the petitioners failed to follow through on their original intent. In three cases, the petitioner withdrew the original petition on the grounds that he or she had decided either to stay in the original status or switch to yet a different one. Only in three cases were petitioners turned down on the basis of problems with their files.Even here, however, it was not the local society that made a negative decision but, rather, intermediary authorities. In one case, the provincial treasury turned down a petition that had been approved by the local society.[46] In the other two, the Moscow Magistracy decided that the petitions were not worth investigating further, one because a letter of freedom was suspect and the other because the kind of mobility requested (a soldier's son entering the society of townspeople) had recently been made illegal.[47]

In archival files, the process of decision making by local societies presents as a simple one. Letters from *soslovie* societies to treasuries or other deciding bodies were often basic statements of fact: we met and are agreed. Even reports of their meetings suggest that the norm was straightforward. One such report, of the Moscow merchant assembly, presented just such a picture. It began with attendance: the town head, Fedor Kozhevnikov, was absent due to illness and thus the meeting at the Office of the Town Society (*Dom gradskogo obshchestva*) was chaired by another merchant. The elected members of that society met to discuss whether to accept a townsman from Ruza, Aleksandr Kraskin, who had presented proofs of his good behavior, trading position in Moscow, and good credit, all supported by guarantors from the Moscow merchant estate. Based on all these reports, the merchant society agreed to accept the man.[48]

Of course, Kraskin's case, and particularly the documents he provided, suggests some sources of possible problems for others seeking to enter new societies. The many pieces of supporting evidence necessary to gain acceptance reflect the concerns of those accepting societies. At base, *soslovie* societies considering new members had many of the same concerns as *soslovie* societies letting their members go. Like those societies, they worried about whether the new members would pay their taxes and fulfill their duties, and they came up with various mechanisms to lend some assurance against arrears. In contrast, however, concerns over public order weighed more heavily in their decision making. After all, the accepting societies were receiving new taxpayers and possible new recruits. But they were also gaining new people to live alongside, whose behaviors might affect the rest of the community. As a result, the accepting *soslovie* societies not only considered carefully the papers of the petitioners but also tried to judge their moral character.

Certainly a major concern for these societies was whether their new members would properly pay their taxes and other dues. In 1746, case of freed serf Nikita Vagin was labeled a risky venture by the Orel merchantry, for just this reason. His documents were all in order, so there was no fear of his turning out to be other than who he said he was, and he did not lack guarantors. But in his petition, Vagin referred to his "old age and illness," noting that what he really wanted was to enter the almshouse of an Orel church. Unfortunately for Vagin, the law said that freed serfs had to enter the tax rolls, so he could not simply move straight into a charity home and register there. As a result, he requested to be entered onto the Orel merchant lists in accordance with his trade as a baker. Since the local merchants would soon be responsible for the duties of a person in the almshouse, who would be unable to pay for himself, they were unwilling to accept him, and the magistracy confirmed their decision.[49] Something similar happened in Kostroma in the 1790s, when three freed household serfs were turned back, in part because the town duma believed that the oldest of them was, at sixty-five years, unlikely to support himself much longer; therefore, they wanted no part of his care.[50]

These concerns continued during the nineteenth century. In 1829, the Rybinsk Town Duma sent in a report to the Iaroslavl' Provincial Administration, which listed its concerns about several new members who had been registered in their society by the provincial treasury. The duma described Rybinsk as a major place for trade, and therefore a place with particular need to safeguard itself against financial risk. Above all, the duma noted, it worried that new members would "fail to pay not only their town duties, but state dues, too, [which would end up] paid for on the society's account"; furthermore, new members would be "unsuitable for military service [and their] recruit obligations would be fulfilled by others."[51] These statements reflected real concerns for societies bound together in large part by their duties to the state.

One way that societies tried to insure against the financial risks that came with taking on new taxpayers was to ask for guarantors of future payments. Beginning in the eighteenth century, local communities demanded that petitioners provide signed statements from guarantors who would take responsibility for making up any arrears that might accrue. Their statements and signatures are omnipresent in magistracies' files. This was not a practice without problems, however. Just as friction began to develop between local and central authorities over competing demands of duty to choose and right to refuse, so, too, friction arose in discussions of these guarantors.

In particular, in 1805, a Senate decree took on this matter of guarantors. At issue was whether local authorities were allowed to demand guarantors from those who had been forced by various manifestos to choose a new status. These "churchmen, returned émigrés, and other people of free status" were exactly those whom local authorities might consider "bad bets" for community stability. But in this decree, those same localities were told in no uncertain terms that they were no longer allowed to demand guarantees from such people.[52]

A later law clarified some of the Senate's thinking; in 1820, it addressed a significant problem with arrears among the empire's merchants. These arrears had accrued despite the fact that guarantors were supposedly meant to ensure proper payments. The Senate looked at a series of earlier laws and agreed that, in the late eighteenth century, proper practice had been to demand guarantors to attest to the ability of new members, or of merchants who received passports to live elsewhere, so as to continue payment of dues. However, it also found that these laws were superseded by new laws that instituted a different method: rather than guarantors, new merchants or merchants leaving towns were to leave a deposit amounting to the payment of future dues. This, the Senate concluded, ought to replace the use of guarantors, and not be established alongside it.[53]

Despite these legal challenges, throughout much of the nineteenth century, town societies continued to demand some sort of guarantee, whether it be a person who ensured future payments and good behavior or a sum of money put down as evidence of future financial stability. In 1854, the townspeople of Riazan' refused to accept the freed serf Grigori Evlampiev because he did not provide a list of guarantors, and other towns also requested attestations of good behavior and reliability.[54] By the end of the century, towns like St. Petersburg even had printed documents for guarantors to sign, attesting that petitioners were well behaved, would pay taxes, and would not draw on public aid; they included spaces to fill in the name of the petitioner and signatories.[55]

But also during the nineteenth century, other methods came into play, as communities continued to worry about protecting their interests. An 1860 description of practices within the Moscow townspeople's administration gave a clear picture of how the process or presenting guarantors normally worked. A man who wished to enter the Moscow society first had to present evidence that he was free to leave his home society. He then had to swear that he was properly Orthodox and not a member of a "dangerous" sect. He also had to swear—with four witnesses and guarantors—that he would accept any service the society called upon him to do, that "he had true means of sustenance," and that he would pay all his dues—but that should he be unable to do so, his guarantors would.[56] Despite efforts on the part of the central state to ease these requirements, societies were adamant about protecting their own rights.

Moreover, despite occasionally trying to eliminate restrictions on mobility, the central state at times affirmed the idea that societies should be protected from disorder. In 1841, the State Council decided a case involving those with the right to choose a way of life, a right that had by then largely trumped the ability of societies to choose their own members. It recognized that movement from *soslovie* to *soslovie* sometimes went along with a significant restructuring of legal households, and it placed limits on how these actions could go together. The State Council decided that the right to register in new societies was made mandatory only for whole households. Essentially, a single petitioner could not leave underaged, elderly, or otherwise economically troubled household members out of his household. According to other laws, those problem cases would also have the right to register, but they would now be a burden on the society forced to take them. By forbidding the dissolution of households, this new law sought to restore responsibility to families themselves, as well as protect the local societies from those who might be unable to pay their dues.[57]

Throughout the period, local *soslovie* societies worried far more (or at least far more obviously) about order when they considered whether to accept new members than when they considered whether to free existing members. In this sense, order could be defined in different ways. For instance, one way new members could affect public order was if they caused the society legal trouble. In much of the eighteenth century, town societies found themselves concerned about what problems or benefits new members might bring them.

Their foremost worry seems to have been that they might accept someone with invalid papers, a fugitive or otherwise compromised person, whose case would be found out, bringing trouble. They were perhaps right to worry, given that documents were indeed challenged. In 1771, Princess Anna Dolgorukaia petitioned the Moscow Magistracy, challenging manumission documents given to several household serfs by her husband several years before. According to Dolgorukaia, because the freed serfs had agreed to continue to live in her household in service, under provisions of the 1649 Law Code dealing with slaves, she had the right to take back their freedom documents and consider them re-enserfed. When one of these freed serfs retrieved his letter and left, she considered him a runaway and a thief.[58] Given that the laws punished those who harbored fugitives, some town societies did not wish to create trouble for themselves by taking in those they should not.

So, in order to protect themselves from this sort of trouble, some local societies began to ask for extra documentation or guarantees. In 1765, the Orel merchantry added a clause to what guarantors of the Ukrainian Ivan Kozlov promised. As a Ukrainian, Kozlov was in principle not registered anywhere, and thus he was free to join the Orel merchantry. However, the merchants wanted to be sure that this was true. Kozlov's guarantors had to promise that he was truly a Ukrainian, "and not a fugitive and not a serf… and if it turns out in the future that Ivan is not a Ukrainian and they gave false evidence, then they will be responsible for him without any refusal."[59] In other words, the locality sought to make the guarantors responsible for any monetary damages that might result from an improper acceptance.

In 1769, something similar happened in Cheboksary, when Petr Shcherbakov, a local artisan, requested entrance into the merchantry. The merchants accepted him, but with a caveat: "we wish to accept [him]… with the note that if it turns out that Shcherbakov and his children are serfs or some other kind of unfree person, and if there follows some sort of exaction of dues, then in that case his guarantors will be totally responsible for him."[60]

Starting in the nineteenth century, *soslovie* societies began to worry more about the character of their new applicants, and to see "trouble" as that caused by unworthy individuals. In 1816, the Iaroslavl' Town Duma found itself in a turf battle with the town magistracy. The duma, as representative of the registered citizens of Iaroslavl', insisted that it had the right to accept or deny entrance to petitioners seeking to join the town society. It presented its case in strong terms. First, given that the country was in the midst of a new revision of the census rolls, the town duma had to have ultimate control over its members in order to be assured that those rolls were properly compiled. But more important, it had a particular duty as "caretaker of the city" to "see all its citizens in person, and to know their position and condition, to evaluate their trade and their character."

Because of this, the duma felt that it was all the more important that it personally evaluate all individuals seeking to enter the town society, so as to prevent those who did not deserve the position from joining such an important provincial capital. In this case, the town magistracy found support for its opposing viewpoint—that the most important thing was simple registration—in the province's treasury board, but that support was trumped by the final decision of the provincial administration. That administration upheld an interpretation of the laws that focused on acceptance and membership, and supported the duma's position.[61]

Nor was this a concern without basis. Documents that record new members of Moscow's merchant society, in particular, include quite detailed physical descriptions of all the family members who had gained such an exalted status. The *Notebooks for Registry* used at the end of the eighteenth century included notations of the height, hair and eye color, shape and coloring of the face, and any distinguishing marks of all new merchants.[62] In other words, the notebook was meant to be a real record of membership, and could be used to ensure that documents proving status were given only to those who were legally entitled to them. Furthermore, later instructions sent on from the Ministry of Internal Affairs emphasized that local administrators were supposed to ensure that they or their underlings knew by sight all members of local societies, to ensure that they would also therefore recognize and observe or even arrest any "new faces," whom the ministry assumed would be dangerous "runaways or vagrants."[63]

This idea, that societies had a particular responsibility to know their members and to evaluate applicants wanting to join them, had later resonance, as well. In 1869, the former household serf Abram Semenov submitted a second petition to enter the Riazan' society of townspeople. He had petitioned the previous year on the basis that he had trade in the town and documentation of freedom from the village in which he had been listed at emancipation. That first petition was refused by the Riazan' townspeople without a full explanation of their reasons. Therefore, Semenov decided to try again and in particular asked:

> for what exactly important reasons they in their town do not accept me, when I have not been and am not now under investigation or under criminal judgment, when I pay all my taxes and am well off, when I am no more than 40 years old, in good physical condition and health, and finally when many citizens and inhabitants of Riazan' know of me and would give assurances of all the above written and that I will fulfill the payment of dues.

In such a case surely Semenov ought to be accepted? But his hopes were again dashed— the townspeople refused to accept him on the grounds that "without seeing him in person we do not agree to accept him."[64]

The fear that new members might cause trouble continued to be a major issue for local communities. Not providing proof of good behavior was a valid reason to refuse a petitioner. The freed serf Ekaterina Ulitskuvna was refused entrance into the Vil'na society of townspeople because she had not provided such proof.[65] So, too, was the peasant Petrunela Tsegion—and in her case, the Vil'na society furthermore decided that she did not really need to join because her home village was close enough that traveling there to renew her passport regularly was not a burden.[66] Because many cases involved people who had been living for years in the communities they sought to join, previous bad behavior could be reason to refuse them membership. In 1849, a state peasant society in Mogilev province refused to accept several new members "solely because of their unruly way of life."[67]

They were perhaps even more likely to worry about new members because of certain new legal restrictions on their ability to punish newcomers. An ukase from 1817 noted that those newly registered as townspeople could not be sent to the military by their society until three years after their registration. This obviously had an impact on the ability of societies to form deals like that involving Stefan Nikiforov, in which a man was accepted in order to enter the military on behalf of a society (and a family) member, but it also had an effect on how towns kept order. Societies were wont to use the draft as a way to rid themselves of problem elements—and this ukase restricted their ability to get rid of someone who turned out to be a problem soon after registry. Of course, the ukase recognized this role of the draft and "in case of bad behavior," allowed societies to hand over such problem members to the police.[68]

Central mandates affected town decisions relating to public order in another way, too. In 1835, the State Council decreed that henceforth no members of certain "particularly dangerous" sects would be allowed to register in town societies, except in those provinces in the Caucasus where sectarian migration had been encouraged.[69] These restrictions were slightly relaxed later, as schismatics were allowed to register in more towns. Even then, though, their residence was always supposed to be limited to towns outside central Russia itself.[70]

Practically, this new restriction affected the paperwork involved in registering new members in societies. According to an 1844 decree, all those who wished to become townspeople or merchants now had to make a formal statement that they did not belong to any "dangerous sects."[71] Such statements became standard in archival files. When the Riazan' townswoman Tat'iana Balantsova petitioned the town duma to become a third guild merchant, she explicitly noted "I have the honor to explain that I am not a member of the *skoptsy* and do not belong to… any dangerous sects."[72] And these statements were at times taken very seriously. In 1865, a freed serf named Ivan Arkhipov petitioned to enter the Egorsk townsperson society. He noted that he was indeed a schismatic, but that his sect was not a dangerous one. The Riazan' Provincial Treasury did not recognize Arkhipov's sect (he followed the Pomorskii Rite), and so turned to the Consistory for more information. The Consistory said that because the Pomorskii Rite was a priestless sect, it was dangerous, even if it was not listed among those officially decreed so. As a result, the treasury responded to Arkhipov, writing that it "did not find it possible to fulfill" his petition.[73]

However, clearly not all authorities were so careful. Two years after Arkhipov's original petition, the Riazan' Provincial Treasury received a notice from the Moscow Provincial Treasury, informing it that Arkhipov had been registered as a townsman in

Kolomna. The Riazan' Treasury wrote back to Moscow, informing the treasury that it had registered a dangerous man, which sparked a bureaucratic tiff between the two provinces. Eventually, the office of the Moscow general governor wrote to that of the Riazan' governor to inform it that, because the official lists had not listed Arkhipov's sect as dangerous, it wasn't; therefore, "the registry of the peasant Arkhipov in the townsperson society was completed with attention to legal formalities."[74]

In addition, town societies specifically worried about the individuals added to their societies without their consent. Former prisoners freed by imperial command or those benefiting from an imperial amnesty were among those granted the right to choose a way of life—and they were among those who caused significant worry to their new societies. When the Rybinsk town duma wrote in 1829 to the Iaroslavl' Provincial Administration, it was complaining about the fact that a number of freed prisoners (five men who had been arrested for vagrancy and then freed for good behavior by an edict of Nicholas I) had just been registered in their society without their consent. The Rybinsk townspeople were unhappy with this decision, in part because they worried about being responsible for taxes on behalf of these men, but also because they feared the possible effect of such newcomers on public order: "the town of Rybinsk is a port for internal trade, where noted commercial figures from various towns gather, and official commissioners, all gathering great sums, and the residence of people who, having corrupt morals which discredit their behavior, will not be tolerated."[75]

These concerns could be so great that communities often flouted the law in deciding to refuse or otherwise keep out undesirable new members. In essence, they were able to circumvent laws that suggested they had no choice in the matter. A decision of the State Council from 1835 stated that priests removed from duty due to bad behavior and who were too old or infirm for military duty or farming should be sent to Saratov, Orenburg, or other far-off places. In 1837, the Kostroma Provincial Administration tried to take advantage of this rule to rid itself of a troublesome defrocked deacon, Mikhailo Iakovlev. Iakovlev was accused of and found guilty of theft after he had already been removed from duty due to ill health; as a result, he was found to be "dangerous" by the inhabitants of his village and "useless" by the church. Because he was too ill and too old (aged 47) for military service or farming, the Kostroma officials decided to take advantage of the State Council's decision, and send him to Saratov to register as a state peasant. But neither Saratov officials nor Iakovlev himself were particularly enthusiastic about this turn of events. Initially, the Saratov Treasury, tasked with formally registering Iakovlev, felt its options limited by the State Council's decision. But Iakovlev, in a series of petitions, gave the Saratov officials ammunition to send him back to Kostroma: he noted that he could not work due to illness, and would be reduced to extreme poverty if forced to live in Saratov province. And, too, he produced legal precedents for why he ought to be returned to Kostroma and placed under the eye of its Office of Public Care. Thanks to this, the Saratov Treasury found reason to send him back.[76]

COMMUNITY OR NOT? MERCHANTS AND TOWNSPEOPLE

The interaction between merchant and townsperson complicated the notion of control over populations. In principle, townspeople and merchants were all formal, legal residents of cities, distinguished only by their relative wealth. But of course, that distinction had significantly larger implications for social status. By the end of the eighteenth century, merchants had won freedom from the soul tax and from military service, a fact that placed them among the privileged; but because their status was based on economic success, not purely on birth, merchant privilege was an uncertain thing. As a result, throughout the eighteenth and nineteenth centuries, a central part of merchant life was its essential instability—and thus its connection to the unprivileged status of mere townsman.

In principle, movement between merchant and townsperson status within a single town was a purely statutory event, guided by financial well-being and nothing else. According to Catherine's Charter to the Towns, merchants and townspeople were distinguished by the amount of capital they possessed; later laws emphasized the paying of proper dues according to status, again emphasizing the economic definition of status. Practically, this meant that merchant societies lacked the right of societies of townspeople to accept their members—and even had fewer options for excluding members for bad behavior.[77] This is apparent in the archival files. A sampling of files of those seeking to enter Moscow's merchant society between 1810 and 1888 shows a very low rate of failure: only 3 of 132 cases. Furthermore, the reason for these failures was not lack of acceptance by the merchant society but, rather, the petitioner's failure to appear.[78]

Largely as a result, this kind of movement has been interpreted as source of individual insecurity based in an unproblematic administrative system rather than as something consciously sought.[79] One mid-nineteenth-century author even described the structure of merchant societies as quite rational, particularly compared to societies of townspeople, in large part because merchant societies were so bound by specific laws that laid out who belonged to the society. Property meant status, and status was applied in very specific ways to family members.[80]

Even within the realm of economics, however, this apparently simple process was anything but simple. In some regions, the decision to move from townsperson to merchant at first seems to have stayed with the townspeople themselves. In Saratov province, townspeople who wished to move into the merchant estate in 1778—shortly after Catherine had laid out a series of economically distinct town statuses, although before the Charter to the Towns itself—filed official documents in which they swore that they possessed the appropriate capital for merchant status, and also that they lived in the town and would pay all appropriate duties.[81] In other words, they were petitioning for entry—there was no automatic change in status when they amassed a certain amount of capital. Nor was Saratov alone in this. Early in the nineteenth century, Moscow townspeople who possessed the financial resources to be considered merchants still had to present the same petitions and attestations as others in order to finalize their new status.[82]

Continued—and, more to the point, changing—demands to declare capital or otherwise prove merchant status or financial well-being could create problems for merchants, throwing yet more sources of uncertainty into their position. After a Senate decree demanded that merchants present proof of capital, some individual merchants were demoted to townspeople because, they claimed, they had been living away from their homes on passports and thus failed to hear of the new demands. The Senate allowed them additional time to clear their status.[83] In other cases, merchants who failed to present their documents on time due to illness were allowed to remain merchants.[84] But despite these moments of generosity, most laws spoke in terms of absolutes that were to be carried out every year, with the names of those who failed to meet them at times even published in local newspapers almost as a public shaming ritual.[85]

A second source of complication for movement between merchant and townsperson status was the unusual (in the context of other *sosloviia*) interaction between status and family. Merchant capital was counted not on an individual basis but, instead, by family; in other words, all the capital belonging to a household was counted toward meeting guild membership levels, and membership in a particular guild was held communally.[86] Furthermore, only the head of the household was the merchant in the family—others were the merchant's sons, wives, daughters, or brothers. Practically, that meant that there was an economic question involved in merchant standing: who received credit, as it were, for the economic success of individuals within a single merchant family.

The 1824 law that restated certain rules for guild membership addressed this point in some detail; for purposes of capital accumulation, a family could consist of a father with sons, unmarried daughters, and grandsons; a widow with sons, unmarried daughters, and grandchildren, "when they all live in one home not separately;" or of brothers and unmarried sisters, again "when they live in one home." Any relatives at further remove needed to gain their own attestations of capital or transfer to the society of townspeople. Within these families, only the main petitioner (in these cases, the father, widow, or one of the brothers) was the true merchant, with attendant rights and privileges; all remaining family members belonged to the category "merchant's son," "merchant's grandson," and so on, with somewhat more limited rights (particularly economic ones).[87]

Practically, this understanding of family had significant implications for mobility. It was normal for entire families to move from one status to another because so much of the labeling of Russian subjects was done in terms of households. But in the case of merchants, there were real differences, particularly when it came to women petitioners. Women were far less numerous among those entering merchant societies than they were among those entering societies of townspeople. When they did, they were nearly always entering as widows with multiple adult sons, whereas women entering the *soslovie* of townspeople were alone or with underaged male children. In other words, widows were serving to bind merchant families, perhaps avoiding the need for brothers to declare the oldest as the head of the household.[88] In addition, laws that spoke of mobility out of the merchant status focused in different ways on the various members of a single household.

That is, demotion to the status of mere townsman affected the merchant and his whole family. But other options for leaving the status—to attend school or join service, for example—were allowed only to the family members of merchants and not to merchants themselves.

In 1826, these issues came together in the case of one Nikolai Istomin, formally a merchant of Moscow. Nikolai, age eleven in 1825, lived with his older, unmarried sisters Tat'iana, Mar'ia, and Nadezhda. Their mother, who held the status of a first guild merchant woman, had died the year before, leaving Nikolai as the official head of the family. Their inherited capital kept them in first guild status. But Nikolai wished to leave the status to enter military service. His request led to questions on two fronts. First, although current statutes allowed members of the merchant *soslovie* to enter the military, they focused on sons of merchants, not heads of households. Second, was a merchant society, unburdened by soul taxes and recruit duties, allowed to demand payment of future dues from its members who wished to leave? The recent Guild Reform gave little guidance. One statute noted that first guild merchants could ask for their sons to be released to join the civil or military service. Requesting release suggested that societies could actually decide the fates of their members. However, a second statute declared first guild merchants to be not a soul-tax paying status, which implied they did not have the same collective responsibility for dues as, say, townspeople.

But of course, the Moscow merchants did not want to accept even a remote possibility that they might have to keep up fees for an absent member. At first, they concluded that "the Moscow merchant society cannot take onto itself responsibility for paying the first guild merchant Nikolai Ivanov Istomin's dues until the next revision."[89] Despite this conclusion, Istomin did eventually receive permission to leave the status in late 1826, but half a decade later questions about his exact status—had he been freed "forever" from the merchants?—reemerged, not to be fully resolved.[90]

The third major issue that complicated movement between townsperson and merchant status was the draft. Townsmen were subject to the draft, merchants were not. The issue affected mobility in two ways. First, there was the question of townsmen becoming merchants: what if a townsman had the capital to qualify as a merchant, but was next in line for the draft? Some of the earlier laws that had emphasized the importance of examining such duties in decisions about mobility addressed one variant of this question. If a townsman wished to enter the merchant society of a different town, thus combining geographic and social mobility, he had to receive proper release, including attention to his draft status. Around the time of the Guild Reform, the idea that townsmen needed freedom to move up into the merchantry had become standard; furthermore, statutes did not clearly differentiate between movement between towns and within a town.[91] Later laws repeated similar statements, usually tying freedom to fulfillment of recruit duties. A law of 1843 did not demand formal release, but it did demand that provincial treasuries look carefully at such cases and ensure that movement would not cause difficulties for societies of townspeople.[92] Several years later, another law again emphasized the importance of the draft. Any townsman or peasant who sought entry into the merchantry during a draft could receive trading rights, but not full membership, until the draft was completed and he remained undrafted.[93]

Throughout this period, at least some town townsperson societies clearly took seriously their role in overseeing mobility even within their towns. The Saratov society, for one, regularly discussed the cases of members who wished to leave, including those who wanted to move up into the local third merchant guild. And at times, they chose to restrict the movement of their members; in 1832, for example, the members refused to release Kozma Malyshkin into the merchantry on the grounds that his family of six souls owed military duties.[94]

In another case, a society of townspeople pursued its interests even after one of its members had been moved into the merchantry. In 1839, the Senate addressed the case of Stepan Mitiushin, a third guild merchant from Gzhatsk who had, he claimed, been unlawfully pulled back into the society of townspeople because of recruit duties. The Senate investigation uncovered the following facts. In 1812, when still a townsman, Mitiushin had formally and legally separated from his family's household. Then, in 1829, Mitiushin entered the merchantry with only his immediate family, while his brother remained a townsman in a separate household. At this time, the brothers' aged parents lived in Stepan's household, supported by him alone. Stepan was elected to several local offices as a merchant, and was listed as a merchant in the eighth revision. However, the provincial administration had begun to check the official lists of those eligible for the draft, and had decided that the entire Mitiushin family—Stepan, his brother, his father, and two sons—had been placed on a single list when the new line system was introduced in the early 1830s, ignoring the earlier legal separation of the household. It therefore decided to pull Stepan back into the society of townspeople in order to keep him in line for the draft. The Senate found the decision unlawful (largely because of the date of the separations of the households), and reinstated Stepan to his merchant status.[95]

Military duties also influenced mobility within towns because of a second question: what happened to merchants who fell into the society of townspeople? In particular, given that this was often a temporary situation brought about by a minor business setback or even just problems with paperwork, should they be protected from the draft? A decision of 1816 said no; although new townsmen from other statuses (primarily freed serfs) were free from the draft for three years after their registry, the same was not true of new townsmen from the merchantry. The decision of the Committee of Ministers was based on a conception of a unified town society: "in as much as there is complete freedom to move from the merchants to the townspeople and back again from the townspeople to the merchants, we should consider townspeople and merchant as one kind of people, differentiated only by capital." And that meant that former merchants were immediately eligible for the draft.[96]

Several decades later, the Ministry of Finance returned to the question with a new variation on the existing laws. The *Digest of the Laws* made it clear that merchants who missed their yearly payments and were demoted to the status of townspeople had a year to return to their former status without major disruption to their social status. With payment of a penalty for late registration (one-fourth of their yearly dues), they could be returned to merchant status "without any formalities," in the words of one provincial correspondent.[97] But did that mean that merchants should not be subject to military duties during that year? The ministry received inquiries from the Belostok Provincial Treasury and petitions from several former merchants, seeking clarification of the laws. The Ministry of Internal Affairs wrote to the governor general of Vil'na (who oversaw Belostok) for his opinion. The governor reported back on the practice in a number of towns in his region (Vil'na, Grodno, and Minsk). In all cases, merchants who were demoted were treated fully as townsmen, which meant they were subject to recruit duties if a draft came up during their time in the lower society. If no such draft occurred during that year, merchants who had reestablished themselves financially would not be held accountable for townsman's requirements. This seemed fair, and this proposal went from the governor to the Ministry of Internal Affairs, to the Ministry of Finance.[98] When that ministry sent the decision to the Senate for confirmation, however, it languished.

At the end of the 1840s, one society's desire to privilege military duties over mobility came to the attention of the State Council. The Bessarabian Treasury Department asked the Ministry of Finance whether societies of townspeople could refuse to allow their members to move up into the merchantry as required by statute. This was a bold question; in principle, the change from townsperson to merchant (or back again) depended purely on individual financial status, not on larger questions of duties. Before presenting its case to the State Council for confirmation, the Ministry of Finance collected several opinions on the subject. The Ministry of Internal Affairs believed that the proposal was simply wrong, and that if townspeople paid their dues promptly, their statutory movement into the merchantry should not be stopped by their local society. The local governor, asked for his opinion, suggested that such townspeople be given extra duties to pay, on the grounds that losing their richest members would create hardship for societies of townspeople, but that extra money might compensate. The Ministry of Finance disagreed with the governor, and instead agreed that mobility trumped the desires of the lower town societies.[99]

INDIVIDUAL AND *SOSLOVIE*: NEW STATUSES

At the same time as central authorities of the imperial state sought to bring clarity to the related statuses of merchant and townsperson, they created various new social categories, some explicitly called *sosloviia*, and some outside of, or perhaps next to, the normal *soslovie* structure, largely in an attempt to adapt the system of *sosloviia* to fit the social, economic, and status demands of the nineteenth century. These attempts show both the continued tensions within the *soslovie* system and the contortions that the imperial state went through in its efforts to fit *soslovie* to the demands of the nineteenth century.

The current system of *sosloviia* did not neatly map on to the economic reality of Russia. As one statistician put it, particularly in towns, and even more particularly in manufacturing, *soslovie* meant little; individual members of a single *soslovie* might be radically different in their economic standing, on the one hand, and single industries might be staffed by men from many different *sosloviia*, on the other.[100] The new categories created through a series of laws sought in part to fix this by aligning occupation with status.

The new categories were wide ranging. Many were based on specific kinds of work, ranging from the quasi-military (merchant sailors), to the semi-professional (medics and teachers, "semi" professions because they were officially state civil servants), to the artistic (those working for the Imperial Theater directorship).[101] And, there was the new *soslovie* of "honored citizen," created in 1832 to fill a gap in the empire's social structures.[102] The status of honored citizen was granted for exemplary acts or service: artists and top university graduates, manufacturers or successful merchants. The status could be hereditary, and thus could give security to those whose status had previously been uncertain. And because it was based on the idea of economic success, it did not tempt manufacturers and others into the less productive ranks of the nobility, while granting them many of the same rights. It was, in other words, a solution to the disjuncture between occupation and rank that consistently complicated the very concept of *soslovie*.

Many of the new categories reflected new economic and social demands or goals, and the laws that established them generally stated that explicitly. The 1834 law that established a new merchant navy society claimed that it was "desiring to promote the use of Black Sea merchant seafaring."[103] The law implied that creation of this new category would also create the people who could carry out this goal. And similar language appeared in other such laws. The establishment of honored citizens was based on an imperial desire "to better bind town inhabitants to their status by new distinctions, on the flowering of which depends the success of trade and industry."[104] Categories not only allowed new behavior but also created it.

The case of the semi-professions was similar, in that statutes touted the ways that establishing these identities would bring real benefit to the imperial state and imperial society through the people who would fill them. The 1834 statute establishing the status of tutor spoke in terms of such grand societal goals, "so tightly bound with the well-being of each and every one."[105] Discussions about medics were somewhat more circumspect, but still spoke to the empire's needs. These new statuses served as models when, several years later, bureaucrats of the Ministry of State Domains discussed the possibility of creating a new *soslovie* of agronomists. In fact, one bureaucrat argued in favor of the new status based on its similarity to the statuses of tutors and medics. The laws establishing those statuses, he argued, had been based on the emperor's "constant concern for the well-being of his subjects."[106] In other words, these new statuses were understood to be based on the needs of Russian society—or, at least, they were supposed to be interpreted that way.

Both the free sailors and the honored citizens were explicitly described as *sosloviia*, either in the initial manifestos announcing them or in later ones clarifying their form and function. This was an important usage of the term. First, it connected official status with economic function; free sailors would engage in merchant trade, honored citizens would be involved in many activities that bring economic well-being to the empire. Second, location was an integral part of the concept of *soslovie* and these statuses were tied to particular locations, to specific towns or ports. The semi-professions, however, were somewhat different. Statutes used the words *zvanie* or *sostoianie*, affirming the connection with work but downplaying both the communal structures of *sosloviia* and their connections with place. These were individual identities, and those who possessed them interacted directly with a representative of the imperial state (the Ministry of Education, the Medical Department of the Ministry of Internal Affairs) instead of through an intermediary *soslovie* organization.[107]

Because these new statuses were created out of whole cloth, mobility—that is, defining how individuals could gain these statuses—was central to the laws that established them. The statutes described, often in great detail, how aspirants could gain these statuses, how they could move up within them, and what happened to them if they left them. The statutes had to deal, on the one hand, with the need to expand these groups to serve society and, on the other, with the social structures that limited individual opportunities.

In some cases, the options for mobility were relatively straightforward. Honored citizens essentially could not come from the taxpaying statuses; they were by definition those who had attained successes not possible without prior release from those statuses. Merchants, for example, had to show longstanding success: ten years in the first guild, twenty year in the second, and never having fallen to a lower guild (or the status of townsperson) nor faced insolvency during that time.[108] As a result, the language of the law establishing this status was more related to those of the nobility—the Heraldry office of the Senate even oversaw all requests for the status—than to those of other *sosloviia*.

Statutes regarding the semi-professions were guided by rather different principles. Honored citizens received their status through extensive, often longstanding action. But the professions were based above all on education or specific training, which could be attained even by those of taxpaying status.[109] The result was legislation that combined talk of attainment with rules governing other kinds of mobility within the soul-tax paying world. Would-be tutors, for example, were supposed to be of "free condition." At the same time, there were instructions for how people belonging to soul-tax paying statuses could nonetheless become tutors: they required, in addition to the attestations of good character and educational achievement, "a freedom agreement from [their] society."[110] Other laws focused on the status of medical students from soul-tax paying societies as they finished their early training and earned lower medical ranks (medics and pharmacy apprentices): they were to be excluded from those societies, having taken on a new social identity.[111]

These new statuses created conflict in the ways they did and did not act like "true" *sosloviia*. Most *soslovie* statuses were permanent, but that was not necessarily true of the new semi-professions. Instead, these statuses came with a warning that lack of work could lead to loss of status. Tutors, for one, had to maintain their position to maintain their freedom from the tax rolls; if a tutor found himself without work for two years, he was then obligated either to rejoin his society of birth or to choose "a different way of life."[112]

Essentially, members of these semi-professional groups were released from the obligations of the "freedom to choose a new way of life" as long as they remained in service. In 1834, the Senate confirmed a proposal from the Committee of Ministers that freed medical apprentices currently in service, but originally from the soul-tax paying population, from the obligation to choose a way of life. The law spelled out what this meant: "freedom both from the necessity of choosing a definite way of life and from all taxes and duties both monetary and in kind, and also from registry in the tax rolls."[113] Without service, however, they had to return to a status equivalent to that of their birth.

A bigger issue with the new statuses was that most *sosloviia* were hereditary; how would that work with the semi-professions? This question had long perplexed authorities. In 1758, a Senate decree tried to make medicine something of a hereditary status when it declared that the sons of doctors or other medical personnel were to remain under the authority of the Medical chancellery and not to enter service in any other field. Furthermore, widows of doctors were exhorted to ensure that their sons be properly trained to follow their fathers' profession—if they did not, their pensions were to be withheld.[114]

This was clearly an unworkable decision, however. By the mid-nineteenth century, laws considered such sons in a different light. They were like the sons of those in service, compelled to serve in some way but with more freedom. They could enter service, certainly, but if they chose not to, they were subject to the soul tax.[115]

Even unsuccessful efforts at creating these new semi-professional statuses show well the degree to which the concept of *soslovie* was linked to ideas of social (and, for that matter, economic) engineering. In 1841, one of the departments within the then still new Ministry of State Domains began to discuss the possibility of creating a new status of agricultural overseers. Members of the committee came up with various projects that in some ways copied the form of the earlier law establishing the status of tutors—setting up, for example, different levels of agronomist with different educational standards and different privileges. One project created both "learned agronomists," who received hereditary freedom from taxpaying status, and "practical agronomists," who did not.[116]

Furthermore, this plan was seen as more than just a practical solution to the apparent backwardness of Russian agriculture. The project eventually approved by the director of the department described a basic problem that this legislation—and other efforts to create professional identities—sought to solve. As the plan's author put it:

It is well known that even from the time of Peter the Great, there have appeared among us… learned people, but without particular rights, without particular and constant protection, they have nearly always disappeared when they did not find supports in the personal goodwill of the Emperor or his magnates.

It was only recently that the state had given "particular rights and privileges to people associated with learning," and thus only recently that a "firm foundation for the education of a particular class of scholars" had been created.[117]

Another draft project, this one authored by Karl Nikolaevich Kleberg, explicitly linked these issues with the notion of *sosloviia* themselves. He believed it was necessary to found "a *soslovie* of farmers [*sel'skii khoziain*]" because only a *soslovie*, "like other *sosloviia* recognized by the State," could find a place in the existing social structures of the empire. Kleberg linked agricultural work to other productive work. He compared the farmer to the merchant, and he noted that the latter "is recognized by the Administration as a member of a particular society, and as such has separate rights, separate privileges vis-à-vis other *sosloviia*." An estate overseer, however, lacked the right to call himself by his true occupation and also was "not a member of a particular society, but due to the lack of a particular to him *soslovie*, he must attach himself to other *sosloviia*, with activities completely foreign to him."

This was one problem—that agricultural overseers did work that was not recognized by any existing *soslovie;* another was that their work could not bring them additional honors. Again, Kleberg drew on recent legislation, noting that merchants were now able to gain "honors and higher rights" by accession to the honored citizenry, something that came to them through their own work and trade. But agricultural overseers had no such opportunities for advancement: "no matter how much he works, how much he tries, he can never and by no kind of effort, by his knowledge and work in his occupation, earn anything similar!"[118]

Finally, Kleberg described the benefits a new *soslovie* would bring to those who joined it:

if every farmer were a member of a society recognized by the Government, of a *soslovie* of farmers! He would have a more honored place in the State, he would know and feel that even his work was considered worthy of particular attention by the Government, he, living in the midst of his colleagues, would have more opportunities to perfect himself, he would have the opportunity and urge to distinguish himself even before the other members of his society! And besides this the Government too would by this means have a better way to know about the needs of farmers, to recognize and to honor the most worthy and by that means to awaken competition, rivalry, in consequence of which there must be the perfection of the science and trade themselves![119]

This was a radically different view of what *soslovie* could mean. Rather than based on a concept of mutual duty—and of mutual restriction—here *sosloviia* appeared as places of opportunity and advancement, serving much the same purpose as professional organizations elsewhere.[120] This seems, on the one hand, a mistaken view of the concept of *soslovie*, despite Kleberg's attention to questions of tax duty and the like in the main body of his plan. But on the other hand, it does reflect some of the trends then developing within the world of *sosloviia* more generally, as questions of access to privilege were increasing in importance. Most of all, though, it reflects the imperial state's general inability to see its society through a lens other than *soslovie*. The *sosloviia* both focused the labor of its population and allowed the empire to see its population. Other options were still underdeveloped—and by no means was it yet willing to accept a population that it could not see.

In his memoirs, A. P. Miliukov, the Moscow townsman freed from his society in order to seek an education beyond the scope of what his status allowed him, remembered his efforts to gain that freedom as a significant moment. Not only was it the moment that allowed him to enter a new life, but it also made him aware of the role of *soslovie* membership in controlling everyday life:

> What was this society, which interfered with my ability to study at the gymnasium, and why did it interfere with me? Was it really true that only nobles were allowed to study, I thought, and from our *soslovie* only the rich?! Or was it true... that it was easier for a camel to pass through the eye of a needle than a poor man go to university? Do they not want us to study?... Is it really dangerous to someone, if there are more educated people among us? Then, for the first time, thoughts of the inequality of *soslovie* began to stir within me, and for the first time I felt envy.[121]

For Miliukov, it was the moment when he came up against the boundary of his *soslovie*, when he sought to leave it, that made its outlines and its role in his life suddenly apparent. The whole concept of *soslovie* seemed unjust, unfair, and against the goals of a society that in principle claimed to want to modernize.

Miliukov came to these conclusions in a flash, as a result of his personal experience of the bureaucracy of *soslovie*, but questions about the fitness of *soslovie* for the kind of society the empire needed in the changing nineteenth-century world developed more slowly. These concerns, however, gained new resonance in the era of the Great Reforms and after, when new ideas of Russia's economic future—a future that might involve significantly more mobility—came into conflict with continued demands to establish and maintain order, a desire based above all in the local constraints of *soslovie* membership. From debates over the Great Reforms to the era of the Stolypin reforms, these issues recurred, creating ever new permutations and definitions of *soslovie*, which were reflected in ever new relationships between individuals, societies, and the state.

5

The Death and Life of *Sosloviia* in the Post-Reform Empire

IN 1846, A man named Ivan Andreev came to the attention of the Ministry of Finance. Several years before, Andreev had been arrested in Riga because he lacked not just proper documents but also a formal place in Imperial Russian society. Born a serf in Vitebsk province, he was freed by his owner Nikolai Paulin in 1819. In 1830, he was drafted into the army on behalf of the Shavli society of townspeople—but this action was declared illegal by the Vil'na court in 1841, and he was released from the army. Although the court gave him a temporary passport, he promptly lost it, and at the time of his arrest he had been living in Riga "without any housing ticket, earning a living in various places as a woodcutter."¹ Now Riga local authorities wanted to know what he was, administratively, and therefore how to deal with him.

Upon further investigation, Andreev's case became even more confusing. According to the records of Riga's town society itself, two brothers, Vasilii and Ivan Andreev, had indeed been freed by the serf owner Paulin in 1819, and the older brother, Vasilii, had registered as a Riga worker—that is, among those with the "right to choose a way of life" who could not find formal acceptance in a society. Riga's files did not record Ivan's fate, but additional investigation proved Ivan's story of improper drafting and eventual discharge was true. Other records suggested that he had come to Riga directly upon gaining his discharge from the army, but because he was ill and impoverished, he had failed to gain the acceptance of Riga's town society for formal registry there, and so his status remained uncertain.

The Ministry of Finance came up with a proposal: "register [Andreev] in the Riga Society without its agreement, but without making the society responsible for paying his dues,"² and turned to the Ministry of Internal Affairs for its approval. In 1848, several years after the initial correspondence, the Ministry of Internal Affairs finally responded, and disagreed. It saw two major questions in the case: first, a theoretical one, about whether such a solution (registry without agreement but without responsibility) was even legally permissible; and second, the specific one of how to deal with the case of Andreev. It first decided that the Ministry of Finance's solution was not a valid one even in theory because of Riga's status as a "privileged" town: one particular statute "positively prohibits the registry of anyone to the *soslovie* societies in 'privileged' towns, without their prior agreement, and… that restriction is in place not only in order to guard societies from untrustworthy and impoverished people, but undoubtedly also in order to restrict the number of individuals having privileges." This was particularly true in Riga, which had "many truly important advantages," and so would be flooded with "a mass of poor people of doubtful reliability, and particularly schismatics."[3]

As far as the specific case of Andreev went, the Ministry of Internal Affairs had a different solution. It had asked for more information on the man, and it found that "he not only is not in the condition to earn himself daily necessities, but also, due to his poor and totally ruined health, has been constantly living on the town's account in the public hospital." This did not bode well for his future abilities even to earn a living, let alone to become the kind of settled citizen who could gain formal agreement from the society. As a result, the ministry suggested a different solution: Andreev had, after all, served in the army for ten and a half years. Why not simply give him the status of a retired soldier and leave it at that?[4]

While this solution seemed ideal, it too turned out to be unworkable in the context of the current state of *soslovie* legislation. The War Ministry, when approached with the idea of granting Andreev military status, concluded that although Andreev had indeed served, the status of "retired soldier" was one only given to those properly drafted from townsman, state peasant, or free cultivator status.[5] Because Andreev should never have been a soldier at all, he could not now be a retired one. After this response, the bureaucrats of the Ministry of Finance found themselves completely at a loss as to what to do. They therefore did the only thing possible in such a case: they wrote up a detailed report recapping all the questions and possible answers, and presented it to the Senate in early 1850. There it sat. And sat. And finally, in December 1855, the Senate sent a response to the ministry, repeating again all the circumstances of the case, and concluding "the Lifland Provincial Administration has reported that Ivan Andreev… died in 1853… therefore, the current matter does not need further decision."[6]

By refusing to solve the dilemma of Ivan Andreev, the Senate in some ways was simply recognizing the fact that in the middle of the nineteenth century the concept of *soslovie* was at once hugely important and strictly controlled by laws, and yet individual lives were messy enough to stymie efforts to bring them into order.[7] Decree after decree had attempted to set out clear lines for *soslovie* membership, and by this time, too, the *Digest of the Laws* had in principle made those lines clear to all.[8] And yet, Andreev's case showed that these efforts to perfect the social world through legislation were not yet, and perhaps would never be, complete. Individuals simply did not necessarily live within the boundaries of the legislation on *sosloviia*. At the same time, the effort put into finding Andreev a proper place (even if that effort eventually went for naught) both shows the continued importance placed on the concept of *sosloviia* in the middle of the nineteenth century and presages the continued efforts on the part of the central state to reform and rethink the very idea of *soslovie*.

In some ways, the Great Reforms, with their goal of making visible the previously hidden bureaucratic and state structures of the Russian state, ought to have been able to solve these problems. But in reality, the Great Reforms failed to do so both because the structures of *soslovie* were far too entrenched and because of the multiple meanings of *soslovie*. The obligations and opportunities that went along with them were relatively easily redefined, but the ways in which *soslovie* also played into ideas of belonging and even hierarchy were harder to eliminate—and, indeed, were too useful to parts of the imperial state to consider eliminating. As a result, in the aftermath of the Great Reforms, *soslovie* retained its position as the organizing principle of Russian society, even as some believed it ought to be eliminated. Even during the Great Reforms, the Ministries of Finance and Internal Affairs had come to have divergent views about the necessity of maintaining *sosloviie*.[9] By the end of the century, both were again interested in their possible reform. During the era of the dumas, other voices called for their reform or elimination—and yet, as some of these voices argued for elimination, they were still caught up in a social world created by and based in *sosloviia*. Eliminating all traces of a vision of society as one defined by official categories was beyond even many of those who wished to abolish this one particular source of stratification.

EMANCIPATION: UNIFICATION AND MOBILITY

By virtually all accounts, the era of the Great Reforms was a turning point in the *soslovie* system. One version sees them as reducing "the estate system to a hollow structure."[10] Others describe them instead as a time when efforts to create, not non-*soslovie*, but all-*soslovie* concepts came to the fore.[11] In this version, efforts to reform the empire did not seek to eliminate *sosloviia* as markers of essential differences, but they did try to create spaces or structures that allowed members of different *sosloviia* to come together for the benefit of society.[12] As a result, even the early Marxist historian Rozhkov could only note that "it is impossible to speak of the complete replacement of the *soslovie* basis by the class[;] it is only possible to notice the strengthening of the latter and the weakening of the former."[13] It led to situations in which reformers spoke at once about "people of all ranks, without distinction" having certain economic rights, but simultaneously reaffirmed that their *soslovie* distinctiveness, and *soslovie* administration, would continue.[14] This approach, however, failed to reconcile the different ways of thinking about *soslovie*: as markers of economic function, of civic status, and of belonging. Some changes reaffirmed and even strengthened the concept of *soslovie*; at the same time, others eliminated some of the bases upon which *soslovie* had rested. The result was a shift in central, local, and individual understandings of what *soslovie* meant, a shift with significant implications for the relationships between these three sets of actors.

The most important of the Great Reforms was the emancipation of millions of serfs by Tsar Alexander II. Emancipation underlay many of the Great Reforms, as it created the social and economic world that allowed for or demanded many of the other reforms to follow. It also had a significant effect on understandings of *soslovie*, in part because after emancipation, for the first time there more or less was a single *soslovie* of peasants that replaced the many different categories of peasants that had existed before.[15] More specifically, it had a short-term effect on mobility, as pent-up desire to change category could be expressed at the moment of emancipation. Notably, however, emancipation had much less of a long-term effect on mobility, a fact largely explained by the ways both it and the other Great Reforms failed to address the multiple meanings of *soslovie* and society.

In one way, emancipation was the culmination of several decades of statutes that had gradually elided differences between separate legal categories of peasants. In 1823, a statute had placed free agriculturists (serfs freed en masse, as entire communities, according to a special provision of Alexander I) under the same rules as state peasants, erasing many differences between those statuses.[16] A few years later, the laws that governed court peasants were extended to "peasants of the Court horse stables," a conclusion that seems obvious but required formal statement.[17] Also that year, a statute essentially redefined two small existing groups—serfs belonging to a particular mining company and those "formerly under the authority of the Commission to Build in Moscow the Cathedral of Christ the Savior"—as state peasants by extending the regulations that governed the social mobility of state peasant to them.[18] These had all historically been separate categories based on occupational differences, for each was associated with a particular trade or project, and each had been subject do a different coordinating authority, but these new statutes spoke to the central state's desire to remove divisions and simplify the social structure.[19]

The 1838 statute that established a new overarching category of state peasants under the jurisdiction of a new ministry, the Ministry of State Domains, was a similar move toward standardization of categories that in some ways set the stage for the eventual melding of peasants into a single post-emancipation category. This reform established formally a single new *soslovie* of state peasants to replace the juridically already largely equal, but differently labeled, groups of peasants. Its first statute described the intent of the reform as "guardianship over the free rural residents (*svobodnye sel'skie obyvateli*)."[20] Later statutes specified who belonged to this group—"state peasants, free cultivators, and foreign settlers"—and emphasized that the first two, at least, were to be treated nearly identically.[21] The goal was clear: as an 1848 imperial decree put it, its goal was to promote "the complete conformity" in the naming of rural inhabitants.[22] And not only did it promote uniformity in naming, it promoted uniformity in administration as well.

An even more significant change came in 1858, when Alexander II "granted to all peasants of the court domains personal and property rights presented to other free rural *sosloviia*."[23] Earlier, court peasants had often been considered to be a particular variety of privately owned serfs with, at times, particular restrictions on their mobility. Laws forbade those with the freedom to choose a way of life from re-enserfing themselves, and other than a brief period in the early nineteenth century, such people could not join court villages because those villages were governed by the laws of serf-owning.[24] Now, however, Alexander was giving them freedom in fact, if not entirely in name—a first step toward formal emancipation, in other words. It also had far-ranging implications. Later that year, a law noted that state peasants were now allowed to join court peasant societies, as both were "free."[25] This was again a conflation of juridically separate statuses, made possible, in Alexander's formulation, by the conception of all being "free."

Finally, the emancipation—or rather, the series of emancipations of private serfs, state peasants, court peasants, and peasants in particular (usually imperial) regions—created a juridically largely unified peasantry. Now, all peasants were subject to the authority of their village and township societies, rather than some to individual owners. The shift was not instant, as the emancipation did not immediately erase all differences between peasants. In the short term, as former serfs moved through the stages of the emancipation process, they passed through juridically separate statuses.[26] Furthermore, well after emancipation in memoirs and other accounts, peasants retained memories of the origins of their villages—even to the point of recalling their villages as formerly belonging to monasteries, now a status that was a century removed.[27] But, still, peasants were increasingly seen simply as peasants, as their place in the social and administrative structures of the empire was made uniform.

Emancipation also had an immediate and obvious effect on mobility. Not every freed serf—and particularly not every freed household serf—wished to remain a peasant, and many clearly took emancipation as an opportunity to radically change their status. Peasants could (and did) refuse the land allotment they were entitled to according to their particular emancipation agreement, and instead receive their freedom to register as something else.[28] This particularly affected certain groups. Fewer new members joined Moscow's merchant society in the 1860s than in the decade before; clearly, those who had the financial status to become merchants were less bound by their serfdom than others, and the last census revision in 1857 had been an opportunity for many to make a change in their position. (Or, in that period when rumors of emancipation were flying, some serf owners may have tried to make deals with their wealthier peasants before rather than wait for the then unknown, but feared to be disadvantageous, emancipation settlement.)[29] Numbers of new Moscow townspeople increased slowly during the 1860s, peaking in 1870, and then falling again—suggesting a steady influx of former serfs as they passed through the stages of emancipation. The chef's guild of the Moscow artisan society, however, saw a huge influx of new members almost immediately after emancipation: 192 new members in 1862, and 939 in 1863, most of them freed serfs. Given the time and the place, many of these new artisans must have been freed household serfs who sought to recognize their previous work rather than take part in the division of lands.

In other places, reports of huge influxes of new members went along with reports of the significant difficulties they caused. In Kostroma province, the provincial treasury tried to institute a rule that former serfs who wished to register in new societies could only do so with their entire family as listed during the last census. The rationale, it seems, was either to simplify the paperwork it had to deal with or to ensure that the break-up of a household would not leave some members unable to maintain themselves in their village of origin. The Senate eventually looked into the case and decided that this was too harsh a solution. Instead, it ruled in part that, in most cases, a family was defined as "a father and a mother and their children—the unmarried sons and daughters." This was a rather limited view of the nuclear family, compared to the extended family so common in peasant society. Perhaps as a result, the Senate made an exception to this general rule: in the case of those recently released from serfdom, a family was whatever the "village assembly defined it as."[30] In other words, if a village wanted to be sure departing peasants took with them aged relatives, it could do so.

Townsperson societies, where many of the freed serfs sought to move, were particularly likely to feel overwhelmed by the numbers of new members. The Saratov Town Duma, for one, decided the best way to deal with the many new petitioners seeking permission to join the local society was to abdicate responsibility for them. Already in mid-1861, mere months after the Emancipation Manifesto, it was receiving dozens of requests from around the province asking about registering former serfs (many of them household serfs) who had already been given their freedom documents. It responded by considering them as it had freed serfs in the past—among those with the right to choose a way of life—which meant those whose registry "depends on the Provincial Treasury without the prior agreement of the society."[31] In other words, it took advantage of earlier decisions to lessen towns' authority over their own membership, and abdicated responsibility for deciding cases it did not wish to assess.

According to some accounts, the uptick in mobility caused by the emancipation particularly affected St. Petersburg and its neighboring towns. In 1864, the St. Petersburg General Governor sent the Minister of Internal Affairs a proposal. According to the governor, many recently freed serfs (particularly household serfs) had registered in nearby Kronshtadt. Their numbers were significant. In the three years since the Emancipation Manifesto, 3,415 male souls had been registered as Kronshtadt townsmen and a further 5,000 petitions remained unresolved. Furthermore, these new members of the Kronshtadt society presented St. Petersburg itself with a major problem. Many had registered in Kronshtadt but were actually living in St. Petersburg, "not worrying about finding themselves work that could provide them with sustenance, occupying themselves with begging." Therefore, to reduce the public display of poverty in the capital, the governor proposed to limit the right of registry of freed serfs in Kronshtadt itself. The Ministry of Internal Affairs responded with sympathy, but refused the request on the grounds that passports allowed anyone from anywhere to live in the capital, and thus restricting one city would fail to affect the actual residents of St. Petersburg.[32]

The possible negative repercussions of these initial surges of mobility could be long-lasting. In 1879, the Ministries of Internal Affairs and Finance dealt with a series of petitions from the town societies of Novaia Ladoga and Shlissel'burg, both complaining about the "great number of people of different *sosloviia* registered in the society of townspeople without its agreement by the Treasury." Like the earlier case of Kronshtadt, the case had been made worse by many former serfs—and also former members of military statuses, released from service in connection with the Army Reform of 1874. According to the Novaia Ladoga society, "the whereabouts of many of them are almost always unknown, and others, being of wanton behavior, lead an idle, drunken life, not paying the dues accruing to them, and avoiding military service, wandering the streets, boldly asking for alms and then immediately drinking them away."[33] The societies asked that the rules about allowing registry without acceptance be curtailed.

In response, the Ministry of Finance stuck with earlier solutions to similar issues, now given all the more force, in its view, in the post-Reform world. It could not see its way to void the provisions of registry in part because of the location of these two towns: it feared that they were so near St. Petersburg, restricting registry in them would force more people even closer to the city itself, creating a problem of public order at the center of power. But also, it noted, "at the present time, when a large part of former household serfs, freed serfs, and those of military status have already been registered, one cannot expect a great increase in the number of people with the right to register without acceptance agreements turning to societies... so the society's petition is untimely."[34]

These were all specific worries about the effect a large movement of people might have on towns, in particular, but at the same time, the emancipation brought certain more general questions about mobility to the attention of the Ministries—questions that were often tied to the new singular concept of "peasant." In 1864, the Minister of Finance wrote to the Minister of Internal Affairs for its opinion on a case arising in Pskov province. A former serf, still under temporary obligation to his former owner, had asked that his son be registered as a merchant in the town of Porkhov. He had been formally freed by their village society, but the local treasury refused to register him on the grounds that he was not yet of age, and therefore barred from entry into merchant status on his own, separate from his family.[35] This was indeed a restriction placed on state peasants, and indicated that the treasury now saw former serfs as one with state peasants.

The Minister of Finance, however, disagreed with this decision. Yes, he wrote, under-aged state peasants were not allowed to enter the merchantry. But the emancipation had stated that former serfs were to be accepted into town societies "by the same method that has been established for people of other free tax-paying conditions." The Minister of Finance argued that because that section of the emancipation did not specifically state that former serfs ought to be subject to the same restrictions as state peasants, he "did not find any particular value in restricting them in their movement into the merchantry, and therefore propose[d] that temporarily obligated peasants [might] enter into this status according to general principles without regard to sex and age.[36] This was, of course, an argument that moved against the general trend of seeing peasants as all alike, instead reaffirming differences based in origin to their legal rights.

The Minister of Internal Affairs responded (nearly three years later) with a rather different interpretation of the emancipation. He agreed that the emancipation "not only does not include any particular statutes that would determine the movement of such individuals into merchant status, but directly and positively it is stated, that temporarily obligated peasants have the right to move into different conditions in accordance with the general laws on that subject." However, he noted, the current trend in legislation was, as he put it, "the amalgamation of peasants of all designations into a single whole." As a result, laws on peasants "should now already obtain general meaning."[37] The minister pointed out the 1858 decree that placed court peasants under the same rules as state peasants as evidence for this trend, and concluded that "allowing temporarily obligated peasants to transfer into town statuses underaged members of their families without those restrictions which are set in relation to the movement of such persons, belonging to peasants of different types, would sooner be like removing those peasants from the influence of general law, rather than extending to them general rules."[38]

The Minister of Internal Affairs also made an important point about the overarching concept of *soslovie* during this period. The problem was this idea of "general rules." There were certain general concepts that seemed widely understood; one relevant to this discussion was that, "according to the general meaning of our laws on conditions and on civil rights, children follow the condition of their father, and may move to a different *soslovie*, to which their father does not belong, only when they come of age."[39] But beyond those concepts that owed little to specific status, defining "general rules" or "general laws" was extremely difficult. Indeed, as he put it, "turning to the actual statutes, it has to be realized, that such 'general laws' that would determine by themselves the conditions of transfer into town statuses individuals of *all* tax-paying statuses in common, have not been set by law."[40] There were simply few truly all-*soslovie* laws, whatever the efforts to create them had been.

Both of these trends—creating consistent categories by which to organize the population, and an increase of mobility associated with certain of the Great Reforms—came to a head in the western provinces. In February 1868, the State Council approved a plan to incorporate two locally specific statuses (*odnodvortsy* and *grazhdane*) into the larger categories of peasant and townsperson. All those who claimed these statuses were instead to register in local town or village societies; if they failed to choose that new registry, it would be done for them, based purely on their current place of legal residence. Beyond these practical measures, the statute stated clearly that this was an effort to eliminate two "particular *sosloviia*," and to create a new more unified social structure in the region. In so doing, it extended the amalgamation of different rural statuses into a single peasant status that had been one focus of the process of emancipation.[41]

The way that this statute played out in the provinces, however, shows the real problems that were faced by town societies, in particular, at this time of increased mobility. The Vil'na Treasury sent a notice to all local administrations under its authority, informing them of the new law and instructing them to make sure that all those affected by the statute be properly registered in their new societies.[42] Quickly, however, it became clear that this was to be no easy task owing to the larger problem of mobility. The administration of the Vil'na Civil (*Grazhdanskoe*) Society decided not to inform higher provincial authorities of the fates of its members in large part because it barely knew anything about them. As the Vil'na administration put it in a report to the town duma, "citizens of Vil'na live all over in various towns, provinces, hamlets and villages, on passports or without them, and the location of the larger part of them is completely unknown." As a result, putting together a "true list" of their members was utterly impossible, and the society hoped that the new policy would simply take the problem off their hands.[43] In addition, other towns and villages from across the region wrote to Vil'na authorities seeking their own members who claimed current residence in the larger city as they sought to clear up their membership rolls.

The effort to register properly all local subjects led to hundreds of pages of letters, reports, and demands sent between town and provincial authorities. The provincial administration, treasury, and eventually the governor himself asked for reports from Vil'na (and, presumably, other towns); within Vil'na, separate *soslovie* and other authorities argued among themselves as to who had responsibility for drawing up reports. From Vil'na, at least, the demands for reports remained unfulfilled, as accurately recording its true membership seemed impossible. Still, the desire for accurate record-keeping, and the desire to hold local *soslovie* societies responsible for their members, drove provincial authorities to push harder for proper reports. And furthermore, their actions reflected the growing conflict between towns and higher authorities that continued in debates over other of the Great Reforms.

TOWNS AND THE TRANSFORMATION OF SOSLOVIE

A second focus of the Great Reforms with significant implications for the system of *sosloviia* was the transformation of town administrations. In some ways, this reform has been treated as a place where the *soslovie* principle was attacked and largely replaced by an all-*soslovie* one where some form of civil society could begin to develop.[44] However, in many of the debates over reforming towns, the real question was not one of eliminating *soslovie* but of defining them. If the emancipation helped to create a new concept of a generalized peasant *soslovie*, and in doing so in some ways helped to reinforce the notion of *soslovie* itself, the eventual town reform had a far more complicated effect on contemporary understandings of *soslovie*.

Debates over the reform of town administration had been largely presaged by the 1846 reform of St. Petersburg's administration. That reform was published in the *Journal of the Ministry of Internal Affairs* and then reprinted as a separate pamphlet, with an introduction that, among other topics, looked specifically at *soslovie*. The reform itself set out two clear sets of administration: one "general for all society" and the second "separate, by *soslovie*."[45] The author of the introduction pointed out how important it was to think about the current social structure of the city, rather than the structure long ago defined by Peter and then Catherine the Great. For one, he noted, some former categories had disappeared (like guests and noted citizens) and others had emerged (honored citizens).[46] The concerns of this author were reflected in the reform itself, which at once reaffirmed and in some ways redefined *soslovie*, while also instituting new all-*soslovie* administrative structures.

A particular problem raised by the St. Petersburg reform was the place of those marginal individuals who had come to towns as those with the right to choose a way of life—for the most part, those who had been counted simply as "workers" or "working people." Initially, the only legal concept of "working people" had been those placed in workhouses used as places of punishment; when a decree of 1816 stated that returned runaways ought to be classified as workers, this created problems.[47] When one such returned runaway sought registry in a Tver' village, local authorities turned him away. The village reported that it had not enough land; he then proved to be too old for the army. But registering him as a "working person" was confusing—there were no such people anywhere in the province except in Tver' itself, but the provincial capital was considered "privileged," and thus free from such registration. The Senate, which was already looking at a similar case coming out of Ekaterinoslav (where there was "no class of working people" and yet people in need of registry as such) simply decided that, based on the earlier statute, there should already be a status of "working people" and if a given locality had no such "class" it was their own fault.[48]

The concept of worker continued to be linked to people whose status was outside the bounds of local town society. In the important 1832 statute about towns and registry, workers were defined as those individuals who could not be refused by societies.[49] This identification, however, was hardly a ringing endorsement of the redefined status. Indeed, the 1842 edition of the *Digest of the Laws* described "workers" in most unflattering terms: "returnees from abroad of bad behavior and unfit for military service ascribed to towns with a place in the townsperson rolls; and also those ascribed to towns of other callings, named below… and registered as working people for their bad behavior and failure to pay their taxes and other duties."[50]

This classification continued to create problems in the context of the current *soslovie* structure, and particularly complicated the reform of St. Petersburg's administration. In 1844, the Minister of Internal Affairs wrote to the Minister of Finance, asking for help in drafting new regulations for the capital. In particular, he wanted help on thinking through the town's social structure. As he put it, "town society is divided into six *sosloviia*. Of them two are comprised of people of non-tax-paying status, owning real estate in the town (nobles and honored citizens with people of various ranks); and the remaining four *sosloviia* are made of people of town condition proper, to which are ascribed merchants, townspeople, artisans, and working people."[31] The problem was with the last of these groups. As the minister put it, "the rights of status are already defined for the first five *sosloviia* in the *Digest of the Laws on Statuses*… only for the working people are there not clear statutes, because the formation of a separate *soslovie* from these people is a new measure."[32] Of particular interest was the fact that working people had been defined as those registered to a town without its local society's acceptance, and that out of this rose the fact that they were to pay taxes individually. However, as the minister noted, "in the laws there are no clear statutes either of the procedure for collecting taxes from them, nor of the scope of their civil rights when it comes to owning property, trade, and so forth."[33]

The regulation put forth in 1846 built on these discussions by reformulating the concept of *soslovie* to fit the currently existing array of people in the town. It listed a rather different set of *sosloviia* (and it used that word) than had earlier statements of town societies: merchants, townspeople, artisans, foreign artisans, and "paid servants and workers."[34] This last group was a way to try to deal with the masses of people of uncertain status in the capital. It included household servants, people working in industries, and "workers proper" (*chernorabochye*). The *soslovie* was technically categorized as an artisan's guild, and it differed from other town soslovie in ways linked to how the category of worker had been developing. Entry into the guild did not require "prior agreement of that guild." And, furthermore, "everyone ascribed to it is personally responsible for proper payment of taxes and for fulfilling other duties."[35] Like other guilds, however, there was both permanent membership and temporary membership, which applied to "townspeople from other towns and peasants of various entitlements coming here for a time, and also for freed serfs, not having in St. Petersburg permanent residence and for serfs coming on passports."[36]

This was a first attempt to better regulate *soslovie* and their governance within the empire's towns, but it was hardly enough. It conflated different kinds of status (workers and artisans and townspeople). It mixed the concepts of individual and of collective responsibility. By allowing registry to be either permanent and not it also confused the issue of the normally hereditary nature of *soslovie*. As a result, it set out a recipe more for greater confusion than for greater clarity. Later reforms did little better.

As the era of the Great Reforms proper took hold, and in preparation for writing the new more general reform, the Ministry of Internal Affairs released a draft project for comment both by other ministries and by representatives from towns themselves. It proposed a kind of all-*soslovie* administration, and in many ways promoted such institutions and concepts. At the same time, it also questioned what it meant to be a member of a town society, a topic that lay at the heart of the concept of *soslovie*, of the demands of registration, and of mobility. In particular, the ministry noted that the currently existing system created a strange situation based on the requirements of registry. First, current laws allowed a number of different people to register as townspeople without gaining formal acceptance. This was certainly not news, but the way that the ministry described these various people emphasized their marginal position:

> illegitimate children of women who do not belong to any tax-paying condition; church people, excluded from religious calling for inability or for suspicion of crimes or misdemeanors; children of bureaucrats who do not have officer's rank; retired soldiers…, all former household serfs and landless peasants who do not wish to use the right to an allotment of land; exiles who have received permission to return from Siberia to the central provinces, and so forth.[57]

The ministry went on to note that in principle such people were meant to be considered as part of a separate category, as "working people" who owed taxes as individuals, not as members of the society. They were not part of the collective responsibility of the community, nor did they "have a voice in the society." However, this distinction was rarely enforced, with the result that these many marginal members of society ended up registered as full members of societies of townspeople.[58]

These were issues of long standing, and in the past the central state had taken a strong stance in favor of their registry. Now, though, at least in the view of this ministry, they gained new importance in the context of debates over changing town administration. The current system had led to a problem in towns, which were legally full of townspeople with doubtful connection to their official residences, while actual residents and property owners with interests in the town were not formally attached to it, and thus had no official role to play in its administration. In an ideal world, according to the ministry, "town society" should "consist of all regular inhabitants of the town who pay some sort of taxes on their real estate or on their trade, no matter to which *soslovie* they belong, and no matter where they are registered as far as state duties."[59] But this ideal world was one laid on top of the existing structures, as in this vision, "the status of town inhabitant is not a distinct status, and every town inhabitant preserves the rights accruing to him by [his existing] status."[60]

The ministry went on to gather comment from other central ministries and from towns themselves. Towns were asked to comment on a number of specific questions, one of which focused narrowly on the idea of mobility, society, and membership: "Under which conditions should people who have settled in towns be considered members of the town society, and into which divisions or *sosloviia* may they be divided?"[61] The official statement went on to clarify what the ministry wished to address with this question:

> Town inhabitants as a group, as a consequence of living together, naturally finding themselves bound together by many general interests, make up one whole—a *society*; but at the same time members of that town society, on the basis of the currently existing laws, finding themselves subject to different duties and having different occupations, fall out into distinct groups or *sosloviia*, made up of those members of

the society who are alike in duties and occupation; such a division into *sosloviia* is all the more necessary because some duties are guaranteed by communal responsibility for one another placed on the inhabitants by these duties.[62]

The ministry's vision was of an ideal town in which *sosloviia* were distinct to a degree not necessarily found in reality. And yet it also expresses the basic idea of *sosloviia* as a source of collective or communal responsibility, which underlay much of the legislation regarding social mobility through the first half of the nineteenth century.

Some of the responses from towns included proposals that were radically different from the then-current hierarchy of town estates. Sixty-six towns argued that there should be no *sosloviia* divisions within towns at all. Most of these towns were arguing from a position of pure necessity. They were small towns, where the mandate to divide up already small populations into subcategories created unworkably small *sosloviia* administrations.[63] Others came up with systems that based divisions on new ideas related to issues raised by the Ministry of Internal Affairs. It had noted that property owners were often excluded from any say in local affairs due to lack of local registry. Many delegates similarly argued that *soslovie* divisions should be based on property ownership. Some believed that towns should be divided into *sosloviia* based on those who were property owning and those who worked; a variant on this proposal suggested three divisions: property owners; a group consisting of merchants, townspeople, and artisans; and a third of peasant-farmers resident in towns. Another suggestion used one of the major real differences between existing *sosloviia* in order to replace current labels with two basic ones: taxpaying and non-taxpaying.[64]

Most towns, however, suggested some variation on the system formalized at the end of the eighteenth century by Catherine the Great, in particular preserving distinctions between merchants and townspeople. Some argued for just those two *sosloviia* and no others. A large group argued for a system that combined attention to property ownership, suggesting a tripartite system of property owners, of merchants, and of townspeople and artisans combined. And the few that suggested new systems of up to seven separate categories got to such numbers multiplying those divisions by ethnic or religious distinctions.[65]

The most radical view came not from the towns themselves but from the Ministry of Finance. It argued that the single most important aspect of the proposed reform was not simply that it removed administration from "the laws of estates" and was "outside any relationship to *soslovie* administration," but that it might actually serve as a first step toward a future without *sosloviia* at all. Its hopes for future involved:

the final abolition of the compulsory corporations that apparently have an unfavorable effect on the development of industry and on the well-being of town inhabitants. All these ways of tying down people by means of *sosloviia*... on the one hand serves as an extraneous constraint on their personal freedom, and on the other hand burdens them with monetary dues under the guise of so-called voluntary contributions, levied above and beyond state and local tax collections, and in many cases even more costly than these last, and very often used not for absolute necessities, but for the luxury or arbitrary desires of the *soslovie* boards.[66]

This was a significant, new approach, one that moved past an all-*soslovie* view to a non-*soslovie* one in the name of freedom and economic growth.

Despite the fact that both the Ministry of Internal Affairs, which set the questions, and the Ministry of Finance, which welcomed the debate, hoped to use the town reform to address basic questions of *soslovie*, that line of reform was shut down by another central authority. As perhaps the administrative body most narrowly focused on the law, the Second Section of His Majesty's Own Chancellery particularly questioned this aspect of the ministry's plan. Although it agreed that *soslovie* could not be totally absent from the plan, it should not feature in any major way. Eventually, it asked that all references to *sosloviia* organization and administration be excluded from the projected reform. Instead, it should focus narrowly on town administration.[67]

The opinion of the Second Section carried the day, and despite the efforts of the two ministries to examine the issue, the eventual town reform essentially ignored the role of *sosloviia*. After the promulgation of the reform in 1870, the Economic Department of the Ministry of Internal Affairs published a special edition of the reform laws with extensive explanations and commentary. In that commentary, the ministry exhorted *soslovie* organs to cooperate with the new all-town administration set up by the new legislation. What exactly their roles were, however, was not just underplayed but, rather, absent in the content of the larger reform.[68] But that very fact—that *soslovie* administrations were to cooperate with the reform, but not otherwise be touched by it—spoke to a basic problem in the vision of the era of the Great Reforms when it came to *soslovie*.

This problem is also visible in another part of the ministry's statements on the reform. In the explanatory introduction, the ministry noted that one of the principle goals of the reform had been to clarify what exactly was meant by "town resident," given that the existing situation was a confusing one: there were those who had a place in towns by occupation or residence, but they were not necessarily town inhabitants "in particular," which meant those who had official town status. Even those town "statuses or *sosloviia*" were confusing, for a few were "collected together into a single corporation," others "made up a corporation of their own," and yet others "not consisting of any kind of corporation, are considered belonging in general to the composition of the town society."[69] This was, it noted, confusing and irrational, and needed to be solved. However, throughout the reform itself, for all its comments on the "all-*soslovie*" or even at times "non-*soslovie*" elements of certain provisions, *sosloviia* themselves were not only not eliminated but were barely touched in their internal workings. This effort at clarification was simply placed on top of the existing system, rather than clearing away the confusing mass of statuses within towns. This meant that the town reform gave, if anything, additional sources of possible conflict between the imperial state and local authorities, particularly over the control of mobility.

As a result, by refusing to allow *sosloviia* to be examined and reformed, the Second Section had essentially condemned the reform to partial success, at best. In principle, it was a reform that aimed to eliminate certain elements of the *soslovie* structure by creating new all-*sosloviia* institutions. But the reform failed to resolve these complexities in any real way. *Sosloviia* and their societies continued to exist and to play real roles in the administration of cities. As the journalist Shchepkin put it, the concept of "*soslovie* distinction" was "eliminated in new laws of self-government, despite the actual existence here of *sosloviia*."[70] Or, as another mid-century commentator put it, the town reform had "completely separated town and *sosloviia* societies" without eliminating the latter. As a result, "this separation generated in practice not a few misunderstandings and fights."[71]

Those "misunderstandings and fights" ranged from relatively simple questions of terminology to more complex ones based on the very nature of *sosloviia* themselves. One example comes from instructions sent out to provincial treasuries in 1864, as part of a reform of accounting principles in those treasuries. The introduction to the instructions stated formally that these rules resulted in provincial treasuries' "losing their revision character."[72] "Revision character" referred to the central role that treasuries had played in maintaining the census records that guided payment of the soul tax. Now, with the end of census revisions (and soon, the end of the soul tax), the treasuries were instead to be considered "the supreme financial agencies in the province." Despite this, the specific accounting rules still included significant work that was much the same as the "revision" work that was no longer an official part of the treasuries' mandate: "the soul and land book of the Treasury should include all data necessary for drawing up tax forms for the collection of taxes and duties." And those books should include "information gathered by the census department of every included or excluded soul."[73] Local *soslovie*-based tax rolls may have lost their central significance with the abolition of the soul tax, but in practice, towns and villages still needed to know who lived in them, who owed local taxes, and who had recourse to the town or village society for public services.

What exactly these societies were was also still unclear. In the 1880s, A. O. Gordon, an attorney for the Saratov merchant and townsperson societies, argued before the Senate against a recent decision by the Saratov Provincial Administration that had at its core the definition of *sosloviia* in the new post-reform world. The case concerned properties mutually owned by the two societies, the income from which went to fund "the needs of the merchant and townsperson societies: for the upkeep of schools, hospitals, pensioners, and the like." In 1882, the societies decided to write a document formalizing the ownership and governance of the properties. However, when they presented the new document to the Ministry of Internal Affairs (via the Saratov governor) for approval, the ministry refused, on the grounds that "the aforementioned property, as something belonging to the two *sosloviia* which made up the town society before the Town Reform of 1870, should go into the management of the Saratov Town Duma." In other words, it should belong to the new all- or non-*soslovie* government of the town rather than to the two *soslovie*-specific administrations. The Saratov Provincial Administration confirmed this decision, and released a statement considering the property as town, not *soslovie* property.[74]

Perhaps unsurprisingly, the two *soslovie* societies protested. Gordon argued for them on a number of counts. The Provincial Administration had claimed that "even individually these *sosloviia* cannot possess property," a claim Gordon found contrary to the laws. The *Digest of the Laws* clearly stated, he claimed, that "'*sosloviia*' may own their own property." The administration had excluded *soslovie* societies from the kinds of corporations that had the right to own property through a faulty understanding of the entire concept of *soslovie*. The laws, Gordon believed, clearly showed that "the expression '*soslovie*' is the same as the expression 'society,' and that a 'society' is a juridical agent." He summarized his argument thus:

> The merchantry and the *soslovie* of townspeople, like the nobility, too, have, independent of the towns's general interests, their own *soslovie* interests. The law by no means ignores these *soslovie* interests. These interests cannot even be ignored, because they entail the urgent needs of life....In order to meet the needs of *soslovie* interests their own property is necessary....These *sosloviia* without their own property cannot survive. They need [to pay] the expenses of their own governance....It falls to them to worry about the interests of the members of their *sosloviia*, disadvantaged by fate (almshouses, schools, etc.)[75]

Gordon was, in fact, summarizing what was just becoming a new source of major conflict between local societies and the central state. The provincial administration, in this case, saw *sosloviia* as mere relics, useful to keep track of the population but now without larger purpose. But Gordon presented a strongly opposing viewpoint, one which claimed continued relevance for *sosloviia*—or at least for *soslovie* administration—even in the face of the post-Reform world. In this view, *sosloviia* were still vital, now not to provide the center with taxes but, rather, to provide services to their members.

TAXES AND THE ELIMINATION OF *SOSLOVIE*

During the era of the Great Reforms, taxes were a third issue that influenced and were influenced by conceptions of *sosloviia*. Over the last half-century of the imperial era, there was a general a shift in the conception of taxes as something mediated by collectives (like the town or village society) to something assessed on an individual basis.[76] The soul tax, which had so affected conceptions of duty and privilege (or, more properly, lack of privilege) was abolished for members of town societies in 1863.[77] Soon thereafter, the Ministry of Finance began to investigate possible methods of abolishing it in the countryside, as well. Around 1872, it gathered the opinions of local authorities—councils of the new provincial (*Zemstvo*) assemblies—on a proposal that aimed to replace the soul tax with alternative forms of taxation. In the process, it found that the dream of a post- or non- or even just all-*soslovie* world was difficult to realize, in large part because it was so difficult to conceive of a way to divorce taxation, in particular, from *soslovie*.

In essence, the ministry's proposal claimed to eliminate reliance on *sosloviia* as intermediaries in the taxation system. It claimed that that process had already been in progress—the soul tax in towns, for example, had been replaced by an all-town, rather than *soslovie*-specific, tax.[78] And it claimed that the system it was now proposing—to replace the soul tax with a land tax—would also reduce the significance of *soslovie*. However, the actual proposal showed the significant limits facing any attempt to eliminate *sosloviia*. The proposed land tax was to be levied solely on lands allotted to peasants. The ministry claimed that this was not *soslovie*-specific because it was the land itself that would be taxed, and therefore those lands would remained taxed if peasants were to sell property, even to members of other *sosloviia*.[79] Commentators from the provinces objected strongly, noting that such a system would simply reduce the demand for land subject to taxes, rather than eventually share the burden of taxation beyond peasants themselves. It might even, one commenter noted, cause peasants to refuse their land allotments, and instead simply rent non-peasant, and thus non-taxed, lands.[80]

Similarly, commentators from the provinces noted that the ministry failed to understand the ways that its proposals were embedded in the world of *soslovie*. Local authorities singled out the way that the commission presented its proposal to introduce a household tax in lieu of the soul tax. The commission claimed that it would do away with the need for communal authority, that basis of *soslovie* society. However, some local authorities disagreed: "collective responsibility, the binding of peasants to a place[,] and the censuses of the population—all these would be just as inextricably linked to a household tax, as with a soul tax, for in both cases the unit of taxation is fictitious."[81]

Ten years later, the Ministry of Finance again brought up the question of eliminating the soul tax in a report to the State Council. Again, it focused on the problems of the soul tax both as a mark of inequality and as something that reinforced the tradition of communal responsibility. The State Council responded to its proposals in ways that focused in part on the very concept of *soslovie*. The Ministry of Finance had commented that it would be difficult to fix the current problem while peasants alone bore so much of the burden of taxation; only with a fairer distribution of the tax burden would a true reform be possible. The State Council found this a troubling precedent on which to base future decisions, in part because it believed that elimination of the soul tax was "not in the strictest sense a mercy" given to relieve the population's current burdens but, rather, "a state measure making it necessary to abolish the system of taxation now hindering the development of the nation's welfare."[82]

Despite this unease, the Ministry of Finance presented further arguments that argued against *soslovie*-specific taxes and regulations. It described many of the Great Reforms as having been based in an effort to "equalize all subjects in their rights and duties towards the state." Emancipation had made peasants equal; the *Zemstvo* reform had allowed for "more or less equal participation of all *sosloviia* in local administrative affairs"; and most of all, the army reform had placed the "privileged *sosloviia* on a totally equal level with others when it comes to this most important state obligation."[83] Now, it argued, the abolition of the soul tax and the general reform of taxation were "absolutely necessary" in order to eliminate "such an enormous contributor to the discord between *sosloviia*."[84]

In this case, too, it focused on the idea that communal responsibility led to a number of real problems for the modernizing Russian world. In particular, it focused on the question of registry and mobility. For one, the soul tax served "on the one hand to bind peasants to the land by means of the passport system so that a taxpayer cannot hide from his obligations, and on the other it promotes unauthorized absence to find better pay." Not only did it recognize that the current system of obligations had an effect on registry and mobility, but it even argued for a radical overhaul of the entire system:

> there can be no doubt of the necessity of the most rapid change of these laws, in light of their extreme inconvenience for members of tax-paying *sosloviia*, in particular due to the possibility of the abuses they allow, and just as much in light of the inevitable complication and frequent confusion in the dealings of administrative bodies when it comes to the re-registry of these people from one society to another.[85]

Essentially, the ministry was altering its earlier attack on *soslovie* by focusing on the specific question of mobility, through encouraging methods to make it easier, rather than to place restrictions on it in the name of preserving local societies. This was part of a general turn in central decision making away from preserving *soslovie* as units of collective responsibility and toward seeing them simply as means of seeing and organizing the population, without necessarily having greater significance.

It was also an argument that had some real resonance outside the halls of various ministries. The mid-nineteenth-century author I. A. Gan put the problem of membership at the center of his discussion of "the current way of life of townspeople in Saratov province." He first pointed out that current legislation listed a large number of different groups allowed to choose their way of life, and he followed by arguing that most of them wound up entering societies of townspeople (he gave figures that suggested that 84.6 percent of freed serfs in the province registered in them) "willingly or unwillingly, but having to register [somewhere] lest they be passed over."[86] Gan further noted that this practice essentially contradicted the concept of town life laid out by Catherine the Great. She had defined towns as places of commerce and trade, but the policy of mandatory registration brought in "people not having the least understanding either of crafts, or of trade, or of industry, like for example a churchman, freed from religious status for inability or for suspicion of crime."[87]

Gan took this argument to a place perhaps not dreamed of by the town officials of the early nineteenth century who sought to retain their right to accept new members. He suggested, instead, that

> there be provided complete freedom of entrance into all *sosloviia*; by the same token, movement from one *soslovie* to another should also not be governed by any restrictions. According to the laws currently in force, town society, speaking particularly of townspeople, has the character of serfdom, both in its origins and in the ways people enter into this *soslovie*, and in movement out of it into another.[88]

Like the Ministry of Finance's proposal, this was a radical departure from the consistent focus on registration and formal group membership that had for so long governed *sosloviia* and the idea of movement. The 1872 inquiry into the soul tax had brought forth agreement that *sosloviia* were waning in importance. One response suggested that anything that "remained grounded in the concept of *soslovie* [*soslovnost'*] stood in clear contradiction to the modern development of our state life."[89] A decade later, as the process of abolishing the soul tax was almost complete, another author went even further. "A person just for himself, and not as an invariable particle of one or the other society, is not recognized here," he wrote. This might have made sense in the time of collective taxation, but now?[90]

Despite this change in attitude toward *soslovie*, its very concept was simultaneously so integral to the way that the imperial state understood its population that eliminating it was almost beyond its powers. Instead, *sosloviia* and *soslovie* societies remained while the world changed around them. For the most part, they hid away behind the larger issues of the day. Occasionally, though, they called out as obstacles in need of reform. Even then, they were discussed, often lambasted, but never fully discarded.

THE EVOLUTION OF *SOSLOVIE*: THE 1896 STUDY

In the last decades of the empire, the central ministries again gave their attention to *sosloviia*, and particularly to the town *sosloviia*. If the Great Reforms had been (in principle, at least) about developing all- or non-*soslovie* administrations, by most accounts the reigns of Alexander III and Nicholas II brought the concept of *soslovie* back into the center of their practices. This ranged from "retreat" from the separation of *soslovie* and town governance in a new Town Statute of 1892; to increased reliance on *soslovie* as a social marker with real meaning that could be used to guide elections; to, in the words of one historian, using *sosloviia* as "one of the several important weapons of Russian statesmen in their struggle against modernity."[91] However, now *soslovie* very clearly took on new meanings. No longer the little, localized societies of the earlier imperial era, now *sosloviia* were increasingly understood as larger, all-encompassing structures, described by Kliuchevskii and explicitly compared to the concept of estates in the West.

In 1896, the Ministry of Internal Affairs sent a circular to all the empire's governors, requesting that they send in information answering specific questions about the status of town *soslovie* societies (merchants, townspeople, and artisans). The request had grown out of an earlier examination of the status of artisans in the empire, an examination that had quickly grown to include the other town *sosloviia*, "primarily that of the townspeople, the numerous limitations of which, shown by practice in recent decades, have often brought on themselves the attention both of the Senate, and of the relevant Ministries."[92] The questions posed in the circular covered basic statistics, including population numbers, taxes, and property; internal governance; the practice of accepting new members, particularly those with the right to choose a way of life; and questions related to the role *soslovie* societies played in individual lives, including charity and public aid. The responses, which included both statistical tables and lengthy written responses, trickled in over the next several years. The statistical tables submitted by provincial officials were obviously at times estimates at best, imaginary at worst. Even so, and particularly when combined with the written documents, they tell a fairly consistent story about the place and workings of *soslovie* societies at the turn of the century.

One of the major concerns of the ministerial inquiry linked to earlier understandings of *sosloviia* was above all about duties; it asked directly: who paid taxes? There were two elements to this question. The first involved numbers. The reports included not just the number of merchants, townspeople, and artisans in the towns but also a usually smaller number of "payers of public dues." The results were confusing, with anywhere from only a third of registered members actually paying dues among Moscow artisans, to St. Petersburg's merchant society enjoying apparently more taxpayers than members. This oddity did nothing but point out the near irrelevance of *soslovie* to the actual payment of taxes and dues.

The instructions for the inquiry asked local authorities to report on whether "collective responsibility" was still in force within their *soslovie* societies when it came to paying taxes. Nearly all the reports concluded that in general it was not, and made no

TABLE 5.1

Percentage of registered male souls paying local taxes in different towns, from 1896 inquiry

	Merchant	Townsperson	Artisan
St. Petersburg	117	25	84
Moscow	95	49	34
Provincial Capitals	47	51	97
District Capitals	39	58	92

Source: RGIA f. 1287, op. 44, dd. 546–48, 550–54.

other particular statement on the subject.⁹³ The only major exceptions involved a particular view of the concept, one that reflected other changes within the late imperial world. In several towns, collective responsibility had been maintained but transformed into responsibility within a single family.⁹⁴ In this understanding, family members were responsible for paying dues collectively, but beyond the household the concept had disappeared.

In addition, the instructions specifically asked for information not only on the number of individuals added to townsperson societies in the recent past but also on both the number who had been added without the societies' formal acceptance and on whether societies used the provision accorded to them in the *Digest of the Laws* to demand formal acceptance after the waiver period. The results varied widely depending on the town. In St. Petersburg, only 25 percent of new townspeople had entered without formal acceptance; in Moscow, 33 percent; in district capitals, 41 percent; and in provincial capitals, 63 percent. These numbers are hard to interpret. The lower percentages in the capitals might suggest that those were places that drew larger numbers of individuals actively seeking a change in their status, rather than those without a place and in need of one. That logic, however, does not necessarily apply to the differences between provincial and district capitals. There, the difference is more likely to be based in the reverse logic: that provincial capitals were more appealing than district ones to those with the right to join without acceptance. By most accounts those with that right were likely to be marginal in some way, either socially or economically. Provincial towns were far more likely to have readier sources of public aid than were district ones.

The narrative accounts from many provinces were consistent in their answer to whether the townsperson societies demanded formal acceptance: that provision of the law almost universally "was not observed."⁹⁵ As with the question of collective responsibility, there were a few exceptions. According to governors, the law still held sway in Irkutsk (but not its district towns), and several individual district towns in provinces where the practice had generally disappeared, including Kozmodem'iansk (Kazan' province), Kologriv (Kostroma province), Chern' (Tula province) and Rybinsk, Mologa, and Romanoborisoglebsk (Iaroslavl' province).⁹⁶ Although there was no note that the provision was followed in Zlatoust, Ufa province, there local authorities did distinguish between the two groups; it was one of the only places where collective responsibility was still in force, but only for those formally accepted by the society.⁹⁷ This exception suggests that collective responsibility had fallen out of use at the same time as the ability to enforce formal acceptance, in large part because the two concepts were connected.

Although most governors contented themselves with similar basic statements of fact, a few went further in their discussion of the question in ways that support this interpretation. The governor of Ekaterinoslav province noted that the law was not followed "because the registry of such people is produced by the order of the Provincial Treasury, without any participation of the Townsperson Boards." The Perm governor wrote much the same.⁹⁸ The governor of Riazan' province failed to answer the question directly, but did note that many of the local townsperson officials complained about having to take in people without formal acceptance, "because that deprives the society of trust and autonomy."[99] And two governors, those of Voronezh and Tambov provinces, explicitly described the process of formal acceptance (and release) as a relic of the past, tied to the now-abandoned soul tax. The Voronezh governor went even further—he believed that now that the soul tax, and therefore collective responsibility, was gone, there was no need for societies formally to accept or release members.[100]

Finally, many of the governors' commentaries directly addressed the idea of removing *soslovie* administrations, leaving only the all-city administrations set up by various earlier reforms. The answers here were at times very basic. A number simply noted that they saw no difficulty with that idea. The report from Tver' stated that the excess of paperwork flooding the townsperson administration meant that it might as well hand over duties to the town.[101] But others had more to say. The governor of Penza province thought it was actively a good idea to get rid of townsperson administrations, for they did little and spent too much money doing it. He believed their property ought to be handed over to the towns, with the note, however, "that the income from these properties and monies should be used exclusively for the aid of the poorest members and families of the townsperson *soslovie*."[102] The report from Smolensk claimed that only in the provincial capital and one other town (Viaz'ma) did the society of townspeople still retain any collective sense of itself as a single unit. In all the small district towns, any such unity had long disappeared, which meant that removing townsperson administration was easily possible.[103]

The most forceful statement against townsperson societies came from Eniseisk. The author of that report described the local townspeople as undereducated and uninterested in their own administration. He believed that the answer to the problem was "the complete eradication of the *soslovie*-townsperson corporation and separate townsperson administrations in Eniseisk province," with all their functions (limited, he noted) to be handed over to town administrations.[104] Part of the problem in that region, a second report suggested, had to do with existing practices among townsperson societies. The second report recommended that even should the administrations not be eliminated, they should be told not to hold meetings in drinking establishments, because that practice had a "dangerous effect" on decision making. According to the report, some bringing cases before the townsperson society turned to those running the drinking establishments, who were known to have undue influence over the decisions taking place in their taverns.[105]

Others supported getting rid of the townsperson administration, but only under certain circumstances. The report from Kronshtadt noted that there was no particular problem with getting rid of the townsperson administration if the rolls of the townsperson society were cleaned up at the same time. According to the report, Kronshtadt was particularly plagued with absent members: although according to their official rolls, 16,000 men and 20,000 women belonged to the Kronshtadt townsperson society, only about 1,800 of them lived in Kronshtadt itself. That meant the city had extremely high levels of unpaid dues, which could be considered nothing but "hopeless."[106]

Several reports, however, reflected the conclusion that there was real value in townsperson administrations. The reports from both Tobolsk and Tomsk wrote about townsperson status and the townsperson *soslovie* with more appreciation than did many of their central Russian counterparts. The various charitable enterprises of townsperson societies in Tobolsk province, as well as their handling of other social issues, meant that they ought to be preserved, as town administrations would be soon overburdened by taking over responsibility for those spheres.[107] The report from Tomsk was even stronger. There, the townsperson society was described as the "foundational and dominant town element," with a real role to play. As a result, removing the townsperson administration would be "advisable" only if the entire *soslovie* was eliminated as well—something that the report did not support.[108] The report from Khar'kov came to a similar conclusion; only in small towns did it make sense to get rid of townsperson administrations; they served a real purpose in larger towns, one that town administrations would be hard-pressed to fulfill.[109] The Riazan' townsperson leadership likewise believed that it would be unwise to eliminate their administration because under its guidance the *soslovie* had prospered.[110]

As these last points suggest, these questions were tightly bound up with the very existence of *sosloviia*. A few authors took that question to heart, and chose to comment both on the concept of *soslovie* in general and on the *soslovie* of townspeople in particular. They also took very different approaches to the question. Some saw *sosloviia* as problematic relics of the past, now outmoded, outdated, and ready to be eliminated. In his report, the St. Petersburg governor, for one, went on at length about the history of the townsperson society from Muscovite times through Catherine's reforms to the present day. In particular, he noted that the practice of mandating the registry of people of "doubtful reputation" had harmed the very name townsperson, tying it with "disgust," making it a "derogatory" word in the minds of others.[111] Out of this, he believed that "the very name townsperson society, due to the obsolescence of its origin, and in consequence of the societal prejudice that has traditionally been tied to it" should be eliminated and replaced by a new name, one without those negative connotations.[112] In a different report, the Riazan' governor also suggested abolishing one particularly problematic aspect of townsperson authority: "it seems right to eliminate completely the right of societies over acceptance and freeing their members, and to introduce administrative naturalization." By this, he meant that any townsperson ought to be allowed to move and settle anywhere, with free right of registry.[113]

Very few of the correspondents actively supported *sosloviia* in their reports. One exception was the author of the Kostroma report. He did not believe that eliminating *soslovie* administration was wise because *sosloviia* themselves had meaning. As he put it, "in Russia the *soslovie* system still has a strong basis in the very conditions of life. To eliminate it, combining all *sosloviia* or the majority of them into a single united mass, this would contradict historically established conditions and the popular way of life."[114]

The kinds of attitudes expressed by the various provincial governors also echoed in the popular press during this period. News of these official debates spread, and journalists and political or social commentators weighed in on the question. As in the official reports, authors took sides both for and against preserving existing structures. One described the debate as simply the most recent of a long history of thinking about eliminating or reforming *sosloviia*. He came down on the side of preserving them, on the grounds, first, that town administration was hardly better than the existing *soslovie* administration; and second, that *sosloviia* had real, different "needs and demands, worries about which demand, therefore, specialized *sosloviia* institutions."[115] Others were more vehement in their support for *soslovie*; another anonymous contributor to the *Moscow News* went on at length about *sosloviia* as "living inheritances of earlier generations," necessary to preserve Russia's uniqueness. As he put it, eliding the three town *sosloviia* into one would be "in actuality a great step towards non-*soslovie*-ness in general, a non-*soslovie*-ness that would contradict both the historical bases of Russia, and the spirit of its people."[116]

Some contributors took stronger stances against *sosloviia* either in general, or against their current organization in principle. A. Samoilov contradicted those who believed that *sosloviia* were age-old concepts that ought to be preserved. He saw them as "artificial" entities, created by the state starting with Peter the Great, and at this point completely irrational. His only major argument with current proposals to combine all town *sosloviia* into one was that that would preserve the concept of *soslovie* itself.[117] Another commentator, this one for the journal *The Week*, did not go quite so far, but did argue that retaining the current *soslovie* was not sensible, given how far the statuses had come from their ideal origins.[118]

In addition to these public statements on the status of *sosloviia* within towns, others sent in comments directly to state ministries. In March 1898, the Ministry of Internal Affairs received a statement by an artisan from Mogilev, arguing for the elimination of the craft guilds and the institution of a general town *soslovie*. He argued that the craft societies, in particular, not only did not fulfill their supposed duty to promote artisanal crafts but in fact were detrimental to their development. As he put it, "they give no help to the artisan in his business, and equally do not bring any benefit to society or to the State." He claimed that supposed mastery of a craft went to those who could pay for attestations, not to those who were actually capable artisans. And, he noted, the artisan societies had failed at their duty to their members. In a postscript to his formal statement, he noted that "as far as the guardianship and help to artisans are concerned, [artisan] board[s] decidedly do not give it, at least I have nowhere happened to find it."[119]

Sosloviia and their administrations were not eliminated as a result of these debates. But the discussion confirms some of the particular issues that complicated *soslovie* governance and membership. *Sosloviia* did have real responsibilities to their members, though not all carried through on them. At the same time, the structures of these societies were not well integrated with larger town functions, nor, perhaps, with the larger societal goals of the Russian state. But because they were so embedded in the administrative structures of the empire, not to mention the individual identities of most subjects of that empire, getting rid of them was, to an extent, unimaginable. Even those commentators who had supported removing *soslovie* administration often still thought of the population as belonging to *soslovie*; they could not see beyond the end of the administration to the end of the label.

By the end of the imperial era, *sosloviia* membership still said something real about who a person was and where his or her place was in the larger social world. It still identified not only a social status but also a place of membership, a place that in principle still owed some responsibility to its members. The last law codes of the empire reiterated the power of *sosloviia* societies over their members, repeating the need for proper registration, for documentation of freedom and acceptance.[120] At the same time, many of its earlier associations had been slowly eliminated. Systems of taxation had changed, as had military recruitment, altering the ways that *sosloviia* stood for obligations. Village communes still had power at the time of emancipation, but the Stolypin reforms greatly reduced that power, even if they failed entirely to eliminate it.[121] Laws had also opened up economic activity in ways that reduced the power of *soslovie* over opportunities.

In the era of the dumas, some voices called for more dramatic measures to eliminate *sosloviia*. They saw the Great Reforms as having gone not far enough in eliminating the limits *sosloviia* placed on individuals. This was the version of *soslovie* described by P. Sokal'skii in his 1907 study of Russia's "middle *soslovie*," by which he meant middle class. For him, *soslovie* was "the closed world, that world, in which people were not moral individuals, but numbered organisms, provided with passports and entered into registers to fulfill their 'state burdens.' "[122] This was a specific view of *soslovie* not as rights-giving statuses but as duty-demanding ones.

Perhaps focusing most of all on this view of *soslovie*, others called for its abolition. One, I. N. Liubchetich, demanded

> the equality of all people before the law—the greatest idea, inspired by the orators of the first Russian State Duma, but... if a *soslovie* of citizens is not founded here, then this idea will turn into a cruel joke on the people belonging to the merchant, "townsperson" and "craft" societies, because the existence in Russia of the last two "societies" in particular is supported only by the system of urgent passports, holding people in quasi-*soslovie* dependence on these "societies," which long ago lost every meaning of the right to existence in life![123]

Again, the idea that *soslovie* was based on passports and registration, not on any real rights, was central to Liubchetich's argument.

But Liubchetich's text also shows the ways that even those with a strong urge to abolish *soslovie* were nonetheless caught up in a vision of society that was indebted to the concept. Liubchetich proposed an alternative to the current system: Russia needed "a *soslovie* of citizens, that is of simple citizens, not touching the existing privileged *sosloviia*."[124] And how would that great mass of simple citizens be recognized? By "a registry of citizens, for recording them in alphabetical order and for giving them documents."[125] Not only that, but in this vision of a future world, "not every town resident has the right to the high status of a citizen."[126] Instead, those unworthy of the status of citizen would be considered "former people" and sent to labor colonies for correction.[127] Not only does Liubchetich's vision eerily predict certain Soviet population policies, but it also displays the difficulty that faced reformers embedded in the *soslovie* system. Even a seemingly radical proposal to eliminate *sosloviia* in the name of equality before the law saw the larger social world as made up of separate parts, some with more rights than others.

The bigger problem in many ways was the fact that at this time *soslovie* was increasingly understood as meaning something much more significant. This was the era when the historian Kliuchevskii explicitly linked the concept of *soslovie* with the concept of social estates as they existed in the West, making the concept of *soslovie* seem at once more meaningful and more archaic. *Sosloviia* were more meaningful because they said something about the relationship of Russia to its Western counterparts. They were more archaic because, as Liubchetich was only the most recent to suggest, they were standing in the way of Russia's full modernization, binding people by documents to particular places and not allowing the full freedom that might make Russia stronger. And yet, even if they were archaic, they were essential to the functioning of Russian society. Liubchetich may have described *soslovie* societies as without "the right to existence in life," but, particularly in many of Russia's largest cities, they actually did continue to provide many services to their members. And, despite the inaccuracies of their image of Russian society, they still provided both individuals and the central state with a way to see each other. They were, therefore, at once obsolescent and vital, even as revolution began to rise.

6

The Evolution of Collective Responsibility

AS IT HAD for decades, in the mid-1890s the St. Petersburg society of townspeople was still regularly making decisions about its membership. By this point, the society had largely regularized certain forms of mobility. Usually, for example, both those wishing to leave the town and those wishing to enter it paid a set fee, and they found their registration confirmed by the board of the townsperson society. That regular practice seemed above all to emphasize that registry was a mere matter of paper, one that reflected the waning importance of *soslovie* as an everyday issue and instead its purely formal nature. Even so, the society still did both decide whether to accept new members and whether its existing members who wished to leave should be allowed to do so. And although at times the those decisions were as pro forma and regularized as the paperwork involved, the society still reserved the right to make decisions in its own best interests.

In the cases of the townsmen Peter Ivanov and Mikhail Vasil'ev, the society did just that, by seeking to make responsible decisions for the health of the society. At the same time, those decisions show well the ways that *sosloviia* were still living institutions with real meaning—but with a meaning that had changed since the earlier parts of the century. Ivanov, aged forty-four when his case came to the attention of the society in 1892, had entered the society as a ward of the Imperial Foundling Home. Since then, he had fallen into arrears by 28 rubles. Inquiry showed that he "turned out not to be in a position to pay, he has no property, and lives in most extreme poverty." Contrary to normal practice, the board decided that it would grant Peter Ivanov his freedom without demanding repayment of those arrears. The case of another former ward, Mikhail Vasil'ev, who wished to leave the ranks of townspeople to become legally a peasant, helps explain the earlier decision, as well. Vasil'ev had a large family, and together they were in arrears by 100 rubles. The board took into account not only the size of the family but also the fact that "when Vasil'ev delivered his petition to the Board, he looked ill, and was also dressed in rags." Again, it decided to free him without repayment, and without paying the normal fee required for such movement. This time, however, the board explained its reasoning: the decision was made "in view of the poverty of Vasil'ev and the large size of his family, which might easily, in the case of Vasil'ev's death, demand from the St. Petersburg society of townspeople aid and charity."[1]

Soslovie membership had evolved by the late imperial era from something based primarily in individual obligation to the society, to something based primarily in the society's obligation to its members. *Soslovie* societies had long worried that by either releasing or accepting members, the society itself might end up harmed. In the eighteenth and early nineteenth centuries, that harm could come from losing an army recruit, from losing a taxpayer, or from gaining a troublemaker. The focus of concern began to shift in the latter part of the nineteenth century, however, as the Great Reforms, and particularly the effect they had on the communal responsibilities of towns and village societies, helped create a new way of thinking about membership in a given *soslovie*. Societies themselves began to worry more about the services they owed to their members, now seeing the concept of membership as one based in the welfare of their members rather than in collective duty. This shift also created new incentives for individuals seeking to change their *soslovie* membership, as some towns, in particular, had something real to offer their members.

This change in the nature of the relationship between *soslovie* societies and their members also had an effect on the relationship between those societies and the central imperial state. In essence, they caused an old battle between center and periphery to gain new life. The Great Reforms shifted the basis of what *soslovie* membership meant by altering the kinds of obligations and opportunities that went along with such membership. This fact changed but did not end both the desire of societies to control their membership and the desire of the imperial state to ensure that every one of its subjects had a formal place within its social structure. This struggle had elements both theoretical, essentially building on the ways that reform efforts had questioned *sosloviia* in the abstract, and practical, as changes to the systems of taxation and military service altered the basis on which *sosloviia* functioned. But it also created new tensions with the central imperial state, which increasingly saw *soslovie* societies as merely a basis for organizing society, as agents of order, while those same societies saw themselves as something much more necessary to the health of their members, and perhaps of the greater society, as well.

SOCIETIES AND COLLECTIVE RESPONSIBILITY

Already by the era of the Great Reforms, both law and practice had well established the fact that *soslovie* societies were not simply conduits for taxes and duties sent from individuals to the central state, but also as suppliers of services of various kinds to their members. Through the first decades of the nineteenth century, the responsibilities of local societies to supply services for their members had become more fully enshrined in law, and by the publication of the 1857 edition of the *Digest of the Laws*, it was clear that these responsibilities were significant. They ranged from relatively straightforward tasks like providing members with documents to more complicated tasks like ensuring public order in part by providing aid to the impoverished or ill.[2] Furthermore, increasing social mobility in the second half of the nineteenth century, something that in particular brought large numbers of peasants into towns, also threw local societies' responsibilities into sharper relief. Those peasant masses were associated with growing poverty, and thus with a growing need for charity, as well as a need to identify those who had a right to charity.[3]

During the era of the Great Reforms, central discussions of those reforms had recognized the idea that *soslovie* societies were both providers of services and responsible for aspects of public order, but they failed to grapple with what that meant in terms of practice. Despite the fact that the Ministry of Internal Affairs had largely focused on more broadly town-based, as opposed to *soslovie*-based, governance as it proposed and refined the reform of town administration, it nonetheless did recognize that *soslovie* organizations played a significant role in the lives of individuals Russians. As the ministry put it, *soslovie* societies were themselves responsible for "the well-being of the *soslovie*" via "measures to protect members of the *soslovie* in emergencies, to give aid to poor members of the *soslovie*, to found charitable organizations and so forth."[4] These functions, however, were not given any new footing in the context of the town reform, leaving *soslovie* societies in an uncertain place as to their specific role.

Moreover, at least according to one late imperial bureaucrat, the ministry's description understated the role played by town *soslovie* societies in the lives of their members—and, furthermore, failed to understand how completely that role had changed over the course of the nineteenth century. Evgenii Blumenbakh was a bureaucrat of the Riga Tax Commission, an institution unique to the Baltics that served essentially as a coordinating body over *soslovie* societies in the town, who eventually wrote two books on *sosloviia* and their governance. Blumenbakh described a significant change in the function of *soslovie* institutions like the Tax Commission over the course of the nineteenth century. When the commission was founded by Catherine the Great, as part of a general regularization of the administration of Riga in line with Russian procedures, it was meant, he wrote, "to deal with the then existing state soul tax." By the end of the nineteenth century, however, Blumenbakh argued that the commission—and town societies more generally—functioned only to collect local taxes and was "in the service of the care of the poor and the healing of the sick."[5]

To Blumenbakh, this was central to understanding not just the general role of *soslovie* institutions but also the specific way that that role was based on a still powerful idea of membership. The responsibilities of *soslovie* societies had shifted from facing outward—from acting as a conduit for the payment of the soul tax to the center—to facing inward, dealing with local taxes and providing services. But these last two issues were tightly linked. As Blumenbakh wrote in his 1899 book on town societies in Russia, "only the tax-paying [*podatnoe*] population… may take advantage of the protection of the town society in case of poverty, infirmity, or illness, because by paying local taxes they gain the right to help from the society."[6] And, furthermore, only those formally registered in the town—its own townspeople and artisans—had the obligation to pay local taxes, and thus were able to call on the town society to help them in their turn. Specific *soslovie* identities, in other words, had real meaning even in the post-Reform, nominally all-*soslovie* world.

The shift described by Blumenbakh had developed slowly over the course of the nineteenth century. Through the 1840s, laws regulating different kinds of hospitals—military and civil ones—laid out rules for payment based on the Offices of Public Care (*Prikazy obshchestvennogo prizreniia*) that Catherine the Great had established as part of her provincial reform of 1775. These boards were responsible for all sorts of public services, from establishing schools, to giving loans, to running hospitals around the empire. Those who could pay for their own medical care did so—laws set out rules for who ought to pay and those who could not. Medical costs for civilians who found themselves in military hospitals and those who were unable to pay for their own treatment there were to be carried by the Board of Social Welfare of the province in which those civilians were registered.[7]

Increasingly, however, laws made it clear that the ultimate responsibility for payment rested with local societies—that they were responsible for the care of their indigent members. A law of 1837 on provincial administration set out a clear rule for public aid. Offices of Public Care were responsible for the medical care and sustenance of those "not having the means for their own keep and treatment, [if they] do not belong to owners or to societies." However, "those belonging to landlords or to town and village societies should also be taken into the care of Public institutions, but with a collection of expenses incurred in consequence from those societies or those landlords."[8] Combined with other laws, this turned into a regular practice by which local authorities had responsibility for medical and other public care costs for those registered as part of their societies.[9] This practice continued even after the duties of the Offices of Public Care were taken over by new provincial *Zemstvo* institutions during the Great Reforms. Then, for example, hospitals run by the provincial administration could collect money from town societies even within their provinces because, as one writer put it, "the town is not a unit of the province… it should worry about the health of its citizens itself."[10] This policy—that care was owed by the place of registry, not residence—continued until the onset of the First World War, when a commission questioned the practice but failed to alter it.[11]

These laws were not simply unfulfilled principles. Some societies found themselves called to account for sometimes significant sums on behalf of their members, and these sums seem to have increased dramatically in the post-Reform era. This was not true everywhere. In 1870, Moscow's society of townspeople estimated it would need to send 458 rubles, 30 kopeks off to other places to pay hospital bills for its members; in reality, it sent out 105 rubles, 30 kopeks, a relatively paltry sum given the size of the population.[12] But others faced much steeper bills. Between 1869 and 1884, the Kaluga society of townspeople ran up unpaid hospital bills of 18,906 rubles, 9 ½ kopeks; and in only seven years, the Tula townspeople and craft societies found themselves facing hospital arrears of 23,617 rubles, 8 ½ kopeks.[13] The wide range likely reflects the fact that provincial towns saw people leave, while Moscow attracted them.

The townsperson society of Kronshtadt was even harder hit by medical costs for its members. Kronshtadt's townsperson society was hardly typical; according to some accounts, its numbers had swelled in the post-emancipation era, as former serfs who wished to register close to St. Petersburg for easy access to the capital swarmed the city.[14] In 1881, a special decision by the State Council had even allowed the Kronshtadt town duma to collect a special hospital fee from all citizens and residents of the city at the rate of one ruble per half year per person. All those who paid the fee would, according to the decision, receive free medical care in the town's Naval Hospital.[15] Despite such attempts to bolster the town's finances, medical fees remained a persistent problem, particularly for the townspeople society. According to the society's account books from the late 1880s and early 1890s, it had outstanding medical bills that it was steadily making payments on, but that still amounted to 165,818 rubles, 84 ¾ kopeks in 1884. On top of these outstanding bills, each year the society sent off money to hospitals around the empire to pay the debts of its members. The detail in the records is incredible—they tell us, for example, that in 1883 the townsperson society sent 59 rubles, 57 kopeks to Saratov for the treatment of two townspeople, Aleksei Evgrafov and Pelageia Stepanova, in a provincial hospital; or that in 1888 it sent 50 rubles, 46 kopeks to Tomsk on behalf of its member Nataliia Fedeeva. These were just a few of those on whose behalf the society sent off money—the total sums were significant.[16]

Aside from the state-run hospitals or institutions of public care to which they might owe money, some local town societies established their own charitable institutions devoted to the welfare of their members.[17] According to a history of its charitable institutions, the Moscow townsperson society had not thought of opening its own institution until the 1830s, believing that "the aged and sick townspeople with no refuge" could find homes in other almshouses around the city. But by the 1830s, the townspeople in these other institutions numbered around 1,000 individuals, and still there were enough poverty-stricken townspeople outside their bounds to create public worry. By the end of the decade the society had rented part of the building of a former hospital to set up its own almshouse. Initially, yearly costs of around 10,000 paper rubles allowed for the housing and care of around 150 residents. Eventually, the society bought its own property, built new buildings, hired medical personnel, and housed more and more residents. By 1866, 994 impoverished, aged, or ill townspeople lived in the almshouse (271 men, 693 women, and 30 under-aged orphans), at a cost to the society of around 20 rubles per person per year. Even this great expansion failed to meet the needs of Moscow's poor, however. Already the almshouse was filled beyond capacity—there were only beds for

820 residents. And at the same time, more than 1,000 other townspeople were housed in other charitable institutions around the town.[18]

In St. Petersburg, the townsperson society faced similar issues. It too eventually ran multiple charitable institutions for its own members, including a House for the Care of Elderly and Infirm Citizens of the St. Petersburg Townsperson Society and a House for the Care of Poor Children of the St. Petersburg Townsperson Society, both founded in the 1870s.[19] In 1884, the society took over the management of another public almshouse in order to ensure more resources for its members. Like the Moscow society, however, the Petersburg townsperson society was also immediately faced with the fact that the needs of the city's poor far outpaced the resources of the almshouse: one sign was that it had far too many applicants for beds. In 1885, only 341 of 613 applicants were accepted; the following year, only 179 of 820 could enter.[20]

Because these public care institutions were expensive (and because there were so many applicants for beds), societies often restricted those who could enter them.[21] Virtually all were open only to members of the societies, usually townsperson, that ran them.[22] The St. Petersburg House for the Care of Elderly and Infirm Citizens allowed private individuals to pay to place dependents in the house, but only if there were vacancies, if the patient was a member of the townsperson society, and if they paid 70 rubles a year, in advance. If the patient "left" the house, the entire sum would stay "for the use of the institution."[23] Some societies placed additional restrictions on entrance. The Kazan' townsperson society required all those asking to enter its almshouse to present a request along with testimony from "no less than three trustworthy individuals, known to the townsperson society, that the petitioner truly cannot provide for himself and does not have relatives or other people required and able to give him the means for life."[24]

These various kinds of aid could place significant financial burdens on societies. In 1900, the Riga Tax Commission submitted reports on the condition of the *soslovie* societies of the town to the Lifland governor. Blumenbakh, the local bureaucrat and author, was involved in compiling the statistics. Riga had an official population (that is, of registered formal residents of the town) of 103,624 men and women. In the previous five years, 3,902 new members had joined the society with the society's acceptance, and 466 had joined without formal acceptance. That meant that Riga's town population had increased by about 4.4 percent through new members in the last half decade. From this population, the society collected yearly local taxes amounting to an average of 1,193,003 rubles, 77 kopeks over the past five years.[25] Although that comes out to an average of 11 and a half rubles per person a year, because local taxes were levied only on men (something of which Blumenbakh did not approve),[26] the actual yearly tax burden per taxpayer was nearly 30 rubles.

Out of these funds, the town found itself responsible for significant monetary outlays in the interest of public aid. As the report noted, "because the Riga society does not run any such establishments or hospitals [of its own], and all such establishments [it once ran] were transferred [to the jurisdiction of] the Town Council, then it must compensate the Council for its expenses in the care and healing of the members of the society."[27] Furthermore, the society could find itself with additional expenses for those of its members living outside Riga: "medical expenses, demanded for care in the hospitals of other cities, are reimbursed with the submission of receipts."[28] Practically, this meant that the Riga town society had to pay for its members' residence in the various "charitable"—but not free—institutions of the town. These included the Nikolaev and Russian Poor Houses, the Refuge for the Incurably Sick, several orphanages, and a Refuge for the Poor. According to the commission's report, over the past five years around 1,300 members of the society were resident in one of the institutions each year. And the costs associated with such residency were high. In 1899 alone, the society paid out 77,280 rubles, 76 kopeks to these institutions.[29] Elsewhere, Blumenbakh estimated that the entire sum paid by the society for various kinds of public aid was even higher: he suggested a figure of around 200,000 rubles per year.[30] Given the yearly tax revenue, that amounted to nearly 17 percent of the yearly income of the society.

The question of these sorts of responsibilities was discussed in the 1896 Ministry of Internal Affairs inquiry into the status of town societies. It requested information that directly addressed some of the concerns often expressed by townsperson and other *soslovie* societies about their responsibilities to their members. In particular, governors were asked to report on charitable institutions built by different societies, and about the funds that many spent on those causes. The reports therefore include extensive listings of the various charitable institutions founded by different societies, or of the monies paid out by them for health care or other charitable goals.[31] Over and over again, the reports mention payments for medical care as either a particular focus of public aid or as a particular worry of individual, usually townsperson, societies.[32]

The responses to the inquiry also showed well that these obligations were now understood as a version of the ideal of collective responsibility, or *krugovaia poruka*, that had for so long been tied to the payment of taxes. The ministry posed a specific question about collective responsibility, asking governors to report on whether town *soslovie* societies still used the method to ensure duties were paid. Few reported that it was still in use as a mechanism to collect taxes, but in a number of towns there was some sort of collective responsibility for one kind of payment: for public aid, and particularly for payments for medical care. In Sterlitomak (Ufa province), collective responsibility was described as being still practiced "for paying hospital bills for insolvent townspeople and outstanding public dues for townspeople who have turned out to be unable to work."[33] Elsewhere, special collections to pay off hospital debts or to care for the poor and indigent were also linked to the concept of collective responsibility.[34] This, now, was a more relevant meaning of the term.

Lurking within these discussions of public care were serious concerns over the idea of mobility and "new" members, and of the responsibility of *soslovie* societies toward them. There was, for example, significant variation in the ways official statutes governing *soslovie* charitable institutions set up policies regarding how long individuals had to have been members of the local townsperson (or other) society in order to gain access to services. Some almshouses were restricted to those members of a given society who had been resident for a certain amount of time.[35] The Moscow Craft Society, for example, opened its almshouse only to those who had been members of the society for at least five years.[36] But others were more open. The almshouse of the Moscow Townsperson Society was open to all members of the society, "without any limit on the time of their registration into the Society; because each member newly accepted by the Society is already both a participant in paying estate dues, and also in using estate resources."[37] This broad acceptance, however, was not as apparent in some of the specific issues that arose between local societies and central administrators over the last decades of the nineteenth century. Instead, conflict became the norm, with individuals seeking aid, or even just a legal place, caught in between them.

SOCIETIES AND BELONGING IN THE LATE NINETEENTH CENTURY

Given the changes that the Great Reforms brought to *sosloviia* and *soslovie* societies, the concept of membership, and therefore of control of membership, took on new dimensions in the late imperial era. Societies did not totally discount questions of taxes, given that local taxes were still an issue even after the abolition of the soul tax. Now, however, the services owed by societies to their members became a major focus of concern. In some ways, villages were least touched by these concerns, although they faced a different issue: access to land. In towns, however, worry over services came to dominate the concerns of local *soslovie* societies, at the same time that the central state continued to see *soslovie* purely in terms of taxation and control.

Village communes gained if anything additional authority over their members in the post-emancipation countryside. Where once many of them were themselves subject to the authority of individual serf-owners, the newly unified status of peasant was governed by communal authorities granted continued and increasing roles in the lives of their members. The rationale behind this expanded role for the commune was the "alleged civic immaturity of former serfs" who required an overarching authority.[38] The result, however was continued control over membership, and therefore over mobility, on the part of the commune.

For the most part, as in earlier eras, the village was primarily a place of exodus, as peasants left the village for new lives in towns. A law of 1849 had even aimed to "ease the movement of state peasants into town *soslovie*," and the emancipation served as a short-term encouragement of movement.[39] But, as in earlier eras, there was also a steady, and perhaps even increasing, trickle of townspeople into villages, wishing to change their status from townsperson (or merchant or, in a few very surprising cases, noble) to peasant. For the most part, entrance into village societies in the post-emancipation era followed practices set earlier for entrance into the state peasant village. Those rules had given peasant villages slightly more control over their membership than townsperson societies had: if a village society did not have land to allot to new members, it could refuse them.

A series of decisions from shortly before emancipation had slightly eased the process of entering village societies—of becoming, legally, a peasant. First, the Senate decided that there was a limit to the right of refusal that had been given to village societies. If a provincial treasury could see that a given village had land in excess of the needs of its current population—in other words, that it was neither land poor nor unable to give new members a sufficient allotment—it was allowed to register those with the freedom to choose a way of life without that village society's consent.[40] Then, in the 1850s, several cases addressed who was allowed to become a peasant. An 1853 decision set out rules for how serfs might be freed to become state peasants, a distinction soon to be made moot, but then a sign of increasing access to the status of peasant.[41]

That year, too, the Ministry of Internal Affairs responded to a query from the Ministry of Finance over yet another permutation: should merchants' relatives (in this case, a nephew) be allowed to register as state peasants? The Kaluga Provincial Treasury believed it was not possible, based on an 1847 circular from the Ministry of Finance that stated that merchants' relatives were not to be registered as townspeople in other towns—it interpreted the circular as restricting mobility outside the town of origin. The Tula Provincial Administration and Tula Provincial Treasury, however, believed that that circular was did not apply for the obvious reason that townspeople were not state peasants. The Ministry of State Domains noted that in the specific case that brought up the question, the state peasant village was eager to accept the merchant's nephew and therefore believed that he ought to be allowed to make the change. The Ministry of Internal Affairs agreed.[42]

Finally, in 1859, a decision of the State Council allowed for greater mobility both by opening up movement into the peasantry to another group and by removing a long-standing restriction on such movement. The issue of the new group came from cases like that of the Riazan' townsman Ivan Ozeritskii, who had petitioned to join a state peasant society. His case had been refused by the Riazan' Provincial Treasury Department on the grounds that "the right of registry in the free agricultural condition… may only be used by townspeople from district towns and settlements, while townspeople from provincial towns are not allowed" to do so.[43] The State Council used clever logic to avoid having to made a radical change: "as every provincial capital is at the same time a district town, then by the literal meaning of [several laws]… the permission for townspeople from district towns to register in the status of a rural inhabitant is extended in equal measure to townspeople of the capitals and provincial capitals."

That decision was an exercise in interpretation, but at the same time, the State Council also decided to remove another, more significant legal restriction on mobility from town to country. The laws then in force, which dated back to the very beginning of the century, noted that any townsperson who himself did not already in engage in agriculture, and furthermore whose father had not engaged in agriculture, was not to be allowed to leave town status. In other words, the laws limited the right to become peasants to those who were demonstratively already engaging in activities appropriate to that status. The State Council now "found, that this restriction is most burdensome for those town inhabitants who would like to occupy themselves with farming," and removed it.[44] That meant that anyone who wished to become an agriculturist would be allowed to do so, even if it meant a significant shift in their own livelihood.

With the Great Reforms also came other changes to village life that affected the conception of membership in a society. In late 1869, the State Council released new guidance for creating and maintaining tax lists. The last of the Petrine census revisions had been carried out in 1857; after that, new lists had to be maintained, now called *okladnye listy*. The 1869 law focused on how these new lists would be drawn up in villages. The world it described, however, was one rather more complicated than might be expected. It made provisions for cases in which a single society (*obshchestvo*) contained multiple villages, and also for cases in which a single village contained multiple societies.[45] This was remnant of the age of serfdom, when residents of a single village might belong to multiple owners, or when a single owner might have viewed the residents of multiple nearby villages as belonging to a single estate.

In addition, the laws described two other variations that veered more sharply from prior practices. Small villages—those with fewer than forty male souls—would now no longer be subject to collective responsibility when it came to paying taxes. And even in larger villages, collective responsibility might not be put in place if that was already the practice. The law here presaged the Stolypin reforms: "peasants having all of the lands of their allotment under their separate command, cannot be attracted to collective responsibility in the proper fulfillment of state taxes and duties for other peasants, even if they belong to the same society or village."[46] Several years later, the State Council again addressed the idea of villages without collective responsibility. In this case, it agreed that in such villages, families no longer needed to pay taxes for those who had left their family, those who were in the military, or those unable to work.[47]

Around this same time, another inquiry came to the Ministry of Internal Affairs, again raising the questions about the parameters of membership in a village society. The question came from Ufa, where the post-emancipation settlement had created a confusing mixture of peoples. Around the province, a number of temporarily obligated peasants had registered as townspeople, but they were still living in the midst of peasant settlements, engaging in agriculture by farming on lands that had been allotted to serf-owners in the division of lands following emancipation.[48] The reports from Ufa were unclear as to what had led to this state of affairs, but most likely these were individuals who had taken the "beggar's allotment" in order to separate from the society, but who had purchased or were renting lands from the former serf-owner in order to farm on their own.

At issue was a basic question of membership: did the fact that these townspeople were living as and among peasants make them part of the village society, whatever their actual current registration? They were refusing to acknowledge any village authority, refusing to pay local taxes to keep up the township administration. And they even refused to contribute to the local priests' salaries and upkeep. Local authorities were asking that, because in their everyday life they "actually make up a single society with the peasants," they be placed under the authority of local peasant administration.[49] The Economic Department of the ministry agreed that this seemed a fair decision, that such legal townsmen ought to be subject to local authority.[50]

In other ways, despite the fact that emancipation brought such a radical change to Russia's social structures, the concerns of village societies over questions of mobility remained largely unchanged. For one, they continued to be concerned about questions of order, and because many new legal peasants were already engaged in agriculture, they could quite well be known as troublemakers. The peasants of Kucheeva, a village in Ufa province, were particularly harsh in their condemnation of the behavior of Usmangalii Shamsutdinov when they refused him entrance into their society. Shamsutdinov had originally been a member of the community, who left to join the Menzelensk merchantry around 1860 and who in 1875 petitioned to return to his peasant origins. But the peasants refused him, in no uncertain terms: "personally Usmangalii Shamsutdinov is a person of not entirely salutary behavior; a week rarely passes, when we the village leaders are not bothered and called to the assembly, and no sooner do we get there than the reason for the problem turns out to be no one other than Shamsutdinov, or a member of his family, involved in fights and arguments."[51] In another case, a village society refused to take back one of its former members after he returned from prison on the grounds that he had been imprisoned.[52] These were cases in which local societies took advantage of the fact that they knew their members, and their potential members as well.

Villages also continued to face an old problem: there was not necessarily enough land to supply new members with proper allotments. Thus, some petitioners who sought to leave town estates to join peasant villages found their applications stymied by a sheer lack of land. In 1876, the peasants of a village in Saratov district agreed to accept the townsman Ivan Ivanov into their society, but refused to grant him "the right to use a land portion." Because of this, the Saratov Treasury found the agreement invalid, a decision with which the Ministry of Internal Affairs agreed.[53] It is unclear why the village peasants wished to accept Ivanov—perhaps he was a blacksmith or otherwise engaged in a craft useful to village life—but their desires in this case were trumped by a basic fact of geography.

Elsewhere, access to land could well stymie efforts to settle firmly in new rural societies. According to one anonymous worker, his father had tried to enter into a peasant society in Krasnoufimsk district, Perm province, in the early 1870s. However, his petition to enter (with his four sons), failed because, as the peasant commune explained, there was not enough land for such a large family.[54] Similar sentiments greeted other petitioners, even in such distant places where one would normally assume there to be plenty of land. In 1875, peasants in Ufa Province refused to accept a member in part because "there is not nearly enough good land in our village."[55] And despite an 1889 law

that eased resettlement into Siberia, those who made the trip could easily find themselves not accepted by a village there, and as a result living outside the margins of official
society.[56]

A rather different case arose in 1880, when the Ivanovo-Voznesensk townsman
Porfirii Babikov petitioned to leave the town in order to enter the peasant community
of a nearby village. In 1876, the Ivanovo-Voznesensk townsperson society had granted
Babikov release—but not a release for him alone. Instead, the freedom document specified that it released Babikov along with his dead father and brother. This conflicted with
his acceptance agreement from the village because, given that he alone would be moving
to the village, the peasants had accepted him alone. But this was not acceptable to the
Ivanovo-Voznesensk townspeople. Despite Babikov's assurances that he would continue
to pay dues for his dead relatives, the townsperson society refused to honor anything but
a full use of its freedom agreement.[57] In other words, the Ivanovo-Voznesensk townspeople saw Babikov's petition as a way to remove two dead souls from their tax rolls.

At the same time, Babikov's case brought up one major change created in the new
post-emancipation rural world. The Ministry of Finance, called in to comment on
Babikov's case, described the change: if Babikov successfully purchased land in the village, then according to the Laws on Peasants, he "would have the total right to register
in the society of peasants without their consent."[58] Land could trump the desires of villagers. Even here, though, a basic idea appeared. Land was central to the definition of a
peasant—as in the case of the Ufa townspeople, use of land was the basis of peasant life.
It represented the supposed unity of economic and social status of the peasantry, and as
such, it made irrelevant the desires of individual communities.

Although the concerns of villages remained largely the same after the Great Reforms,
towns were faced with more significant changes. Moreover, town *soslovie* societies felt
an increasing estrangement from the ideals expressed by laws and bureaucrats from St.
Petersburg. As town societies weighed questions of membership and mobility, public
aid began to come more and more to the forefront of their calculations. Furthermore,
this was a particular problem when it came to issues of mobility. One mid-century commentator on the state of Moscow's *soslovie* societies, M. P. Shchepkin, described this in
stark detail. He noted the particular set of problems that faced townsperson societies: as
he put it, "many expenses, totally insufficient income, and the *soslovie* itself taken as a
whole cannot boast either of its welfare or of its improving position." He also located the
particular problem that faced the society with the permeability of its boundaries: "the
constantly shifting, changing mass, which now constantly accepts new members from
the lower, formerly enserfed population... now releases others, always the stronger and
healthier members, who have sought space for themselves in the merchantry, which, in
its turn, returned [to the society of townspeople] its insolvent members."[59] Mobility, in
other words, particularly challenged *sosloviia*.

In an effort to deal with this problem, some town societies began demanding proof
that new members would not be a drain on their civic resources. In several cases in the

1890s and early 1900s, the Riga Deputies' Meeting considered placing limits on accepting new members into the taxpaying population. In 1893, it suggested that potential new members who were more than forty years old had to possess capital, property, or other security that proved they would be able to fulfill their duties; to show medical evidence that they were healthy and capable of work; and to show some sort of attestation of their moral worth.[60] A decade later, it considered another proposal. Factory workers should not be allowed to register in the society; other workers should have to prove they earned a salary of at least 300 rubles; all new entrants into the society of townspeople had to prove they had finished at least the first class at the district school, or at a comparable school; and no unmarried and impoverished women should be allowed to register at all.[61] The society was, in essence, declaring itself out of bounds for most of the migrants flooding into such cities in this period of rapid industrialization.

Nor were these mere proposals. At the end of the nineteenth century, the Riga Tax Commission actually did collect many documents as it decided the cases of those seeking entrance. These included things like birth, marriage, or baptismal certificates that proved who people were and that they had the right to act on their own behalf; passports; police certificates proving residency; receipts that petitioners had paid their entrance fees (20 rubles in 1898); and documents proving that petitioners did not "belong to any dangerous sects." In some cases, too, petitioners provided evidence that they were healthy, as in a signed, stamped, and sealed doctor's note giving "evidence of the fact that Andreas Tsuker, his wife Ol'ga Tsuker, and their five-year-old son Al'fons, from external examination seem to me to be completely healthy and without any kind of organic problems."[62]

Similarly, when the St. Petersburg townsperson society started to use printed forms for guarantees of good behavior, it also included phrases about public aid as part of the promises made when individuals were accepted into the society. The text ran:

> We, the undersigned, this do aver, that [name] who has expressed a desire to register in the St. Petersburg society of townspeople, has good behavior and, with registry into the society will not demand aid from it, or care in either the St. Petersburg townsperson or other almshouses open only to St. Petersburg townspeople, and will pay all future social/local dues.[63]

Again, the townsperson society was attempting to avoid undue expenditures for new members, or to avoid those seeking entrance to the society purely out of a desire for public aid.

Even so, some new members clearly did intend to make use of public services—and the society seems to have made them pay for the privilege. At the turn of the century, some individuals petitioning to enter the St. Petersburg society of townspeople had to submit a fee with their application. Taxpaying men paid 25 rubles, explicitly as guarantee for the first years of their tax burden, but women had no such fees levied on them. However, in 1898, the four oldest women to petition to join the society of townspeople, all aged fifty or higher, submitted sums of anywhere from 50 to 200 rubles with their applications. In one case, Matrena Kalinina, aged eighty-four, submitted 50 rubles "for use in the community almshouse." But seventy-six-year-old Anna Akulova not only gave 200 rubles for the almshouse but specifically asked that "when I am registered in the Society place me in the St. Petersburg Townsperson Almshouse."[64] In these cases, petitioners simply purchased access to the services provided by the society.

The standard fees demanded of St. Petersburg's petitioners were one example of a tactic other town societies began to use regularly. Around the middle of the nineteenth century, town societies started to demand other kinds of financial guarantees from new members, sometimes explicitly linked to issues of public aid. The fees varied. In the Baltic provinces, petitioners to enter town societies were required to put up money as guarantee of their payment of future dues. But the various cities of the Baltic region demanded different amounts, leading to significant discontent on the part of petitioners. Some of them turned to the governor of the region with complaints about the "onerous guarantees" required of them. In 1866, the governor turned to the Senate for clarification of official policy. He reported that the amount of guarantee demanded by cities in the Baltic ranged widely. The city of Revel' (Tallinn) "even from women demands the presentation of a guarantee of from 15 to 25 rubles);" in Lifland province, towns demanded 42 rubles as guarantee for those entering the worker lists, and 70 rubles for those entering the society of townspeople; and in neighboring Kurliand province, the guarantee never exceeded 30 rubles.[65]

These fees, however, also began to bring towns into conflict with other parts of the state apparatus. After receiving the report, the Senate decided that town societies had been exceeding their authority; guarantees had been allowed by Senate ukase in 1858, but were not to exceed 30 rubles. But it also noted that a major change had come in when an ukase of 1863 abolished the soul tax in towns, replacing it with a property tax. In such a situation, did it make sense to continue to allow guarantees from individuals who would no longer be paying the communally based soul tax? The Senate concluded that it did not. It argued that the guarantees were only appropriate for individuals who owed "personal" taxes—and neither the property tax nor the kinds of local taxes based on property, trade, or craft that funded town societies and their works counted.[66]

Clearly, however, some town societies quietly continued to collect fees from those entering their ranks, a fact that sometimes brought them to the attention of higher authorities. In 1879, the Enisei Treasury Department questioned the practices of the Krasnoyarsk townsperson society. The townspeople had been demanding a fee of 30 rubles per person as a "guarantee for the payment of taxes and dues"; it even demanded such a fee from women seeking to enter the townsperson society with their sons, including those who had been born after the last (10th) revision. The treasury particularly questioned this last policy, in large part because "sons born after the last revision do not have to pay dues until the new revision," which meant that these charges were simply extortive, not guarantees of anything.[67] A half decade later, the Vyshnii Volochek townsperson society also decided to start demanding "donations" from those seeking to enter its numbers, a fact that came to the attention of the ministries when a peasant soldier's widow, Mariia Fedorova Saimonova, complained that they had refused her petition. These sums were controversial and restricted by law. In Saimonova's case, however, the fact that the Vyshnii Volochek townspeople were levying one was not enough for the ministries to intervene on her behalf. Instead, they noted, all cases of problems with townsperson societies and their actions rested with provincial administrations.[68]

At times, townsperson societies tried to institute special collections from populations they deemed particularly likely to need future public aid. In 1885, the St. Petersburg townsperson board made a proposal to the St. Petersburg mayor (*gradonachal'nik*) that they be allowed to collect a one-time fee of 5 to 10 rubles from every woman entering the local society of townspeople. They saw this as a way to find "sources to increase the income of the society's coffers, especially to cover the yearly expenses of keeping up the charitable organizations of the townsperson society." The mayor was leery of this proposal, in part because it posed far too great a burden for entering women and also because St. Petersburg, he claimed, was awash with charitable institutions that removed much of this possible burden from the society itself.[69]

Perhaps because the practice of collecting fees as guarantees was widespread, in the 1890s it was recognized as a legitimate practice by the State Council. In April 1893, the State Council released an opinion paper "On the confirmation of the decisions of townsperson societies regarding the collection of monetary fees from individuals, entering into those societies by their own desire." It clarified that these were to be fees "guaranteeing punctual payment of local dues," and decided that such fees should be allowed.[70] Once the State Council released this opinion, local societies were expected to decide on their rates. In one case, the Lifland Provincial Governor wrote to the Riga Tax Commission (and presumably to other towns, as well), asking it to meet and make a formal proposal for the governor's approval. When the Riga society met, it recommended that all petitioners—that is, both men and women—should be subject to the same levy. Those entering the society of townspeople should pay 30 rubles, the craft societies 25 rubles, and both the servants' and workers' ranks 20 rubles. Furthermore, it suggested that these monies should be placed in a single fund and used for certain expenses: "in case of general emergencies, like epidemics or flooding, if members of the Riga society are victims of such circumstances," to pay for arrears, and, from the interest income only, to pay regular expenses of the society.[71] The proposal apparently passed, and a separate account for these monies was set up; by December 1914, it held 96,425 rubles in a savings account and an additional 1,177 rubles, 96 kopeks on hand, in petty cash.[72]

Fees demanded of petitioners to enter societies came to be seen as legitimate sources of insurance and income, but some town societies went further and began to make other exactions in the name of public aid. Already in the 1850s, petitioners seeking to leave the St. Petersburg craft society were encouraged to make "donations" (of unspecified but "significant" amount) to the society's almshouse.[73] A bit later, the St. Petersburg townsperson society levied a special fee on "single townswomen living separately from their male relatives" of 60 kopeks per each adult woman; they had special permission from the Minister of Internal Affairs to levy such an unusual (i.e., on women, usually tax-exempt) fee in the name of the public good.[74]

These sorts of fees remained controversial, even as administrators realized the real financial problems arising in many communities. In 1873, authorities in Tver' were told that they could not levy extra fees on passports, even to help pay medical fees, on the grounds that such fees would "increase the already existing inconvenience of the passport system."[75] In 1908, the Vereia townsman Vasilii Nazarov petitioned to leave the society of townspeople and enter the peasant society of the village in which he lived. As he put it in a petition to the Moscow governor, not only did he have property there but his father had originally been a peasant in the village (Timofeevo) before exiting into the Vereia society of townspeople. Nazarov found himself wanting not only to live there but also to be a legal member of the local society. The Vereia townspeople were willing to give him freedom, but only if he paid 25 rubles "to help pay the debt accruing to the society for medical care of townspeople in various hospitals." The townspeople believed that Nazarov was well able to pay this fee, as he owned land and ran a brick factory, but Nazarov demurred, claiming that despite appearances he was not able to do so—hence his protest to the governor's office. The Vereia town elder explained the position of the townspeople: the society was paralyzed by its health-care debts, which currently stood at 2,978 rubles, 92 ¾ kopeks. Unable to make up the money through regular collections, it had decided to charge for exit papers—"the most modest sum"—even knowing that such fees would hardly make a difference in its debts. In this case, the Vereia townspeople ran into a problem: the Moscow governor demanded that any future decisions to assess extra fees on members be run by him for approval. The Vereia townspeople could do nothing but acquiesce.[76]

At the same time that town societies began to collect fees to guarantee their financial status, other concerns over membership brought them into increasing conflict with the central authorities. There had long been tension between local societies and the imperial state over the right to accept members.[77] Although that conflict was resolved on paper by allowing different kinds of registry, some with full rights in the society, some without full membership, and thus full oversight, in reality it continued to fester. For one thing, local societies continued to protest as additional groups were granted the right to join societies without their permission during the middle decades of the century.[78] Furthermore, local authorities regularly asked that those registered as belonging to their societies without their agreement be removed from their rolls; rarely, however, were these requests granted.[79] The existing standards ruled, which demanded registry, but in principle, at least, solved societal demands by removing the idea of communal responsibility for paying dues.[80]

There was already significant precedent for thinking in terms of the duties that societies owed their members, both in individual decision making and in the institutional structures that governed charity and popular welfare; but particularly after the abolition of the soul tax, the concerns of central and local authorities began to diverge more. Local communities now saw themselves primarily as suppliers of public services to their members, and as a result, their decisions turned more and more on the question of whether they would need to provide such services to new or existing members. This manifested itself in different ways. It could complicate an individual's efforts to leave a society, as in the case of the Moscow townsman A. A. Dmitriev. In 1908, he most indignantly petitioned for redress in his heretofore unsuccessful attempt to gain freedom to join a peasant society. The sticking point in his case was his request to be released alone—which meant leaving behind parents (identified as "elderly" by the townsperson society) and two sisters. From his point of view, he wanted to strike out alone without the responsibility for these people. From the point of view of the townsperson society, due to their age, the parents might well have to turn to public aid without their son. In one (of many) petitions, Dmitriev clarified his point of view: "in light of the fact that my father is fifty-five years old, and will be freed from dues from January 1, 1909, and members of the female sex do not have any dues, and beside that my parents are still able to provide for themselves materially through their work," they were no burden to anyone. In the end, the Moscow townspeople were convinced, and they gave him his freedom.[81] But this was perhaps because of the way he cast his argument. He did still draw on the language of taxpayers, but now also addressed the bigger concern by implying that his parents would not need to draw on the services of the society.

More often, societies worried about the burdens new members might place on them— and particularly they worried about those whom they in principle had no right to refuse. Those with the "freedom to choose a way of life" continued to be a particular problem for townsperson societies. The Tula townsperson society explained its outstanding debts to the provincial hospital in part because many of those who had run up bills had been "registered without the agreement of the society and they serve only as a burden to it."[82] The Kaluga society tried much the same tactic in an effort to convince the provincial hospital to forgive its debts, but found its efforts rebuffed. In that case, the *zemstvo* argued that hospital officials had no way of knowing whether an individual townsperson had been registered with or without the townsperson society's acceptance. They treated townspeople as townspeople, and they deserved payment.[83]

The issue came to the attention of the Ministries of Finance and Internal Affairs during the 1860s, when local authorities from both Moscow and St. Petersburg brought to them problems with the current system. First, a Moscow-based commission on public aid produced a report that placed the blame for the "existing poverty in the townsperson *soslovie*" on "the acceptance into its midst of new members, without proper proof either of their solvency, nor of their ability to gain their livelihood." After their initial waiver period, when they were freed from taxes and duties, such people—people with the freedom to choose a way of life—were supposed to present formal documents of acceptance to be considered full members of the townsperson society. If they did not, they were to be considered workers and given individual responsibility for fulfilling their duties. However, the commission found, in practice, this distinction did not exist. Everyone ended up a townsperson. While the ministries agreed with certain elements of the commission's proposal to make the difference between those formally accepted and those not more explicit, for the most part they refused to take further measures, on the grounds that the laws were clear and responsibility lay with the town duma.[84]

Soon thereafter, however, a second inquiry came from St. Petersburg, an inquiry that raised new questions. The St. Petersburg townsperson society complained that the provincial treasury had added 5,891 souls to their society without their agreement, and furthermore that the treasury now considered them to be full members. Upon investigation, the provincial treasury explained its reasoning: the townsperson society was itself responsible for informing the treasury that these souls had not gained full acceptance. In its view, "not having in sight the statement of the townsperson board about excluding someone into the worker status, and believing because of that, that the townsperson society willingly accepts responsibility for those people for the payment of duties by them, registered them, at the end of the waiver period, finally in the townsperson ranks."[85] Furthermore, it noted, this was the only sensible thing to do. If all those souls were excluded, and given individual responsibility for payment of dues, that would mean that local tax authorities would be faced not with "only one tax register, coming from the townsperson society, [...but] hundreds and thousands of such registers, that is, from each individual having a place in the worker's ranks separately."[86] Based on these findings, the Ministry of Internal Affairs came up with a solution that explicitly drew on the fact that the soul tax had just been abolished for townspeople: eliminate the category of workers, because "at the current time it does not have sufficient meaning" and because "collective responsibility" without the soul tax "cannot be burdensome for townsperson societies."[87]

The divergence in ideas of membership was made clear in a law from 1865, regarding the fate of "former household serfs who, due to old age or illness, are incapable of supporting themselves." The Ministries of Finance and Internal Affairs decided that such individuals—assuming they had no capable adult relatives who could bear responsibility for them—ought to be registered in townsperson societies "only for the count," and not placed on tax rolls.[88] Again, from the ministries' point of view, this solved all problems. It gave such individuals a formal place, with a formal registry, and did not demand anything of town societies in the way of increased taxes. But such individuals had become exactly those for whom towns did not want responsibility—and the law made it unclear whether being registered "only for the count" entitled them to the public services of their new *soslovie* status.

Just over a decade later, the issue arose again. Then, the Kovno Provincial Treasury wrote to the Ministry of Finance with a report on the terrible state of the province's townsperson societies. At the time of the last census revision in 1857, 10,380 Christian townsmen had been registered in the province. Now, in 1877, there were 42,813. The vast majority of that increase had come from those "registered as choosing a way of life, without the agreement of societies, with personal responsibility in paying taxes, from the *soslovie* of free people and *odnodvortsy* [registered at the elimination of their societies in 1864 and 1868] and members of the former Polish nobility not confirmed in their nobility [who were required on the basis of a decree of the Senate from September 23, 1864 to register in tax-paying *sosloviia*.]"[89] The problem, of course, was that many of those who had been registered in towns had left, had died, had gone into the army, or had otherwise disappeared; and despite the fact that they had supposedly individual, not communal, responsibility for paying taxes, the town societies still felt the burden of these missing members.

In this case, the Ministries of Finance and Internal Affairs agreed to a solution that they believed should solve many of these problems. Two years before, they had allowed villages to exclude the aged and infirm from their tax rolls—they were still members "for the count," but would not be subject to state taxes. Now, the ministries agreed to extend these provisions to townsperson societies, as well.[90] The resulting decree, confirmed by the State Council and Senate, allowed all those registered in town societies without those society's consent, and who had for "various reasons" left, to be excluded from the tax rolls.[91] Again, however, the alternative concept of collective responsibility was ignored.

In 1891, the Riga Tax Commission wrote to the Ministry of Finance with a complaint about the provincial treasury department that echoed the earlier correspondence. According to Riga officials, the treasury had been adding people to the city's rolls without the agreement of the local society. In particular, the society brought up the case of Amalia Zemberg, who wished to enter the Riga society of townspeople after the death of her (foreigner) husband. The society strongly objected to her inclusion, however, because "she is now seventy-two years old and one must suppose that she, as a poor woman of elderly years, will be a burden to whichever society she is registered in, and will require oversight and aid." The society claimed it had greater rights to refuse even those with the duty to choose a way of life, on the basis of Riga's special status as a "privileged" city within the empire. Eventually, after several years of additional complaints, the society received a response: according to the Ministries of Internal Affairs and Finance, the society's concerns were "not worthy of attention," in large part because "the law cannot be paralyzed by the lack of agreement of individual societies to accept [certain individuals] into their midst."[92]

Based on this decision, the Riga authorities had no choice now but to consider many they did not wish to accept as members of their society. However, they very clearly also refused to see them as full members. Also in 1891, the commission decided that because it had not agreed to take on responsibility for such new members, it would not take on responsibility for their care.[93] This decision again provoked controversy when it refused to pay for charitable aid given to one Andrei Ivanov, a retired soldier turned Riga townsman. In 1897, the Commission on Aid to the Poor of the Riga Town Council inquired about Ivanov's status, and on what basis the town society refused to pay for his welfare (although the reason for the inquiry was left unstated, it seems likely that the commission had given Ivanov aid and hoped to recoup its costs from his society). The society responded that it still did not believe that it had responsibility for anyone it did not accept; therefore, those like Ivanov, added to their rolls without their full acceptance, "did not have the right to receive aid and health care on the account of the Riga society."[94] In this, at least, they did have the support of the higher authorities. By the mid-1890s, the Senate had decided that societies did not have to pay the medical fees of those they had not formally accepted.[95]

Concerns about public services also changed the way that societies viewed women. As in the case of Amalia Zemberg, societies worried that even though women did not owe taxes, they still might call on the obligations of societies to care for them. Nor was this a new concern. In 1845, the freed serf Avdot'ia Kolotukhina petitioned the Minister of Internal Affairs himself for aid in her attempt to register in the St. Petersburg society of townspeople. She had a basic problem: "Not having any kind of means for registry... I beg you to write to the townsperson board and whoever else is necessary to accept and register me in the society without any kind of fees, due to my poverty."[96] The ministry did push forward with her case, writing to the St. Petersburg Governor General for further information. In the course of the correspondence that ensued, the St. Petersburg townsperson society came to a decision on her case. They were happy to accept her, "if when she appears in front of the elders she turns out to be capable of feeding herself and not too old."[97] Of course, because as a freed serf Kolotukhina would be considered among those with the right to choose a way of life, the society ought not have any right to refuse her. And yet, it strove to maintain its authority in this case where it feared increased obligations.

These concerns grew because, despite the fact that women paid no (or at least, few) local taxes, it appeared that women were more likely than men to draw on public aid.[98] In St. Petersburg in 1877, there were nearly four times as many town and artisan women as men in charitable institutions—in this case, not including any special townsperson establishments.[99] Similar ratios were found in Moscow, where in the 1880s five public care institutions specifically for members of the town estates (merchants, townspeople, and craftspeople) housed 737 men and 2,064 women.[100] Furthermore, some evidence suggests that the problem was getting worse. The St. Petersburg City Poor House had always housed more women than men, but the proportion of women residents grew significantly toward the end of the nineteenth century. In 1829, 73.4 percent of its residents were women; by 1887, 84.9 percent of them were.[101]

Pressures like these brought a new, and fairly radical, shift in attitudes toward accepting women. Earlier in the nineteenth century, societies did actively consider whether to admit women into their midst, but they did not seem unduly concerned with issues of public care. When a large group of women petitioned to enter the Vil'na townsperson society at the time of the eighth census revision, the local society for the most part agreed to accept them all. The women were freed serfs, "residents" without previous registration, and women who could not prove their (largely Polish) noble ancestry, and thus had been stripped of their noble status. The Vil'na society only refused entrance to one woman: Ekaterina Ulitskuvna, who did not provide evidence of her good behavior.[102] A decade later, when another large group of women of similar social origins petitioned, all were accepted.[103]

Later, however, societies became much more wary of accepting women, and much more argumentative about whether they could be forced to do so. A very strong statement of this point of view came from the Arkhangel'sk townsperson society in the 1880s, when it refused entrance to three impoverished peasant women. The society had a clear reason: "such a registry is combined with expenses for the society in the care and healing of its members, in the case of their poverty, in hospitals, and right now the Arkhangel'sk townsperson society has debts just to the local hospital of the Office of Public Care, for the care of poor townspeople, amounting to more than 3,000 rubles, not even counting the fees for hospitals in other towns that care for members of the society who have left home on passports."[104] Although the women were not immediately ill, the very concept of taking in three women seemed likely to add to the debts of the society, in their opinion.

While local societies may have come to see women as a particular possible burden, the central state still saw *soslovie* membership in terms of taxpaying male souls obligated to perform military service, and in need of ordering by a local authority. This culminated in a circular sent out by the Ministry of Finance to all provincial treasuries and administrations in 1888, which included an update to the *Digest of the Laws*: all peasant and townswomen whose households contained no male souls (i.e., single women or women with only daughters) could "re-register in other towns by only their requests, without presenting acceptance agreements."[105] In other words, the central government gave women, the group that local societies most worried about when it came to public services, unusual freedoms. In so doing, it removed the possibility of local societies' managing their intake in the way they most desired.

OUTSIDE THE COMMUNITY

As in the earlier nineteenth century, the presence of statuses allotted to the individual, not by a society, complicated the understanding of *soslovie* and of collective responsibility. Statuses that were based on professional attainment or education—particularly the status of honored citizen—were (initially, at least) based in individual accomplishment, not birth. Moreover, acquisition of the status of honored citizen placed those who possessed it outside any collective *soslovie* society—it was a status of individuals (or perhaps of families) rather than of societies. Over the course of the later nineteenth century, many kinds of professional attainment were added to the list of those that could attain the status of honored citizen, which recognized their individual achievement. Graduates of new educational institutions, including technical and agricultural schools, and individuals ranging from "artists of the Imperial theaters" to doctors to surveyors to musicians all gained eligibility.[106]

Both honored citizenship and certain professional identities gave individuals status outside the boundaries of a specific *soslovie* society. That fact, however, meant that those individuals were—like the "workers" not granted the right of membership in a townsperson society decades before—without access to sources of collective security. Evgenii Blumenbakh, the Riga bureaucrat, singled out such individuals as those who lacked such collective security, and thus as those who, "having fallen into poverty or illness, are at the whim of fate."[107] Concerns over welfare and membership were also prominent in discussions of other *sosloviia* that badly fit the model of communal responsibility. Particular concerns about the welfare of individual members of the clergy meant that the post-reform clerical estate, which had become a much more porous status due to recent changes, maintained its status as a distinct *soslovie*.[108]

Similarly, although their legal status granted them no such protections, various late-nineteenth century efforts to organize professionals were often as concerned with their members' economic well-being as they were with larger issues of their professions. The Russian Theater Society was concerned with the "development of theater affairs in Russia," but it grew out of philanthropic organizations that attempted to aid impoverished theatrical artists.[109] Even the Pirogov Society, particularly lauded for its role in developing a medical profession, was concerned with the poor economic status of doctors, even planning insurance programs to provide aid.[110]

Such individuals were likely those who "did not know to which *soslovie* [they] belonged" at the start of the twentieth century.[111] When local authorities in the town of Gatchina carried out a census of the population in the early 1890s, they found their efforts complicated by the fact that "rather a lot did not completely indicate the *soslovie*, to which they belonged." Of course that might have indicated unwillingness to indicate *soslovie* rather than inability, but it did suggest that for a certain group, *soslovie* was no longer a relevant consideration. The Gatchina authorities also noticed something in particular about those who did not indicate *soslovie*: they were among those who tended to come to Gatchina for temporary residence, not the town's permanent residents. And who were those temporary residents? Some were *dachniki*—summer cottagers from St. Petersburg, who were almost certainly from these professional classes. The rest, according to the account, were from the "working class."[112] These two groups (who not coincidentally mapped on to the bourgeoisie and proletariat) were increasingly defined outside the *soslovie* system.

Perhaps most complicated by changes in the conception of *soslovie* membership, though, was the vexing question of the relationship between merchant and townsperson. This relationship was based in part on this same opposition between group membership and individual status. Townspeople were definitely members of a society, with all that enailed. Merchants, however, were in some ways members of a society, but in others were treated as individuals. During and after the Great Reforms, central and local authorities continued to question this relationship, and by extension questioned the social and economic definitions of *soslovie*.

In 1859, the Kiev governor's office sent an inquiry to the Ministry of Finance that brought this issue to the fore. It asked, just how much of a role ought local town dumas have over townspeople who wished to enter merchant societies in other towns? Such townspeople needed to be freed from their home society—all sides agreed on this. But exactly what paperwork was necessary to prove that freedom was unclear, and different treasuries in the region were handling the process differently. One required only a freedom document, while others demanded a separate document from the duma "or other institution governing *soslovie* affairs," in large part to avoid "alienating town dumas from participation in the movement of citizens" (the file was unclear about the practical difference between these documents). The governor supported those who asked for extra documents, but the Ministry of Internal Affairs decided otherwise. It argued that requiring multiple documents proving freedom was demanding too much, and that requiring less paperwork was the better choice.[113]

In 1866, the State Council returned to the question and approved a formal proposal by the Ministry of Finance to clarify the rules for townspeople moving into new societies, based in part on this earlier correspondence. A townsman wishing to move now had to present a freeing agreement "from his society" that contained specific information: that he was not in line for the draft; that he had no debts or outstanding dues, and that he had paid all state dues through the rest of the year; that he was under no criminal investigation, and that he did not belong to any dangerous "schismatic sects"; that if he was underage, he had the approval of his parent; and that if part of the household to which he belonged was to remain in his society of origin, it was self-sufficient without him. The agreement, verified by the town duma, was then to be presented to a provincial treasury, which ought to accept it without additional verification. If a townsman proved to be improperly registered in a new society and turned out actually to be subject to the draft, then those members of his society who claimed he was not, and the duma who verified their claim, were to be held responsible.[114]

This was a straightforward decision, but it did not assuage town desires to continue to control their membership. The issue reemerged late in the nineteenth century when local authorities in Riga wrote to the Lifland Provincial Treasury complaining about the lack of regularity in the process of transferring townspeople into the merchantry. Because the treasury had not established any regular process, the Riga *soslovie* authorities (the Tax Authority) had created their own procedure: those wishing to register as merchants were to bring their supporting documents to the Tax Authority. It considered the documents, and if it agreed that a petitioner was deserving of merchant status, it sent the petitioner to the Board of Trade for specific evidence of his financial status. Only then should the petitioner turn to the treasury to finalize his status. However, the authority complained, the treasury was accepting individuals who only had approval from the Board of Trade and not from the Tax Authority, despite the fact that the former had "no societal power" and therefore could not rule on whether an individual was worthy of the social status of merchant. The treasury disagreed, believing instead that merchant status was an individual economic one, and that it therefore had full authority to adjudicate any such cases.[115]

In the late 1880s, a case originating in Kiev merchant society brought together many of these issues of local *soslovie* control. The case began around 1888, when the elder of the Kiev Merchant Society turned to the Kiev governor with a complaint about the actions of the provincial treasury. The elder alleged that the treasury regularly "allowed all those who wished not only to enter into the number of merchants, but also to be ascribed to the local merchant society, without the agreement of the *soslovie* administration." That is, it was conflating the idea that "merchant" was both an occupation and an actual social status that implied membership. This was, according to the elder, contrary to regulations; statute stated clearly that potential merchants had to present either the agreement of the society or "the approval of six trustworthy citizen-householders and the agreement of the Kiev Merchant Elder."[116]

The governor had already been in correspondence with the provincial treasury over its practices with regard to the registration of Jews as merchants in Kiev (it is unclear from the archival file whether this came out of another complaint or originated with the governor). In this case, the treasury had laid out its point of view clearly. It demanded four types of documents from all those seeking status as a merchant: passports from the petitioner and his family; a formal statement of the members of his family; a document from the local police stating that the petitioner "fulfills all moral conditions" that statute demanded; and a receipt for payment of the appropriate merchant guild dues. The treasury based its practices on a different statute than the one cited by the elder: "the note to statute 521... in which is literally stated the following: 'for entrance into the merchantry the agreement of the merchant society is not required.' "[117] If the laws were contradictory, the treasury chose to follow the one that gave it fuller authority.

The governor, in his query to the Ministry of Internal Affairs, also brought up issues that lay within the case. He differentiated between registry into the merchantry as an occupation and into the merchant society as a social status, a distinction he believed the treasury was ignoring. In his view, "entrance into the merchantry signifies obtaining only temporarily the right to buy and sell, as for a trade, while ascription to the merchant society constitutes an act of gaining known rights and privileges, the receipt of which cannot be limited only by the payment of some known sum, but is determined also by other demands of the law, common for entrance in general into the number of the members of town *sosloviia*."[118] At base, the question was whether becoming a merchant was an economic act or whether, "despite all the changes going on at the current time in the laws on statuses... the legislative power has not found it possible to equalize, or even completely eradicate the merchantry, as a separate *soslovie*, consisting of a separate kind of status of town inhabitants."[119] The treasury was wrong, in his opinion, to believe that the provisions of statute 521 applied not just to "the right to engage in retail activities" but also to acquisition of the rights belonging to the merchant *soslovie*.[120]

Finally, the governor wrote, this policy of the treasury necessarily led to a reduction in the prestige of Russia's merchants. After all, he noted, if even townspeople had the right to agree to accept members, what did it mean if the merchants lacked that right? How could they ensure that new merchants were of proper moral worth? He concluded with what he clearly meant to be a disturbing thought: too much reliance on treasuries, and not the societies that knew their members, "creates a condition by which worthless individuals not only can escape their townsperson society, but even gain by payment of a given sum the higher rights allotted by law to merchants of the first guild."[121]

The Ministry of Internal Affairs turned to the Ministry of Finance for its opinion. After a long gap in correspondence (from October 1888 until March 1892), the Ministry of Finance approved of the treasury's actions, for several reasons. First, guild certificates gave "above the right to trade, merchant rank and the personal privileges that go along with it," which meant that the distinction between individual merchant status and entrance into the merchant *soslovie* was irrelevant. Second, "becoming a part of the merchantry occurs unconditionally according to the wishes of the person holding the certificate himself," which meant that the wishes of the society were irrelevant. And third, this fact was linked to another way that merchant status was different from other town statuses: "exit from the merchantry is allowed not by the agreement of the society, but solely by the personal discretion of the one leaving." Merchants were different, and they were not bound by their society in the same way that townspeople or artisans were. The Ministry of Finance then suggested that the Ministry of Internal Affairs turn to the Codification Department of the State Council (which had replaced the Second Department of His Majesty's Own Chancellery as the state department responsible for updating the *Digest of Laws*) to clarify the laws that underlay this whole process.[122]

When applied to, the Codification Department gave yet another new spin on the discussion. It reported on the longer legislative history of the statutes at question, and looked particularly at a law of 1810 that provided the first indication that the fact that merchants and townspeople owed duties differently (as individuals or communally) had implications for mobility.[123] The current edition of the *Digest* was indeed contradictory, and so the department asked a basic question: "can there be situations, when agreement by the merchant society to accept people wishing to enter it is demanded?"[124] This was a turnabout from the original question raised by the Kiev governor. Where he had presented the right to accept as the norm and its lack as an aberration, the Codification Department saw the lack of consent as the norm and asked whether there could in principle be times when it was not.

Furthermore, the Codification Department could find only one place where laws suggested that official acceptance might be necessary. It noted that the laws on peasants stated that those who wished freedom from their peasant society had to present an acceptance agreement from the society into which they wished to move.[125] In other words, peasants needed proof of a place to go before they could be given the freedom to go there. The Codification Department then turned this question back to the Ministry of Internal Affairs, asking whether it found it necessary to keep that provision. Internal correspondence within the ministry came up with a simple answer. The current law was unworkable and posed undue hardships for peasants. Removing it posed no problems.[126]

Finally, in August 1893, after the Ministry of Internal Affairs had received a second inquiry from the Kiev governor, wondering if any progress had been made on his question from five years before, the Codification Department sent what turned out to be the final word on the matter. The next revision of the *Digest of Laws* would maintain the statement currently attached to statute 521. Entrance into the merchantry did not require the formal agreement of a society. And, too, the law describing the duties of the merchant elder would read differently: the duty to "collect agreement from the society for the acceptance of new petitioners" was to be removed from the list.[127]

This end result was certainly not what Kiev's merchant society had desired. The society, via its elder, had approached the governor to protect and maintain its authority over its social milieu, an authority perhaps given all the more importance owing to the radical changes in economic authority created by the Great Reforms. But the society found itself caught in a strange way by its own privilege within the *soslovie* structure. The freedom from collective responsibility that had allowed increased flexibility for merchants also, from the point of view of St. Petersburg, removed any need they might have had to have a say in their fellow members. But from its point of view, contradictions still remained, contradictions that would appear and reappear in further discussions of the very idea of *soslovie* in the late imperial world.

The meaning of different town statuses arose again in the era of the dumas. In May 1911, the Volyn' Provincial Treasury wrote to the Ministry of Finance regarding the current understanding of merchant status. The treasury had been conducting a review (*proverka*) of the lists of merchants in the province, and had discovered that in many towns individuals were claiming the status of merchant despite not having been registered as such by the treasury itself. In other words, towns were allowing merchants to act as merchants, and confirming them in that status, without regard to provincial authority. Now, the treasury wondered if it ought to exclude all those individuals from the status of merchant, despite the fact that many had been successfully trading as such for years, or whether it should ask them to petition formally for inclusion into the status. It also asked for guidance about whether the merchants who petitioned should be formally registered as of the date of their petitions, or retroactively to the time they initially started trading as merchants.[128]

More than a year later, the Ministry of Finance responded by chastising the treasury for allowing this to have happened, and also by arguing in support of the continued relevance of *soslovie*. Something odd had happened in this case, and thus the ministry decided that all those who had been living and working as merchants could be confirmed in that position as long as they now went through the process of formally registering with the treasury. As rationale, the ministry wrote that "only Provincial Treasuries"—in other words, not town societies—had the authority to finalize registration as merchants. Anyone who wished to trade was required to petition the treasury, and to present proper documentation that he had left his previous status. The ministry added a new reason for demanding such documentation even in the supposedly freer post-Stolypin world: "for according to the law no one may use the rights of two statuses."[129]

This solution was a just one, in that it sought not to punish individuals for larger administrative failures. But it also reflected a particular problem in justifying the continued reliance on *soslovie* as anything other than a form of social control. The ministry here used the idea of *soslovie* as a system of rights and hierarchy that marked individuals totally. In its argument, peasants and townspeople ought to give up their earlier statuses in order to take on that of merchant. This made a certain amount of sense, but its hollowness was soon laid bare.

In February 1914, the Kherson Provincial Treasury wrote with the news that it, too, had uncovered cases of unregistered people living and acting as merchants. Twenty such supposed merchants had been trading in Odessa, paying their merchant dues—one since 1870!—but never formally registered by the treasury. The Kherson Treasury asked if it could follow the decision given to Volyn', and simply register all the merchants in action as merchants in name, and gave an additional argument in favor of its inclination. The ministry responded several months later, agreeing to extend its earlier decision to Kherson, as well.[130]

Left unsaid in the ministry's decision was the fact that this change in status made no sense in any context other than its own desire to control the population. In this particular case, the unregistered merchants all possessed existing statuses that were higher than that of merchant: one noble, two dentists, and the remainder honored citizens.[131] These were statuses that had traditionally been impossible to leave—and, in fact, that could at times be held in conjunction with rights to trade. Here, the *soslovie* ideal had always proved tricky, precariously balancing its identification with status and with occupation. Now, in the last gasp of the empire, the center attempted to hold on to its desire to classify, regardless of the rationality of that classification.

In 1872, the academician and journalist M. P. Shchepkin published an account of the financial status of Moscow's merchant society. He pointed out that this was a difficult task because imperial Russia's individual *soslovie* societies had developed in large part out of public view. In so doing, Shchepkin echoed other nineteenth-century commentators on the role of *soslovie* societies in Russia's social structure. An author for the journal *Russian Messenger*, for one, noted that a particular problem with understanding the inner workings of the societies of townspeople was that many of the decrees that governed their workings "did not go into the *Digest of Laws*" and were instead locally specific.[132] As Shchepkin put it, these societies were "nearly a mystery" to outside observers. The internal workings of *sosloviia* were "a secret matter, inaccessible to the public, and therefore even into our periodical press almost nothing from their enchanted world slips out other than a bit of petty gossip and domestic spats, not worthy of any attention."[133]

Shchepkin's description highlights the particular difficulty in conceptualizing *soslovie* in the late nineteenth century. The conflicts between local *soslovie* societies—which were, as he put it, operating in a hazy world outside what appeared to be the normal legal structure—and the central state were at base an expression of the complicated understanding of *soslovie* in the late imperial era. On the one hand, the central state saw *sosloviia* primarily as a means of governability—a means of categorization that allowed it to see its population. In a way, it saw *soslovie* more as the overarching concept of a true estate than the localized societies that had developed in large part due to its policies. But at the same time, those localized societies still had real roles to play in the lives of their members, and they used this as the basis to demand that their authority—that their real existence—was still essential.[134]

7

Soslovie in Context

LIFE STORIES

IN 1841, A serf from Voronezh named Egor Mikhailov sought his freedom. His owner, one Chertkov, argued with his serf over the cost of that freedom, particularly over the price he planned to charge to free Egor Mikhailov's daughter. But through a combination of financial incentives and personal appeals, Egor Mikhailov was able to gain freedom for himself and his family. According to the memoirs of his descendants, Egor Mikhailov immediately started to fix his family in their new, non-serf status. He apprenticed one son, Mikhail, to a bookbinder in a nearby provincial town. He began to work as an estate manager in southern Russia, where his other sons, Mitrofan and Pavel, joined him. Soon Pavel went to work for a merchant in nearby Taganrog, and Mitrofan followed the same path in Rostov. Eventually, both sons settled in those towns in town societies; Pavel also married a merchant's daughter and began to raise a family. In general, Egor Mikhailov's sons became examples of those many urban inhabitants whose social status occasionally wavered, shifting between merchant and townsperson depending on their financial position in a given year.

Another round of mobility, however, affected the next generation of the family. Pavel Egorevich took seriously the idea of having moved on to a new status; despite frequent financial setbacks, he sent his sons first to the local Greek school, and then to the Taganrog secondary school, and according to one son's memoir, even hired a French tutor for his children. Most of his children moved on, too, to even higher educational institutions in Moscow, often supporting their own studies through work giving lessons. As a result, although some of the grandsons and granddaughters of Egor Mikhailov continued in trade, a number of others moved on to radically new statuses by the end of the imperial era. One granddaughter became a teacher, while a grandson became a painter. Even greater heights were reached, however, by one grandson, the third son of

Egor Mikhailov's son Pavel. This grandson moved on from his background of shifting merchant and townsperson status through education; he attended the Taganrog secondary school and went on to study medicine in Moscow, eventually qualifying as a doctor, and thus gaining individual status and freedom from a *soslovie* society. At the same time, however, he, like his brothers, began to publish short stories first under a pseudonym and later, as his renown as a writer grew, under the family name his father and grandfather had taken from their place of origin: Chekhov. Anton Pavlovich Chekhov, son of trade, grandson of a serf, became the voice of fin-de-siècle Russia, embodying all the social complications that had accrued alongside, or on top of, official *soslovie* status.[1]

Chekhov did not himself leave many explicit statements about his origins; one comment in a single letter has become his most famous statement on the topic: that he had had to "squeeze the slave out of himself drop by drop."[2] Nevertheless, those origins linger both in his writings and in the interpretations of others. As one biographer has put it, "the family had passed, within half a century, first through serfdom and then through shopkeeping to the liberal professions… the social transformation of the clan into a milieu which can never have figured in Grandfather [E]gor Chekh's wildest nightmares."[3] Another describes it as "telling" that upon first arriving in Moscow to study, the writer Chekhov "registered with the police as a [townsperson]."[4] But it was less telling than it was recognition of the still vital role of *soslovie* in everyday life. Even in 1879, even for a brand-new student in the medical faculty of Moscow University, the identity recognized by the police was by definition one that included *soslovie*.[5] *Soslovie* was malleable, as his family history showed, but still a real part of individual identity.

Thousands, tens of thousands, perhaps hundreds of thousands of individual subjects of the Russian empire, together with their families, effected changes in their official status over the course of some two hundred years. Those moments of change were only single events (even if at times long, drawn-out ones) in longer lives, but single events with sometimes significant after effects. The act of changing status influenced not simply the remainder of these individuals' lives but also the lives of their descendants. The ways that that longer history of *soslovie* could play out varied significantly. Some were barely affected by a change in their official status; others moved once, and then went on to move again. In many cases, as in the case of Chekhov, the next generation saw the most significant change, as grandsons and granddaughters of those who initially altered their *soslovie* went on to do sometimes great things, things likely unimaginable in the worlds of their forefathers' (or foremothers') birth. And, too, some of those who changed their status simply disappeared from view, hidden outside the archival records that allow some glimpses into the world of *soslovie* during the imperial era.

Few of those who changed their status, or who were descended from those who had, left as extensive written records as Anton Chekhov. Furthermore, even those who might have written extensively, like Chekhov, did not necessarily directly address the role that mobility had played in their lives or the lives of their families. Some records, however, do provide both direct commentary on social mobility and non-narrative data on what happened to those who initially changed their status. Several memoirs, all of former peasants or serfs turned merchants, townspeople, or artisans, comment not only on the reasons to change *soslovie* but also on the results of those changes. Archival records from Moscow and St. Petersburg include not only lists of the individuals who entered those towns' *soslovie* societies but outlines of their later fates, as well. Together, these sources paint a picture of mobility as often having real meaning, and real effect, on the lives of those who accomplished it. None went on to the heights of Chekhov's fame, and some, in fact, failed to prosper. But all were transformed, if sometimes transformed only partially, while still marked, internally or externally, by their status of origin.

FOUR LIVES

The four life stories discussed here show that individuals came to change their *soslovie* for very different reasons and in very different ways: the first not by his own choice, the second to avoid duties, and the third and fourth through specific desire for schooling and thus exit from their status of birth. All four also show ways in which these authors found themselves at odds with their new status, whether by coming up against the limitations of even sought after statuses or because of uncertainty about their own place in society. And all were not only transformed as individuals by their moments of change but also transformed in ways that were multiplied among their descendants.

Venedikt Malashev's life story involves three generations of changing *soslovie*, from his father's fall into serfdom, to his own freedom and acceptance of a new *soslovie*, to his son's exit from the constraints of a *soslovie* society and installation in a new semi-professional identity. As a result, his story encompasses not only many of the ways in which individuals either sought to change their status, or found their status changed, from the late eighteenth through the early nineteenth centuries but also the longer aftereffects of such changes. His father was caught up in the large-scale changing of statuses that often went with the empire's expansion into new territories; Malashev himself did not actively seek his freedom, but was granted it, and he used that freedom to choose a new way of life; his son chose to make his work his identity, and sought and gained not only a new semi-professional status but also freedom from a *soslovie* society. Social identity affected their later lives and the choices they went on to make.

Like many memoirists, Malashev began his story about himself with the story of his parents; because of the peculiar fate of his father, this choice immediately emphasizes the issue of social mobility. According to his account, his father, Mikhail Malashevich, had been a member of the Polish minor nobility who had come to work as an overseer in a village belonging to a Polish magnate. Already this signified a change in Mikhail's status from (in principle) noble to a man in service—but he faced a far bigger change after the first partition of Poland. In the restructuring of lands, and concomitant restructuring of social relations that followed, Catherine II gave the village in which Mikhail served—Krugloe, in Mogilev district—to one of her favorites, Princess Dashkova. Suddenly, according to family lore, Mikhail was enserfed.[6]

Despite this huge change in its legal status, in some ways Malashev's family continued in much the same patterns as it had before. Mikhail continued to serve as the estate steward, a position of some authority within the village, though of course it was an odd authority, based in part on his own unfree status.[7] Furthermore, Malashev, born according to his account in either 1782 or 1783, and his sister Sophia both also found themselves separate from the majority of the village serfs. Both became personal servants—household serfs—to Dashkova herself starting in the mid-1790s. Nor were they common household serfs; Malashev became an even more rarified kind of serf when he was trained in music and began to play in Dashkova's private orchestra.[8]

Already Malashev's family had seen significant change in their social status, from (extremely minor) nobility to serf, but Malashev's life changed even more radically, and suddenly, after Dashkova's death in 1810. First, all the household serfs in the village were told to go to Dashkova's Moscow house for further instructions. There, they discovered that Count M. S. Vorontsov, who inherited Krugloe, had decided to free about forty souls—including Malashev—as a mark of his favor and in thanks to Dashkova. Suddenly, Malashev was free—or at least, free to choose a new *soslovie*. He described his immediate actions:

> In 1811, I, Venedikt, receiving my freedom document, appeared in the Moscow Provincial Administration, [and then at the] Moscow Town Magistracy, from where by means of an ukase [I] was transferred into the *soslovie* of artisans of the craft board; for according to the existing IMPERIAL decree, according to which people freed by their lords, having found a way of life, must register in societies right away... therefore I was accepted into the society of the artisan guild![9]

Malashev knew well the language of *soslovie*, but his specific choice shows that even those statuses chosen rather than inherited might be disconnected from the way individuals actually lived. Moscow's artisan guild was subdivided into twenty-four subguilds, and individuals belonged to one or the other of those guilds. Some were based on obvious crafts, like cooking, carpentry, or hat-making, but Malashev joined one of the more unusual guilds: the barber's (*fershel'nyi*) guild. Despite its name, it officially included an odd hodgepodge of crafts and trades: not just hairdressers and hair dyers but also those making pomades, perfumes, and rouges; tobacconists, including cigar makers; and those who made "chalk for card games."[10] None of these seem to have much to do with Malashev's life before his freedom—and nor did they reflect his next actions.

In essence, Malashev's registry was simply one of convenience. Registry in the guild gave Malashev status in Moscow, but he immediately set off to work elsewhere. He went to nearby Tula province, where he found work first as a scribe and then as an overseer for a local noble landowner. He soon married a local household serf, thereby adding another level of social mobility to his family story, for she would have had to have been freed in order to marry him. For the next twenty years, he and his wife lived in the village, raising children, as Malashev held several different jobs in the area. He continued to be registered in Moscow, though he himself rarely, if ever, traveled to the capital. His normal way of dealing with the disconnect between his registry and his residence was to rely on his employers. They, usually local landowners, delivered Malashev's dues and picked up his new passport on their trips to Moscow. For the most part this practice worked well, although it did leave Malashev liable to trouble if his employer proved untrustworthy.[11]

After years of living for the most part at peace with his hybrid life, registered in one place, living in another, and working in the same kind of estate administration that his serf father had, suddenly, in 1837, Malashev found himself facing the reality of his actual *soslovie* membership. He described it in dramatic terms:

on the 17th day of May, there was revealed to us, and to our whole family, the uncertain fate of the human race; on the 17th day of May a Warrant was received by me from the Land Court in Bogoroditsk, No. 1521 from the 17th of May 1837, by which warrant I was ordered to appear at the Land Court to hear an injunction from the Moscow artisan administration… and I, appearing at the Bogoroditsk Land Court on the 18th of May, was informed… that I was to appear in Moscow in haste, in order to fulfill the military duties placed on my family.[12]

This was a sudden, shocking reminder that membership in a *soslovie* had real meaning, even for those living far from their place of registration, seemingly separate from their official status. Malashev's account emphasizes the personal drama (the sudden appearance of "uncertain fate") contrasted with the emotionless bureaucracy (the repetition of dates, the recitation of the specifics of the warrant number, the colorless administrative language). In the end, the drama was of short duration, for Malashev was able to pay someone else to act as a draftee on behalf of his family. Clearly, however, the anxiety of the event lingered. In his memoir, Malashev only writes of the challenges of gaining passports and paying dues after this event, though he had clearly managed to maintain his position for more than a quarter-century by that time.

Malashev's account also touches on the next generation, and the ways that his sons were affected by their father's *soslovie* status. Obviously, one might have had to enter the army because of the draft demands of the Moscow artisans. But more, despite the fact that Malashev himself worked as an agricultural overseer, not at any of the various trades associated with his legal identity, his sons were truer members of their *soslovie*. His sons moved from the village to the capitals, and trained as barbers. Furthermore, one son, Petr, made yet another move. Around 1847, he sought his freedom from the Moscow artisan's *soslovie* based on his work as a hair dresser for the imperial theater in

St. Petersburg. For the sum of 240 paper rubles, the artisan's society gave him his free-dom, and he therefore gained new semi-professional status—off the tax rolls—under the auspices of the theater directorship.[13]

In a way, these three generations came full circle. Malashev's father had been born free and was considered an individual in the eyes of the law. When enserfed, he became sub-ject to the whims of his owner and registered as part of a village society (despite his work as an overseer). Malashev himself remained officially a serf belonging to an owner while registered in a particular village, though he occupied himself not with agriculture, but as a musician. Upon his manumission, Malashev was freed from the personal author-ity of his owner, but he was still subject to the communal authority of his new *soslovie* society. And though he lived much of his life as if that communal authority was simply a paper authority—something accessed through passports and ensured by payment of dues—his experience of the demand for military duties suddenly showed him that it was much more real than that. Finally, one son used his occupation to free himself from that communal authority, ironically despite the fact that it was an occupation that was well aligned with one associated with the authority, and to gain status as an individual, a fact marked by his exit from the tax rolls.

A second life story, that of Nikolai Chukmaldin (1836–1901), was a nineteenth-century Russian version of a classic rags-to-riches success. In the introduction to the 1902 pub-lication of Chukmaldin's *Notes on My Life*, the conservative journalist S. F. Sharapov described the author as "a Siberian peasant boy turned Moscow merchant-millionaire," a trajectory that in its bare outlines fulfills the image of the self-made man that had become so familiar in the popular press by that time.[14] That was an image of a world without *soslovie*, and with permeable class boundaries, where by sheer force of will a boy could make his fortune and find himself among the world's elite.

That might fit the outline of Chukmaldin's story, but its specifics show instead the story of a boy and then a man deeply embedded in Imperial Russia's *soslovie* society, with its local communities and overarching meaning at times at war with one another. Even the introduction suggests something of the sort; it claims that through his whole life, whatever heights he reached, Chukmaldin retained a certain "peasant point of view" that colored his memoirs.[15] In other words, at least in the mind of this Slavophile commentator, whatever his attainments in the world of class, Chukmaldin was forever marked by his *soslovie* of origin.[16]

Chukmaldin, born in 1836, was by origin a state peasant from Tobolsk province. His village, Kulakovo, was a medium-size one, of around 600 male souls, and by Siberian standards close to the town Tiumen'. In his account of his life, Chukmaldin portrays his family as in various ways somewhat atypical peasants. For one, his nuclear family lived apart from their larger extended family. He recalled the family moving into a single hut, where his father worked in one corner making parts for carts and his mother in another weaving rugs, work that made the family more financially successful than most.[17] The family also clearly had high ambitions. Although Chukmaldin's father was illiterate, he wanted to be sure his son learned to read. He hired a teacher to come to the village to teach young Nikolai at the cost of 5 rubles a month, plus living expenses. There were limits to this, of course—it was decided that Nikolai had learned well enough after only three months of study with the tutor. Still, this moment in some ways started to separate Chukmaldin from his official status.

Other events conspired to mark Chukmaldin as different. When he was ten years old, his father was named the elder of the village, a fact that in principle was a mark of respect but in practice was a real burden. Because his father was illiterate, Chukmaldin was taught to keep accounts (one of the major jobs of the elder was to collect and keep track of dues and taxes), and he became the village scribe not just during his father's tenure as elder but for later elders, as well. This meant not only that he became part of the village administration, but because he also served as scribe for many fellow villagers, he started to come into contact with the outside world, in the form of the township administration, as well.[18] Furthermore, Chukmaldin followed his parents' example of hard work; he began to build cart bodies like his father, and he wrote "when for the first time there appeared in my hand a half-imperial, earned by me personally, I felt in myself a proud understanding of my own self-worth."[19]

These were sentiments that could appear in any story of the poor boy made good, but the next phase of Chukmaldin's memoir places his story firmly within Russia's world of *sosloviia*. Just as he was coming into his own as a productive worker, in his mid-teens, Chukmaldin faced the reality of his *soslovie* status. In his case, it was a recognition that whatever his hard work, whatever his value to the village, he might end up an army recruit. This threat, moreover, reflected not simply a regular peasant duty but specifically the role that registration had on individual lives. Although Chukmaldin's father had physically moved his immediate family into a separate household, the official records of the village—the tax rolls—still listed the extended family as a single unit. That meant that the entire household, which practically meant the families of both Chukmaldin's father and his uncle, was considered as a whole when it came time to providing recruits. And, as Chukmaldin noted, because his uncle's two sons were both disabled, he was the only viable recruit for a family of six working souls. The moment he came of age, he was likely to be taken away to serve.[20]

Fortunately for Chukmaldin, his family had connections that helped him escape this threat. Although Chukmaldin had inherited his father's peasant status, his mother had relatively more exalted connections: one sister was married to an artisan and a second ran an inn with her husband.[21] Thanks to these connections, in 1852 Chukmaldin was sent to Tiumen' to live with a "wealthy relative," I. A. Reshetnikov, the head of a local merchant family and an uncle of some sort on Chukmaldin's mother's side. Reshetnikov himself ran a leather factory, while the oldest of his sisters had a shop in the local merchant arcade, where she sold "manufactured goods." Chukmaldin first worked at the factory, but whatever his talents at peasant manufacturing, he did not find an easy home there. Soon, he started to work in the shop, and there he found his true calling.[22]

Despite the family's connections in Tiumen', the idea of actually changing *soslovie* was not immediately apparent to them. The initial plan was that Chukmaldin would work for his relative, getting close enough to him to be able to borrow money to purchase a replacement recruit when he came of age.[23] It was only after Chukmaldin became acquainted with a local townsman, V. P. Shmurygin, that the idea of changing *soslovie* came up. Shmurygin, who had served as the elder of the Tiumen' townsperson society, suggested that if Chukmaldin's immediate family not only legally separated from the larger household but also left the village formally and became Tiumen' townspeople, many of their problems would be solved.[24] Although that process involved real effort and a "great and demeaning fuss," Chukmaldin reported the family's success with glee: after formalizing the family's registration, "I returned to Tiumen already the son of a townsperson family."[25]

It soon became clear, however, that this change in official status did not immediately alter much about the lives of Chukmaldin and his family. For one, the bulk of his family continued to live in the village, although they had returned their land allotment to the village society as part of gaining freedom. Instead, their earlier manufacturing activities became their major source of income, while Chukmaldin continued to work in Tiumen'. After a year or so of this stasis, Chukmaldin again found himself under the threat of the draft. Townspeople, after all, were subject to the draft just like peasants. The splitting of the household had created a buffer of safety for Chukmaldin, as it meant that as the only son of his household, he was considered ineligible for the draft. But a change to the recruiting system—the introduction of a lottery—now placed even single sons at risk. As Chukmaldin put it, this gave him three choices: "to buy a recruit receipt, to find some sort of alternate, or, finally, to register me in the third guild [of merchants]." With the help of his wealthy relative, the family chose the last of these options. The result, as far as Chukmaldin was concerned, was that he was forever freed from the threat of the draft.[26]

Despite the fact that he had already left his peasant status, and despite the fact that he recalled all his efforts to change his status as purely practical measures taken to avoid military service, rather than as actively seeking a new life, this last change does seem to have strengthened Chukmaldin's position as something new. Often still with the help of his family, he continued to develop his business interests in and around Tiumen'. According to his memoirs, between 1861 and 1872, his capital increased from 2,926 rubles to 69,445 rubles; as a result, toward the end of this period he had moved up into the second merchant guild, and began traveling as far as the Nizhnii Novgorod market to trade in "raw Siberian products and primarily wool in all its aspects." In addition, it was only after Chukmaldin rose to the merchantry that his family sold its property in the village and fully moved to the city. Initially they lived with one of his aunts, but eventually Chukmaldin bought his own house for all of them. In so doing, Chukmaldin made possible a different kind of generational mobility—he not only moved himself, and not only allowed future generations to move, but he also pulled past generations with him into the new status.[27]

In 1872, Chukmaldin accomplished yet another kind of mobility: he moved to Moscow. Initially, this purely geographical move was even more of a challenge than his earlier movement from status to status. The problem was not purely one of a new environment. Instead, he recalled, business ran differently in Moscow. According to Chukmaldin's memoirs, in Tiumen' loans were handed out freely to close acquaintances; if someone had extra money, he would lend it to a friend, and if someone needed money, a friend would always lend it. He claimed that "the money was always returned in time, in full, at least in our circle." But Moscow practices were far more formal, demanding bills of exchange and interest. Chukmaldin found this practice "unpleasant and even very egotistical."[28] Soon, however, he adjusted. He quoted a maxim: "don't go to a different monastery with your own rules." And, indeed, he adjusted well to business practices in Moscow, eventually even traveling to Berlin to extend his trade and reaching the end point of his journey of success. He became the "Moscow merchant-millionaire" he was supposed to become.

Chukmaldin's account of his life is one in which *soslovie* underlaid nearly everything. Although he was born a peasant, his extended family contained within itself many different *soslovie* identities. Thanks in large part to these connections, Chukmaldin was able to try on a number of these identities until he found the one that best fit him. As a merchant he prospered, even to the point of moving from the society in which he had longstanding connections to one in which he had to be only a single individual. At the same time, Chukmaldin described his life as one bounded less by the opportunities associated with particular *soslovie* identities than by the restrictions that went along with them. In his account one issue, and only one issue, guided his and his family's social mobility: the draft. That threat trumped any positive association with a particular status or society, and it proved to be the major motivating factor in his story.

The third and fourth stories are those of two peasants who used schooling to exit their status of birth. In this, they are different from the stories of Malashev and Chukhmaldin, in that they themselves were motivated to change their status out of a positive impulse, rather than forced into change like Malashev or motivated by fear like Chukmaldin. But while these two stories—and these two memoirs—are similar in at least the beginnings of their movement through Russian society, they could not be more different. Not only did the two men lead eventually startlingly different lives but even the ways their memoirs were compiled hint at the very different men they were.

The modesty of Konstantin Klepikov's (1821–1907) life story is reflected in its physical form. His *Autobiography of Konstantin Ignat'evich Klepikov* is a tiny pamphlet of just a few pages, published in his home of Viatka in 1902. The autobiography gives the bare outlines of the life of a man who had already made a name for himself as a local historian of Viatka. In contrast, Ivan Stoliarov's (1882–1953) memoir was not only a differently scaled document, one much longer than that of Klepikov, but also one clearly meant to be and to do something different. While the document is in part a personal memoir of Stoliarov's early life, it is equally an ethnographic exploration of his home village, written by a man trying to come to terms with a disjuncture between his origins and his later life. Clearly, Stoliarov's peasant origins weighed on him, and his apparent ambivalence is reflected in his text. At times he writes almost as an outside observer of his home village. But his memoir is still a personal document of one man's childhood, of his family, and of his dreams. The personal is interspersed with larger comments on the peasant village—and the contrast shows well the ways that this one man did not fit the society into which he was born.

Both authors describe the villages in which they were born, but in very different ways. Klepikov gives a bare sketch of his home village: Klepikovskoe, a tiny settlement of six households, in Viatka province. The settlement was an outgrowth of a larger village (Kobra), twelve versts away (about eight miles), and its peasants were some kind of state peasant (unusually for a memoir, Klepikov does not specify the kind of village it was).[29] Stoliarov, in contrast, begins his memoir with an extensive physical and ethnographic description of his home village Karachun, in Voronezh province. He describes folk sayings and local domestic practices, and, in particular gives a harsh accounting of the overall state of the local peasants. In his description they were "badly dressed and badly shod," they were "short of stature, poorly formed, all shriveled, of sallow complexion." This was all the more perplexing, he wrote, because their neighboring village was not that way; the peasants there were better dressed, looked healthier, and even spoke more modern Russian. The difference dated back to before the emancipation, but did not, as Stoliarov put it, reflect an expected distinction. Karachun had always been a village of state peasants, while the peasants of the neighboring village had been privately owned serfs. Even then, however, the serfs had been in such better economic shape that they "fled" from the idea of intermarrying with the nominally free state peasants of Karachun.[30]

Like many memoirists, the two authors move on to a description of their families and of the role they played in their early education. Klepikov introduces the reader to his father with a brief, but vivid description. He was an illiterate but religious man, described by his son as "walking in bast peasant shoes, who lived to age 92," and who had already (at least according to the autobiography) begun calling himself by the family name Klepikov. Given the relatively early date of Klepikov's birth, this fact may mean that his father was engaged in manufacturing or trade of some kind that brought him into regular contact with people outside the village. Certainly, according to his son, the elder Klepikov was at least well acquainted with merchants in the nearby district town Orlov, for it was thanks to that contact that Konstantin was set on a path unusual for a peasant of that time. The Orlov merchants advised Klepikov senior to have Konstantin, the youngest of three brothers, sent to school. And so, in the winter of 1829–1830, Konstantin was sent to Orlov to live with "an elderly, literate, unmarried townswoman,

Evdokiia Toropova." Over the course of the winter, Konstantin learned his alphabet, and after another summer spent in the village and in the fields, he went off to another district town to attend the parish school. The following year he moved on to the district school, and in 1833 he graduated and received a diploma.[31]

Stoliarov's picture of his parents is both more detailed and describes a very different kind of peasant life. His father was a dreamer who came back from his military service literate and trained in a richer trade—bootmaking—but who, in the face of his family's disapproval, left it behind to do what everyone else in the village did: make crude clay pots. His mother, who on the one hand was practical enough to risk opprobrium by selling her long braids for 3 rubles (a sum Stoliarov calls a strong inducement) while her husband was in service, on the other hand refused to think seriously of one of her husband's dreams of moving to land-rich Siberia to escape the poverty of their village. Despite that unwillingness to escape the village, Stoliarov's parents nonetheless did dare to move beyond the norms of peasant society: they opened a small shop in front of their house, one meant to supply villagers with everyday necessities and a few extra trinkets. Although their trade went badly (Stoliarov claims their failure came out of their kind-heartedness, and willingness to extend credit to their fellow peasants), their vision of a life in trade was too seductive to leave. As Stoliarov put it, "like those poisoned by alcoholism, they could not abandon their shop, and return to their prior 'normal' peasant way of life."[32]

The image of another life also attracted Stoliarov, but his goals were different from his parents'. Like so many memoirists, he wrote of the particular hold that the promise of education had for him. He remembered the moment when, in 1890, the village priest announced that a school would be opening in the village:

> now it is difficult for me to express that feeling, which this news called up in me. The very word "to study" sounded to me unusual, not like other words of normal peasant speech sounded. It seemed to me that in the very word some sort of secret was hidden, which would be revealed to me, as soon as I began to study.[33]

The reality of the village school, however, disappointed young Stoliarov. He showed up with the family's one book, a religious tome given to his father upon leaving the army, but he was told to leave it aside for simpler exercises. Indifferent school masters drilled the students in rote exercises, and they could not answer Stoliarov's many questions. As a result, Stoliarov described these early years as at best a half-education. Still, Stoliarov was one of the few villagers to receive a certificate for finishing his primary schooling. He was, as he put it, a "pioneer" of learning in the village.

Both peasants ran into difficulties in moving on from their initial forays into education. Konstantin's father supported his son's education, and indeed seems to have been the driving force at least for its first stage, but even parental support could not overcome the restrictions of *soslovie*. According to his account, in September 1833 Konstantin went to Viatka to enroll at the local secondary school. He was not accepted, however, both because it was too late in the year to enroll and because, as a peasant, he did not have the right to enter the secondary school at will. He was informed that he had to present a freedom document from his village society in order to move on in his studies. The description of the result of this moment is one of the few places in his autobiography in which Klepikov directly describes his own desires, and also a certain separateness from peasant life. The next year he spent back at home in the village; as he put it, "I worked at homely peasant work, I walked in bast shoes, but I very much wanted to study."[34]

Study he eventually did, but not without going through the process of gaining release from his home society. In May 1834, Konstantin and his father went before not just a gathering of the local peasants but in front of

> a big assembly of peasants in the township administration, the bailiff was there and the priest from Kobro led the peasants in the oath. Father gave the administration a petition, that he wished to send his son to study at the gymnasium, and that he needed freedom from the society; the petition was read out to the society; the society did not [initially] agree to give the freedom, pointing out that the society would be expected to pay money for the schooling, but the priest and bailiff said that there would be no fee for the schooling and they [right away] gave [me] freedom.[35]

According to the accounts of others, this was an unusually easy process of gaining freedom; once the society understood that the change would cost them nothing new, it was perfectly willing to grant the boy freedom. The reason for this ease likely lies in the specifics of Konstantin's birth year. He had been born in 1821, after the seventh revision of the tax rolls, and he was seeking release in 1834, just before the eighth revision. In other words, although he was a peasant by birth, he had not yet been made official in the eyes of the central state by placement on the tax rolls. His mobility was not as confined as those only four years his senior, nor as it would have been had he sought release two years later. Thanks in part to this lucky timing, Konstantin went to try again with the freedom document and diploma in hand, and after passing an entrance exam, was admitted to the provincial secondary school.

Stoliarov's path to furthering his education was more convoluted. He spent five years after finishing his primary education living and working in the village. His schooling, though, had set him apart. For one, he had begun singing in a church choir and assisting the priest and deacon with their duties. This led to a first attempt to go on to more schooling, when his mother took him, then aged fifteen, to Voronezh to enroll in a monastery choir school. Their trip proved to be unsuccessful, for Ivan sang well but could not read music, and the choir masters were unwilling to put effort into training a singer on the cusp of adolescence, whose voice might be about to change for the worse. But this moment, he recalled, gave him a new focus. "I even more sharply began to feel my estrangement from the world of Karachun, and even more began to think of how

I could break the chains binding me, to break through to knowledge, to learning." It also made him realize a particular hindrance he faced: his parents. His mother only wished him to leave the household to enter some sort of religious status; his father did not wish him to leave at all. Perhaps because his dreams had remained unfulfilled, he believed his son ought to stay at home, plying the same trade everyone in the village had plied for generations.[36]

Soon thereafter, however, Stoliarov found himself on a new path through a combination of his own determination and random chance. The latter played a role when the village scribe told him of a school for medics in Voronezh that might have an opening for him. Overjoyed at the thought, Stoliarov then forced the issue by facing his parents' opposition with a threat: if they did not allow him to study, he would run off to Voronezh and find work in a tavern. Faced with the idea of such a dishonorable action, his parents agreed to allow him to study—but at a rural agricultural school (the Lower Agricultural Kon'-Kolodezskii school, commonly called the Konevskii school), not in the city. Stoliarov happily agreed. As he put it, all he knew was that he wanted to study more; the school itself did not matter.[37] At the new school, Stoliarov excelled. At the end of his four years at the lower school, he applied for entrance to the Mariinskii Middle Agricultural School in Saratov. He was accepted, and then he had to face the question of funding: he had received a scholarship from the province for his study at the lower school, but going to Saratov required outside funds. Initially, the head of his school held a fundraiser on his behalf, but he refused the money, asking that it be given to other poor students. In the end, he received a scholarship from the Ministry of Agriculture to attend the Mariinskii School.[38]

At this point in his memoir, Stoliarov skips over the moment when his educational goals required a change in his official status. In order to attend schools like the Mariinskii School, peasants needed to receive formal freedom from their home societies. Stoliarov, who did describe the documentary evidence needed for his earlier schooling, does not describe this process in his memoir. In the published version of his memoir, however, the facsimile of the letter of freedom he received at this time appears in an appendix. The formal language of the letter in many ways simply expresses a feeling Stoliarov had long had: "the present certificate is given to Ivan Iakovlev Stoliarov, age 22, stating that the society and the township administration have no objections to excluding him from the peasant society of the village of Karachun."[39] Perhaps Stoliarov did not mention this moment in his memoirs because he had already felt separate, even excluded, from his village for years. This document only confirmed formally what he had already long felt.

This feeling of separateness was one that affected both boys as they entered their schools. Although both were formally excluded from their peasant societies, that did not, of course, mean that they were suddenly no longer peasants. Instead, they found themselves in very different worlds from the ones they had known before, in ways that were both thrilling and frightening. Within his secondary school, Klepikov was unique. As he put it, "during my studies at the school there was not one student from the peasantry" besides himself.[40] Beyond this, and beyond some mention of school uniforms and the like, he does not go into much detail about what his experience there was like. Stoliarov, however, vividly described how it felt to be a peasant among students from towns and even from the gentry. On the one hand, as he put it, "in school they cut our hair, they dressed and shod us all identically. Thus social difference disappeared." But, too, despite the fact that these new clothes erased visible differences between the students, other differences remained. "I took off my peasant clothes and put on the school uniform. I was in no ways different from all the other students and all the same I still was a stranger among them."[41]

Neither Klepikov nor Stoliarov finished their higher education, and their eventual fates were quite different. Klepikov left the gymnasium during his fifth year there, "because of not having funds and weakness of health." But rather than return to the village, he took on a new identity, registering as a townsman in Viatka. Through this new identity, he became firmly a part of Viatka society. He worked for a first guild merchant for nineteen years, eventually becoming his primary agent. At one point he even lived in St. Petersburg for several months on business (his major memory of the capital was that the city was in the midst of a cholera epidemic). He attained merchant status himself. He also served in the civil administration of Viatka in many capacities over the years.[42] He was, in other words, fully a part of his new town status, fully a part of his new society.

Furthermore, Klepikov confirmed his town status through marriage and by passing that status down through future generations. He and his wife had many children, who went on to establish themselves firmly in local and other merchant societies. Two sons became Moscow merchants, another moved to Semipalatinsk as a merchant, and a fourth gained a higher education, and then moved to Kineshma, where he worked as a factory inspector, joined the Moscow branch of the Imperial Technological Society, and became a great patron of the local theater. His daughters married well, six to merchants and one to a bureaucrat (and one last daughter entered a monastery at age 16). One daughter, Elena Konstantinovna, became one of the first women to graduate from a Moscow agricultural academy. And her son—one of the seventeen grandsons and fourteen granddaughters Klepikov had by 1900—was A. V. Chaianov, eventually known as one of the most important peasant theorists in Russia.[43] In an odd way, he brought the story of the family back to its beginning, from the man born to a peasant father to his highly educated grandson who studied the phenomenon of peasants.

Taken as a whole, Klepikov's story is one of modest success, in terms of both his worldly affairs and, it seems, his ability to rationalize his place within the larger social world of imperial Russia. He moved from townsman to merchant, and placed not only himself but also his larger family firmly within that last *soslovie*. But he was never the showy "merchant-millionaire" that Chukmaldin apparently became; instead, he ends his memoir with a far more modest boast: "in the whole span of my life, in trade and industry, I have never been indebted to anyone, and was never fined nor brought before the court."[44] At the same time, although he does not quite address this directly, he seems to have been able to reconcile his peasant origins with his later status without significant difficulty. He had been born a peasant, of course, and that peasant origin was part of his life story, but that peasant life was far removed. When he moved to Viatka, he clearly became as if a native. By the end of his life he was an "old-timer" of Viatka, a well-established local merchant, who could remember his peasant origins but who had, according to his descendants, become fully ensconced in his new life.

Stoliarov's fate, on the other hand, was bound up with the times in which he studied, and it reflected both a more radical time and greater difficulty in reconciling his peasant status with his place in the larger society. He entered the Saratov agricultural school in 1902, and he, then in his early twenties, was soon caught up in the revolutionary spirit of the times. He explained his transformation as being essentially based in his *soslovie* of origin. Earlier in his memoir, Stoliarov had described his awareness of being marked as different and lesser because of his peasant status. As he put it, "from early childhood we were subjected to many humiliations on the part of the higher *sosloviia*. The administration (lords, rich merchants, bureaucrats) had complete power over the peasant and could even resort to beatings. Unexpected curses often rained down on a peasant, and he could not protect his rights. Local authorities used every opportunity to offend or beat him.... The peasant knew that he would always be guilty before the lord. He had to bear everything."[45] While at school in Saratov he "became a revolutionary" not, he claimed, out of reading economics or politics, but simply because of his origins: "I was forced into it by that which I had been witness to since childhood."[46]

In fairly short order, Stoliarov was arrested after he and several revolutionary friends decided to liberate the school's ancient cannon, and he was sent to Voronezh, his official place of residence. Rather than returning to his home village, where he no longer belonged, he fell in with other revolutionaries and through them found a position as a surveyor on the extensive estates of S. V. Panina, herself eventually a leader within the Kadet party. He soon became embroiled in the events of 1905, particularly in the Peasant Union, and, again with the help of Panina, he fled the country to escape arrest, settling in France. His life story, therefore, moves completely out of the bounds of the story of *soslovie* in Russia (for although he did eventually return to Russia, it was not until 1916— and he then became embroiled in the many stories of the early Soviet era).

Perhaps because his life in Russia was interrupted, Stoliarov seems not to have been able to reconcile his peasant past with whatever his present became as successfully as Klepikov did. For the most part, he treats the village of his childhood and youth as an outsider, and he writes of his feelings of estrangement from his peasant surroundings. And yet, even these sections are intercut with bright moments of purely personal storytelling. He tells, for example, of lazy conversations about everything and nothing with other boys on a hot summer day, and he throws into this universal memory something utterly specific: the ground in Karachun was littered with pottery shards from the local industry, and on hot days those shards burnt their bare feet.[47] His memories of school also bespeak a discomfort with his origins. On the one hand, life in school was perfect and perfectly classless; on the other, he was internally marked as a peasant despite his haircut and uniform. In the end, he found himself in part frustrated by his peasant past, in part frustrated by those who claimed to speak of or for the peasantry. He scorned Chekhov and Gorky's depictions of peasants as nasty and brutish, but at the same time felt that "the tsarist regime did everything in order to erect an impassible, impenetrable wall between my people and me."[48]

EVOLVING *SOSLOVIIA*: THE HIDDEN STORIES OF ASCRIPTION

In some ways, the most basic part of being a member of one of imperial Russia's *soslovie* societies was having one's name written down in the pages of a book.[49] The act of listing names in a book or on a document had both evidentiary and symbolic importance. Ascription was the source of proof that an individual had certain rights and privileges. At times, too, particular kinds of ascription were given even higher symbolic weight. In 1807, as part of a larger manifesto granting privileges to the newly honorable *soslovie* of merchants, Alexander I called for a new "velvet book of notable merchant families" to be drawn up and kept in the Ministry of Commerce.[50] The process of ascription here granted honor rather than duty.

More generally, ascription was a basic element of individual *soslovie* identity. Many of the provisions of Catherine the Great's Charters to the Nobility and to the Towns focused on the kinds of evidence an individual had to supply in order to be properly written down in a given society's books. Evidence based on these sorts of books—and also on the parallel registries based in parishes, the metrical books—came to be required for all sorts of activities. Stoliarov, for one, recalled that in order to gain admission to the lower agricultural school, he had to provide three documents: a certificate of vaccination against smallpox, which the local medic gave him without charge; a diploma for having finished primary school, which he already possessed; and metrical evidence, which the local priest would provide, but only in return for 3 rubles, a sum Stoliarov's mother thought outrageous.[51] Fees for ascription also played into the regular running of town societies. When Emel'ian Griaznov entered the Moscow merchant society in 1865, he paid a whole series of fees, including 1 ruble for a passport, and 15 rubles for "ascription into the town resident book."[52]

The books kept by the Moscow Artisan Society to record its members fulfill both these goals: to supply evidence and to symbolize importance or honor. The latter is accomplished most of all through sheer physical size; they are imposing volumes, their great size making even the very act of pulling the books off a shelf difficult, let alone moving them from shelf to desk. Then, when opened, they cover an entire reading desk. Even the motion required to turn the pages can barely be accomplished while sitting down, and not at all without exaggerated gestures. They seem meant above all to strike those consulting them by their grandeur and importance. For such impressive books, however, their contents are far more ordinary and geared toward the everyday sorts of evidence that might be required by imperial Russia's system of *sosloviia*. They include a long numbered list of households ascribed to the society, with orderly columns to record names, ages, and other basic information about those households' members.

Although the volumes seem at first glance to be static images of Moscow's artisan society—the formal title of one such volume, *Household List of Moscow Artisans of the Cooking Guild Compiled in 1874*, suggests, after all, a particular moment in time—they soon reveal themselves to be instead constantly changing, almost living documents. For one, the book includes not only all households of the guild as of 1874 but was continued past that date to include all those who registered in the society through 1897. In addition, sometimes well after one hand had listed the names of all these members in the neat script of a chancellery clerk, later writers filled the empty spaces on the huge pages with annotations tracing out later developments in the lives of these many individuals. Records of their marriages, the births of their children, and their deaths all give greater depth to the story of their lives. So too do moments when their lives came into contact with the state, through changing or gaining a name, through problems with the law, or through leaving the society to pursue some other vision of their future. The marginalia here makes the simple enumeration of people into something constantly evolving.

As a result, the life stories traced out in the household lists of both the Moscow artisan and townsperson societies, and also in the books of registrations in the St. Petersburg townsperson society, show some of the ways that a moment of movement into a town *soslovie* played out over the ensuing decades. They give glimpses into the broader paths of individual lives—mere outlines, true, but outlines that are nonetheless at times almost haunting. They speak to the ways that individuals found themselves a place via marriage or via finding work. They speak to the family connections that at times drew people to new places and at times bound them to their old, despite their best efforts to break free. And, too, they speak to those for whom a change in status was only temporary, or unsuccessful, or at base a matter of paper registration rather than real change.

In 1876, a man named Ivan Golovkin entered the Moscow townsperson society.[53] By origin a peasant from Orel province, Golovkin was forty-one years old and entered the society along with his immediate family. Over the next several decades that family expanded. A daughter, Vera, was born in 1877, and a son, Fedor, in 1879. When an older son married, his wife and eventual children were added to the household's numbers. In the new century, though, a new kind of change began to affect the family. Vera left the household and the townsperson society in 1901, becoming a non-trading merchant in Grodno. One of Ivan Golovkin's grandsons, Nikolai, born in 1890, left the society as well. In 1916, he gained the rank of collegiate registrar—the lowest rank on the Table of Ranks—and as a result, he gained his release from the townsperson society. These events suggest a story of success for the Golovkin family, one where the former peasants came and prospered in their new status. But notes in the record books of the townsperson society also portray a more difficult part of the family's fortunes. Son Fedor was twice arrested, in 1903 and 1912, and sent to prison for theft. His end bespoke a different fate, one of dislocation and disgrace.

Golovkin's family was only one of hundreds registering in Moscow or St. Petersburg in the second half of the nineteenth century. Between 1859 and 1896, 652 individuals were registered as new heads of household in the townsperson books of Sretenskaia neighborhood, just one of Moscow's thirty-three separate townsperson administrative groups. The group was nearly evenly split between men and women: women accounted for 47 percent of the new entrants. The St. Petersburg townsperson society similarly took in many new members, although its record-keeping practices make direct comparisons difficult. However, in just three years—1883, 1892, and 1899—the society took in 1621 new members, 70 percent of them women. These many individuals often brought with them families, and as a result thousands were affected by these initial moments of change.

Golovkin's family may have been one of many but its specific later fate was unique to it. Nonetheless, the twists and turns of that larger family life—changes that accrued through birth, death, disgrace, or personal achievements—do highlight some of the ways that the decision to change status played out for many subjects of the Russian empire. From the expansion of families through marriages and births, through further movement for original petitioners or their descendants, even to the signs of trouble, whether it be theft, early death, or disappearance, all were possible fates reflected in the *soslovie* records of Moscow and St. Petersburg.

First, the most basic future facing many of those who entered the townsperson or artisan societies of the capitals might best be described as a simple domestic success reflected in the growth of their families. Individuals came in with families and those families expanded through another generation (or even two), or they married in their new status and began the process of settling down. In so doing, they solidified their position as townspeople or artisans of Moscow or St. Petersburg. These were figures like Matvei Gaidash, a state peasant from Grodno province, who entered the St. Petersburg townsperson society in 1859 along with his wife and two daughters. Soon after, Gaidash and his wife had several sons. Although Gaidash himself died in 1873, his descendants continued to be members of the townsperson society for an additional forty years—and all were associated on paper with that initial moment of gaining membership, recorded on the very decree that established Gaidash's new social status.[54] Or, they were figures like Konstantin Rudnev, a soldier's son turned St. Petersburg townsman in 1883. He came to the society a twenty-year-old bachelor, but he married, had children, and saw them marry and have children before his eventual death in 1905.[55]

The close connection of family and *soslovie* could nonetheless lead to complications based in the moment of change. In October 1825, the peasant Nikon Mikheev (sometimes called Matrosov) joined the Moscow merchant society, initially with a woman he called his wife, Matrena Dmitrieva. Soon, however, he admitted that his family situation was rather more troubled. In December, Nikon submitted a statement to the Moscow Town Society, stating "I have a lawful wife Elizaveta Ivanova and not Matrena Dmitrieva, with whom I was registered by an ukase of the Treasury Department." Further investigation showed that Nikon and Elizaveta had been estranged ever since Elizaveta ran off with some of her husband's merchandise. They lived apart, and a case for the dissolution of their marriage sat with local authorities. This might not have caused problems, but for the fact that Nikon changed his status. That change meant that if his legal wife was not also made a merchant, she would remain without a proper place in society. For her purposes, this was important most of all because she would be left without documents granting her the right to live where she wished. In the end, one document listed Elizaveta as Nikon's wife, but her documents were withheld on the grounds that their court case was still in progress.[56]

Even within this basic idea of establishing not just oneself but also one's family, even including later generations, in a new status, there were many possible paths. Some initially entered a society alone, leaving children either in a previous status or without status (as in the case of illegitimate children); eventually, some of these children found their status regularized as they were added to their mothers' (usually) households. Such was the case of Iakobina Shpats, by origin a German colonist from Lifland province.[57] She entered the St. Petersburg townsperson society in 1883, alone. Soon, however, her two illegitimate children (a son born in 1880 and a daughter born in 1882) were added to her household, as was a second illegitimate son born in 1888. Shpats eventually herself married, as did her two oldest children. That son saw his children born St. Petersburg townspeople before his death in 1910. The second, Ivan, also acted in a way to solidify his place in St. Petersburg: in 1916, during the First World War, when anti-German sentiment was rampant in the country, Ivan Shpats legally changed his last name to Sedov.[58]

Another permutation of the role of families involved another way of building them: adoption. In some cases, these adoptions were clearly examples of legitimizing illegitimate children. Sergei Chernetsev, a freed serf who entered the Moscow artisan society in 1863, adopted his wife's illegitimate son Mikhail, an act that gave Mikhail a patronymic (Sergeev) and a last name (Chernetsev).[59] In others, the relationship was less clear. Avgust Tishler, who entered the St. Petersburg townsperson society in 1883 as a twenty-nine-year-old peasant from Estliand province, never married, but did eventually adopt a peasant girl born in 1898. He died in 1909, and the following year the young girl began acting in part on her own behalf, as she herself signed for a passport.[60] Ivan Volkov, a landless peasant from Pskov province, also entered the St. Petersburg townsperson society in 1883. He married there, and in 1887 he and his wife adopted a sixteen-year-old illegitimate daughter of a Swedish citizen.[61] Varvara Bobrova, a widowed landless peasant from Penza province who entered the St. Petersburg society in 1892 with her son, eventually also adopted the illegitimate daughter of a peasant from

Nizhnii Novgorod in 1908.[62] All these cases are straightforward on the page, but they suggest mysteries in their specifics. What was the connection between Volkov and the "Swedish citizen" whose child he adopted? Did Tishler adopt his own illegitimate child, in so doing giving her status she otherwise lacked?

At the same time that the records show families growing, the way households were defined means that some examples of the act of establishing a family are obscured by the very practices of record-keeping. In particular, women who entered townsperson societies disappear from the record at what might have been the very moment of settling themselves: marriage, as in the case of Iakobina Shpats, above. Not many of these women went on to marry. Just under 10 percent of the women who joined the St. Petersburg townsperson society in several years in the second half of the nineteenth century later married; only a slightly higher percentage of women who entered Moscow's townsperson society—15.6 percent—did the same. When they did marry, however, they left the household they had created by entering a society on their own behalf and entered that of their husband. As a result, archival records from the town townsperson and artisan societies simply list the dates that women, be they heads of their own households or daughters within larger household, married, and their further life is cut off from that of their family. Nor do the records indicate whether these women found themselves possessed of a new status upon their marriage; their husbands (and their ranks) are simply not listed. (For that matter, nor are the statuses of origins of those women who marry into the households.)

Despite these limitations, memoir accounts, at least, suggest that marriage—perhaps particularly the marriage of daughters—played an important role in establishing families as full members of a new status and society. Women who themselves changed their status might not be likely to marry but dependent women, the daughters or granddaughters of men who changed status, often did. Furthermore, they often did so in ways that seemed explicitly to formalize either status in a particular place or the idea of upward mobility within the family. Aleksandr Berezin waited until he had not simply moved from monastery peasant to merchant of the second guild, but had further moved up to the first guild, before he married a fellow merchant's daughter. Furthermore, he noted, his children married well—one daughter to a merchant, another to an architect with the civil rank of captain.[63] This latter result was certainly not an uncommon one. Vasilii Barkov, who began life as a factory serf, also described such a result of his own social movement into the town estates. He gladly saw one son and one daughter marry into wealthy merchant families.[64] Other archival sources confirm the idea that marriage was particularly important in more firmly establishing status. The file recording Ivan Khludov's entry into the Moscow merchant society in 1824 includes a marriage certificate for one of his sons, Taras. He married the daughter of a Moscow merchant, one Avdot'ia Iakovleva, a sixteen-year-old girl of medium height, with a pale face, gray eyes and blond hair.[65] The marriage was another way of fixing the family into the society of Moscow merchants.

A second major outcome of a single instance of change of status, and one also visible in the case of Golovkin, was the possibility of yet more social mobility. Some evidence suggests that one experience of changing status might have inclined individuals (or their family members) to move yet again. In 1892, the St. Petersburg townsperson board decided on thirty-six cases of those wishing to leave the society. Only seven of those individuals (19 percent) came from families that had been in the society as of the last census revision in 1857.[66] And the records from Moscow and St. Petersburg show that a small but distinct minority of those who entered town societies either went on to yet further new statuses themselves or saw some member of their family do so. Within that minority were a number of sources of variation, based on type of mobility, gender, and generation.

The records show four main types of future movement by these new townspeople and their descendants: to other town societies either locally or at a distance; by attainment of the status of honored citizen; by joining a peasant society; and through release from the town society for educational access and the attainment of a professional (or quasi-professional) status. Those who moved into another town society were in one way simply taking part in the regular movement of townspeople between *meshchanin* and merchant status (and sometimes back again). Those who became honored citizens were at once affirming their status in the town, but also separating themselves from the idea of communal responsibility that was embedded in the *soslovie* ideal. They were, in other words, attaining status as individuals, while also maintaining their association with Moscow or St. Petersburg. The few who joined peasant societies were leaving the town for the village, and taking on peasant status as they did so. And the last group were those who attained individual status through educational achievement, through profession, or through service to the imperial state.

Women were consistently less likely than men to see future mobility in their families. This held true in both Moscow and St. Petersburg, even when wards of the foundling

TABLE 7.1

Percent of new townspeople and artisans with future mobility in their families, by gender, c. 1858–1899

	Moscow Artisans	Moscow Townspeople	St. Petersburg Townspeople
Total	6.7	8.6	8.2
Men	6.7	11.6	23.1
Women		5.2	3.5
Women without wards			8.1

Source: *TsIAM f. 6, op. 1, d. 12; TsIAM f. 5, op. 1, dd. 209–13; TsGIASPb f. 222, op. 1, d. 360–61, 421–22, 506–507, 1108.*

home, who very rarely changed their status—only 0.6 percent, or 4 of 688 total wards, were recorded as eventually moving on to some new status—are removed. Certainly this fact is partially explained by the fewer choices open to women. State service (other than service in the imperial theaters) was not generally open to them, and their opportunities to engage in the kinds of educational institutions that required (or allowed) release from the society were far more limited than those of their male counterparts. While a few became tutors or midwives, for the most part women simply had fewer places to move to, and thus moved less.

In addition, women were almost by definition less likely than their male counterparts to have established families. Women who entered the societies as heads of household were always unmarried, and only some of them had children. Among the new towns-people in Moscow, 86 percent of men and 33 percent of women entered the society with families; in St. Petersburg, singletons were generally more common, but men were still more likely than women to enter with families: 49 percent to 17 percent of new towns-people, even discounting the many wards of the imperial foundling home who by def-inition entered without family but who may have had some connections due to that earlier status. This fact likely influenced the lower rate of future social mobility among the families of new women in the societies in two ways. For one, they simply had fewer total family members to go on to new statuses later on. In addition, they had less sup-port to make moves made possible by economic success, like movement into the status of merchant or honored citizen.

A second source of variation affecting social mobility is the generation in which that later mobility took place. In some cases, those who had initially changed their *soslovie* themselves went on to new statuses; in the remaining cases, one or more descendants of those who initiated movement into one of the capital societies moved on to new sta-tuses. The three societies had different patterns here; compared to their descendants, new artisans were most likely to stay put in their new status while new St. Petersburg towns-people were most likely to move on to yet another new position. Furthermore, the initial migrants and their descendants varied significantly by type of future mobility—to other town society, honored citizenry, peasant, or profession. In particular, those who had initially moved into lower town statuses themselves were more likely than their descen-dants to move into other town *soslovie* societies. Their descendants, however, were more likely to leave those societies, taking on radically new positions as honored citizens, as professionals, or even as peasants.

Consistently, among all three groups, those who moved on themselves were more likely than their descendants to move locally, to other town societies—merchant, artisan, or townsperson—in either Moscow or St. Petersburg. Even in St. Petersburg, where the overall rate of movement into another St. Petersburg society was lower than it was for those in either the townsperson or artisan's societies of Moscow (17.5 per-cent of movement, compared to around a third of movement in both Moscow groups), first-generation migrants were far more likely to stay within the boundaries of town

TABLE 7.2

Percent of future movement of new townspeople and artisans, by destination and generation

| | Moscow Artisans | | Moscow Townspeople | | St. Petersburg Townspeople | |
	Self (N = 39)	Descendants (N = 60)	Self (N = 29)	Descendants (N = 27)	Self (N = 94)	Descendants (N = 49)
Local town *soslovie*	56.4	23.3	44.8	11.1	21.3	10.2
Other town *soslovie*	25.6	20.0	10.3	7.4	17.0	4.1
Honored Citizen	0.0	1.7	13.8	37.0	23.4	28.6
Peasant	10.3	11.7	0.0	7.4	4.3	6.1
Professions, service, education	7.7	40.0	31.0	48.1	34.0	55.1

Source: TsIAM f. 6, op. 1, d. 12; TsIAM f. 5, op. 1, dd. 209–13; TsGIASPb f. 222, op. 1, d. 360–61, 421–22, 506–507, 1108.

society than were their descendants. In addition, a similar decline in rates of movement from generation to generation occurred in a different kind of mobility, to town societies in other towns. New members of the Moscow and St. Petersburg town societies and their descendants at times changed their registry to a similar status in other towns. Moscow artisans and townspeople moved into nearby town societies in Sergeev Posad, Voskresensk, or Kolomna, and also to farther places, including Viatka, Odessa, Orenburg, and even Vladivostok. St. Petersburg townspeople moved mostly locally, to Tsarskoe Selo or Iamburg, with one outlier, Vladimir Kudriashev, who registered as a merchant in Usman, Tambov province, in 1865, six years after he had joined the St. Petersburg society as a freed serf. But consistently, migrants themselves were more likely to make such moves than were their descendants.

Movement into the honored citizenry was slightly more complicated. In one way, the three groups were alike: in every case, descendants of initial migrants were more likely to attain the rank of honored citizen than the migrants themselves. The two townsperson groups also share certain similarities; in both cases, around a quarter of all mobility involved attainment of honored citizen status. However, and likely in large part because of the very different patterns of local movement in the two societies, the generational change was far greater in Moscow than in St. Petersburg. Furthermore, the Moscow artisan society had a completely different pattern. Of the 1,521 individuals who moved into the Moscow artisan society of chefs, and of the 99 who went on to move into some other status, only one saw a descendant attain that rank: one Petr, the youngest son of Makar Chulkov, a freed serf who entered the society in 1863, attained the status of hereditary honored citizen in 1911.[67] In part, this may reflect the differences in the overall rates of future change for the three societies. St. Petersburg's new townspeople were the most likely to move themselves, and were similarly more likely to move into the honored citizenry, than were their Muscovite fellows. It may also be the necessary flip side of the higher rate of Moscow's townspeople moving into other town societies. In either case, however, it suggests that town status was either more important or had higher value in Moscow, while in St. Petersburg the goal of moving into the honored citizenry was more pronounced.

A few of those who went on to move to new statuses became peasants. Their numbers were never large but increased from first-generation migrants to following generations. And their stories show a variety of possible motivations. Some returned to former places of residence. Matvei Iakovlev, a freed serf who joined the St. Petersburg townsperson society in 1859, returned to his home district in Novgorod province sixteen years later. In his case, remaining a peasant may always have been his goal, but one that was not possible in the waning years of serfdom.[68] After initially fixing his place according to where it was easiest to move (a townsperson society), he later returned to this earlier place and earlier status. In so doing, he was, perhaps, fixing a feeling of dislocation common to many migrants of the era.[69]

The paths of others were more complicated. Prokofii Osipov, a soldier's son who had entered the Moscow artisan society in 1863, was transferred into a society of temporarily obligated peasants in 1866.[70] Perhaps this was a new society, or perhaps a parent had belonged to the village, and had maintained connections that Prokofii eventually solidified. The descendants of initial migrants who moved into the peasantry followed at times widely different paths. Ivan Krysin, a freed serf from Vitebsk province, joined the St. Petersburg townsperson society in 1859. In 1906, his grandson, then only age sixteen, moved with his wife to a peasant society in St. Petersburg district, apparently into the household of his father-in-law. Here, he was clearly solidifying his place in a family by changing his status. Fedor Ivanov, another freed serf, joined the Moscow artisan society in 1863 with his wife, two sons, and a daughter. One son, Grigorii, who was seventeen at the time of transfer, married and had children, including a son Mikhail, in 1886. That son, a grandson of the original migrant, transferred into a peasant society with his wife in 1912. The following year, his father, then about sixty-seven years old, and mother and sisters joined them as peasants.[71]

Far more migrants, and particularly their descendants, moved into a variety of other statuses that all involved some sort of educational or professional attainment. These sorts of professional, semi-professional, or service statuses accounted for nearly or just over half of the mobility of the descendants of initial migrants. Furthermore, both men and women attained freedom from their townsperson status by gaining these statuses. Sons

and daughters, grandsons and granddaughters—all attained new statuses through finishing certain levels of schooling. Many became teachers or tutors. Some women became
midwifes. Some men entered some sort of state service and eventually gained the rank
of collegiate registrar. Particularly in St. Petersburg, some children began to work in the
arts, as actors or ballerinas in imperial theaters, work that gave them freedom from the
townsperson society and a new status.

These overall patterns hide many possible variations between and within families—
and, it seems, many possible futures. In 1883, Fedor Nikolaev Burmistrov, a former serf
from Kaluga province, became a St. Petersburg townsman. He brought with him his
wife, a son, and six daughters. The family clearly prospered. Burmistrov himself became
a personal honored citizen in 1887. In 1892, two of his daughters entered the service of
the imperial theaters and gained their exclusion from the society. And in 1904, a third
daughter, Ekaterina, also entered the service of the theaters as a ballerina.[72] She was still
performing as a ballerina during the stormy revolutionary era, dancing for the Mariinskii
Theater as the Queen in *Sleeping Beauty* and as the sovereign princess in *Swan Lake* in
1918 and 1919.[73] In 1892, one Dmitrii Fedoseev entered the St. Petersburg townsperson
society with a similarly large family: a wife, three sons, and three daughters. Originally
peasants (and from before emancipation, state peasants) from Moscow province, the
family had for the most part an average fate in St. Petersburg, with marriages and a next
generation. One son, Sergei, born in 1877, eventually attended and graduated from St.
Petersburg University with a degree in physics and math. As a result, he was excluded
from the townsperson society in 1905.[74] As far as the townsperson society was concerned,
his story ended there. But other sources give hints as to where he went next. The records
of the Russian State Historical Archive list one Sergei Dmitrievich Fedoseev, born 1877,
as a bureaucrat in the Department of the State Treasury as of 1906.[75]

Burmistrov and Fedoseev were married men with families, but even those with more
marginal positions could find similar successes in their new statuses. In 1892, Mariia
Ivanova Kryzheva, by birth a landless peasant from Iaroslavl' province, entered the St.
Petersburg townsperson society as an unmarried mother of a son and daughter in their
early teens. Despite these seemingly inauspicious beginnings, Kryzheva's children prospered. Kryzheva had a second daughter after her registry in the capital, and all three
children were granted a common last name: Kerbloi, in the records, which seems to
have been transformed into Kerblai at some point. All three children were eventually
excluded from the townsperson society. The oldest daughter, Evdokiia, became a tutor in
1896; her younger sister gained the same status in 1904. The son, Semen, finished studies
at the Technological Institute and was granted the rank of personal honored citizen in
1904.[76]

He went on to significant further success. His expertise with electricity kept him in
good standing in the early years of the Soviet era. According to one account, he was
central to the project of electrifying Petro/Leningrad; in addition, he both worked as
an engineer in a series of factories around the city and taught at institutes there, and

continued to work as a lecturer at a military school during the evacuation of Leningrad. His daughter Tamara, a physicist in her own right, helped evacuate a factory during the blockade and went on to live outside Moscow.[77]

ALTERNATIVE PATHS: DISGRACE AND DISAPPEARANCE

Of course, not everyone prospered in their new status. Some individual early archival documents indicate such fates. Avdei Nikitin, an economic peasant, was accepted into the Moscow merchant society in 1815, after more than ten years' residence in the city. With three sons, a daughter, two daughters-in-law, and five granddaughters, Nikitin might have had a strong enough base to prosper. But soon his oldest son, the father of the five granddaughters, died, and the family fell on hard times. A follow-up report in their file notes that they had failed to pay proper merchant dues, and had therefore never really been registered as merchants. They were dunned for all dues accruing to their former status since their acceptance, and furthermore placed in the town's townsperson society.[78] Similar troubled fates are reflected even in the bare notations in the registry books. Some fell into trouble with the law, like Fedor Golovkin, jailed twice for theft in the waning years of the empire. Others had to seek out the mercy of their society's charitable institutions. And yet others simply disappeared, their fates completely lost.

The number of those who faced criminal prosecution of some sort was never large. Fewer than 1 percent of those who entered Moscow's artisan society and St. Petersburg's townsperson society were eventually jailed or exiled, and only a slightly larger proportion of those entering Moscow's townsperson society (3 percent) did the same. The reasons for their interactions with the law also varied. The most common crime mentioned in the records is theft. Efronsinia Niniianova, a freed serf who had entered the Moscow townsperson society in 1863 was sentenced to prison for three months in 1878; others found themselves repeatedly in trouble, like Georgii Zimin, the descendant of a peasant turned townsperson, convicted of theft several times in the early years of the twentieth century. A few were given harsher sentences for apparently the same crime, as they were sent into exile for theft (perhaps for repeated theft).

Exile to Siberia was not uncommon among the punishments, though the reasons for those punishments are not always clear. Several new members of the Moscow artisan society were sent either to Siberia in general or to specific places there—usually Tobol'sk—in particular. Lavrentii Aleksandrov, who entered the society in 1863 as a household member of his father, a freed serf, was sent "for residence in Tobol'sk province" in 1870. Two years later, another freed serf turned artisan, Pankratii Petrov, was sent to Tobol'sk "for permanent removal." In a very few cases, more abstract reasons for exile appear. Nikolai Semenov, another serf's son brought in to the artisan society with his family, got in trouble a decade after his initial registry. In 1873, then aged twenty-three, he was sent to Tobol'sk "due to being unaccepted by the society."[79] And in 1908, the same year her brother was sent to Olonets province for robbery, Antonina Kudriavtseva, the daughter of a soldier turned Moscow townsperson, was sent to Tobol'sk for "revolutionary activities."[80]

A case involving the harshest punishment is particularly evocative. In 1870, two sisters, Solomonida and Avdot'ia Savel'eva, registered in the Moscow townsperson society. They were both unmarried—and never married—peasants from Vladimir province. Solomonida was fifty at the time of their entry, her sister forty-three. The two women were Old Believers associated with the Rogozhskoe community in Moscow. That community had certain aspects that made it a self-sufficient world within the larger city; among other things, it had its own charitable institutions for members. Something, though, clearly went wrong with the Savel'eva sisters and their lives in Moscow. In 1884, Avdot'ia, then fifty-seven years old, was sentenced to six years of hard labor—by far the harshest sentence of any listed in these documents—for arson.[81] In rural Russia, arson has most of all been associated with protest, whether against landlords or against prosperous fellow peasants, and was considered a most serious crime.[82] In old, wooden, highly populated Moscow, that crime was all the more a sign of possible serious tragedy.

Some of those who entered societies eventually found themselves or their family members turning to local charitable institutions for support. Overall, few did: 3.7 percent of new Moscow townspeople, and less than 1 percent of the other groups. Here, though, gender and initial family size had a strong influence on patterns. Virtually all who entered almshouses were without families to support them. The one case of someone with a living family member entering an almshouse among new Moscow artisans is the wife of Gerasim Shabarshin. The two had entered the society in 1865 (unusually, their status of origin was not indicated in the record books). The wife entered the almshouse in 1878, the year before Gerasim died—perhaps he was already failing and unable to support her. The records suggest that she lived there until her death in 1891.[83]

As a rule, and unsurprisingly, women, and particularly women without family support, entered almshouses. Every one of the twenty-four cases of Moscow townspeople entering almshouses is a women. And the eighteen cases of new St. Petersburg townspeople or their descendants who entered almshouses almost all involve women, either those who had joined the society on their own or who were widowed and left without support. Only in two cases did men move into an almshouse. In 1899, Ivan Maksimov and his wife—former landless peasants from Smolensk province who had just entered the St. Petersburg society that year—both entered the almshouse. He died in 1901, she in 1911. Petr Evpiov, who had entered the society as a single freed household serf in 1859, became a resident of the almshouse in 1871, at age forty-eight. He died two years later.[84]

The family histories of the women who entered almshouses usually highlight their solitariness. Only five of the twenty-four women who first became Moscow townswomen, and later entered the society's (or the Rogozhskoe society's) almshouse, had families; those five entered as the single mothers of daughters. The remaining nineteen women were all single, either never married or widowed, and at least officially, never married after their entry into the society. Their single state, does not, however, mean that these women were necessarily condemned to solitude and the almshouse from the moment of their entry. The average age at entry of the women who ended up in the almshouse was forty-five, with a range from twenty-seven to seventy-two, higher than the overall average age (thirty-two) of women at registry. But despite this, the average length of time between entry in the society and entry into the almshouse was seventeen years—seventeen years in which the women lived on their own.

The range here, too, was significant. Akulina Morozova, a widowed peasant from Serpukhov district outside Moscow, was fifty-nine when she entered the townsperson society in 1877. She almost immediately entered the almshouse and died the following year, suggesting that her entrance into the society had been perhaps a means of gaining access to the almshouse itself. On the other end of the spectrum, Fekla Iakunina entered the society in 1861 as a thirty-two-year-old soldier's widow. She eventually also entered the almshouse—but not until 1902, forty-one years after her initial registry.

A last possible future reflected in the household books is, at base, the absence of one. Or, at least, the absence of a record of one. This reflects, in part, a consistent complaint of some local societies about policies of, in particular, mandatory registration. In many cases, it became quite clear that the major benefit of *sosloviia* from the point of view of the center—that they allowed it to see its people—was limited, if not totally illusory. Much effort had been put into arguing that everyone needed membership in a *soslovie* society in order to give the individual a voice, a place in society and in view of the state. But the problem was that many of those registries were on paper only. An accounting of the Odessa townsperson board for 1865, for example, noted that the single biggest problem facing the new board was the fact that it could not find many of the townspeople who were supposed to be its members.[85] Some members signed up on paper, and then disappeared.

Records from Moscow and St. Petersburg give new insight to this process, perhaps particularly as it was affected by large-scale movements of population. The Moscow artisan society's cooking guild saw a huge influx of new members in the aftermath of emancipation. The five years from 1862 to 1866 brought 1,295 new members with their families; 1,171, or 90.4 percent of them, were freed serfs. In contrast, the Moscow townsperson society saw no such huge increase in the number of new members during those years. The Moscow artisan society also saw a major difference: far more of those written into its household books simply disappeared from the records after that initial moment of ascription. That is, the household books, filled as they usually were with marginal notations about the future lives of the society's members, were in these cases nearly blank. In 12.7 percent of all cases (and over 14 percent of cases who entered during two of the primary years of movement), individuals were written in and, apparently, never heard from again. Of those who disappeared, 61.5 percent were single men, 29.9 percent married men with only a wife (or in six cases, a mother), and 8.6 percent men with larger families. Unsurprisingly, the single and unattached were more likely to disappear.

Something similar happened with another group of unattached singletons in St. Petersburg. There, large numbers of young women who had been wards of the Imperial St. Petersburg Foundling Home were listed as townswomen upon reaching their majority. In three years during the second half of the nineteenth century, 688 of them were added to the townsperson society rolls; 607 of them, or 88.2 percent, disappeared, or at least left no traces of themselves in the archives.

There are many possible explanations for the disappearance of these many young men and women. Unofficial mobility was clearly rife in late nineteenth-century Russia. Even official mobility, made possible by passports and other documents, took many men or women far away from their place of registry, from whence news of their lives lived may not have made it back to the capitals. The fate of the young women—most left the foundling home around age twenty-two—could have had other complications. Their status as townswomen might have fallen to the yellow tickets carried by prostitutes in the era.[86] But all in all, these missing people do suggest that the choice of a new *soslovie* identity, while it may have made possible successful families and future mobility for some, did not necessarily take root in the lives of others. Perhaps those who disappeared found success elsewhere. If so, their moment of change had been rendered irrelevant.

What, in the end, was the role of *soslovie* in individual lives? For the administration of individual *soslovie* societies, this version of status was, even as revolution began, intensely important. These administrations maintained records of their members in such great detail that the individual fates of thousands and thousands of low-ranking townspeople can be at least partially reconstructed. For those individual townspeople, the question was more mixed. Those who disappeared from view presumably found their *soslovie* status essentially meaningless, as they ignored its strictures and lived outside its authority. For others, though, continued movement through and beyond the *soslovie* system either found them gaining great successes or occasionally falling into decline.

According to memoirists, meanwhile, the role of *soslovie* was often nothing. Once a new status had been attained, figures like Chukmaldin and Klepikov seem to have happily lived new lives without thinking that much about their place of origin. But also according to memoirists, at times *soslovie* meant everything. When it restricted educational opportunities, or when it suddenly demanded a dreaded service, it had the power to alter radically individual lives. For figures like Stoliarov, *soslovie* and the very fact of a society based on such divisions was part of his awakening as a revolutionary. It was in understanding his position and the restrictions it always placed on him that he became conscious. That, then, may be the best understanding of *soslovie* in individual lives during much of the imperial era: it was nothing until it was everything.

Conclusion

DURING THE FIRST World War, the Ekaterinoslav Treasury Department found itself perplexed by one particular aspect of the refugee crisis that had overwhelmed the country, as millions fled the vast areas occupied by enemy forces. By mid-1916, some 242,000 refugees had registered in Ekaterinoslav province, many in the provincial capital itself, where they now constituted 25 percent of the population.[1] The flood of new people created many issues for municipalities dealing with influxes of new residents who arrived with little means of support. But the treasury department was particularly concerned with what might seem a question of semantics: how to reconcile the many, everyday hardships facing refugees with its own particular duty to oversee the bureaucratic process of ascription into a specific *soslovie*.

Treasury departments had long had the responsibility of overseeing this process: they gave out the final documents that stated an individual had changed his or her *soslovie*, from priest's son to merchant, from townsman to peasant, or any one of many other possible trajectories. According to statute, changing *soslovie* required documents, in particular documents stating that an individual was free to leave his or her society or community of origin, and that he or she had been accepted into a new society or community. But the flood of refugees from occupied territory had created a problem with this system. Those who wanted to register in a new *soslovie*—that is, to establish themselves more fully in their place of residence—were supposed to provide documents from their home towns or villages, but those from occupied territory were unable go back to get the appropriate paperwork. Faced with this conundrum, the Ekaterinoslav Treasury wrote to the Ministry of Finance on October 26, 1915, asking for guidance. As the treasury noted, "people are presenting petitions, [and] have handed over to the Treasury only the acceptance documents demanded by §563 [of the Tax Code], but the freedom agreements demanded by §572 of that same Code, they are not currently able to present due to the circumstances of the war."[2] What, the treasury asked, should be done about such cases?

The Ministry of Finance and its frequent correspondent in matters pertaining to *soslovie*, the Ministry of Internal Affairs, were slow to respond—unsurprising given other more important matters they faced during wartime. The Tax Department of the Ministry of Finance wrote to the Ministry of Internal Affairs for comment in December 1915, but no response came. In July 1917—after the end of the tsarist regime—the Ekaterinoslav Treasury wrote again, asking if its question had received a formal response, "in light of the fact that such petitions continue to be presented even up to the present day, and people who have already submitted theirs very often come in with questions about how they are coming along."[3] Finally in August, the two ministries came to a conclusion: allow "Treasuries to ascribe refugees from occupied territories without presenting documents it is impossible for them to obtain, but with the note that such documents should be presented after the war ends."[4] With this, the Ministry of Finance drew up a circular, dated September 4, 1917, to send to all treasuries announcing the new policy. Only two months later, the new bolshevik regime would abolish the entire institution of *soslovie*, making the treasury's question and the ministries' decision moot.[5]

As this correspondence suggests, *soslovie* persisted as a relevant factor in individual lives, in local administration, and in central decision making even as the Russian Empire was in its death throes. The ability to fix oneself to a place gave certain kinds of security to individuals. Local societies worried about those for whom they were responsible by ascription. And the central state considered *soslovie* a way of seeing its population, a way of counting and knowing who it governed. Even in the chaos created by the First World War—and given the role that a kind of identity politics turned out to play on the home front in that war, perhaps because of that chaos—these seemingly obsolescent identities still resonated at all three levels of the Russian state and society.[6]

From the early eighteenth century through the First World War, individual subjects of the Russian Empire chose to alter their official, legal social status (their *soslovie*) through bureaucratic act. They were men and women, by origin freed serfs and state peasants, townspeople and merchants, churchmen and soldiers' wives, and they petitioned to become something different. That is, they strove to leave the social rank and specific local community to which they belonged, usually because of birth, both to gain a new social rank and either to become a member of a local community or to gain status as an individual. In their specifics, these thousands of cases varied widely, but all were united in their recognition that official *soslovie* status meant something real.

Soslovie had meaning for more than just individuals. The regulation of *sosloviia* occurred at both central and local levels. Local *soslovie* authorities conceived of their duties in terms of what they owed the central state, and what they owed their members. Both of these sets of duties brought them into conflict. The duties they owed the center—control of the population, and extraction of service and dues—could easily bring them into conflict with their members. It was not just in the act of collecting those duties that conflict could arise, but also at the moments when individuals sought to sever or start their relationship with a local society. Leaving and joining were often restricted by these issues of duty. The duties that local societies owed their members could also cause conflict. They feared that the demands of their members might tax their limited resources. And they consistently resisted central demands that they take in new members, first to avoid duties to the center, later to avoid duties to individuals.

For the imperial state, *soslovie* was simpler. It was a way of understanding and categorizing its population, and therefore of ensuring public order and public fiscal well-being. From the early eighteenth century, categorization was above all concerned with resources and order. Even then, though, a second thread began to develop, as it believed that policy on *sosloviia*, and on not-quite-*sosloviia* like the professions, had the power to transform society in ways it desired. To an extent these transformative goals were a success, as merchants and others sought status as honored citizens, and as education began to increase the number of professionals in the late nineteenth century. Towards the end of the nineteenth century, one part of the central administration, the Ministry of Finance, began to see *soslovie* as something that placed too many strictures on the population, thus limiting its economic potention; this was a complete shift from a century before, when Russia's empresses saw it as a way to promote service and encourage growth. But more often, the central state's refusal to eliminate the language of *soslovie* even as it sought goals more exalted than mere resource extraction condemned those goals to limited, if any, success.

All of these levels came together to construct imperial Russia's society of *sosloviia*. That society evolved over more than two centuries, as new categories appeared, others disappeared, and as regulations defining their boundaries altered their very nature. *Soslovie* always had multiple meanings. It suggested social status, it suggested economic activity, it suggested privilege and the lack thereof. It also denoted specific, local identities, and at times also much larger ones. And it gave individuals a place within the larger society of imperial Russia, allowing them both to be seen by the state and to be heard by it. At the end of the imperial era many of these functions were still more or less in place, and still providing something to individuals and the different levels of the state, whatever voices decried or celebrated its apparent obsolescence. Even as it was eventually abolished, however, the role it played lingered. This particular version of viewing the population through categories that defined their opportunities and obligations, their places within the social hierarchy and on the map of the empire, died. But, of course, it was soon replaced by other versions of categorization, other efforts by an imperial state to see its population, and unfortunately for many, other ways of using those categorizations to further imperial and political goals.

Appendix

ARCHIVAL SOURCES

The statistical data cited throughout the text was gathered in archives around the former empire, in Moscow, St. Petersburg, Iaroslavl', Riazan', Saratov, Tver', Riga, and Vilnius. The archival fonds of local *soslovie* societies and administrative bodies include both thousands of small files in which individual cases were recorded and smaller numbers of large files that record many cases of mobility either in a specific geographic region or in a specific chronological period. They are, as a result, difficult to parse without reference to the different styles of record-keeping and attention to possible anomalies in their files.

Files from many of the eighteenth-century magistracies were gathered in the middle of the nineteenth century into the Moscow Archive of the Ministry of Justice, one of the foundational archives of the current Russian State Archive of Ancient Acts.[1] The archival registers (*opisy*) for the magistracy fonds list hundreds of cases of individuals changing their *soslovie*, among many other files pertaining to various civil suits between townspeople, regulating bills of exchange and promissory notes, or governing trade in towns. However, some files were unavailable due to their condition, and while basic information on some of these can be retrieved from the archival registers themselves, others were not described in enough detail to allow for any analysis. As a result, the discussion in this book is principally based on 357 separate cases of individuals moving from one status to another, collected from the archival holdings of seventeen town or provincial magistracies: Aleksin', Astrakhan', Belev, Briansk, Cheboksary, Iaroslavl', Kursk, Moscow, Orel', Pereslavl' Zalesskii, Rostov, Rzhev, Saratov, Selenginsk, Sol'vychegodsk, Suzdal', and Ustiug Velikii.[2]

Because records were kept according to different rules in different places, there are practical limits on what these files can tell us. The files of some individual magistracies seem already to omit certain aspects of the social system and to emphasize others, whether by chance or by design. For example, the records of the Suzdal' Magistracy include only a few files that touch on movement between statuses, and all are on the same kind of movement: from townsman or merchant into a church status (usually entry into a monastery).[3] On the one hand, the prominent religious institutions in and around Suzdal' could have impelled more individuals to seek refuge in monasticism. But on the other hand, it seems unlikely both that there were no other cases of movement into or out of the towns' societies over the several decades that elapsed between the first and last of these cases and that such movement into monasteries was so much more prominent here than in other towns, given the many monasteries in the Russian heartland. As a result, the total sample may be skewed toward more movement into church statuses and away from town societies.

The Central Historical Archive of Moscow (TsIAM) and Central State Historical Archive of St. Petersburg (TsGIASPb) both hold the records of the many local administrative bodies that governed (or attempted to govern) the capitals and their provinces. Among them are the boards and other units that administered the capitals' merchant, townsperson, and artisan societies. As in the eighteenth century, record-keeping practices varied by place, by authority, and over time, in ways that make broad comparisons challenging.

Moscow's merchant society is represented in the archives by three different administrative bodies. The files of the Moscow Merchant Guild (*Moskovskaia kupecheskaia gil'diia*, f. 397) covers the second half of the eighteenth century. The Merchant Division of the Moscow Town Society (*Kupecheskoe otdelenie doma Moskovskogo gradskogo obshchestva*, f. 2) picks up in 1793, and runs through 1863. Then the Moscow Merchant Board (*Moskovskaia kupecheskaia uprava*, f. 3) administered the society through the end of the century. Two sets of archival documents help illuminate mobility into the merchant *soslovie*. First, a *Notebook for the Registry into the Moscow Merchantry People of Various Statuses* records all new members of the merchant society in 1795, and it includes information on the social and geographic origins of these new merchants plus detailed information on their families.[4] Second, the archival registers for two nineteenth-century merchant institutions—the merchant division of the Moscow town society before the reform of town administration in the early 1860s, and the Moscow merchant board after reform—include basic information on those who entered the society from 1810 until 1888.[5] Although these files may not be complete, and also list all those who sought entry into the society, rather than those who completed the process of changing *soslovie*, they can be taken as a reasonable comparison with the eighteenth-century files. A sample of the larger data set suggests that failure was rare: out of 132 cases, only 3 did not lead to a finalized change of status, a failure rate of just over 2 percent.

Townsperson societies, so much larger than those of merchants, were forced to keep records differently. And, despite various central efforts to standardize bureaucratic practices, by the middle of the nineteenth century the townsperson societies of Moscow and St. Petersburg came to keep records of their new members in different ways. In Moscow, the local townsperson board (*uprava*) recorded all of the society's members in giant "neighborhood books."[6] These books reflected the division of the town's population into a series of neighborhoods or suburbs (*slobody*). Each neighborhood had two sets of books, one listing "male" households (those with male heads of households, or those with female heads of household but with male "souls" included in their count) and one listing "female" households (those consisting of only women, usually single, but sometimes family groups of women, as well). They list all the members in a household at the time when the list was drawn up, their ages, and, if relevant, their social origin. These books were then updated as new members joined the society and as households already listed underwent changes in their composition due to births, deaths, marriages, or release into a new *soslovie*.

In St. Petersburg, on the other hand, records were kept differently. Perhaps because the capital's society had been created with the new city in the early eighteenth century, it lacked Moscow's history of separate economic divisions. As a result, it instead handled its vast numbers of townspeople in part by dealing with them year by year. The St. Petersburg townsperson board used the ukases from the provincial treasury that finalized the registration of new members to keep track of new members and their families. All ukases from a single year were bound together, divided again by gender (a male book and a female book).[7] Then, those ukases became the same sort of basis for notes about the future fates of the households described in the original documents, as later hands wrote marginal notations on their pages.

Similar files kept in provincial archives add another dimension to the study. The archives of town dumas, magistracies, provincial treasuries, and provincial administrations all contain both files representing individual stories or issues, and those that bring together information from multiple years or places. Like the files from Moscow and St. Petersburg, they are tricky to use because of differences in record-keeping. However, evidence from archival *opisy* from Iaroslavl', Riazan', Saratov, and Tver' was pulled together to make a single, large database recording movement between *sosloviia* societies. These data cannot say anything about overall numbers because it is unclear exactly how some materials made it into *opisy* and how others did not; nor can it necessarily say anything about increases or decreases in numbers from the early part of the nineteenth century to the later part of that century, for the same reason. It can, however give some sense of what kinds of movement occurred and how their prevalence changed over time.

INTRODUCTION

1. Alfred Rieber, *Merchants and Entrepreneurs in Imperial Russia* (Chapel Hill: University of North Carolina Press, 1982); Edith W. Clowes, Samuel D. Kassow, and James L. West, eds., *Between Tsar and People: Educated Society and the Quest for Public Identity in Late Imperial Russia* (Princeton: Princeton University Press, 1991); Barbara Alpern Engel, *Between the Fields & the City: Women, Work, & Family in Russia, 1861–1914* (Cambridge: Cambridge University Press, 1996); Joseph Bradley, *Voluntary Associations in Tsarist Russia: Science, Patriotism, and Civil Society* (Cambridge, MA: Harvard University Press, 2009); Sally West, *I Shop in Moscow: Advertising and the Creation of Consumer Culture in Late Tsarist Russia* (DeKalb: Northern Illinois University Press, 2011); Alexander M. Martin, *Enlightened Metropolis: Constructing Imperial Moscow, 1762–1855* (Oxford: Oxford University Press, 2013).

2. N. M. Korkunov, *Russkoe gosudarstvennoe pravo* (St. Petersburg: M. M. Stasiulevich, 1909), vol. 1, 275. Historians have seen the intersection of estate and signs of modernization, like an emergent civil society, as something "incongruous." See Murray Frame, *School for Citizens: Theatre and Civil Society in Imperial Russia* (New Haven: Yale University Press, 2006), 4.

3. I. Sal'nikov, "O gorodskikh obshchestvakh," *Russkii vestnik* 25, no. 2 (February 1860): Sovremennaia letopis', 230.

4. V. Snegirev, for one, claimed that by the mid-nineteenth century "already for a long time there were no *sloboda* at all," even if there was a memory of them. V. Snegirev, *Moskovskie slobody* (Moscow: Moskovskii rabochii, 1947), 3. For an account from the mid-nineteenth century, see M. Makarov, "Moskovskie meshchanskie slobody," *Moskovskie gubernskie vedomosti. Pribavlenie* (March 21, 1842): 249–52. On the use of the *chasti*, or police districts, to define neighborhoods, see Martin, *Enlightened Metropolis*, 227–43.

5. On the early history of the *slobody*, see L. O. Ploshinskii, *Gorodskoe ili srednee sostoianie russkogo naroda, v ego istoricheskom razvitii, ot nachala Rusi do noveishikh vremen* (St.

Petersburg: V. P. Poliakov, 1852), 109–11; E. I. Indova, "Moskovskii posad i podmoskovnye dvortsovye krest'iane v pervoi polovine XVIII v.," in *Goroda feodal'noi Rossii* (Moscow: Nauka, 1966), 479–85.

6. The records appear at TsIAM f. 5, op. 1, dd. 210, 213.

7. Over the course of the 1860s, hundreds of thousands of soldiers were given their discharge; many had been drafted during the Crimean War, and were aging out of useful service. By the end of the decade, all those who had been drafted before 1856 were released from service, and in October 1870, a law proclaimed that all those drafted before March 1, 1857 were as well (*PSZ* 2, vol. 45, no. 48826 (October 20, 1870). P. A. Zaionchkovskii, *Voennye reform 1860–1870 godov v Rossii* (Moscow: Izdatel'stvo Moskovskogo Universiteta, 1952), 78–79.

8. Alison K. Smith, "Freed Serfs without Free People: Manumission in Imperial Russia," *American Historical Review* 118, no. 4 (October 2013): 1029–51; and "'The Freedom to Choose a Way of Life:' Fugitives, Borders, and Imperial Amnesties in Russia," *Journal of Modern History* 83, no. 2 (June 2011): 243–71.

9. Joseph Bradley, *Muzhik and Muscovite: Urbanization in Late Imperial Russia* (Berkeley: University of California Press, 1985)

10. There were, of course, limits to that. See, for example, Elise K. Wirtschafter, "Social Categories in Russian Imperial History," *Cahiers du monde russe* 50, no. 1 (2009): 231–50.

11. On Elena Sergeevna, see Sofia Andreevna Tolstaya, *My Life*, John Woodsworth and Arkadi Klioutchanski, trans. (Ottawa: University of Ottawa Press, 2010), 321n.; Tolstaya furthermore notes that in 1870 Tolstoy first mentioned his desire to write a novel about a "woman who had fallen out of her upper-class Petersburg social circle," the eventual *Anna Karenina* (158).

12. Boris Mironov briefly touches on the question of mobility in his *Social History of Russia*, but focuses on its demographic impact rather than its effect on the notion of *soslovie* itself. He notes, for example, that both town *sosloviia* and the nobility grew more rapidly than a natural rate of increase, a fact he credits to movement into those *sosloviia* from others. *Sotsial'naia istoriia Rossii perioda imperii, XVIII-nachalo XX v.: genezis lichnosti, demokraticheskoi sem'i, grazhdanskogo obshchestva i pravovogo gosudarstva* (St. Petersburg: D. Bulanin, 1999), vol. 1, 133–40.

13. A major issue in the historiography of *soslovie* has been the difficulty of trying to encompass the entire system. Some grapple with this by focusing on either only a few *sosloviia* or by running through one group after the other separately instead of pulling them together into a coherent narrative. See, for example, Elise Kimerling Wirtschafter, *Social Identity in Imperial Russia* (DeKalb: Northern Illinois University Press, 1997); N. A. Ivanova and V. P. Zheltova, *Soslovnoe obshchestvo Rossiiskoi imperii* (Moscow: Novyi khronograf, 2010).

14. Maiia Lavrinovich makes this argument, that the boundaries of town statuses in the reign of Catherine the Great were defined in part by the process of registry of peasants. See Maiia Lavrinovich, "Sozdanie sotsial'nykh osnov imperii v XVIII veke: zakonodatel'nye praktiki v otnoshenii gorodskogo naseleniia Rossii i ikh zapadnoevropeiskie istochniki," *Ab Imperio* 3 (2002): 120.

15. Elise Kimerling Wirtschafter argues that the category of the *raznochintsy* did something similar; see *Russia's Age of Serfdom, 1649–1861* (Malden: Blackwell, 2008), 84–5.

16. "Besedy s gorozhanami: o vliianii diety na chelovecheskii organizm," *Ekonom* 5, no. 117 (1843): 98; Review of *Putevye zametki*, by T. Ch, *Biblioteka dlia chteniia* 85 (1847), "Kritika": 28; "Preduvedomlenie," *Zhurnal obshchepoleznykh svedenii* 5, no. 1 (1837): 2.

17. On terminology, see Gregory L. Freeze, "The Soslovie (Estate) Paradigm and Russian Social History," *American Historical Review* 91, no. 1 (February 1986): 15–19; and Rieber, *Merchants and Entrepreneurs*, xxii.

18. The volume of the *Digest of the Laws* that directly addresses social categories is titled the "laws on *sostoianiia*," but it includes many references within to *soslovie*. Some of them include *SZ* 1833, "Zakony o sostoianiiakh," § 332, 369.

19. *Sbornik imperatorskogo russkogo istoricheskogo obshchestva* (henceforth *SIRIO*), vol. 4 (1869), 94, 132, 151, 152154, 163, 164, 170; vol. 8 (1871), 215.

20. Michael Confino, "The *Soslovie* (Estate) Paradigm: Reflections on Some Open Questions," *Cahiers du monde russe* 49, no. 4 (2008): 699.

21. Some contemporary authors also wrote about *sosloviia* by comparing them to the West, but in a negative way, arguing that they were importations that never quite fit their new Russian home. See L., "O sovremennom gorodskom obshchestvennom upravlenii," *Vestnik Evropy* vol. 3, no. 9 (September 1866): Istoricheskaia khronika, 59; Korkunov, *Russkoe gosudarstvennoe pravo*, vol. 1, 274. Later, V. O. Kliuchevskii, in his famous late nineteenth-century lectures on the history of *sosloviia*, developed the habit of comparing Russian *sosloviia* with Western estates. See *Istoriia soslovii v Rossii*, in *Sochineniia v deviati tomakh*, vol. 6 (Moscow: Mysl', 1989), esp. 250–51. This question then infuses many later attempts to grapple with the subject. See the conclusion of Ivanova and Zheltova, *Soslovnoe obshchestvo*, 721–24. For a counter-argument, see Confino, "*Soslovie* (Estate) Paradigm," 693–95.

22. Kliuchevskii argued that it was Catherine the Great's Charter to the Nobility, in particular, that marked the beginning of *soslovie* formally within Russia (*Istoriia sosloviia*, 225), while I. Beliaev looked instead to Peter the Great's censuses as particularly important dividing lines in the history of social categorization (I. Beliaev, *Krest'iane na rusi* (Moscow: Universitetskaia tipografiia, 1860), 10). Gregory Freeze moves the other way, and places a more formal conceptualization of *soslovie* in the first half of the nineteenth century. Freeze, "The Soslovie (Estate) Paradigm," 20.

23. Elise Kimerling Wirtschafter, *Structures of Society: Imperial Russia's "People of Various Ranks"* (DeKalb: Northern Illinois University Press, 1994), and "Social Categories," develops the idea of the "porosity, amorphousness, and malleability of Russia's official social categories" ("Social Categories," 242). Descriptions of *sosloviia* that emphasize that porosity include Reginald E. Zelnik, *Labor and Society in Tsarist Russia: The Factory Workers of St. Petersburg 1855–1870* (Stanford: Stanford University Press, 1971), 15–16, 229–30.

Others, however, focus on the barrier between *sosloviia*. Ia. E. Vodarskii argues that by the time town *sosloviia* had been fully developed in the reign of Catherine the Great, "exit from serfdom and registry in a town was extremely difficult," in *Issledovaniia po istorii russkogo goroda (fakty, obobshcheniia, aspekty)* (Moscow: Institut rossiiskoi istorii RAN, 2006), 28–30. Other statements that emphasize the difficulty of leaving or entering *sosloviia* include Bradley, *Muzhik and Muscovite*, 108–109.

24. As Michael Confino points out in "The *Soslovie* (Estate) Paradigm," 685, the notion that *sosloviia* were "flourishing" even in the very late imperial period was the "really novel element" in Gregory L. Freeze's earlier article. Some work on the First World War emphasizes the ways that *sosloviia* as a scheme of categorization still had significant weight in public discourse and state action. See Peter Gatrell, *A Whole Empire Walking: Refugees in Russia during World War*

I (Bloomington: Indiana University Press, 2005), esp. 90, 197–98; and Eric Lohr, *Nationalizing the Russian Empire: The Campaign against Enemy Aliens during World War I* (Cambridge, MA: Harvard University Press, 2003), 109–10. Charles Steinwedel has also argued that *soslovie* was the dominant classification in Bashkiria well into the 1890s, and only then did it begin to lose some of its potency in the face of other systems of categorization. See his "Making Social Groups, One Person at a Time: The Identification of Individuals by Estate, Religious Confession, and Ethnicity in Late Imperial Russia," in *Documenting Individual Identity: The Development of State Practices in the Modern World*, ed. Jane Caplan and John Torpey (Princeton: Princeton University Press, 2001), 71–72.

25. So, for example, Freeze's work is affected by his earlier study of *The Parish Clergy in Nineteenth-Century Russia: Crisis, Reform, Counter-Reform* (Princeton: Princeton University Press, 1983); Elise Kimerling Wirtschafter's by the military statuses she explored in *From Serf to Russian Soldier* (Princeton: Princeton University Press, 1990); J. Alfred Rieber's "The Sedimentary Society," in *Between Tsar and People*, draws on his work in *Merchants and Entrepreneurs in Imperial Russia* (Chapel Hill: University of North Carolina Press, 1982). And although Confino does look more broadly, he also notes that "when we speak of the *soslovie* system, we think mainly (though implicitly) of the nobility and in terms of the nobility" ("*Soslovie* [Estate]," 690).

26. On the high-level debates, see, for example, Abbott Gleason, "The Terms of Russian Social History," in *Between Tsar and People: Educated Society and the Quest for Public Identity in Late Imperial Russia*, ed. Edith W. Clowes, Samuel D. Kassow, and James L. West (Princeton: Princeton University Press, 1991), 26, where he describes "the reassertion of the sosloviia" in late imperial Russia.

27. Cyril E. Black notes that the "corporative organization of the social strata…tended to isolate them from each other." See "The Nature of Imperial Russian Society," *Slavic Review* 20, no. 4 (December 1961): 570. On the many separate societies within the larger overarching *soslovie* structure, see also Jane Burbank, "An Imperial Rights Regime: Law and Citizenship in the Russian Empire," *Kritika* 7, no. 3 (Summer 2006): esp. 403–406. On the importance of local identities in Muscovy, see Nancy Shields Kollman, "Concepts of Society and Social Identity in Early Modern Russia," in *Religion and Culture in Early Modern Russia and Ukraine*, ed. Samuel H. Baron and Nancy Shields Kollman (DeKalb: Northern Illinois University Press, 1997), 37–38.

28. Ivanova and Zheltova, *Soslovnoe obshchestvo*, 132–48. The importance of the local is also explicitly linked with the gaining of "corporate rights" for the nobility in N. A. Rozhkov, *Gorod i derevnia v russkoi istorii*, 2nd ed. (Moscow: Skororpech, 1904), 67–68. Nor was this only Imperial practice; Nancy Shields Kollmann notes that even collective petitions to right crimes against honor included "discrete, not generalizing, descriptions of their collectivity, citing region and rank," in *By Honor Bound: State and Society in Early Modern Russia* (Ithaca: Cornell University Press, 1999), 60.

29. Several scholars have looked closely at the role of local loyalties within noble society. See, for example, Mary W. Cavender, *Nests of the Gentry: Family, Estate, and Local Loyalties in Provincial Russia* (Newark: University of Delaware Press, 2007); and Catherine Evtuhov, *Portrait of a Russian Province: Economy, Society, and Civilization in Nineteenth-Century Nizhnii Novgorod* (Pittsburgh: University of Pittsburgh Press, 2011). See also Korkunov, *Russkoe gosudarstvennoe pravo*, vol. 1, 279, on this idea.

30. Richard Pipes, *Russia under the Old Regime*, 2nd ed. (London: Penguin Books, 1995). See also Roger Bartlett, "Serfdom and State Power in Imperial Russia," *European History Quarterly* 33, no. 1 (2003): 35, for comment on the idea of the "universality of duties" and the idea that "the regime as a whole was based on concepts of hierarchy and obligation."

31. A. de Gurowski, *Russia as It Is* (New York: D. Appleton, 1854), 137–38.

32. Jane Burbank calls *soslovie* "a typical strategy of Russian imperial rule, one of the several registers through which the polity was governed." See "Thinking Like an Empire: Estate, Law, and Rights in the Early Twentieth Century," in *Russian Empire: Space, People, Power, 1700–1930*, ed. Jane Burbank and Mark von Hagen (Bloomington: Indiana University Press, 2007), 197. It was also, of course, only one of many kinds of categorization the empire used to describe and define its subjects, a point Nicholas Breyfogle makes in *Heretics and Colonizers: Forging Russia's Empire in the South Caucasus* (Ithaca: Cornell University Press, 2005), 313.

33. On patterns of temporary migration, see Joseph Bradley, *Muzhik and Muscovite*, 25–26; Boris Gorshkov, "Serfs on the Move: Peasant Seasonal Migration in Pre-Reform Russia, 1860–61," *Kritika* 1, no. 4 (Fall 2000): 627–56. On more permanent migration, see Willard Sunderland, "Peasants on the Move: State Peasant Resettlement in Imperial Russia, 1805–1830s," *Russian Review* 52, no. 4 (1993): 472–85; and *Taming the Wild Field: Colonization and Empire on the Russian Steppe* (Ithaca: Cornell University Press, 2004), 29–31 42, 75, 112, 138.

34. Ivanova and Zheltova argue that the first stage in the development of a peasant *soslovie* occurred with the Kiselev reforms of the 1830s that created a single *soslovie* of state peasants, while the creation of a singular peasant *soslovie* was much slower to develop. See their conclusions at Ivanova and Zheltova, *Soslovnoe obshchestvo*, 653–54.

35. N. P. Druzhinin, *Meshchanskoe dvizhenie 1906–1917 gg* (Iaroslavl': Golos, 1917), 3. Some exceptions to the tendency to ignore the *meshchanstvo* in particular include Iu. M. Goncharov and V. S. Chutchev, *Meshchanskoe soslovie zapadnoi sibiri vtoroi poloviny XIX-nachala XX v* (Barnaul: AzBuka, 2004); and A. P. Kaplunovskii, "Meshchanskaia obshchina," in *Ocherki gorodskogo byta dorevoliutsionnogo Povol'zhia* (Ul'ianovsk: Srednevolzhskii nauchnyi tsentr, 2000), 294–415.

36. Laurie Manchester, *Holy Fathers, Secular Sons: Clergy, Intelligentsia, and the Modern Self in Revolutionary Russia* (DeKalb: Northern Illinois University Press, 2008).

37. Gregory L. Freeze, "Social Mobility and the Russian Parish Clergy in the Eighteenth Century," *Slavic Review* 33, no. 4 (December 1974): 641–62. On entry into monasteries, see Scott Mark Kenworthy, *The Heart of Russia: Trinity-Sergius, Monasticism, and Society after 1825* (New York: Oxford University Press, 2010).

38. Lindsey Hughes, *Russia in the Age of Peter the Great* (New Haven: Yale University Press, 1998), 182–85.

39. *PSZ* vol. 23, no. 16914 (October 26, 1790).

40. *PSZ* vol. 29, no. 22418 (January 1, 1807). See also *PSZ* 2, vol. 2: 1631 (December 21, 1827).

41. At the end of the imperial era, His Majesty's Own Chancellery decided whether to allow nobles and others of "privileged" status to give up those privileges in order to become, legally, peasants or others of lower rank. Examples include RGIA f. 573, op. 12, d. 13724.

42. This created a boom in historical studies by Ukrainian nobles during the early nineteenth century, as each sought to prove his noble ancestry and thus to ensure his rights within the empire. See Taras Koznarsky, "Izmail Sreznevsky's *Zaporozhian Antiquity* as a Memory Project," *Eighteenth-Century Studies* 35, no. 1 (Fall 2001): 92.

43. Andreas Kappeler summarizes the "socio-ethnic structure of the periphery of the Russian empire" as "a very complex state of affairs," in *The Russian Empire*, trans. Alfred Clayton (Harlow: Pearson, 2001), 124, and further discusses the interaction of *soslovie* and ethnicity at 289–90.

44. On the military statuses, see Wirtschafter, *From Serf to Russian Soldier* and her article "Social Misfits: Veterans and Soldiers' Families in Servile Russia," *Journal of Military History* 59, no. 2 (April 1995): 215–35.

45. As a result, these facts complicated the administration of such groups. The Ministry of State Domains, for example, investigated procedures for allowing those of military status to register formally as state peasants. According to its registers, between 1842 and 1856, 104,723 retired soldiers did so. See RGIA f. 383, op. 2, d. 27,010, ll. 1–30b.

46. On the general idea of the distinction between class and *soslovie* as it developed in the later parts of the imperial era, see N. A. Ivanova and V. P. Zheltova, *Soslovno-klassovaia struktura Rossii v kontse XIX-nachale XX veka* (Moscow: Nauka, 2004).

47. Madhavan K. Palat refers to them as "mutant *soslovie*," in "Casting Workers as an Estate in Late Imperial Russia," *Kritika* 8, no. 2 (Spring 2007): 307–48.

48. The idea of multiple identities is one suggested by Alfred Rieber in "The Sedimentary Society." On professions, see William Pomeranz, "'Profession or Estate'? The Case of the Russian Pre-Revolutionary *Advokatura*," *SEER* 77, no. 2 (April 1999): 240–68.

49. Although she does not frame her argument explicitly in terms of *soslovie*, Michelle Lamarche Marrese does focus on what was essentially a *soslovie*-based privilege of noble-women in *A Woman's Kingdom: Noblewomen and the Control of Property in Russia, 1700–1861* (Ithaca: Cornell University Press, 2002). In many other general attempts to grapple with *soslovie*, however, women disappear.

50. See Alison K. Smith, "The Shifting Place of Women in Imperial Russia's Social Order," *Cahiers du Monde russe* 51, no. 2–3 (April-September 2010): 353–67.

51. *SZ* 1833, "Zakony o sostoianiiakh," § 2. This is the version that appears over and over again in references to *soslovie*.

52. A variant on this system was an eight-part division of society in parish records (where, for example, household serfs were separated out from peasants, and Old Believers were their own group. See B. N. Mironov, *Russkii gorod v 1740–1860-e gody: demograficheskoe, sotsial'noe i ekonomicheskoe razvitie* (Leningrad: Nauka, 1990), 81.

53. K. I. Arsen'ev, *Nachertanie statistiki Rossiiskogo gosudarstva*, vol. 1 (St. Petersburg: Imperatorskii Vospitatel'nyi Dom, 1818), 63.

54. Black, "The Nature of Imperial Russian Society," 569; *SIRIO* 4, 125.

55. On this as the great distinction see Freeze, "Soslovie Paradigm," 21; Bartlett, "Serfdom and State Power," 41.

56. O. Eikhel'man, "Ocherki iz lektsii po russkomu gosudarstvennomu pravu," *Universitetskie izvestiia*, 13, no. 6 (June 1890): Part II, 144.

57. Korkunov, *Russkoe gosudarstvennoe pravo*, vol. 1, 277.

58. Kliuchevskii even argued that laws are the only valid source for studying *sosloviia*, describing other sources as merely the "fruits of individual consciousness," in *Istoriia soslovii*, 244.

CHAPTER 1

1. N. M. Chukmaldin, *Zapiski o moei zhizni* (Moscow: Tipo-litografiia A. V. Vasil'eva i Ko., 1902), 88–89.

2. This hyper-bureacratization is indicated by the role played by the treasury offices; these were, as O. V. Moriakova put it, "among the most bureaucratized" elements of local control in the itself highly bureaucratized Nicholaevan era. See O. V. Moriakova, *Sistema mestnogo upravleniia Rossii pri Nikolae I* (Moscow: Izdatel'stvo Moskovskogo universiteta, 1998), 137.

3. "Sokrashchennaia zhizn' pokoinogo Sanktpeterburgskogo kuptsa pervoi gil'dii Aleksandra Petrovicha Berezina, pisannaia po ego vole nezadolgo do konchiny sego Bogom blagoslovennogo muzha i nakonets soglasno obrazu ego zhizni i deianii vnov' sochinennaia N. N., v pamiat' potomstva ego, po soizvoleniiu liubezneishei ego docheri i ziatia S.-Peterburgskogo vtoroi gil'dii kuptsa Petra Iakovlevicha i suprugi ego Pelagei Aleksandrovny Tufanovykh, urozhdennoi Berezinoi, v 1807 godu, Ianvaria dnia," *Russkii arkhiv* 17, 1, no. 2 (1879): 230; A. P. Miliukov, *Dobroe staroe vremia. Ocherk bylogo* (St. Petersburg: A. F. Bazunov, 1872), 179–80. Similarly, the process of leaving one status and entering another comes into the historiography as either an enormous burden that hugely limited mobility, as in Bradley, *Muzhik and Muscovite*, 108–109; or as "harassments," not "serious impediments," as in Zelnik, *Labor and Society*, 16; or Daniel Morrison, *"Trading Peasants" and Urbanization in Eighteenth-Century Russia: The Central Industrial Region* (New York: Garland, 1987), 22.

4. State concern over vagrancy and runaways was persistent. See accounts in *Materialy dlia istorii krepostnogo prava v Rossii* (Berlin: Behr, 1872), 138–39; and a fuller discussion of the issue in N. V. Kozlova, *Pobegi krest'ian v Rossii v pervoi treti XVIII veka* (Moscow: Moskovskii universitet, 1983). On later periods, see Daniel Brower, "Urbanization and Autocracy: Russian Urban Development in the First Half of the Nineteenth Century," *Russian Review* 42, no. 4 (October 1983): 385–86, 389–90, and his *The Russian City between Tradition and Modernity, 1850–1900* (Berkeley: University of California Press, 1990), 82–83.

5. For the pre-Reform peasantry, see L. B. Genkin, *Pomeshchich'i krest'iane Iaroslavskoi i Kostromskoi gubernii pered reformoi i vo vremia reformy 1861 goda* (Iaroslavl': Iaroslavskii gos. pedinstitut, 1947), 40; and Gorshkov, "Serfs on the Move." For the post-Reform peasantry, see Robert Johnson, *Peasant and Proletarian: The Working Class of Moscow in the Late Nineteenth Century* (New Brunswick: Rutgers University Press, 1979), 28–50; Bradley, *Muzhik and Muscovite*, 26–28, 33–34; James H. Bater, "Transience, Residential Persistence, and Mobility in Moscow and St. Petersburg," *Slavic Review* 39, no. 2 (June 1980): 239–54.

6. Boris Mironov argues that during the eighteenth century, fewer than 3 percent of town populations had formally registered, and that "the majority of migrants" had less permanent, if not actively illegal, positions there; by the late nineteenth century, though many did, their numbers were still swamped by those simply living in the town. See his *Russkii gorod*, 102–103, 126.

7. On another version of using administrative acts to change legal status, see Alessandro Stanziani, "Serfs, Slaves, or Wage Earners? The Legal Status of Labour in Russia from a Comparative Perspective, from the Sixteenth to the Nineteenth Century," *Journal of Global History* 3 (2008): 183–202, esp. 196–99.

8. Elise Kimerling Wirtschafter comments on the limitations of such sources in *The Play of Ideas in Russian Enlightenment Theater* (DeKalb: Northern Illinois University Press, 2003), ix.

9. GARO f. 49, op.1, d. 182, l. 1 (1853); d. 311, l. 1 (1856).

10. As early as 1733, a woman named Mar'ia Semenova found herself in trouble with religious and secular authorities in part for demon possession, but even more for transgressing laws on mobility. See Christine D. Worobec, *Possessed: Women, Witches, and Demons in Imperial Russia* (DeKalb: Northern Illinois University Press, 2001), 30–31.

11. *PSZ,* vol. 15, no. 11364 (November 28, 1761); vol. 21, no. 15296 (10 December 1781); V. M. Kabuzan, *Narodonaselenie Rossii v XVIII-pervoi polovine XIX v.* (Moscow: Akademiia Nauk SSSR, 1963), 65.

12. The two were D. Pokkova, a merchant's wife who sought to formalize her status as a merchant on her own behalf in 1766, and Anna Ilzhina, a fugitive economic peasant who wished to register as a *meshchanka* in Moscow. RGADA f. 713, op. 1, d. 401; RGADA f. 308, op. 2, d. 196.

13. John P. LeDonne, *Ruling Russia: Politics and Administration in the Age of Absolutism, 1762–1796* (Princeton: Princeton University Press, 1984), 125-27; Simon Franklin, "Printing and Social Control in Russia 1: Passports," *Russian History* 37 (2010): 213–24; V. G. Chernukha, *Pasport v Rossii, 1719–1917* (St. Petersburg: Liki Rossii, 2007). See also comments by delegates to the Legislative Commission on requiring peasants to use passports, at *SIRIO* 4, 117, 123.

14. *SZ* 1857, vol. 14, "Ustavy o pasportakh," §§ 1, 48. On the further development of the legislation and practice of documentation in the later nineteenth century, see Steinwedel, "Making Social Groups, 73–78; Jeffrey Burds, *Peasant Dreams & Market Politics: Labor Migration and the Russian Village, 1861–1905* (Pittsburgh: Univeristy of Pittsburgh Press, 1998), 56–57; Paul Werth, "Between Particularism and Universalism: Metrical Books and Civil Status in the Russian Empire, 1800–1914," paper presented at Citizenship, Nationality, and the State in Imperial Russia and the Soviet Union Conference, Davis Center, 2004, and http://daviscenter.fas.harvard.edu/seminars_conferences/WERTH.pdf, accessed August 24, 2009; Eugene M. Avrutin, *Jews and the Imperial State: Identification Politics in Tsarist Russia* (Ithaca: Cornell University Press, 2010).

15. Bulkin, "Neskol'ko slov o Moskovskom meshchanskom obshchestve," *Russkii vestnik* 25, nos. 1–2 (1860): 55.

16. Bulkin, "Neskol'ko slov o Moskovskom," 55. The other documentary demands were hardly less rigorous. The residence ticket was handed out through much the same procedure as a passport, cost 15 kopeks, and lasted a year. The ticket listed the head of household who received it; the number of male souls in the household; how many were underaged, of working age, and over 60; the occupation of the head of household; and a statement of whatever real estate he owned. Furthermore, if the wife or daughter of the ticket holder lived separately "in service," she needed extra documentation that cost 30 kopeks. The other tickets, for short-term absence, or for living in the province, required similar documentation, of similar costs (56).

17. RGIA f. 1088, op. 3, d. 956, ll. 1–3 (1830).

18. TsIAM f. 32, op. 9, d. 1297, l. 7 (1815); RGIA f. 1088, op. 3, d. 956, ll. 5–60b (1835); RGIA f. 1287, op. 38, d. 479, l. 1 (1864); LVIA f. 937, op. 2, d. 1739, ll. 7–70b (1869); RGIA f. 1287, op. 44, d. 905, ll. 26–260b (1903); TsIAM f. 54, op. 57, l. 1 (1908). On the ways village authorites used passports to exert control over members of their communes, see Burds, *Peasant Dreams*, 58–61, 64-70.

19. *PSZ,* vol. 36, no. 27745 (March 31, 1819). Paul's decree is at *PSZ* vol. 26, no. 19443 (June 7, 1800).

20. *PSZ* 2, vol. 6, no. 4538, § 11 (May 6, 1831). The ban on women's mobility was ended in *PSZ* 2, vol. 7, no. 5842 (December 22, 1832; published by the Senate on January 18, 1833): § 6.

21. John L. Keep, *Soldiers of the Tsar: Army and Society in Russia, 1462–1874* (Oxford: Clarendon Press, 1985), 145.

22. Alison K. Smith, "Authority in a Serf Village: Peasants, Managers, and the Role of Writing in Early Nineteenth Century Russia," *Journal of Social History* 43, no. 1 (Fall 2009): 157–73;

Wirtschafter, *From Serf to Russian Soldier*, 5–9, on mutilations, and 20–22, on the line system; Rodney D. Bohac, "The Mir and the Military Draft," *Slavic Review* 47, no 4 (Winter 1988): 652–66; Edgar Melton, "Household Economies and Communal Conflicts on a Russian Serf Estate, 1800–1817," *Journal of Social History* 26, no. 3 (Spring 1993): 569–77.

23. Rieber, *Merchants and Entrepreneurs*, 31; Brower, "Urbanization and Autocracy," 389.

24. Chukmaldin, *Zapiski*, 60–61.

25. Chukmaldin, *Zapiski*, 88–89.

26. A. V. Stupin, "Sobstvennoruchnye zapiski o zhizni akademika A. V. Stupina," *Shchukinskii sbornik* 3 (1904): 375.

27. *PSZ*, vol. 24, no. 17695 (December 29, 1796).

28. Smith, "Freedom to Choose," 265–67.

29. GARO f. 49, op. 1, d. 770, ll. 77–78.

30. Linda Bowman, "Russia's First Income taxes: The Effects of Modernized Taxes on Commerce and Industry, 1885–1914," *Slavic Review* 52, no. 2 (Summer 1993): 258; Yanni Kotsonis, "'Face to Face': The State, the Individual, and the Citizen in Russian Taxation, 1863–1917," *Slavic Review* 63, no. 2 (Summer 2004): 223–25.

31. Rieber, *Merchants and Entrepreneurs*, 83–84.

32. Jerome Blum, *Lord and Peasant in Russia from the Ninth to the Nineteenth Century* (Princeton: Princeton University Press, 1961), 485–86.

33. Blum, *Lord and Peasant in Russia*, 442–52.

34. N. Shcherban', "Vospominaniia krepostnogo, 1800–1868," *Russkii vestnik* 130, no. 9 (September 1877): 38–39.

35. L. A. Travin, "Zapiski L. A. Travina," *Trudy Pskovskogo arkheologicheskogo obshchestva* 10 (1913–1914): 90.

36. Nikolai Shipov, *Istoriia moei zhizni. Rasskaz byvshego krepostnogo krest'iana* (St. Petersburg: V S. Balashev, 1881), 1, 15. A list of serfs freed from Count Sheremetev's Ivanovo estate included twenty-one households responsible individually for anywhere from 3.5 to 40 *tiagla* (work units). Other documents from the Sheremetev files confirm similarly high demands from individual wealthy families. See RGADA f. 1287, op. 5, d. 5674, ll. 1–2 (undated) and op. 6, d. 301, ll. 6–7, 10–100b (1826). This likely hid the fact that some serfs themselves virtually owned other serfs; their purchase of serfs had had to be done in the name of their owner, Count Sheremetev, but within the village it was understood that they were the true authorities. In one case, after a wealthy serf was freed, the serfs who had formerly considered themselves belonging to him were shocked at having to pay more *obrok* now that that fictitious layer of ownership was removed. See RGADA f. 1287, op. 6, d. 329.

37. Those fees could be a true burden, however, leading some women to petition higher authorities for aid in the form of a waiver from paying fees for registration. See RGIA f. 1287, op. 37, d. 330, ll. 1–10b (1846) and GARO f. 49, op. 1, d. 553, l. 10 (1860).

38. In this there are later (sometimes much later) echoes of other experiments with social welfare based in localities. Elizabethan England saw the rise of Poor Laws that built on parish responsibility to provide charity for the "known" poor (Paul A. Fideler, *Social Welfare in Pre-Industrial England* (Basingstoke: Palgrave, 2006), 85, 99-102), while the structures of poor relief in late-eighteenth-century Prussia were also based on an immobile population connected to their localities; increased restrictions on movement were tied to concerns over such policies (Hermann Beck, *The Origins of the Authoritarian Welfare State in Prussia: Conservatives,*

Bureaucracy, and the Social Question, 1815-70 (Ann Arbor: The University of Michigan Press, 1995), 149-53.

39. On late imperial charitable institutions, see Bradley, *Muzhik and Muscovite*, 249–337; and Adele Lindenmeyr, "A Russian Experiment in Voluntarism: The Municipal Guardianships of the Poor, 1894–1914," *Jahrbücher für Geschichte Osteuropas*, Neue Folge, 30, no. 3 (1982): 429–51; Lindenmeyr notes that the Moscow municipal government gave "almost nothing" for publich charity, though its *soslovie* societies had their own institutions (431).

40. On eighteenth-century precedents, see N. V. Kozlova, *Liudi driakhlye, bol'nye, ubogie v Moskve XVIII veka* (Moscow: ROSSPEN, 2010); and A. R. Sokolov, *Blagotvoritel'nost' v Rossii kak mekhanizm vzaimodeistviia obshchestva i gosudarstva (nachalo XVIII-konets XIX vv.)* (St. Petersburg: Liki Rossii, 2007), esp. 204–12. On how these various elements played out in one region, see Kaplunovskii, "Meshchanskaia obshchina," 390–97.

41. Adele Lindenmeyr, *Poverty Is Not a Vice: Charity, Society, and the State in Imperial Russia* (Princeton: Princeton University Press, 1996), chs. 2–3.

42. Freeze, *The Parish*, 171–79.

43. *SZ* 1857, vol. 14, "Ustav o preduprezhdenii prestuplenii," st. 257, which immediately follows the exhortation that serfowners properly watch over their serfs.

44. Miliukov, *Dobroe staroe vremia*, 171–72.

45. RGADA f. 742, op. 1, d. 477, ll. 1, 3 (1749).

46. For example, RGADA f. 713, op. 1, d. 500, ll. 1, 2 (Briansk, 1768); TsIAM f. 32, op. 9, d. 586, l. 1 (1814); d. 646, l. 1 (1815); op. 12, d. 1787, l. 1 (1832).

47. Kenworthy, *The Heart of Russia*, 56–61, 126, 134–36.

48. RGIA f. 571, op. 1, d. 1796, ll. 7–8 (1857).

49. TsGIASPb, f. 222, op. 1, d. 503, ll. 347–49 (1898).

50. Evgenii G. Blumenbakh, *Dokladnaia zapiska i proekt reorganizatsii soslovnykh obshchestv i uchrezhdenii v Rossiiskom Gosudarstve* (Riga: V. F. Gekker, 1917), 5.

51. RGIA f. 1287, op. 38, d. 1674.

52. For a comprehensive examination of the many, many laws produced by the imperial state on these subjects, see particularly the exhaustive accounting of them, by *soslovie*, in Ivanova and Zheltova, *Soslovnoe obshchestvo*.

53. On the complications implicit even in simply defining the town delegates to the Commission, see François-Xavier Coquin, *La grande commission législative, 1767–1768. Les cahiers de doléances urbains (Province de Moscou)* (Paris: Béatrice-Nauwelaerts, 1972), esp. 44–56.

54. *PSZ*, vol. 12, no. 9201 (July 19, 1745); vol. 14, no. 10486 (December 1, 1755), Tamozhennyi Ustav, pt. 10.

55. *PSZ*, vol. 22, no. 16188 (April 21, 1785).

56. *PSZ*, vol. 25, no. 18663 (September 12, 1798); no. 18822 (January 17, 1799); no. 18814 (January 10, 1799).

57. For a lengthy discussion of the problems facing trading peasants and merchants in the early nineteenth century, see RGIA f. 1374, op. 5, d. 200, which includes two proposals for dealing with the "problem" of trading peasants, with commentary from the Ministry of Justice, from around 1802.

58. *PSZ*, vol. 39, no. 30,115 (November 14, 1824); *PSZ* 2, vol. 1, no. 422 (1826).

59. Rieber, *Merchants and Entrepreneurs*, 84–85.

60. Yanni Kotsonis, *Making Peasants Backward: Agricultural Cooperatives and the Agrarian Question in Russia, 1861–1914* (New York: St. Martin's, 1999), 20–21.

61. For a discussion of some of these issues, see P. A. Berlin, *Russkaia burzhuaziia v staroe i novoe vremia* (Moscow: Kniga, 1922), 94-95.

62. Travin, "Zapiski," 95.

63. "Sokrashchennaia zhizn'," 230–31.

64. GARO f. 49, op. 1, d. 214, l. 1 (1854); RGIA f. 1088, op. 3, d. 1051, l. 380b (1855). Similar general arguments include that of Nikita Titov, who asked to enter Moscow's merchant society "for the most convenient pursuit of trade." TsIAM f. 2, op. 1, d. 1877, l. 1 (1825).

65. RGIA f. 1088, op. 3, d. 1051, l. 120–1200b (1855)

66. RGADA f. 742, op. 1, d. 358, l. 1.

67. RGIA f. 1088, op. 3, d. 1058, ll. 1–20b (1856).

68. RGIA f. 1088, op. 3, d. 1058, ll. 18-180b (1855).

69. V. D. Barkov, *Istoriia Vasiliia Dmitrievicha Barkova, potomstvennogo pochetnogo grazhdanina* (St. Petersburg: P. O. Iablonskii, 1902), 74–75.

70. Chukhmaldin, *Zapiski*, 66, 81.

71. Records from TsIAM ff. 2 and 3.

72. See John Bushnell, "Did Serf Owners Control Serf Marriage? Orlov Serfs and Their Neighbors, 1773–1861," *Slavic Review* 52, no. 3 (Autumn 1993): 419–45.

73. Shipov, *Istoriia moei zhizni*, 9, 15.

74. It was, however, one of the main sources of social mobility in eighteenth century theater; Wirtschafter, *Play of Ideas*, 95-98.

75. RGADA f. 695, op. 1, d. 1972, l. 1 (1778). His petition was eventually granted. RGADA f. 695, op. 1, d. 1995 (1779).

76. For a general statement, see Wirtschafter, *Structures of Society*, 8–9,139–41; for specific fields, see Nancy Mandelker Frieden, *Russian Physicians in an Era of Reform and Revolution, 1856–1905* (Princeton: Princeton University Press, 1981), 23, 205–206; Lynn Sargeant, "A New Class of People: The Conservatoire and Musical Professionalization in Russia, 1861–1917," *Music & Letters* 85, no. 1 (2004): 41–61.

77. V. V. Dodonov, *Piatidesiatiletie Imperatorskogo Gatchinskogo Nikolaevskogo Sirotskogo Instituta (1837-1887)* (St. Petersburg: V. S. Balashev, 1887), ix, 44.

78. F. D. Bobkov, "Iz zapisok byvshego krepostnogo cheloveka," in *Vospominaniia russkikh krest'ian XVIII-pervoi poloviny XIX veka* (Moscow: 2006), 601. See also the various figures profiled in M. D. Kurmacheva, *Krepostnaia intelligentsiia Rossii vtoraia polovina XVIII-nachalo XIX veka* (Moscow: Nauka, 1983), as well as A. Shch., "Nezateilivoe vospitanie. Iz zapisok A. Shch.," *Atenei* 5–6 (1858): 492–93, 44, 126–27.

79. John MacKay points out that a particular concern with writing may be endemic to such accounts simply because "it was literacy above all that both made the composition of the narratives possible and distinguished these serf narrators from the majority of their fellow bondspeople." See his *Four Russian Serf Narratives* (Madison: University of Wisconsin Press, 2009), 16.

80. A. V. Nikitenko, *Moia povest' o samom sebe* (St. Petersburg: A. S. Suvorin, 1900), 74, 116.

81. Nikitenko, *Moia povest' o samom sebe*, 185–86, 210–11. Nikitenko was not alone. Konstantin Klepikov and A. P. Miliukov both also sought to change their status in order to further their education. See [K. I. Klepikov], *Avtobiografiia Konstantina Ignat'evicha Klepikova* (Viatka: Maisheeva, 1902), 3–4; and Miliukov, *Dobroe staroe*, 161–63.

82. TsIAM f. 5, op. 1, dd. 210, 213.

83. "Zabytaia 'Myslitel'naia mashina' professor A. N. Shchukareva," http://ukrainiancomputing.org/Shchukarev_r.html, accessed August 25, 2013.

84. E. A. Shabunin, "Obrazovanie i pravoslavie," www.orthedu.ru/kraeved/924-10.html, accessed August 25, 2013.

85. "Lobachev Vladimir Grigor'evich," http://pozhproekt.ru/enciklopediya/lobachev-vladimir-grigorevich and M. M. Iakovlev, "Lobachev G. G.," http://dic.academic.ru/dic.nsf/enc_music/4483/Лобачёв, both accessed August 25, 2013.

86. Miliukov, *Dobroe staroe*, 150–61.

87. NIOR, f. 358, karton 240, ed. khr. 3, l. 5 (1893).

88. ARGO, f. XIV, d. 104, "Naruzhnost' i semeinyi byt russkikh zhitelei goroda Chistopolia i ego uezda," ll. 2–3 (1853).

89. On the idea of migrants as living liminal or marginal lives, see Brower, *The Russian City*, 85–91.

90. GARO f. 49, op. 1, d. 770, ll. 91, 117, 124 (1867); TsIAM f. 32, op. 9, d. 15, l. 1 (1813); d. 598, l. 1 (1815).

91. RGADA f. 695, op. 1, d. 1902, ll. 1–2 (1776).

92. RGIA f. 1088, op. 3, d. 1051, ll. 30–31 (1855); d. 1052, ll. 2–20b (1855); d. 1058, ll. 18–190b (1855).

93. GARO f. 49, op. 1, d. 394, l. 1 (1857); TsIAM f. 32, op. 9, d. 89, l. 1 (1813), d. 177, l. 1 (1814); d. 300, l. 1 (1814); d. 606, l. 1 (1815); d. 953, l. 1 (1815); d. 1082, l. 1 (1815).

94. RGADA f. 796, op. 1, d. 616, ll. 2, 6.

95. RGADA f. 768, op. 1, d. 1000, ll. 1–10b, 2.

96. RGADA f. 713, op. 1, d. 767, l. 1 (1774); also f. 764, op. 3, d. 86, ll. 13–130b (1773).

97. TsIAM f. 2, op. 1, d. 86, ll. 1–2.

98. Manchester, *Holy Fathers*, 171. See also Freeze, *The Parish Clergy*, 155–64 on the "disjuncture" between *soslovie* and service among the clergy.

99. He also noted that he did not fit his *soslovie* of origin, having "neither home nor livestock in the village," and thus "being not used to peasant work or farming." RGIA f. 515, op. 5, d. 4, ll. 2–20b (1798).

100. RGIA f. 383, op. 20, d. 27018, 9 (1859).

101. There are many such cases. For *meshchane* seeking to enter peasant societies on the basis of being, in essence, peasants, see GASO f. 94, op. 1, d. 719, l. 66 (1845); GARO f. 49, op. 1, d. 120, l. 1 (1851); GARO f. 49, op. 1, d. 232, l. 1 (1854); GARO f. 49, op. 1, d. 313, l. 1 (1856); TsIAM f. 54, op. 57, d. 61, l. 2 (1908). For those seeking to enter town societies, and citing their existing trade, property, and longtime residence as reason, see LVVA f. 1394, op. 1, d. 1, ll. 52–520b (1794); RGIA f. 515, op. 5, d. 4, ll. 16–160b (1798); TsIAM f. 54, op. 7, d. 486, l. 1b (1812); GASO f. 94, op. 1, d. 782, ll. 65 (1845); GASO f. 94, op. 1, d. 783, l. 70 (1845); GASO f. 94, op. 1, d. 785, l. 181 (1847); GARO f. 49, op. 1, d. 818, ll. 1–2 (1869); LVIA f. 937, op. 2, d. 2144, l. 27 (1870); RGIA f. 1287, op. 44, d. 905, ll. 41–410b (1903).

102. RGIA f. 515, op. 5, d. 22, l. 12b (1798).

103. TsIAM f. 54, op. 1, d. 524, l. 1 (1793).

104. RGADA f. 796, op. 1, d. 1037, ll. 1, 4. A few other petitions in Cheboksary around the same time were accompanied by similarly detailed descriptions, as in d. 1044, for Savelei Smirnov.

105. TsIAM f. 32, op. 3, d. 1331, l. 2 (1815).

106. RGIA f. 1287, op. 38, d. 665, l. 1 (1866).

107. GARO f. 49, op. 1, d. 530, l. 1–2 (1859).

108. Burds, *Peasant Dreams*, 114-17; Engel, *Between the Fields and the City.*

109. Such feelings were also common among the nascent worker intelligentsia, who often found themselves feeling doubly alienated: from their social equals by education and from their places of origin by work. On the latter, see Mark D. Steinberg, *Proletarian Imagination: Self, Modernity, and the Sacred in Russia, 1910–1925* (Ithaca: Cornell University Press, 2002), 154–55, 178.

110. "Sokrashchennaia zhizn'," 227.

111. Chukhmaldin, *Zapiski*, 66–71.

112. Valerie Kivelson, *Cartographies of Tsardom: The Land and its Meanings in Seventeenth-Century Russia* (Ithaca: Cornell University Press, 2006); Steven L. Hoch, *Serfdom and Social Control in Russia: Petrovskoe, a Village in Tambov* (Chicago: University of Chicago Press, 1986); Smith, "Authority;" Jane Burbank, *Russian Peasants Go to Court: Legal Culture in the Countryside, 1905–1917* (Bloomington: Indiana University Press, 2004).

113. Travin, "Zapiski," 37–58.

114. Shipov, *Istoriia moei zhizni*, 24–25; Nikitenko, *Moia povest'*, 18–37.

115. Steinberg, *Proletarian Imagination*, 76.

116. Aleksandre Avdeev, Alain Blum, and Irina Troitskaia, "Peasant Marriage in Nineteenth-Century Russia," *Population-E* 59, no. 6 (2004): 726–27. See also Stephen P. Frank, "Popular Justice, Community and Culture among the Russian Peasantry, 1870–1900," *Russian Review* 46, no. 3 (July 1987): 239–40.

117. The term is used by Barbara Engel to describe the majority of women who migrated to towns, primarily in the later imperial period. See *Between the Fields and the City*, 43–44.

118. On women merchants and their prospects, see Galina Ulianova, "Merchant Women in Business in the Late Eighteenth and Early Nineteenth Centuries," trans. Roger Bartlett, in *Women in Eighteenth-Century Russian Culture and Society,1700-1825*, eds. Wendy Rosslyn and Alessandra Tosi, 144-67 (Houndmills: Palgrave, 2007).

119. *SZ*, "Zakony o sostoianiiakh," st. 5; M. N. Palibin, ed., *Zakony o sostoianiiakh (Sv. Zak. t. IX, izd. 1899 g.) s dopolnitel-nymi uzakoneniiami, raz"iasneniiami Pravit. Senata i Sv. Sinoda, tsirkuliarami Ministerstva Vnutrennikh Del i alfavitnym ukazatelem* (St. Petersburg: N. K. Martinov, 1901), st. 3.

120. Alexander Etkind, *Internal Colonization: Russia's Imperial Experience* (Cambridge: Polity, 2011), 102.

121. Abby M. Schrader, *Languages of the Lash: Corporal Punishment and Identity in Imperial Russia* (DeKalb: Northern Illinois University Press, 2002), 11–13, 22–26. See also a discussion of awareness of social distinctions within the nobility, but also between the nobility and other estates, in Priscilla Roosevelt, *Life on the Russian Country Estate: A Social and Cultural History* (New Haven: Yale University Press, 1995), 159; and a description of this as a moment when the nobility were reimagined as "the empire's first citizens" in John Randolph, *The House in the Garden: The Bakunin Family and the Romance of Russian Idealism* (Ithaca: Cornell University Press, 2007), 32.

122. Kollman, *By Honor Bound*, 47.

123. A. B. Kamenskii, *Povsednevnost' russkikh gorodskikh obyvatelei* (Moscow: RGGU, 2006), 159–60, 174; Burbank, *Russian Peasants Go to Court.*

124. Alfred Rieber notes that Peter's inclusion of merchants on the rolls of soul-tax payers was a blow to their status; Catherine's reforms later switched merchants to a tax system based on capital. See Rieber, *Merchants and Entrepreneurs*, 5, 13.

125. See Richard Hellie, *Slavery in Russia, 1450–1725* (Chicago: University of Chicago Press, 1982), 698–99. For other ways in which the soul tax altered social groups, see Hughes, *Russia in the Age of Peter the Great*, 138; and E. V. Anisimov, *Podatnaia reforma Petra I: vvedenie podushnoi podati v Rossii, 1719–1728 gg.* (Leningrad: Nauka, 1982).

126. Stupin, "Sobstvennoruchnye zapiski," 370, 379.

127. A. I. Kupriianov, *Gorodskaia kul'tura russkoi provintsii. Konets XVIII-pervaia polovina XIX veka* (Moscow: Novyi khronograf, 2007), 390.

128. I. S. Belliustin, *Description of the Clergy in Rural Russia: The Memoir of a Nineteenth-Century Parish Priest,* trans. Gregory L. Freeze (Ithaca: Cornell University Press, 1985), 194.

129. Genkin, *Pomeshchich'i krest'iane*, 114; he discusses the general trend of serfs living completely cut off from their villages, and yet still remaining serfs, earlier (40).

130. David L. Ransel, *A Russian Merchant's Tale: The Life and Adventures of Ivan Alekseevich Tolchenov, Based on His Diary* (Bloomington: Indiana University Press, 2009).

131. Shcherban', "Vospominaniia krepostnogo," 38–39.

132. "Sokrashchennaia zhizn'," 228.

133. Wirtschafter describes a set of petitions by serfs that show "a striking desire for liberation" in *Structures of Society*, 120. Richard Stites notes that such thoughts could also lead to (presumably less legal) flight. See Richard Stites, *Serfdom, Society, and the Arts in Imperial Russia: The Pleasure and the Power* (New Haven: Yale University Press, 2005), 34–35. For a larger discussion of the concept of freedom in the world of Russian serfdom, see Smith, "Freed Serfs without Free People."

134. Nikitenko, *Moia povest'*, 176. See also P. Bakhmetev, "Osvobozhdenie moego ottsa ot krepostnago iga," *Trudy saratovskoi uchenoi arkhivnoi komissii* 31 (1914): 205–206.

135. Steinberg, *Proletarian Imagination*, 89–90, 123–24. See also Chris J. Chulos, *Converging Worlds: Religion and Community in Peasant Russia, 1861–1917* (DeKalb: Northern Illinois University Press, 2003), 5, 66–81, for thoughts on the role of pilgrimage in late imperial Russia, as well as on restrictions on mobility in earlier periods. See also Engel, *Between the Fields and the City*, 31–32, for a discussion of women's desires for freedom and social advancement.

136. RGIA f. 571, op. 1, d. 1796, ll. 261–261ob (1851).

137. Rieber, "Sedimentary Society." Iu. M. Goncharov and V. S. Chutchev argue that the end of the imperial era saw a general flattening of the social hierarchy, in *Meshchanskoe soslovie zapadnoi sibiri*, 34.

138. On the moratorium, see *PSZ*, vol. 23, no. 17357 (July 13, 1795).

139. TsIAM f. 397, op. 1, d. 121, l. 427.

140. Wayne Dowler, "Merchants and Politics in Russia: The Guild Reform of 1824," *SEER* 65, no. 1 (January 1987): 38–52.

141. Daniel Morrison argues that an increase in the proportion of serf migrants to towns at the end of the eighteenth century—and particularly the fact that most serfs ended up as *meshchane* rather than merchants—means that many more than "a wealthy few" were able to purchase their freedom; it may instead mean that many were freed without their consent. Morrison, "Trading Peasants," 219–20.

142. See chapter 3, this volume.

143. On such habits, see my "Freed Serfs without Free People."

144. Wirtschafter, "Social Misfits, 220–21."

145. *Materialy dlia polnoi i sravnitel'noi statistiki Moskvy*, vol. 1 (Moscow: Universitetskaia tipografiia, 1841), 264. The exact dates listed are 1788–1794 and 1834–1840.

146. V. P. Androssov, *Statisticheskaia zapiska o Moskve* (Moscow: Semen Selivanovskii, 1832), 66.

147. TsGIASPb f. 222, op.1, d. 1095.

148. GASO f. 94, op.1, d. 1321. Two women, both freed serfs, also joined the society with sons.

149. GASO f. 94, op. 1, d. 1685; that same record lists 15 women who entered the society: 6 from peasant societies; 7 merchants, one soldier's wife, and one "skipped" in a previous count. The book does not make it clear whether these are all the women who joined in that year, or just those who joined with male family members.

150. Nikitenko, *Moia povest'*, 211.

CHAPTER 2

1. RGADA f. 742, op. 1, d. 358, l. 1.

2. RGADA f. 742, op. 1, d. 358, ll. 10b-7.

3. Dating the moment when *sosloviia* were fully developed as concepts is a central point of contention in the historiography. Kliuchevskii sees *soslovie* as perfected with Catherine the Great's Charters (*Istoriia sosloviia*, 225); for a similar argument, see V. V. Eremian and M. V. Fedorov, *Mestnoe samoupravlenie v Rossii (XII-nachalo XX vv.)* (Moscow: Novyi Iurist, 1998), 91 or the discussion in A. B. Kamenskii, "Soslovnaia politika Ekateriny II," *Voprosy istorii* no. 3 (1995): 29–45. B. N. Mironov describes the town *sosloviia* as fully developed by that point, but the larger *sosloviia* structure as continuing to evolve (*Sotsial'naia istoriia Rossii*, vol. 1, 112, 522–23). Others follow Mironov by restricting the notion of full development to certain *sosloviia*; Freeze, at least, notes that the eighteenth century did see the "recasting of the clergy into a closed hereditary estate" ("Social Mobility and the Russian Parish Clergy," 642).

4. There were two sides to this. One the one hand, it recalls what Valerie Kivelson has called "not the overwhelming might of…central authority, but the astounding helplessness of the state as it confronted the enormous sprawl of its own lands and administration" in *Cartographies of Tsardom*, 35; this contrast is further developed (50–55). In addition, it reflects the fact that for all that *soslovie* in principle implied occupation, in reality it often did not. On the persistence of such issues at the end of the eighteenth century, see George E. Munro, *The Most Intentional City: St. Petersburg in the Reign of Catherine the Great* (Madison: Fairleigh Dickinson University Press, 2008), 57–59.

5. On the *raznochintsy*, see Wirtschafter, *Structures of Society*, 25–26.

6. Kliuchevskii, *Istoriia soslovii*, 292.

7. Kliuchevskii, *Istoriia soslovii*, 353.

8. Kliuchevskii, *Istoriia soslovii*, 366–68.

9. Richard Hellie, *Enserfment and Military Change in Muscovy* (Chicago: University of Chicago Press, 1971), 240–42. Igor Filippov looks at the historiographical debates surrounding the rise of serfdom in "La naissance du servage russe. Un survol de l'historiographie contemporaine," in *Noveaux servages et société en Europe (XIIIe-XXe siècle). Actes du colloque de Besançon, 4-6 octobre 2007*, ed. N. Carrier, 333-82 (Caen: AHSR, 2010).

10. This version of the results of the *Ulozhenie* dates back at least to the mid-nineteenth century, in Ploshinskii, *Gorodskoe i srednee sostoianie*, 112; and Andrei Prigara, *Opyt istorii sostoianiia gorodskikh obyvatelei v vostochnoi Rossii*, vol. 1 (St. Petersburg: V. Golovin, 1868), 65–66. Modern statements of the same include Rieber, *Merchants and Entrepreneurs*, xxi. Nancy Shields Kollman also descries a Muscovite world of "little social mobility" in "Concepts of Society," 37.

11. Keep, *Soldiers of the Tsar*, 145. The levies called for a certain proportion of recruits, generally one or two soldiers per several hundred souls, although the rates varied widely over the eighteenth and early nineteenth centuries. See Blum, *Lord and Peasant in Russia*, 466.

12. Hughes, *Russia in the Age of Peter the Great*, 138. The original call for a census, aimed at military efficiency, appeared in 1718, and was soon followed by a series of other ukases giving more specific information about the census and including more and more groups in the census population. *PSZ*, vol. 5, no. 3245 (November 26, 1718); no. 3287 (January 22, 1719); vol. 6, no. 3747 (February 28, 1721).

13. I. P. Rukovskii, "Istoriko-statisticheskie svedeniia o podushnykh podatiakh," in *Trudy Kommissii vysochaishe uchrezhdennoi dlia peresmotra sistemy podatei i sborov*, vol. 1 (St. Petesrburg: V. Bezobrazov i Komp., 1866), 92–93. I. Beliaev also saw the institution of the revision as a major event, bringing with it a new era of serfdom that bound peasants to their lords and their lords to service. Beliaev, *Krest'iane na rusi*, 251-69.

14. Laws against fugitives were frequently reiterated. See *PSZ*, vol. 2, nos. 981–82 (1682); vol. 6, no. 3512 (February 9, 1720); no. 3743 (February 19, 1721); no. 3939 (April 6, 1722); and no. 3958 (April 11, 1722). See also E. V. Anisimov, "The Struggle with Fugitives during the Reform Period," Hugh F. Graham, trans., *Soviet Studies in History* 28, no. 1 (Summer 1989): 59–77. There was one major exception: fugitives who had fled abroad, who were increasingly treated completely differently, and, indeed, allowed to return to Russia to "choose a new way of life." On this, see Smith, "'The Freedom to Choose a Way of Life.'"

15. *PSZ*, vol. 5, no. 2812 (May 26, 1714). N. V. Kozlova has described the early eighteenth century as a period of "active struggle with runaways," as the "fiscal interests of the state" demanded better control of its population. See Kozlova, *Pobegi krest'ian*, 128.

16. Elise Kimerling Wirtschafter discusses this in the case of the *raznochintsy*. See Wirtschafter, *Structures of Society*, 40–48. For an example of the shifts in specific categorization that occurred in the eighteenth century, see I. A. Bulygin, "Osobaia kategoriia feodal'no zavisimykh krest'ian v pervoi chetverti XVIII v.," in *Dvorianstvo i krepostnoi stroi Rossii XVI-XVIII vv.*, ed. N. I. Pavlenko (Moscow, 1975), 190–212.

17. The ukases regulating the second and third revisions are found at *PSZ*, vol. 11, no. 8619 (September 17, 1742); no. 8835 (December 16, 1743); and vol. 15, no. 11364 (November 28, 1761). Archival files involving primarily registering the as-yet unregistered include RGADA f. 768, op. 1, dd. 46, 47, 65.

18. Instructions for the second census appear in *PSZ*, vol. 11, no. 8836 (December 16, 1743).

19. Richard Hellie, "The Impact of the Southern and Eastern Frontiers of Muscovy on the Ulozhenie (Law Code) of 1649 Compared with the Impact of the Western Frontier," *Russian History* 19, nos. 1–4 (1992): 99–115. See a similar discussion of the ways that the concept of freedom was different on the borderlands of Muscovy in Valerie Kivelson, "Muscovite 'Citizenship': Rights without Freedom," *Journal of Modern History* 74, no. 3 (September 2002): 486.

20. Mironov makes this argument in *Russkii gorod*, 89.

21. Martin, *Enlightened Metropolis*.

22. See V. M. Kabuzan, *Emigratsiia i reemigratsiia v Rossii v XVIII-nachale XX veka* (Moscow: Nauka, 1998), 13–48, for a painstakingly thorough enumeration of the various patterns of migration within the empire during the eighteenth century.

23. Linsdey Hughes particularly argues that the goal of the law was to support the state, not to free the individual. See Hughes, *Russia in the Age of Peter the Great*, 184, and on the Table more generally, 182–85.

24. *PSZ*, vol. 6, no. 3708 (January 16, 1721), Gl. V.

25. Peter established the *tsekhi* in *PSZ*, vol. 6, no. 3980 (April 27, 1722); the Senate clarified some of his statements a few months later in no. 4054 (July 16, 1722). In October, another Senate decree repeated the demand that all who engaged in crafts register with town Magistrates; no. 4102 (October 4, 1722). Later, however, an exception was noted: non-Orthodox free men could not join *tsekhy*. See *PSZ*, vol. 12, no. 9012 (August 3, 1744).

26. On their failures, see J. Michael Hittle, *The Service City: State and Townsmen in Russia, 1600–1800* (Cambridge, MA: Harvard University Press, 1979), 126–29.

27. See *PSZ*, vol. 6, no. 3754 (March 7, 1721); no. 3923 (March 20, 1722); vol. 7, no. 5161 (September 20, 1727); vol. 11, no. 8577 (July 2, 1742).

28. *PSZ*, vol. 3, no. 1666 (January 1, 1699); no. 1723 (November 24, 1699); vol. 4, no. 1775 (March 11, 1700). This idea was reaffirmed as one point in a general law on duties to be paid on trade, vol. 4, no. 1819 (December 22, 1700).

29. Prigara, *Opyt istorii*, 129.

30. For laws focusing on registering people according to their occupation, see *PSZ*, vol. 7, no. 4312 (September 27, 1723); no. 4318 (October 1, 1722); no. 4336 (October 23, 1723); no. 4398 (December 20, 1723). On tax duties, see *PSZ*, vol. 7, no. 4373 (November 28, 1723). A Senate ukase of 1722 did note that newcomers to towns ought to be sent back to their prior homes and statuses, but it was followed soon thereafter by another Senate ukase that instead stated that merchants and peasants should not be returned, but instead registered in new statuses. *PSZ*, vol. 6, no. 4026 (June 1, 1722); no. 4059 (July 19, 1722).

31. *PSZ*, vol. 7, no. 9372 (February 13, 1747).

32. The 1747 law lists one previous decision that refers to peasants who had been freed by their owners, but none of the other prior decisions make any mention of such a necessity, nor does the final decision in this law. Prigara claims that a Senate decree of 1714 stated that serfs and other peasants had to remain in their prior statuses (Prigara, *Opyt istorii*, 130–31), but the law he cites (*PSZ*, vol. 5, no. 2770 [February 4, 1714]) seems instead to state that peasants could not leave behind their former tax responsibilities—a fact repeated in a later Petrine law (*PSZ*, vol. 7, no. 4566 [September 16, 1724]). On the other hand, these two laws do suggest that there were different kinds of registration allowed, and individuals could be simultaneously registered in towns while still belonging to their owners.

33. *PSZ*, vol. 15, no. 11426 (January 31, 1762). The last point reiterates that contained in the 1714 law above. Among the first laws to restate some of these points for other kinds of social mobility was one that stated that peasants seeking to enter monasteries had to prove their freedom and the continuation of their tax payments with written evidence. See *PSZ*, vol. 19, no. 13454 (April 29, 1770).

34. Richard Wortman, *The Development of a Russian Legal Consciousness* (Chicago: University of Chicago Press, 1976), 9–10.

35. *PSZ*, vol. 20, no. 14632 (July 25, 1777).

36. *PSZ*, vol. 19, no. 13453 (April 29, 1770).

37. *PSZ*, vol. 21, no. 15578 (November 8, 1782).

38. *PSZ*, vol. 20, no. 14275 (March 17, 1775).

39. *PSZ*, vol. 9, no. 7070 (September 28, 1736); vol. 10, no. 7169 (February 6, 1737).

40. *PSZ*, vol. 12, no. 9113 (February 28, 1745).

41. *PSZ*, vol. 20, no. 14343 (July 1, 1775).

42. During the lengthy process of writing and rewriting the manifesto that would establish these new institutions, certain revisions specifically focused on regulations governing movement both between places and between social categories. The Senate, in particular, focused on the role of Magistracies in ensuring social stability and fighting against runaways, by including language that ordered unregistered individuals to be sent away from their illegal place of residence, and also clarified regulations about allowing military servitors to register as townspeople—those still classified as serfs were not allowed in to town rolls. In the end, the magistracies were given responsibility for serving not just as judicial organs in towns but as clerical ones too, drawing up plans of towns and making sure that the right people were registered in them. See Vodarskii, *Issledovaniia po istorii russkogo goroda*, 215–17; *PSZ*, vol. 6, no. 3708 (1721).

43. Hittle, *The Service City*, 132–37.

44. During the eighteenth century, "his" is usually appropriate, as most cases involved men. This changed dramatically around the turn of the century, however, when women began to figure heavily in the lists of those changing estate.

45. RGADA f. 742, op. 1, d. 1020, l. 1 (1771). Not using stamped (*gerbovaia*) paper could lead to fines later on, as in RGADA f. 820, op. 2, d. 1518, l. 8 (1777).

46. RGADA f. 742, op. 1, d. 1020, l. 1 (1771).

47. For example, the petition at RGADA f. 308, op. 2, d. 184, l. 1 (1779) from Sergei Ushakov, a fugitive economic peasant from Serpukhov district seeking entry into the Moscow merchant estate. On this larger process, see Smith, "'The Freedom to Choose a Way of Life.'"

48. RGADA f. 807, op. 1, d. 511, ll. 2–3, 7–12, 13–18, 36, 38, 39. Other cases in which petitioners included extra information as a buffer against the illegality of their requests include RGADA f. 695, op. 1, d. 1067, ll. 1–60b (1737) and RGADA f. 695, op. 1, d. 1117, ll. 1–6 (1743).

49. In Zukov's case, this was a copy of his manumission papers from Khotmyshskii district, at RGADA f. 742, op. 1, d. 1020, l. 2.

50. RGADA f. 764, op. 3, d. 33, l. 13 (1764).

51. RGADA f. 742, op. 1, d. 1020, ll. 5–6.

52. RGADA f. 820, op. 2, d. 9, ll. 9–30, 54–540b, 63 (for the multiple acceptances/rejections) and d. 19, l. 5 for Timofei Epifanov.

53. For Zukov, RGADA f. 742, op. 1, d. 1020, l. 8.

54. The Kursk Civil (*grazhdanskii*) Elder gave the merchants' agreement to accept Zukov at RGADA f. 742, op. 1, d. 1020, l. 7.

55. RGADA f. 742, op. 1, d. 1020, l. 10.

56. RGADA f. 768, op. 1, d. 113, l. 4. Something similar happened in 1777 when the College of the Economy (the college that administered former monastery lands) instructed the local treasury officer on how to handle one of its former peasants who had been registered as a merchant: "in the census books do not exclude the petitioner by erasing [his name] but only note down 'Registered in the merchantry' so that until the next census revision all his dues are collected according to the Ukase" (RGADA f. 308, op. 2, d. 137, l. 6).

57. Zukov only swore an oath that he would be a good merchant, at RGADA f. 742, op. 1, d. 1020, l. 11.

58. For example, RGADA f. 308, op. 2, d. 190, l. 8.

59. Such was the case with Il'ia Efimov Svinin, who had asked for a 15-year waiver from service obligations after acceptance into the Solvychegodsk merchantry. They refused this request, and the magistracy called him in to hear of the decision. See RGADA f. 695, op. 1, d. 1972, ll. 9–90b.

60. Marc Raeff, "Preface," *Catherine II's Charters of 1785 to the Nobility and the Towns*, trans. and ed. David Griffiths and George E. Munro (Bakersfield: Charles Schlacks,, 1991), xii.

61. "Predislovie," *PSZ*, vol. 1, xx.

62. RGADA f. 707, op. 1, d. 12, ll. 1, 5; d. 15, ll. 1–2; d. 14, ll. 1–2, 4.

63. RGADA f. 742, op. 1, d. 733, l. 1.

64. RGADA f. 742, op. 1, d. 358, ll. 1, 6.

65. RGADA f. 713, op. 1, d. 685, ll. 1–4.

66. RGADA f. 308, op. 1, d. 100, ll. 1, 11–14.

67. RGADA f. 308, op. 1, d. 140, ll. 1–20b.

68. RGADA f. 807, op. 1, d. 46, ll. 1–10b, 6–16, 29–30.

69. RGADA f. 768, op. 1, d. 1005, ll. 1, 8, 14.

70. RGADA f. 764, op. 3, d. 33, ll. 1, 19–22, 23. This particular group would continue to receive special (though not necessarily better) treatment by the laws. In 1774, a Senate decree was released in the case of the falconer turned Pereslavl' Zalesskii merchant Andrei Popov. The Senate agreed that falconers had to keep up their duties in their old estate, because not doing so would hurt the Empress's ability to enjoy the hunt. However, this of course meant that falconers who joined new estates might be subject not just to the double tax but to double service duties, as well. RGADA f. 691, op. 1, d. 1436, ll. 1–60b.

71. RGADA f. 764, op. 3, d. 31, l. 1–5, 7–120b, 14).

72. RGADA f. 291, op. 1, d. 13038, ll. 1, 6. On the history of the *odnodvortsy*, see Carol Stevens, *Soldiers on the Steppe: Army Reform and Social Change in Early Modern Russia* (DeKalb: Northern Illinois University Press, 1995), 140–57.

73. RGADA f. 707 op. 1, d. 93, ll. 1–1, 3–4, 9–90b.

74. *PSZ*, vol. 15, no. 11426 (January 31, 1762).

75. *PSZ*, vol. 6, no. 3512 (February 9, 1720); vol. 7, no. 9372 (February 13, 1747).

76. *PSZ*, vol. 6, no. 3980 (April 27, 1722).

77. For a discussion of similar practices, see N. V. Kozlova, *Rossiiskoi absoliutizm i kupechestvo v XVIII veke* (Moscow: Arkheograficheskii tsentr, 1999), 249–60.

78. Examples are found at RGADA f. 591, op. 1, d. 1940, ll. 1–10b, 6; d. 1945, l. 1 (1746, reiterating the rules for registry into the craft guilds); f. 691, op. 1, d. 1450, l. 1 (1764, reiterating rules on registering peasants as merchants); f. 820, op. 2, d. 710, l. 1 (1766, on not registering economic peasants without freedom from the economic college); f. 291, op. 1, d. 14171, ll. 1–7 (1767, on not registering runaways as peasants).

79. RGADA f. 1069, op. 1, d. 137, l. 420b.

80. RGADA f. 713, op. 1, d. 1, ll. 1–30b.

81. RGADA f. 1069, op. 1, d. 137, l. 50 (1780).

82. Of course, some simply registered people without comment: the Sol'vychegodsk Magistracy accepted church peasants in 1743 (RGADA f. 695, op. 1, d. 1116, ll. 1, 70b–190b) and a state peasant in 1779 (d. 1995, ll. 27–280b); the Pereslavl' Zalesskii Magistrate accepted a

particular kind of state blacksmith in 1760–1761 (RGADA f. 691, op. 1, d. 3721, ll. 1–11; d. 3749, ll. 1–90b).

83. RGADA f. 705, op. 1, d. 49, ll. 1–13.

84. In 1745, the Rostov district court peasant Ivan Ivanov Nikanov was accepted into the Pereslavl' Zalesskii merchants on a passport with this caveat (RGADA f. 691, op. 1, d. 4011, ll. 1–200b); in 1780 the Serpukhov *meshchanin* Ivan Ivanov Krymov entered the Moscow merchantry on a passport; in this case the Moscow Magistracy even wrote to Serpukhov to confirm his dues (RGADA f. 308, op. 2, d. 191, ll. 1, 7–8).

85. RGADA f. 705, op. 1, d. 53, ll. 1–7; d. 56, ll. 1–9; d. 57, ll. 1–33, and d. 58, ll. 1–29.

86. RGADA f. 820, op. 2, d. 1446, ll. 1–2, 7; d. 1508, ll. 1–5; d. 1512, ll. 1, 2, 5; d. 1518, ll. 1, 8; f. 796, op. 1, d. 1606, ll. 1–2, 10.

87. RGADA f. 820, op. 2, d. 1444, ll. 1, 10 (1776).

88. RGADA f. 705, op. 1, d. 58, ll. 33, 37–38.

89. For example, *PSZ,* vol. 12, no. 9256 (February 6, 1746).

90. RGADA f. 291. op. 1 d. 11217, ll. 1–10b, 10.

91. RGADA f. 1069, op. 1, d. 175, ll. 10–13.

92. RGADA f. 1069, op. 1, d. 93, ll. 4–5.

93. Something similar happened in Krasnoiarsk, where several *raznochintsy* and peasants were allowed to register despite having only passports, expired or otherwise. RGADA f. 291, op. 1, d. 15329, ll. 1–3 (1769).

94. RGADA f. 1069, op. 1, d. 137, ll. 6, 14, 21.

95. RGADA f. 807, op. 1, d. 14, ll. 1–10b, 10–11.

96. RGADA f. 695, op. 1, d. 1902, ll. 1–2, 7–8, 11.

97. RGADA f. 820, op. 2, d. 1575, ll. 1, 5.

98. RGADA f. 707, op. 1, d. 71, ll. 2, 7 (1768).

99. RGADA f. 291, op. 1, d. 7702, ll. 1–4, 8 (1756); see also d. 7519, ll. 1–2, 10–11 (1756) and d. 8445, ll. 1–20b, 11–12 (1757).

100. RGADA f. 807, op. 1, d. 513, ll. 1–2, 11–13, 23–4, 26–270b.

101. RGADA f. 291, op. 1, d. 6242, ll. 2–3 (1747). Similar cases include that of Prince Peter Repnin, whose Rostov district serfs had been registered in the Iaroslavl' merchant estate (RGADA f. 308, op. 2, d. 10 [1747]).

102. RGADA f. 291, op. 1, d. 7917, ll. 1–10b.

103. RGADA f. 820, op. 2, d. 876, l. 1.

104. RGADA f. 712, op. 1, d. 345, ll. 1–5, 6, 9.

105. RGADA f. 820, op. 2, d. 2, ll. 4–6, 9–12, 24–26.

106. Wortman, *Development of a Russian Legal Consciousness,* 12, 8.

107. *PSZ,* vol. 15, no. 11092 (August 16, 1760).

CHAPTER 3

1. TsIAM f. 32, op. 9, d. 1327, ll. 2, 3, 4.

2. Paul Dukes, *Catherine the Great and the Russian Nobility* (Cambridge: Cambridge University Press, 1967), 218.

3. On Catherine's Enlightenment ideals, the *Nakaz,* and *soslovie,* see Lavrinovich, "Sozdanie sotsial'nykh osnov imperii," 117-19 and Kamenskii, "Soslovnaia politika," 33-35.

4. "Predislovie," *SIRIO* 8, xxiii.

5. *SIRIO* 8, 140–41 (Ivan Ikonnikov, delegate from Zaraisk); 160 (Stepan Samoilov, delegate from Eniseisk, who noted that many local *raznochintsy* were trading despite their lack of proper registry and hoped that further laws would insist that they enter the local merchant estate); 163 (Ivan Bol'shoi Efimov, delegate from Riazhsk, who focused on the need for craftsmen to register in the *tsekhi*); 182–83 (Ivan Kobelev, delegate from Kazan', who claimed that many local Tatars were illegally engaging in manufacture and asked that they be forced to follow the laws); 258 (Stepan Fomin, delegate from Tomsk).

6. *SIRIO* 8, 185. Blaznov's fiery rhetoric (he also claimed that merchants were so harmed by peasant trade that they were going abroad to seek better conditions) got him censured by the marshal overseeing the discussion. On peasant trade as a danger to agriculture, see also 100 (statement of Petr Khlebnikov, merchant of Elatma, who grudgingly agreed that *raznochintsy* could and should join merchant societies if they wished to trade) and 328 (statement of Galich district noble Iurii Lermontov).

7. *SIRIO* 8, 313–15. Similarly, debates over peasants joining craft guilds also went back and forth over the desirability of permanent or temporary registry. *SIRIO* 4, 122, 125–26.

8. *SIRIO* 8, 170. Fedor Polezhaev, a state peasant from Kungur, echoed these statements and noted that merchants in his area were abusing the rights of agriculturists, much to his fellow peasants' dismay (332–33).

9. See particularly the statement of the Tikhvin delegate Samoila Solodovnikov, who quoted not just the *Ulozhenie*, laws of Peter the Great, and the Nakaz, to prove his point, but even scripture (*SIRIO* 8, 152–56); also see the statement of Ivan Karyshev, delegate from Barnaul, who provided a extremely long list of legal precedents for his argument in favor of mandatory registration (193–200); and a second statement by Andrei Blaznov, who listed law after law to prove that peasants had no business trading (224–27).

10. On the latter point, see the statements of Abdul murza Daushov, *meshcheriak* of Isetsk province, who noted that local conditions created a need for more flexibility in trade laws to ensure that agriculturists and state servitors alike had sufficient income (*SIRO* 8, 191–93); Gavrilo Bozhich, delegate from the *shliakhta* of Nezhin and Baturin, who described Ukraine's unique (he claimed) *soslovie* structure (215); Rakhmankul Alkin, delegate from the service Tatars of Kazan' district, who noted that language could also serve as a deterrent to trade in the regions (223–24).

11. *SIRIO* 8, 147–48. These problems were also felt in places that had long since ceased to be border regions. Vialsh Elgushev, a Tatar delegate from near Kasimov, soon to be part of Riazan' province, commented on many of the same issues (too few merchants, Tatars and murzas listed in positions incompatible with their actual occupation) in this place that had long been part of the Russian core (10).

12. *SIRIO* 8, 163.

13. *SIRIO* 8, 66–67.

14. *PSZ*, vol. 21, no. 15277 (November 16, 1781).

15. *PSZ*, vol. 21, no. 15278 (November 16, 1781); no. 15296 (December 10, 1781).

16. *PSZ*, vol. 21, no. 15459 (July 2, 1782).

17. *PSZ*, vol. 21, no. 15578 (1782). There is no specific date listed for this ukase, but it appears between two others dated November 7. Perhaps the contradiction between this law and the others from earlier in the year is simply caused by it being misplaced by the compilers of the *Polnoe*

sobranie. If the ukase were actually from earlier in the year, it would have been basing its argument on the then existing legal statutes. Even so, it failed to recognize the power of Catherine's 1775 Manifesto, which explicitly stated that freed serfs, at least, could join the *meshchanstvo*.

18. Isabel de Madariaga sees Catherine's policies as a shift away from thinking in terms of social estate and toward thinking purely in terms of "straightforward stratification according to wealth." Isabel de Madariaga, *Russia in the Age of Catherine the Great* (New Haven: Yale University Press, 1981), 281. Alfred Rieber, however, defines Catherine's goal as "to transform the merchantry into a genuine full-fledged soslovie," and finds her policies mostly successful in so doing. Rieber, *Merchants and Entrepreneurs*, 13. And Maiia Lavrinovich sees the end results of Catherine's reforms as creating a *soslovie* "structure" based on "maximal limitations on the possibility of vertical mobility" in "Sozdanie sotsial'nykh osnov imperii," 134.

19. *PSZ*, vol. 22, no. 16188 (April 21, 1785), st. 11, 139.

20. *PSZ*, vol. 22, no. 16188 (April 21, 1785), st. 63–68. Catherine used the term *posadskie*, an older term for the poorer townspeople, which had seemed to be superseded by the definition of *meshchane* in the 1775 Manifesto.

21. *PSZ*, vol. 22, no. 16188 (April 21, 1785), st. 80–91. *Posadskie* appeared in st. 138–45, but appear to be much the same as the *meshchane* in earlier laws.

22. The confusing use of language in the Charter was pointed out by several later authors. See *Novoe obshchestvennoe ustroistvo S. Peterburga* (St. Petesrburg: Ministerstvo Vnutrennykh Del, 1846), 4n.; and Ia. M. Vileishis, *Sistematicheskii sbornik zakonov o meshchanskikh upravleniiakh s pozdneishimi raz"iasneniiami Pravitel'stvuiushchego Senata, Ministerstv i dr. uchrezhdenii* (Kherson: Khersonskoe gubernskoe pravlenie, 1914), i. In 1888, an attorney representing the Saratov *meshchanin* and merchant societies even argued that that confusing usage had led to later improper decisions on the part of the Ministry of Internal Affairs. See Abram Osipovich Gordon, "Po delu ob imushchestve Saratovskikh kupecheskogo i meshchanskogo soslovii," *Zapiski Senata* 97 (1888): 13.

23. *PSZ*, vol. 22, no. 16188 (April 21, 1785), st. 5–6.

24. *PSZ*, vol. 22, no. 16188 (April 21, 1785), st. 138.

25. *PSZ*, vol. 22, no. 16188 (April 21, 1785), st. 56.

26. *PSZ*, vol. 22, no. 16188 (April 21, 1785), st. 71, 78.

27. *PSZ*, vol. 22, no. 16187 (April 21, 1785), st. 72-90 (on the books); 91-92 (on forms of evidence).

28. David Griffiths and George Munro, trans. and eds., *Catherine the Great's Charters of 1785 to the Nobility and the Towns* (Bakersfield: Charles Schlacks, 1991), 69–74.

29. N. Varadinov, *Istoriia Ministerstva Vnutrennikh del*, Part II, book 2 (St. Petersburg: Ministerstvo Vnutrennikh del, 1862), 566.

30. Rozhkov, *Gorod i derevnia*, 68.

31. *PSZ*, vol. 26, no. 19576 (September 27, 1800).

32. *PSZ*, vol. 26, no. 19579 (September 28, 1800). More generally, since the Charter to the Towns, other laws had also dealt with the double tax duty. In 1785, an imperial ukase stated that peasants whose status had changed because their village had been made a town—and all its inhabitants had been made merchants or *meshchane*—only owed duties as townspeople, but that all other peasants who had entered merchant or *meshchanin* societies by moving to towns owed the double duty as laid out in the Charter to the Towns. *PSZ*, vol. 22, no. 16254 (September 4, 1785). Almost a decade later, another law focused on a different kind of double tax

duty, stating that artisans who registered as merchants had to pay dues for both statuses. *PSZ,* vol. 23, no. 17157 (October 5, 1793).

33. *PSZ,* vol. 29, no. 22278 (September 18, 1806).

34. *PSZ,* vol. 30, no. 23240 (August 19, 1808).

35. For example, *PSZ,* vol. 31, no. 24136 (February 28, 1810), or vol. 37, no. 28389 (August 19, 1820), which reiterated a specific earlier rule as part of a larger effort to clarify the use of guarantors or guarantees. As new routes of mobility were decided, too, the double tax was applied, as when a Senate decision allowed free agriculturists to join new societies. *PSZ,* vol. 38, no. 29715 (December 24, 1823). In 1821, another Senate decree gave specific rules to the timing of registry, in part to eliminate "diversity," but also to make sure taxes were properly allotted. *PSZ,* vol. 37, no. 28653 (June 20, 1821). At various points, the Senate censured provincial treasuries for not following instructions. See cases cited decided in 1818 and 1821, reported in P. Khavskii, *Sobranie zakonov o kuptsakh, meshchanakh, posadskikh i tsekhovykh, ili Gorodovoe Polozhenie so vkliucheniem zakonov predshestvuiushchikh i posleduiushchikh s 1766 po 1823 god* (St. Petersburg: Tipografiia pravitel'stvuiushchogo Senata, 1823), 275–79, 314–18.

36. *PSZ,* vol. 23, no. 17357 (July 13, 1795).

37. *PSZ,* vol. 31, no. 24680 (June 19, 1811).

38. TsIAM f. 397, op. 1, d. 121.

39. *PSZ,* vol. 26, no. 19694 (December 19, 1800).

40. The laws cited a decree from Paul's reign, in which the emperor stated that he wished to have final authority on any such case. *PSZ,* vol. 26, no. 19434 (May 27/June 16, 1800); Alexander allowed the Synod to maintain its authority over such matters. *PSZ,* vol. 26, no. 19897 (May 30, 1801); vol. 28, no. 21278 (April 30, 1804). Another law emphasized that townspeople who wished to move to new towns had to receive formal freedom from their old society, as well. *PSZ,* vol. 28, no. 21693 (March 31, 1805).

41. *PSZ,* vol. 30, no. 23092 (June 14, 1808). Other decisions that emphasize the importance of proper documents include *PSZ,* vol. 31, no. 24364 (September 30, 1810).

42. *PSZ,* vol. 24, no. 17695 (December 29, 1796).

43. *PSZ,* vol. 28, no. 21484 (October 24, 1804). In 1806, another decree described treasuries acting against the law, and instituted forms to regularize the system. *PSZ,* vol. 29, no. 22366 (November 22, 1806). And in 1810 another decree repeated that the 1804 law was still in effect, focusing in particular on the need for proper freedom documents, with due consideration to all these concerns. *PSZ,* vol. 31, no. 24248 (May 30, 1810).

44. TsIAM f. 2, op. 1, d. 915, ll. 1–20b (1820).

45. *PSZ,* vol. 37, no. 28659 (June 26, 1821). For perhaps the same reason, in 1822 he forbade state peasants in one district of Novgorod province from entering town societies (perhaps, because the decree only stated the prohibition). *PSZ,* vol. 38, no. 29096 (June 30, 1822).

46. *PSZ,* vol. 31, no. 24441 (November 28, 1810).

47. RGIA f. 1151, op. 1, d. 170, ll. 90b–10.

48. *PSZ,* vol. 26, no. 19932 (June 30, 1801); vol. 27, no. 20942 (September 18, 1803); vol. 29, no. 22232 (August 7, 1806).

49. LVIA f. 937, op. 1, d. 12, l. 13 (1815).

50. There is one major exception. In 1826, increased obligations were placed on court peasants who wished to become merchants, on the grounds that it was in the best interest of the tsar's

family (and, supposedly, peasant villages themselves) "to complicate as much as possible" such movement. *PSZ* 2, vol. 1, no. 721 (December 4, 1826).

51. RGIA f. 1341, op. 15, d. 1175, ll. 12–120b (Senate decision, 1814).

52. Daniel Brower argues that in this reform, "Kankrin sought to discourage peasant inter-lopers," and that although "in this precise hierarchy some social mobility was unavoidable," its general purpose was to constrain mobility. See "Urbanization and Autocracy," 387–88. Wayne Dowler sees it as expressing the central state's "ambivalence about the correct balance between old social arrangements and new economic forces and needs" in "Merchants and Politics in Russia," 48.

53. *PSZ*, vol. 39, no. 29823 (February 29, 1824). Later, because some provincial treasuries had questioned whether they really meant to eliminate the need to prove freedom from military service, the Senate clarified why it had made the law: the previous standard had given Jews an advantage, as they did not owe military service; thus, by eliminating the requirement for "towns-people of Jewish and Christian origins," that advantage was eliminated. *PSZ*, vol. 39, no. 30187 (December 31, 1824).

54. *PSZ* 2, vol. 2, no. 1123 (May 26, 1827). It echoed a law from 1824 that gave this right to townspeople seeking to move from one town to another. *PSZ*, vol. 39, no. 30099 (October 29, 1824).

55. Described in Petr Ivanov, *Obozrenie prav i obiazannostei Rossiiskogo kupechestva i voob-shche vsego srednego sosloviia, s prisovokupleniem izlozheniia Postanovlenii, otnosiashchikhsia kak do sudebnykh mest, uchrezhdennykh dlia sosloviia sego, tak i lits izbiraemykh iz onogo k razli-chnym dolzhnostiam* (Moscow: P. Kuznetsov, 1826), 182–83, and reported in S. M. Seredonin, *Istoricheskii obzor deiatel'nosti Komiteta Ministrov*, vol. 1 (St. Petersburg: Gosudarstvennaia tipografiia, 1902), 317. The statute appeared only later, at *PSZ*, vol. 39, no. 30120 (November 17, 1824).

56. Seredonin, *Istoricheskii obzor*, 317. In *PSZ* 2, vol. 5, no. 3513 (March 4, 1830), which extends the provisions to free agriculturists, another rationale appeared: "merchants and *meshchane* are obligated to pay taxes and dues in two statuses only when they have establishments in state vil-lages, on state lands." Therefore, those state peasants and others who had left behind the land ought not owe duties there.

57. Walter McKenzie Pintner, *Russian Economic Policy under Nicholas I* (Ithaca: Cornell University Press, 1967), 58–59.

58. Seredonin, *Istoricheskii obzor*, 317.

59. The limitations were enumerated in *PSZ* 2, vol. 1, no. 173 (February 28, 1826).

60. *PSZ* 2, vol. 5, no. 5842 (December 22, 1832; published by the Senate on January 18, 1833).

61. *PSZ* 2, vol. 5, no. 5842 (December 22, 1832), §§ 1–5.

62. For example, in 1833 the Senate confirmed an opinion of the Minister of Finance that age restrictions ought to be in place for state peasants and others seeking to enter *meshchanin* societies. The rationale for placing the age limit at the age of legal adulthood was, in part, that taking responsibility for underaged boys was too much to ask of towns. *PSZ* 2, vol. 8, no. 6531 (October 28, 1833).

63. *PSZ*, vol. 7, no. 4373 (November 28, 1723).

64. Gregory L. Freeze, *The Russian Levites: Parish Clergy in the Eighteenth Century* (Cambridge, MA: Harvard University Press, 1977), 186–204.

65. *PSZ*, vol. 7, no. 9372 (February 13, 1747).

66. Among many such examples, see RGADA f. 796, op. 1, d. 1037, ll. 1, 4 (1767); d. 1044, l. 4 (1767); f. 768, op. 1, d. 944, ll. 1–7 (1778).

67. RGADA f. 291, op. 1, d. 11327, ll. 10–11 (1762) and d. 20229, l. 10b (1780). Variations appear at RGADA f. 291, op. 1, d. 15329, l. 2 (1769); f. 712, op. 1, d. 345, l. 5 (1774), which actually notes that the "Belyi merchants have certified and accepted" petitioners; f. 691, op. 1, d. 4106, ll. 22–22ob (ukaz of the Main Magistracy to the Pereslavl' Zalesskii Magistracy, April 26, 1776).

68. RGADA f. 778, op. 1, d. 160, l. 3 (December 20, 1757). Similar formal statements appear at RGADA f. 764, op. 3, d. 32, l. 3 (Rostov, 1764); d. 52, ll. 7–8 (Rostov, 1766); f. 796, op. 1, d. 1951 (Cheboksary, 1769); f. 713, op. 1, d. 685, l. 9 (Briansk, 1771); f. 1069, op. 1, d. 137, l. 28, (Iareisk, 1771); f. 768, op. 1, d. 1005, l. 4 (Saratov, 1780); f. 796, op. 1, d. 1804, l. 5 (Cheboksary, 1780).

69. RGADA f. 695, op. 1, d. 1972, ll. 5, 8.

70. *PSZ*, vol. 12, no. 9383 (March 16, 1747).

71. *PSZ*, vol. 22, no. 16404 (June 5, 1786). The ukase only examined this issue; the Charter was formally extended to the region a year later (with many notes and regionally specific addendums) at no. 16584 (October 12, 1787).

72. *PSZ*, vol. 22, no. 16235 (July 30, 1785).

73. *PSZ*, vol. 22, no. 16723 (October 24, 1788). In 1811, the State Council affirmed that townspeople wishing to register as peasants had to present not only a document from their home society freeing them, but "the same sort of agreement from the peasant society, too, stating that they accept them, they will answer for the payment of dues on their part, and that their villages had sufficient land for the newcomers. *PSZ*, vol. 31, no. 24517 (February 9, 1811).

74. *PSZ*, vol. 26, no. 19576 (September 27, 1800).

75. In the mid-nineteenth century, N. Beliaev argued that it was Elizabeth's revision that started to demand registry even of the supposedly "free, "that sought to ensure that "no one remained without a position." Beliaev, *Krest'iane na Rusi*, 282–83.

76. *PSZ*, vol. 10, no. 7533 (March 10, 1738).

77. *PSZ*, vol. 21, no. 15853 (October 20, 1783). The law referenced an earlier ukase granting the "freedom to choose a way of life," with the same caveats on the general and individual good, to Polish prisoners who had converted to Orthodoxy. *PSZ*, vol. 21, no. 15198 (July 28, 1781).

78. The earlier Manifesto stated that "all those freed by serfowners, we do not allow, today and in the future, to register themselves as the property of anyone, but instead . . . they should declare into which sort of Our service they wish to enter." *PSZ*, vol. 20, no. 14275 (March 17, 1775).

79. Tracing this evolution exactly is difficult, as some decrees are referenced by later laws, but not in the "complete" collection itself. So, for example, an 1804 law defining who was allowed to "register in the status of single householder," in passing referenced ukases from 1784 and 1803 that defined those "presented with the freedom to enter into a way of life that they themselves choose, such as: service; or to register in the merchantry, the *soslovie* of townspeople, or craft guilds; or to become one of the state peasants." Those earlier decrees, however, are not in the *Complete Collection of the Laws*, at least under the dates specified in the 1804. *PSZ*, vol. 28, no. 21332 (June 6, 1804); these earlier decrees, dated March 29, 1784, and June or July 9, 1803 (different laws cite different months), were cited in later laws, too.

80. *PSZ*, vol. 24, no. 18223 (October 26, 1797); vol. 26, no. 19852 (April 1801); vol. 30, no. 21811 (June 28, 1805); vol. 32, no. 25677 (August 30, 1814).

81. TsIAM f. 54, op. 1, d. 524, l. 1. Other petitions using the phrase include those at TsIAM f. 54, op. 1, d. 539, l. 1 (1793) and RGIA f. 515, op. 5, d. 22, l. 12b–12bob (1798), as well as dozens

more from the early nineteenth century. Meanwhile, the provision that stated that these "free" people could not become serfs created a slight problem in the early nineteenth century. When Paul reorganized the court lands, he stated that court peasants should be treated legally like private serfs. But that meant that free people could not become court peasants. In 1806, the Senate decided that this was an exception to the general rule, and that former church people and others with the right to choose a way of life could, indeed, join court peasant villages if they so chose. *PSZ*, vol. 29, no. 22181 (June 28, 1806).

82. TsIAM f. 32, op. 9, d. 28, l. 1 (1813). See also d. 6, l. 2–2a (1812); d. 652, l. 1 (1815).

83. TsIAM f. 32, op. 9, d. 300, l. 1; also, d. 177, l. 1 (1814); d. 606, l. 1 (1815); d. 953, l. 1 (1815); d. 3783, l. 1 (1817), a petition from a freed serf, noting he had received "perpetual freedom with the choice of a future way of life." Slight variations also appeared, as in d. 598, l. 1 ("I wish to be in a different way of life," 1815). The phrase continued through much of the nineteenth century. TsIAM f. 2, op. 1, d. 973, l. 1 (a townsperson "freed to choose a different way of life," 1820); f. 32, op. 12, d. 1519, l. 5 (manumission included the "freedom to choose a way of life," 1821); f. 32, op. 12, d. 1570, l. 1 (1830); f. 54, op. 14, d. 3, l. 1 (1845); f. 2, op. 1, d. 5808, l. 4 (a manumission document "for choosing a way of life," 1859); GARO f. 49, op. 1, d. 552, l. 1 (1860); TsIAM f. 54, op. 57, d. 70, l. 1 (1908).

84. TsIAM f. 32, op. 12, d. 1572, ll. 1, 5 (petition, report, 1830).

85. At the same time, the "choice" could be made multiple times. At various points individuals sought first to register in one status, and later to move into a different one. See, for example, TsIAM f. 32, no. 9, d. 1327, ll. 2, 4 (1815), or later cases at GARO f. 49, op. 1, d. 270, l. 1 (1855); d. 278, l. 3 (1853); d. 394, op. 1 (1857); d. 687 (1863).

86. TsIAM f. 54, op. 14, d. 4, ll. 1–3, 6. The same threat was levied on two postal workers removed from duty due to drunkenness. See RGIA f. 571, op. 1, d. 1414, l. 12 (1827).

87. TsIAM f. 32. op. 9, d. 775, ll. 1–2, 8.

88. GARO f. 49, op. 1, d. 278, l. 6.

89. *PSZ*, vol. 33, no. 25998 (November 16, 1815). This was restated in later decrees, as well: *PSZ*, vol. 38, no. 29483 (May 23, 1823).

90. Among many later cases, see descriptions of fines levied on individuals who failed to register, or threats to treat them as vagrants under the law at RGIA f. 571, op. 1, d. 1414, l. 12 (1827); GARO f. 49, op. 1, d. 278, l. 6 (1856); GARO f. 4, op. 100, t. 14, d. 9680, l. 1–2 (1860).

91. "Meshchanskoe soslovie v Moskve (za 1845 god)," *ZhMVD*, ch. 17 (January 1847): 73–74.

92. This fact was recognized by various nineteenth-century writers, and argued during hearings about the new Town Statute of 1870. See I. A. Gan, *O nastoiashchem byte meshchan Saratovskoi gubernii* (St. Petersburg: Tipografiia Sht. Otd. Kor. Vnutr. Strazhi, 1860), 23; *Materialy otnosiashchiesia*, I: 192 n.

93. *PSZ*, vol. 30, no. 21811 (June 28, 1805).

94. Something similar happened in 1820s Prussia, where state officials legislated on "the obligation of communes to accept newcomers," in large part due to concerns over social welfare. See Beck, *Origins of the Authoritarian Welfare State*, 153-4.

95. RGIA f. 571, op. 1, d. 1414, ll. 10–160b (1827).

96. *PSZ*, vol. 30, no. 23130 (June 30, 1808).

97. *PSZ*, vol. 30, no. 23597 (April 20, 1809).

98. *PSZ*, vol. 31, no. 24795 (September 28, 1811). The ukase gave the Ministry of Police authority to place Roma in towns by executive order.

99. On these manifestos more generally, see Smith, "The Freedom to Choose a Way of Life."

100. RGIA f. 1286, op. 2, d. 103, ll. 44–45.

101. RGIA f. 1286, op. 2, d. 103, ll. 66–68ob.

102. RGIA f. 1286, op. 2, d. 103, ll. 76–77 (1816).

103. RGIA f. 571, op. 1, d. 1414, l. 8.

104. RGIA f. 571, op. 1, d. 1414, ll. 9a–9aob. These decisions figured in shortened form at *PSZ* 2, vol. 5, no. 3663 (May 14, 1830). The same phrase—that being without a status meant being without a voice—appeared elsewhere, as at *PSZ* 2, vol. 14, no. 12742 (October 3, 1839).

105. *PSZ* 2, vol. 3, no. 2149 (July 11, 1828).

106. RGIA f. 571, op. 1, d. 1414, l. 130b.

107. RGIA f. 571, op. 1, d. 1414, ll. 48ob–49 (1831).

108. RGIA f. 571, op. 1, d. 1414, ll. 46ob–47 (1830).

109. *PSZ* 2, vol. 7, no. 5425 (June 9, 1832).

110. *PSZ* 2, vol. 7, no. 5842 (December 22, 1832; published by the Senate on January 18, 1833); § 7.

111. Such laws include *PSZ* 2, vol. 17, no. 16195 (November 10, 1842) (on Siberian exiles who had completed their sentence and returned to European Russia).

112. For examples, see GARO f. 49, op. 1, d. 176, ll. 4, 35 (1853); d. 286, l. 1 (1856); d. 319, l. 1 (1857); d. 390, ll. 8–9 (1857); d. 543, l. 2 (1860).

113. GARO f. 49, op. 1, d. 231, ll. 1, 3–4 (1854).

114. GARO f. 49, op. 1, d. 195, ll. 1, 10.

115. RGIA f. 571, op. 1, d. 1548, ll. 2–7, 22–230b (1840–1844).

116. RGIA f. 571, op. 1, d. 1455, ll. 40b–5, 7–70b, 2–3; Kursk was not alone in its missing *meshchane*; at various points over the next decades, the Saratov Town Duma complained to higher authorities that its townsperson society was overly burdened by the arrears accruing to members who had been registered without their agreement, and who had been "at the time of their registration in places unknown." GASO f. 94, op. 1, d. 787, ll. 64 (1849); see also d. 1040, l. 320ob (1851).

117. *PSZ* 2, vol. 9, no. 6723 (January 16, 1834).

118. Vileishis, *Sistematicheskii sbornik*, 3. Similar language appeared in *PSZ* 2, vol. 9, no. 7295 (July 24, 1834), which extended the rules on registry without acceptance to new groups, and vol. 14, no. 11918 (January 4, 1839), on exiles to Siberia.

CHAPTER 4

1. Miliukov, *Dobroe staroe vremia,* 3–11. This consciousness of a life based most of all as "old Russian" stands in contrast to John MacKay's comment that serf narrators did not so much see themselves in larger "Russian" terms. See *Four Serf Narratives*, 13. Miliukov's experiences of a life not normally bounded by strict *soslovie* distinctions, however, does echo the greater "fluidity in the social order" in Nicholaevan Moscow identified by Alexander Martin, in *Enlightened Metropolis*, 222.

2. Miliukov, *Dobroe staroe vremia*, 82–86, 150, 161.

3. Miliukov, *Dobroe staroe vremia,* 170.

4. Miliukov, *Dobroe staroe vremia,* 172.

5. Miliukov, *Dobroe staroe vremia,* 172–79.

6. Miliukov, *Dobroe staroe vremia*, 170.

7. On the idea that *soslovie* failed to reflect reality, see, for example, Munro, *The Most Intentional City*, 57–59; Evtuhov, *Portrait of a Russian Province*, 110–12. A variant notes that places classified as towns were often underdeveloped, while some places classified as villages were bustling centers of trade. See V. A. Nardova, *Gorodskoe samoupravlenie v Rossii v 60-kh-nachale 90-kh godov XIX v.* (Leningrad: Nauka, 1984), 11.

8. TsIAM f. 32, op. 9, dd. 17, 86, 586, 598, 606, 646, 953, 1082, 1541; op. 12, d. 177.

9. RGIA f. 1287, op. 38, d. 479, ll. 1–10b (1864).

10. GARO f. 49, op. 1, d. 313, ll. 4–5 (1856).

11. RGIA f. 571, op. 1, d. 1796, ll.7–8 (1857).

12. GARO f. 49, op. 1, d. 120, ll. 1, 6 (1851); d. 606, ll. 3–4 (1860); TsGIASPb f. 222, op. 1, d. 34, l.1 (1858).

13. RGADA f. 1069, op. 1, d. 137, l. 50.

14. LVIA f. 937, op. 1, d. 2721.

15. *PSZ*, vol. 26, no. 19576 (September 27, 1800).

16. *PSZ 2*, vol. 1, no. 396 (June 8, 1826).

17. GASO f. 94, op. 1, d. 719, ll. 24–37. See also the case of Ivan Afanas'ev Beliaev, who tried to exit the Moscow *meshchanstvo*; because he did not explain how he intended to keep up dues, his petition was rejected by the town society. TsIAM f. 32, op. 9, d. 606, l. 4 (1815) (similar files include d. 300, l. 3 (1814) and d. 586, l. 3). That same year the Moscow craft society refused to free one of its members unless he "brought in all state dues and other fees until the next revision" right away. This was obviously unfeasible, given the amount that might be required and the fact that no one knew when the next revision might take place. TsIAM f. 32. op. 9, d. 598, l. 4 (1815).

18. GASO f. 94, op. 1, d. 782, ll. 57–69 (original case in 1841, second petition in 1845).

19. TsGIASPb f. 792, op. 4, d. 9, ll. 9–10 (1857).

20. RGADA f. 1287, op. 5, d. 5674, l. 1; see also a petition by Ivanovo peasants addressed to Sheremetev, complaining about the fact that by freeing the wealthiest members of their society the remainder of the peasants had trouble meeting their obligations at RGADA f. 1287, op. 6, d. 327, ll. 18–190b (1830).

21. RGIA f. 1287, op. 38, d. 479, ll. 1, 4–5 (1864).

22. Wirtschafter, *From Serf to Russian Soldier*, 20; see also Keep, *Soldiers of the Tsar*, 148–49.

23. *PSZ 2*, vol. 6, no. 4677 (June 28, 1831), §§ 67–69.

24. RGADA f. 1069, op. 1, d. 137, l. 50.

25. RGADA f. 308, op. 2, d. 137, ll. 5–60b.

26. GARO f. 49, op. 1, d. 214, ll. 1, 3–4, 5–6. Other cases in which the Riazan' townspeople refused to free members due to recruit duties include those of Dmitrii Nikiforov Baskakov, Nikolai Ivanov Polovin, and Nikolai Dmitriev, at GARO f. 49, op. 1, d. 770, ll. 7, 78, 106 (1867), and that of Nikolai Petrov Makarov, at d. 840, l. 7 (1870). The St. Petersburg townsperson society also demanded formal statements about whether those seeking freedom had fulfilled their recruit duties. See TsGIASPb f. 222, op. 1, d. 23, ll. 25–250b; 137–38 (1854).

27. GARO f. 49, op. 1, d. 109, ll. 2–3 (1851).

28. GARO f. 49, op. 1, d. 393, ll. 5, 14.

29. GASO f. 94, op. 1, d. 719, ll. 67–68 (1845).

30. RGADA f. 768, op. 1, d. 365, l. 3 (1770).

31. *SIRIO* 4, 125–26, 128.

32. RGIA f. 1341, op. 1, d. 694, ll.2–20b (1804)

33. *PSZ* 2, vol. 1, no. 721 (December 4, 1826).

34. "Sokrashchennaia," 230.

35. *Nastavlenie sel'skim prikazam po vysochaishemu o imperatorskoi familii Uchrezhdeniiu v udel'nykh imeniiakh uchrezhdennym* (St. Petersburg: Tip. Gub. Pravleniia, 1799), 12–13.

36. Sometimes this manifested itself in odd caveats, as when the Sevsk Provincial Chancellery added a restriction to its approval of Trofim Andreev's freedom. The former priest wished to enter the Briansk merchantry, and while the provincial chancellery agreed to allow him to move from Sevsk to Briansk, it noted that he was not allowed "to go between them nor buy Turkish or foreign things." RGADA f. 713, op. 1, d. 685, ll. 8–10.

37. RGADA f. 705, op. 1, d. 49, l. 1; d. 53, l. 1; d. 56, ll. 1–9.

38. GARO f. 49, op. 1, d. 182, ll. 1, 3, 5–6 (1853). Soon thereafter another Riazan' townsman, Afanasei Kharitonov Fedorov, petitioned to be released into a state peasant village. Not only did he have no arrears, but he clearly stated in his petition where he lived (the village). In his case, the townspeople agreed to free him. GARO f. 49, op. 1, d. 232, ll. 1, 3–4 (1854).

39. It is hard to imagine that there were not more such cases, but there is surprisingly little evidence of them in the archival files that I have seen.

40. GARO f. 4, op. 100, t. 1, d. 255, ll. 6–9.

41. GARO f. 49, op. 1, d. 134, ll. 6, 8, 14 (1852).

42. RGIA f. 571, op. 1, d. 1475, ll. 47–48 (1839).

43. RGIA f. 1287, op. 38, d. 665, ll. 1, 3–4, 5.

44. *PSZ* 2, vol. 24, no. 22955 (January 24, 1849).

45. Chukmaldin, *Zapiski*, 88–89.

46. TsIAM f. 32, op. 9, d. 3.

47. TsIAM f. 32, op. 9, dd. 230, 1333.

48. TsIAM f. 2, op. 1, d. 127, l. 3 (1814).

49. RGADA f. 820, op. 2, d. 5, ll. 1–2, 4.

50. V. I. Semevskii, *Krest'iane v tsarstvovanie Imperatritsy Ekateriny II*, vol. 1 (St. Petersburg: F. S. Sushchinskii, 1881), 329. In this case, the Senate eventually decided that the two younger men (37 and 52) should be taken into the town, while the men's owner had to take the 65-year-old back into service.

51. GAIaO f. 79, op. 1, d. 729, l. 16 (1829).

52. Described in Ivanov, *Obozrenie prav*, 185–86 (decree of June 28, 1805).

53. *PSZ*, vol. 37, no. 28389 (August 19, 1820).

54. GARO f. 49, op. 1, d. 231, ll. 3–4. Other example of petitioners providing guarantors include that of Ivan Senkov into the Vilnius *meshchanstvo* at LVIA f. 937, op. 1, d. 2722, l. 2.

55. TsGIASPb f. 222, op. 1, d. 503, l. 5.

56. Bulkin, "Neskol'ko slov," 54.

57. *PSZ* 2, vol. 16, no. 14361 (March 17, 1841).

58. RGADA f. 291, op. 1, ch. iv., d. 16491. Unfortunately, only the petition is filed, with no resolution.

59. RGADA f. 820, op. 2, d, 616, l. 4.

60. RGADA f. 796, op. 1, d. 1951 l. 7.

61. GAIaO f. 79, op. 2, d. 149, ll. 1–10b, 10–11, 14–140b (1816).

62. TsIAM f. 397, op. 1, d. 121, "Tetrad 1795 goda dlia zapiski v Moskovskoe kupechestvo raznogo zvaniia liudei postupivshikh s kapitalom na 1796 god,"

63. *Materialy dlia istorii krepostnogo prava v Rossii*, 41–42.

64. GARO f. 49, op. 1, d. 818, ll. 1–2, 3.

65. LVIA f. 937, op. 1, d. 1909, ll. 10–11 (1835).

66. LVIA f. 937, op. 2, d. 1739, ll. 7–70b, 10–100b.

67. RGIA f. 571, op. 1, d. 1722, ll. 6–7 (1849). The Senate decided that this was not a valid reason in large part because the men were the sons of a vagrant, landless peasants who needed to be registered somewhere.

68. Ivanov, *Obozrenie prav*, 43. The ukase is from January 1817.

69. *PSZ* 2, vol. 10, no. 8167 (May 27, 1835). On those migration patterns, see Breyfogle, *Heretics and Colonizers*.

70. *PSZ* 2, vol. 27, no. 26336 (June 3, 1852), allowing registry in every Caucasus town except Tiflis; vol. 35, no. 35910 (June 12, 1860), allowing registry in towns in Pri-Amurskii krai.

71. *PSZ* 2, vol. 19, no. 17748 (March 21, 1844).

72. GARO f. 49, op. 1, d. 530, l. 1 (1856). Shortly before, another would-be merchant was informed that he needed to produce proof of his religious status to finalize his registry. See GARO f. 49, op. 1, d. 282, l. 1 (1856).

73. GARO f. 4, op. 100, t. 14, d. 9695a, l. 5 (1865).

74. GARO f. 4, op. 100, t. 14, d. 9695a, ll. 18, 35 (1867).

75. GAIaO f. 79, op. 1, d. 729, ll. 15–16. In the end, the Iaroslavl' Provincial Administration told the Rybinsk Town Duma that the men had been registered lawfully and thus could not be removed. The duma could collect all normal dues from them, but nothing more (l. 20). Something similar happened decades before, when three fugitive serfs sought entrance into the Kolomna townsperson society under the auspices of an imperial manifesto that had granted them amnesty. They found the new society wary of accepting them, largely because they had already run away once. The Kolomna elder reported that his society would accept them only if they received a promise that the petitioners would not ask for additional help from the society and if the society did not become responsible for them. Despite their caveats, the Main Magistracy decided that because these petitioners had to be registered somewhere to avoid idleness and to feed themselves, they would be registered as Kolomna townsmen despite the local society's uncertainty. RGADA f. 291, op. 1, d. 20229, ll. 1–4 (1780).

76. GASO f. 2, op. 1, d. 1606, ll. 1–3, 15–16, 22, 23–24.

77. *SZ* 1833, "Zakony o sostoianiiakh," § 252. Ivanova and Zheltova make particular note of this, including of moments when mechant societies sought to change this, in *Soslovnoe obshchestvo*, 386, 448–49.

78. TsIAM f. 2, op. 1, d. 120 (1812); d. 126 (1814); f. 3, op. 1, d. 4 (1863).

79. Rieber, *Merchants and Entrepreneurs*, 31–39.

80. Bulkin, "Neskol'ko slov," 64.

81. RGADA f. 768, op. 1, d. 944, ll. 1–7.

82. For example, TsIAM f. 2, op. 1, d. 440, ll. 1–3 (1817).

83. *PSZ*, vol. 36, no. 27856 (June 26, 1819).

84. *PSZ*, vol. 38, no. 29646 (November 12, 1823).

85. For example, "O Moskovskikh kuptsakh, ne ob"iavivshikh na 1841 god kapitalov i pere-chislennykh v meshchanstvo," *Moskovskie gubernskie vedomosti* (March 22, 1841): 84–86; "O litsakh, ne ob"iavivshikh kapitalov v kupechestvo," *Moskovskie gubernskie vedomosti* (March 2, 1846): 54–55.

86. Rieber, *Merchants and Entrepreneurs*, 27.

87. *PSZ*, vol. 39, no. 30, 115 (November 14, 1824).

88. On this, see Smith, "The Shifting Place of Women," 363–64.

89. TsIAM f. 2, op. 1, d. 1934, l. 230b (1826), also ll. 5, 15–16, 20–210b.

90. TsIAM f. 2, op. 1, d. 1934, l. 151 (1832).

91. *PSZ* 2, vol. 1, no. 458 (July 11, 1826), p. 8.

92. *PSZ* 2, vol. 18, no. 17299 (November 8, 1843).

93. *PSZ* 2, vol. 22, no. 21813 (December 22, 1847).

94. GASO f. 94, op. 1, d. 445, ll. 21–25.

95. RGIA f. 571, op. 1, d. 1475.

96. *PSZ*, vol. 33, no. 25313 (June 12, 1816). A later law stated that any townsman who had risen to the merchantry and then fallen back to the status of townsman ought to be credited with any military service on the part of his family completed while he was first a townsman, as well. *PSZ* 2, vol. 18, no. 17243 (October 18, 1843).

97. RGIA f. 1286, op. 7, d. 603, l. 9.

98. RGIA f. 1286, op. 7, d. 603, ll. 21–24, 26–28aob.

99. "Zapiska iz dela po voprosu o rasprostranenii sily 219 st. V t. Sv. Zak. ust. o pod. na vsekh meshchan perekhodiashchikh v kupechestvo, bez soglasiia obshchestva, s razresheniia Gg. Ministrov Finansov i Vnutrennikh Del," *Materialy Gosudarstvennyi sovet* 7 (1850), np. This case echoes one from earlier in the century, in which *meshchanin* societies worried about the effect losing members might have on their recruit obligations. See *PSZ*, vol. 30, no. 23092 (June 14, 1808).

In other cases from nearly the same time, recruit duties were privileged. In the early 1850s, the Ministries of Interior and Finance looked into a problem in Orel Province. There, the provincial treasury had moved a number of people out of the Bolkhov *meshchasntvo* without the approval of that society and despite the fact that several were in line for military service. In this case all men were moved back into the *meshchanstvo*. RGIA f. 1287, op. 37, d. 794, ll. 1–30b, 16–160b.

100. Androssov, *Statisticheskaia zapiska*, 54, 59–60.

101. For example, in 1817, the Senate had agreed to allow those working in the Imperial Theaters (72 individuals, ranging from tailors and hairdressers to actors and musicians) to be excluded from their prior taxpaying status. Only in 1839 did a statue lay out a series of regula-tions that formalized a new status for them. *PSZ*, vol. 34, no. 27186 (December 17, 1817); *PSZ* 2, vol. 14, no. 11934 (January 15, 1839).

102. *PSZ* 2, vol. 7, no. 5284 (April 10, 1832).

103. *PSZ* 2, vol. 9, no. 6745 (January 26, 1834).

104. *PSZ* 2, vol. 7, no. 5284 (April 10, 1832).

105. *PSZ* 2, vol. 9, no. 7240 (July 1, 1834).

106. RGIA f. 398, op. 5, d. 808, ll. 20b–3.

107. For more on the tension between *soslovie* and profession in the Great Reform era and after, see Pomeranz, "'Profession or Estate'," 245-7.

108. *PSZ* 2, vol. 7, no. 5284 (April 10, 1832).

109. On debates within the musical world about the role formal education ought to play in defining who was truly a musician, see Sargeant, "A New Class of People," 43–8.

110. *PSZ* 2, vol. 9, no. 7240 (July 1, 1834), §§ 3 14, 16.

111. *PSZ,* vol. 40, no. 30342 (May 13, 1825); no. 30517 (September 30, 1825); *PSZ* 2, vol. 1, no. 398 (June 8, 1826). Several decades later, rules tried again to open up some professions. In one case, an imperial decree gave new rules for becoming a surveyor, in the hopes of increasing their number (just before emancipation). *PSZ* 2, vol. 34, no. 34480 (May 11, 1859).

112. *PSZ* 2, vol. 9, no. 7240 (July 1, 1834), § 32. On the other hand, if they served long enough, because the statute placed tutors under the auspices (and control) of the Ministry of Education, they could gain rank. Later laws looked at exclusion from some of these statuses. One from 1855 noted that those freed from the status of free sailor should be registered as *meshchane. PSZ* 2, vol. 30, no. 29411 (June 13, 1855).

113. *PSZ* 2, vol. 9, no. 7013 (April 21, 1834).

114. *PSZ,* vol. 15, no. 10872 (August 25, 1758).

115. *PSZ* 2, vol. 15, no. 13861 (October 14, 1840). An earlier law had stated that sons of personal nobles or low-ranking bureaucrats were even allowed to register as state peasants (with appropriate agreements from the peasant society). *PSZ* 2, vol. 14, no. 12042 (February 22, 1839). The Senate later examined cases based on these kinds of laws, including RGIA f. 571, op. 1, d. 1475, ll. 57–580b (1839) and ll. 135–360b (1843).

116. RGIA f. 398, op. 5, d. 808, ll. 63–64.

117. RGIA f. 398, op. 5, d. 808, ll. 97–98.

118. RGIA f. 398, op. 5, d. 808, ll. 59–60.

119. RGIA f. 398, op. 5, d. 808, ll. 59–60.

120. A 1834 law formalizing the various ranks of medical personnel in some ways does much the same thing, proposing as it does a clear hierarchy of position and service, with rank allotted accordingly. *PSZ* 2, vol. 9, no. 7118 (May 24, 1834). William Pomeranz argues that that this positive view of *soslovie* also existed in proposals to create the *advokatura*, in "'Profession or Estate',", 245. And Lynne Sargeant describes the petitions of a group of musicians who found their status much less secures than those who had a formal *soslovie* identity in "A New Class of People," 45.

121. Miliukov, *Dobroe staroe vremia,* 179–80.

CHAPTER 5

1. RGIA f. 571, op. 1, d. 1631, ll. 1–10b.

2. RGIA f. 571, op. 1, d. 1631, ll. 30b.

3. RGIA f. 571, op. 1, d. 1631, ll. 250b–260b.

4. RGIA f. 571, op. 1, d. 1631, ll. l. 260b–27.

5. RGIA f. 571, op. 1, d. 1631, ll. 30–32.

6. RGIA f. 571, op. 1, d. 1631, ll. 360b–7.

7. Elise Wirtschafter describes similar problems of the "uncertainties of social definition caused by the demands of the service state" in "Social Categories," 235.

8. On the *Svod zakonov* as central to a "strictly *soslovie*" understanding of Russia's social structure, see Goncharov and Chutchev, *Meshchanskoe soslovie,* 30.

9. Alessandro Stanziani notes similar divergences between ministries and their opinions on *soslovia* in his discussion of census politics. See "Les sources démographiques entre

contrôle policier et utopies technocratiques. Le cas russe, 1870-1926," *Cahiers du monde russe* 38 (1997): 464-70.

10. Seymour Becker, *Nobility and Privilege in Late Imperial Russia* (DeKalb: Northern Illinois University Press, 1985), 25. See also Daniel Field, "The 'Great Reforms' of the 1860s," in *A Companion to Russian History*, ed. Abbott Gleason (Maldon: Wiley-Blackwell, 2009), 207–208.

11. Nardova, *Gorodskoe samoupravlenie*, 49; Zaionchkovskii, *Voennye reformy*, 304-05.

12. On the Great Reforms as they leveled trading rights between *soslovie*, and on merchants' unhappy reaction, see Rieber, *Merchants and Entrepreneurs*, 47–48, 84–85. On the ways that the Great Reforms and their aftermath did and did not affect tax structures, see Bowman, "Russia's First Income Taxes." For more general comments on this concept of all- but not non-estateness, see Freeze, "*Soslovie* (Estate) Paradigm," 26–27.

13. Rozhkov, *Gorod i derevnia*, 81.

14. Zelnick, *Labor and Society*, 132. See other examples of the Great Reforms failing to follow through on the promise of reducing *soslovnost'* in Samuel D. Kassow, "The University Statute of 1863: A Reconsideration," in *Russia's Great Reforms, 1855–1881*, ed. Ben Eklof, John Bushnell, and Larissa Zakharova (Bloomington: Indiana University Press, 1994), 256.

15. This is one of the arguments made by Ivanova and Zheltova in *Soslovnoe obshchestvo*, 653.

16. *PSZ*, vol. 38, no. 29715 (December 24, 1823). And later laws repeated elements of this law, sometimes for specific groups, sometimes to recognize other changes in legislation or administration. Among them are *PSZ* 2, vol. 22, no. 21657 (October 28, 1847), and vol. 32, no. 32277 (October 15, 1857).

17. *PSZ* 2, vol. 3, no. 1899 (March 38, 1828).

18. *PSZ* 2, vol. 3, no. 1960 (April 16, 1828), § 334; no. 2525 (December 17, 1828).

19. There were limits to this. In 1836, the Senate reaffirmed one special status: Okhta residents, who were ascribed to the Okhta gunpowder factory just outside St. Petersburg, and under the authority of the Naval Ministry. They had been particularly restricted in their mobility; a law of 1823 had stated that even after they stopped working in the factory, they "did not have the right to choose a way of life," but instead "must have their residence in the Okhta villages forever, and nowhere else." The Senate, however, found this to be an unduly harsh restriction, and allowed Okhta residents to register as merchants or *meshchane*—as long as they had stopped working in the factory and reached sixty years of age. *PSZ* 2, vol. 11, no. 9580 (October 6, 1836).

20. *PSZ* 2, vol. 13, no. 11189 (April 30, 1838), § 1.

21. *PSZ* 2, vol. 13, no. 11189 (April 30, 1838), §§ 32, 84A–B.

22. *PSZ* 2, vol. 23, no. 22444 (July 15, 1848). There were other, similar efforts to unify separate groups later on, as well. *PSZ* 2, vol. 29, no. 27872 (January 20, 1854); vol. 35, no. 35936 (June 17, 1860). In some imperial spaces, there were yet other possible arrays of categorization—and yet during this period, many of them were conflated, as well. See Paul W. Werth, *At the Margins of Orthodoxy: Mission, Governance, and Confessional Politics in Russia's Volga-Kama Region, 1827–1905* (Ithaca: Cornell University Press, 2002), 130–31, 151.

23. *PSZ* 2, vol. 33, no. 33326 (June 20, 1858).

24. Furthermore, court lands administrators took these rules seriously, and refused the registry of such people. See correspondence refusing registry in several court villages around St. Petersburg at RGIA f. 472, op. 2, d. 546.

25. *PSZ* 2, vol. 33, no. 33724 (November 4, 1858).

26. Additional statutes clarifying emancipation procedures often focused on these differences, as in *PSZ* 2, vol. 37, no. 38892 (November 7, 1862).

27. Among them, M. G. Gordeev, *Polveka unizhenii i bor'by* (Moscow: Trud i kniga, 1925), 11–12; and Ivan Stoliarov, *Zapiski russkogo krest'ianina/Récit d'un paysan russe* (Paris: Institute d'études slaves, 1986), 15.

28. RGADA f. 1287, op. 5, d. 8199 holds a series of notifications from the local township board informing a former serfowner of peasants who made such decisions.

29. Count Sheremetev, at least, did this in 1855, when he sent out a notice to all his villages inviting his serfs to make him an offer for their freedom. Many took him up on the offer. RGIA f. 1088, op. 3, dd. 1051-53.

30. *PSZ* 2, vol. 37, no. 38893 (November 7, 1862).

31. GASO f. 3, op. 1, d. 3612, l. 4 (1861).

32. RGIA f. 1287, op. 38, d. 423, ll. 3–4, 6–70b.

33. RGIA f. 1287, op. 38, d. 1675, l. 1 (1879).

34. RGIA f. 1287, op. 38, d. 1675, ll. 40b–5.

35. RGIA f. 1287, op. 38, d. 472, ll. 1–10b (1864).

36. RGIA f. 1287, op. 38, d. 472, ll. 3–30b.

37. RGIA f. 1287, op. 38, d. 472, ll. 50b–6 (1867).

38. RGIA f. 1287, op. 38, d. 472, II. 7.

39. RGIA f. 1287, op. 38, d. 472, II. 7.

40. RGIA f. 1287, op. 38, d. 472, ll. 50b–6 (1867).

41. *PSZ* 2, vol. 43, no. 45505 (February 19, 1868).

42. LVIA f. 937, op. 2, d. 1284, ll. 16–160b.

43. LVIA f. 937, op. 2, d. 1284, ll. 19–200b.

44. For example, Brower, *The Russian City*, 92–100; Mironov, *Sotsial'naia istoriia Rossii*, 500; W. Bruce Lincoln, "N. A. Miliutin and the St. Petersburg Municipal Act of 1846: A Study in Reform under Nicholas I," *Slavic Review* 33, no. 1 (March 1974): 55–68; and his "Reform in Action: The Implementation of the Municipal Reform Act of 1846 in St Petersburg," *SEER* 53, no. 131 (April 1975): 202–209. Contemporaries pointed this out, too; see L., "O sovremennom gorodskom obshchestvennom upravlenii;" Sal'nikov, "O gorodskikh obshchestvakh;" and Korkunov, *Russkoe gosudarstvennoe pravo*, vol. 2, 593–4.

45. *PSZ* 2 vol. 21, no. 19721 (February 13, 1846).

46. *Novoe obshchestvennoe ustroistvo S. Peterburga*, 8, 4n.

47. On the initial association, *PSZ*, vol. 22, no. 16566 (August 27, 1787); for the later decree, see vol. 33, no. 26363 (July 20, 1816).

48. *PSZ*, vol. 37, no. 28597 (March 21, 1821).

49. *PSZ* 2, vol. 7, no. 5842 (December 22, 1832), st. 9.

50. *SZ* 1842, vol. 9, § 466.

51. RGIA f. 571, op. 1, d. 1617, l. 1.

52. RGIA f. 571, op. 1, d. 1617, l. 10b.

53. RGIA f. 571, op. 1, d. 1617, l. ll. 10b–2.

54. *PSZ* 2, vol. 21, no. 19721 (February 13, 1846), st. 3.

55. *PSZ* 2, vol. 21, no. 19721 (February 13, 1846), st. 86–87.

56. *PSZ* 2, vol. 21, no. 19721 (February 13, 1846), st. 88.

57. *Materialy otnosiashchiesia do novogo obshchestvennogo ustroistva v gorodakh imperii*, I: 192.

58. *Materialy otnosiashchiesia do novogo*, I: 193, 193n.

59. *Materialy otnosiashchiesia do novogo*, I: 206.

60. *Materialy otnosiashchiesia do novogo*, I: 206.

61. *Materialy otnosiashchiesia do novogo*, I: 10.

62. *Materialy otnosiashchiesia do novogo*, I: 10.

63. *Materialy otnosiashchiesia do novogo*, I: 39, 41.

64. *Materialy otnosiashchiesia do novogo*, I: 44–46.

65. *Materialy otnosiashchiesia do novogo*, I: 47–48.

66. *Materialy otnosiashchiesia do novogo*, I: 539–40.

67. *Materialy otnosiashchiesia do novogo*, I: 470; II: 422–23.

68. *PSZ* 2, vol. 45, no. 48498 (June 16/28, 1870), §§ 6–8.

69. *Gorodovoe polozhenie s ob"iasneniiami* (St. Petersburg: Tipografiia Ministerstva vnutren-nikh del, 1873), 21.

70. M. P. Shchepkin, *Opyty izucheniia obshchestvennogo khoziaistva i upravleniia gorodov*, vol. 1 (Moscow: M. P. Shchepkin, 1882), 16.

71. M. I. Mysh, *Sbornik uzakonenii, pravitel'stvennykh i sudebnykh raz"iasnenii o meshchan-skikh i remeslennykh upravleniiakh* (St. Petersburg: N. A. Lebedev, 1886), iii.

72. *Instruktsiia Kazennym palatam. Na vremia opyta edinstva kassy* (St. Petersburg: V. N. Maikov, 1864), 1.

73. *Instruktsiia Kazennym palatam*, 52–53.

74. Gordon, "Po delu ob imushchestve," 1.

75. Gordon, "Po delu ob imushchestve," 4, 25.

76. Kotsonis, "'Face-to-Face,'" 221–2; Yanni Kotsonis, "'No Place to Go': Taxation and State Transformation in Late Imperial and Early Soviet Russia," *Journal of Modern History* 76, no. 3 (September 2004): 537–45.

77. *PSZ* 2, vol. 38, no. 39119 (January 1, 1863).

78. *Kratkii svod zamechanii zemskikh uchrezhdenii na proekt, sostavlennyi osoboi kommissiei pri Ministerstve finansov, o zamene podushnykh sborov pozemel'nym i podvornym nalogami* (St. Petersburg: V. Bezobrazova i Komp., 1872), 8.

79. *Kratkii svod zamechanii zemskikh*, 8.

80. *Kratkii svod zamechanii zemskikh*, 8–9, 11.

81. *Kratkii svod zamechanii zemskikh*, 14.

82. "O zamene podushnoi podati drugimi nalogami," *Materialy Gosudarstvennogo Soveta* 142 (1882): Delo 173, document 1, l. 4.

83. "O zamene podushnoi podati," document 3, l. 17.

84. "O zamene podushnoi podati," document 3, l. 17.

85. "O zamene podushnoi podati," document 3, ll. 19, 20–21.

86. Gan, *O nastoiashchem byte*, 23–24.

87. Gan, *O nastoiashchem byte*, 25.

88. Gan, *O nastoiashchem byte*, 25–26.

89. *Kratkii svod*, 5.

90. F. Voroponov, "Pasportnaia reforma," *Vestnik evropy*, 20, no. 12 (December 1885): 850.

91. Gleason, "Terms of Russian Social History," vii. On the reign of Alexander III in a turn-ing point that led back to a defense of *soslovie* privilege, see Becker, *Nobility and Privilege*, 58–66.

92. RGIA f. 1287, op. 44, d. 545, l. 8. Thanks to Aleksandr Kaplunovskii for telling me about this inquiry.

93. Exceptions included Minusin (Eniseisk province) (RGIA f. 1287, op. 44, d. 547, l. 640b); two district towns in Vologda province (RGIA f. 1287, op. 44, d. 546, ll. 121–210b); and Tetiush (Kazan' province) (RGIA f. 1287, op. 44, d. 548, l. 170b).

94. Variations on this understanding appeared in reports about Kazan' and Arsk (Kazan' province) (RGIA f. 1287, op. 44, d. 548, l. 170b); several district towns in St. Petersburg province (RGIA f. 1287, op. 44, d. 550, ll. 139–390b); and Zvenigorod (Moscow province) (RGIA f. 1287, op. 44, d. 548, l. 224–240b).

95. That phrase is first used in the report from Arkhangel'sk (RGIA f. 1287, op. 44, d. 546, l. 30b); another variant was "is not practiced" (l. 196). In Kursk province, the law was "rarely observed." RGIA f. 1287, op. 44, d. 548, l. 126; in Saratov, "in the majority of cases in practice it is not observed." RGIA f. 1287, o. 44, d. 550, l. 1640b.

96. RGIA f. 1287, op. 44, d. 547, l. 930b; d. 548, ll. 180b, 1190b; d. 551, ll. 740b, 182.

97. RGIA f. 1287, op. 44, d. 551, l. 94.

98. RGIA f. 1287, op. 44, d. 547, l. 52; d. 550, l. 21.

99. RGIA f. 1287, op. 44, d. 550, l. 1020b.

100. RGIA f. 1287, op. 44, d. 546, ll. 187–870b. The Tambov governor also tied acceptance to the soul tax. RGIA f. 1287, op. 55, d. 551, l. 190b.

101. RGIA f. 1287, op. 44, d. 551, ll. 350b–36. Similarly, the report from Irkutsk suggested that too much administration was now falling on the *meshchane*, the poorest townspeople. To correct this, taking their responsibilities onto the town as a whole made sense. RGIA f. 1287, op. 44, d. 547, ll. 103–1030b.

102. RGIA f. 1287, op. 44, d. 550, ll. 10b–20b. The Kursk report agreed with the first part of this, noting that local *meshchanin* leaders were largely illiterate and uninvolved; eliminating them would be an active good. RGIA f. 1287, op. 44, d. 548, l. 1280b. The Kostroma report had a note similar to the second point, and suggested getting rid of the artisans society, as long its property went to help out poor artisans. RGIA f. 1287, op. 44, d. 548, l. 117.

103. RGIA f. 44, d. 550, l 2440b. The Kaluga report made a similar point, that the *meshchanin soslovie* did not make up "a mass united by general interests, but consists of individuals to so speak completely separate one from the other, solely united by common administration." RGIA f. 1287, op. 44, d. 548, ll. 32–320b. And the Arkhangel'sk report claimed that most societies owned no property, and barely existed as organizations. Removing them was no problem. RGIA f. 1287, op. 44, d. 546, l. 5.

104. RGIA f. 1287, op. 44, d. 547, l. 60.

105. RGIA f. 1287, op. 44, d. 547, l. 810b.

106. RGIA f. 1287, op. 44, d. 552, ll. 114–15.

107. RGIA f. 1287, op. 44, d. 551, ll. 510b–52.

108. RGIA f. 1287, op. 44, d. 551, ll. 590b–60.

109. RGIA f. 1287, op. 44, d. 551, l. 114. The Samara and Vladimir reports agreed that the *meshchanin* administration had a real function that would burden other administrations were it to be eliminated. RGIA f. 1287, op. 44, d. 550, d. 129; d. 546, l. 1080b.

110. RGIA f. 1287, op. 44, d. 550, ll. 106–1060b. The same was true in Voronezh. RGIA f. 1287, op. 44, d. 546, ll. 182–820b.

111. These phrases came from a special report for the capital itself. RGIA f. 1287, op. 44, d. 553, ll. 10–100b. But the report from St. Petersburg province included similar language, labeling those registered without acceptance as likely to be "unreliable." RGIA f. 1287, op. 44, d. 550, ll. 1470b–48.

112. He suggested *gorozhanin, obyvatel', zhitel'*, or *grazhdanin*. RGIA f. 1287, op. 44, d. 550, l. 11.

113. RGIA f. 1287, op. 44, d. 550, ll. 111–110b.

114. RGIA f. 1287, op. 44, d. 548, l. 1170b.

115. "Preobrazovanie gorodskikh soslovnykh uchrezhdenii," *Moskovskie vedomosti* (October 30, 1899): 2.

116. "K preobrazovaniiu gorodskikh soslovnykh uchrezhdenii," *Moskovskie vedomosti* (December 1, 1899): 2.

117. A. Samoilov, "K reorganizatsii gorodskikh soslovii," *Russkie vedomosti* (December 3, 1899): 4.

118. "Gorodskie sosloviia," *Nedelia* (November 21, 1899): 1543–46.

119. RGIA f. 1287, op. 44, d. 490, ll. 69–700b. The author of the letter was Nikolai Faustinovich Sekerskii.

120. Palibin, *Zakony o sostoianiiakh*, st. 561–80.

121. Corinne Gaudin, *Ruling Peasants: Village and State in Late Imperial Russia* (DeKalb: Northern Illinois University Press, 2007), 16–19, 170–72.

122. P. Sokal'skii, *Rost srednego sosloviia v Rossii kak sledstvie ostanovki v roste gosudarstvennoi territorii* (Odessa: Slavianskaia, 1907), 12–13.

123. I. N. Liubchetich, *Proekt organizatsii gorodskogo sosloviia i trudovykh kolonii* (Khar'kov: Pechatnoe delo, 1907), 3.

124. Liubchetich, *Proekt organizatsii gorodskogo sosloviia*, 6.

125. Liubchetich, *Proekt organizatsii gorodskogo sosloviia*, 8.

126. Liubchetich, *Proekt organizatsii gorodskogo sosloviia*, 7.

127. Liubchetich, *Proekt organizatsii gorodskogo sosloviia*, 7–10.

CHAPTER 6

1. TsGIASPb f. 222, op. 1, d. 428, ll. 30–300b, 49–50.

2. On mutual assistance and charity within *soslovie* societies, in the Reform era and after, see Sokolov, *Blagotvoritel'nost' v Rossii*, 506–10; Lindenmeyr, *Poverty Is Not a Vice*, 48–51, 57–60; O. K. Pavlova, "Soslovnoe prizrenie i blagotvoritel'nost' peterburgskogo kupechestva vo vtoroi polovine XIX-nachale XX v., in *Blagotvoritel'nost' v istorii Rossii: Novye dokumenty i issledovaniia*, ed. L. A. Bulgakova (St. Petersburg: Nestor-Istoriia, 2008), 288–89.

3. For example, Bradley, *Muzhik to Muscovite*, 249-337 and "The Moscow Workhouse and Urban Welfare Reform in Russia," *Russian Review* 41, no. 4 (October 1982): 427-44, and on the connection between urban poverty and crime, see Joan Neuberger, *Hooliganism: Crime, Culture, and Power in St. Petersburg, 1900-1914* (Berkeley: University of California Press, 1993), 235-43, 277-9. Nor was this unique to Russia; mobility has been tied to new concerns over local responsibility for social welfare elsewhere, as well. See Fideler, *Social Welfare in Pre-Industrial England*, 69–77.

4. *Materialy otnosiashchiesia do novogo obshchestvennogo ustroistva v gorodakh imperii*, I: 13

5. Blumenbakh, *Dokladnaia zapiska*, 3.

6. Evgenii Blumenbakh, *Grazhdanskoe sostoianie (soslovie) v Rossii, a v chastnosti v Pribaltiiskikh guberniiakh. Ego prava i obiazannosti* (Riga: Ernst Plates, 1899), 30.

7. *PSZ* 2, vol. 14, no. 12360 (May 18, 1839); vol. 21, no. 20415 (September 10, 1846).

8. *PSZ* 2, vol. 12, no. 10303 (June 3, 1837), § 188.

9. Among the laws are *PSZ* 2, vol. 9, no. 7273 (July 12, 1834), laying out definitions for those eligible for no-cost health care. For a later discussion, see RGIA f. 1287, op. 44, d. 432 (1894).

10. K. M. Goreleichenko, *Gde i kakie bol'nitsy dolzhno stroit' zemstvo? O gubernskoi zemskoi bol'nitse. Dom umalishennykh, bogadel'nia* (Ekaterinoslav: N. Ia. Pavlovskii, 1885), 6.

11. Bradley, *Muzhik and Muscovite*, 311.

12. *Otchet Moskovskoi meshchanskoi upravy o summakh postupivshikh na prikhod i izraskhodo-vannykh v 1870 godu* (Moscow: Iv. Smirnov, 1872), 22–23.

13. "O nedoimki v 1890b r. 9 ½ k., nakopivsheisia na meshchanskom obshchestva za lechenie meshchan g. Kalugi," *Doklad Kaluzhskoi gubernskoi zemskoi upravi* 20 (1885); "O nedoimki, chisliashcheisia za lechenie nesostoiatel'nykh meshchan, tsekhovykh i byvshikh oruzheinikov," *Doklady Tul'skoi gubernskoi zemskoi upravy* 8 (1872): 4.

14. RGIA f. 1287, op. 38, d. 423.

15. *PSZ* 3, vol. 1, no. 205 (May 26, 1881).

16. *Otchet Kronshtadtskoi meshchanskoi upravy o prikhode, raskhode i ostatke denezhnykh summ za 1883 god* (Kronshtadt: E. Barsova, 1885); *Otchet Kronshtadtskoi meshchanskoi upravy o prikhode, raskhode i ostatke denezhnykh summ za 1884 god* (Kronshtadt: A. E. Barsova, 1886), 36–37; *Otchet Kronshtadtskoi meshchanskoi upravy o prikhode, raskhode i ostatke denezhnykh summ za 1888 god* (Kronshtadt: Kronshtadtskii Vestnik, 1890).

17. Among them: Kazan' in 1870 (*Ustav Mariinskoi bogadel'ni s sirotskim otdeleniem Russkogo meshchanskogo obshchestva v g. Kazan', utverzhdennyi Gospodinom Ministrom Vnutrennikh Del, 17 Noiabria 1871 goda* (Kazan': Gubernskaia tipografiia, 1871[?]); Novgorod in 1870 (*Pravila o poriadke soderzhaniia Novgorodskoi gorodskoi obshchestvennoi bogadel'ni so bol'nichnim i sirots-kim pri nei otdeleniiami, utverzhdennye Novgorodskoi gorodskoi dumoi na osnovanii p. 10 st. 55 Gor. Polozh. 15 Iiunia 1870 g. (t. II ch. I Sv. Zak. 1876 g. st. 2002 p. 10* [Novgorod: N. I. Bogdanovskii, 1883]); Iaroslavl in 1898 (*Ustav meshchanskoi bogadel'ni v gor. Iaroslavle* [Iaroslavl': E. G. Fal'k, 1898]); and Tsaritsyn in 1913 (*Ustav doma prizreniia dlia bednykh meshchan Tsaritsynskogo mesh-chanskogo obshchestva, uchrezhdennogo v pamiat' trekhsotletiia Tsarstvovaniia doma Romanovykh* [Tsaritsyn: V. R. Fedorova, 1913]). According to A. I. Kupriianov, Siberian towns began to build such almshouses in the 1850s. See his *Russkii gorod v pervoi polovine XIX veka: obshchestvennyi byt i kul'tura gorozhan zapadnoi sibiri* (Moscow: AIRO-XX, 1995), 49. More examples are found in Goncharov and Chutchev, *Meshchanskaia obshchestva*, 94–95.

18. *Materialy dlia istorii Pokrovskoi Bogodel'ni i Aleksandro-Mariinskogo remeslennogo uchil-ishcha Moskovskogo meshchanskogo obshchestva*, vol. 1 (Moscow: I. M. Mashistov, 1892), 6–17, 22. Around 1865, the society spent 21,544 rubles on the almshouse. M. Shchepkin, *Biudzhety trekh Moskovskikh soslovii: kupecheskogo, meshchanskogo i remeslennogo* (Moscow: Grachev i Kop., 1865), 35. By 1870, the society was spending 42,587 rubles, 48 kopeks a year on the almshouse and additional aid. *Otchet Moskovskoi meshchanskoi upravy*, 22–23.

19. *Ustav Doma prizreniia prestarelykh i uvechnykh grazhdan i doma prizreniia maloletnikh bednykh S.-Peterburgskogo Meshchanskogo Obshchestva* (St. Petersburg: Iu. Vigandt, 1876).

20. I. E. Andreevskii and P. K. Ugriumov, *Gradskie bogadel'ni v S.-Peterburge* (St. Petersburg: Shreder, 1889), 39–41. The authors cautioned readers not to read too much into these numbers, as beds were still occupied by paying patients, as well (41–42).

21. In 1884, Kazan's Mariinskii almshouse had expenses of 11,640 rubles, 17 kopeks to aid 24 adults and 30 orphans. *Otchet o sostoianii Mariinskoi bogadel'ni s sirotskim otdeleniem*

kazanskogo russkogo meshchanskogo obshchestva za 1884 god (Kazan': Tipografiia Gubernskogo pravleniia, 1885), 2–4.

22. The almshouse of the Moscow *meshchanin* society was open only to Moscow *meshchane* (*Materialy dlia istoriia Pokrovskoi*, 28); that of the Moscow craft society was open only to crafts-people (in this case, additionally, those over 60 years of age, although younger residents could be accepted with permission of the board of directors) (*Pravila dlia popechitelei i Ekonoma Moskovskoi obshchestvennoi remeslennoi bogadel'ni* [Moscow: A. A. Levenson, 1893], 5); that of the Kazan' *meshchanin* society only to Kazan' *meshchane* (*Ustav Mariinskoi bogadel'ni*, 1); and that of the Iaroslavl' *meshchanin* society only to Iaroslavl' *meshchane* (*Ustav meshchanskoi bogadel'ni v gor. Iaroslavle*, 3). In contrast, Novgorod's almshouse was open "primarily to those from the local merchant and *meshchanin sosloviia*, men and women" (*Pravila o poriadke*, 1).

23. *Proekt ustava Doma prizreniia prestarelykh i uvechnykh grazhdan i Doma prizreniia malo-letnykh bednykh S. Peterburgskogo meshchanskogo obshchestva* (St. Petersburg: E. Treiman, 1875), 4–5.

24. *Ustav Mariinskoi bogadel'ni*, 7. Tsaritsyn's house was not to accept anyone with living relatives "able and obliged to take care of the aged and infirm ones." *Ustav doma prizreniia*, 2.

25. LVVA f. 1394, op. 1, d. 261, ll. 30b–4.

26. Blumenbakh, *Dokladnaia zapiska*, 5.

27. LVVA f. 1394, op. 1, d. 261, ll. 51–52.

28. LVVA f. 1394, op. 1, d. 261, l. 52.

29. LVVA f. 1394, op. 1, d. 261, ll. 11–120b, 79.

30. Blumenbakh, *Grazhdanskoe sostoianie*, 30.

31. The Kazan' report included a particularly long list of charitable institutions and funds. RGIA f. 1287, op. 44, d. 548, ll. 140b–15, 18. See also lists for Kostroma province (RGIA f. 1287, op. 44, d. 548, ll. 119–1990b); Vladimir province (RGIA f. 1287, op. 44, d. 546, ll. 880b–91); and Vologda province (RGIA f. 1287, op. 44, d. 546, l. 1210b.

32. See reports from Riazan' (RGIA f. 1287, op. 44, d. 550, ll. 1030b–4); Smolensk (RGIA f. 1287, op. 44, d. 550, l. 2440b).

33. RGIA f. 1287, op. 44, d. 551, l. 94.

34. Among them, in Samara (RGIA f. 1287, op. 44, d. 550, I. 122); Saratov (RGIA f. 1287, op. 44, d. 550, l. 163); and all towns in Irkutsk province (RGIA f. 1287, op. 44, d. 547, l. 92).

35. The estate societies may have taken a cue from parish almshouses; in St. Petersburg, at least, parish almshouses only accepted people who had lived in the parish for a certain amount of time—"in most at least a year, and in a few, at least half a year." P. P. Semenov and I. E. Andreevskii, *Prikhodskie blagotvoritel'nye obshchestva* (St. Petersburg: Vtoroe otdelenie Sobstvennoi E. I. V. Kantslarii, 1875), 47.

36. *Pravila dlia popechitelei*, 5.

37. *Materialy dlia istoriia Pokrovskoi*, 20.

38. Gaudin, *Ruling Peasants*, 16–17; also Burds, *Peasant Dreams*, 45–88.

39. For the 1849 law, see *PSZ* 2, vol. 24, no. 22955 (January 24, 1849).

40. *PSZ* 2, vol. 10, no. 8080 (May 22, 1835).

41. *PSZ* 2, vol. 28, no. 27491 (August 4, 1853).

42. RGIA f. 1287, op. 37, d. 1420, ll. 4–5.

43. GARO f. 49, op. 1, d. 393, ll. 1, 8, 11, 14 (1857). A second, similar, case made it out of Riazan' Province to the Ministry of Finance. RGIA f. 383, op. 20, d. 27018, ll. 1–20b, 11 (1857, 1859).

44. *PSZ* 2, vol. 34, no. 35235 (December 14, 1859).

45. *PSZ* 2, vol. 44, no. 47687 (November 17, 1869, published December 11, 1869), ss. 1–2. In both cases, the smaller unit ought to have its own *okladnyi list*.

46. *PSZ* 2, vol. 44, no. 47687, ss. 3–4.

47. *PSZ* 2, vol. 50, no. 55452 (December 30, 1875, published February 3, 1876).

48. RGIA f. 1287, op. 38, d. 1571, ll. 4, 5 (1873).

49. RGIA f. 1287, op. 38, d. 1571, l. 50b.

50. RGIA f. 1287, op. 38, d. 1571, l. 7.

51. RGIA f. 1287, op. 38, d. 1723, ll. 3–30b.

52. RGIA f. 1287, op. 38, d. 2448, l. 20b (1887).

53. RGIA f. 1287, op. 38, d. 1679, ll. 3–4.

54. NIOR f. 358, op. 24, d. 16, l. 1.

55. RGIA f. 1287, op. 38, d. 1723, ll. 3–30b.

56. Sunderland, *Taming the Wild Field*, 179, 181–82.

57. RGIA f. 1287, op. 38, d. 2040, ll. 1–2. Earlier laws had suggested that such freedom agreements were not valid, and that dead relatives were explicitly not supposed to be legally transferred to merchant societies. See *PSZ* 2, vol. 13, no. 11167 (April 25, 1838).

58. RGIA f. 1287, op. 38, d. 2040, l. 3.

59. Shchepkin, *Biudzhety*, 44.

60. LVVA f. 1394, op. 1, d. 312, l. [1].

61. LVVA f. 1394, op. 1, d. 312, l. [2]. Such conversations call into question arguments by some historians that bureaucracy kept workers from joining.

62. LVVA f. 1394, op. 1, d. 2691, "Metricheskie vypiski, spravki s mesta raboty, politsii i podpiski o ne sostoianie vo vrednykh sektakh predstavliaemye litsami pri pripiske k obshchestvu" (1898). The file is a collection of smaller paper files (that is, individual large pieces of paper folded in half serving as thin file folders), each for a different person, containing the documents that person brought in to get his or her acceptance. The files are unnumbered and unpaginated.

63. TsGIASPb f. 222, op. 1, d. 503, l. 5.

64. TsGIASPb f. 222, op. 1, d. 503, ll. 260–62, 347–49.

65. LVVA f. 1394, op. 1, d. 584, l. 5.

66. LVVA f. 1394, op. 1, d. 584, ll. 50b–6.

67. RGIA f. 1287, op. 38, d. 1674, ll. 4–7 (1879). Of course, the 10th revision was the last revision.

68. RGIA f. 1287, op. 38, d. 2270, ll. 1–2, 5–50b.

69. RGIA f. 1287, op. 38, d. 1674, ll. 54–55 (1885).

70. LVVA f. 1394, op. 1, d. 585, unpaginated newspaper clipping (*Pravitel'stvennyi vestnik* [June 9, 1893], 1).

71. LVVA f. 1394, op. 1, d. 585, unpaginated draft of record of the meeting of deputies, August 20, 1893.

72. LVVA f. 1394, op. 1, d. 585, unpaginated report of deputies meeting, December 30, 1914.

73. TsGIASPb f. 792, op. 4, d. 9, l. 21, passim.

74. *Proekt ustava Doma prizreniia*, 3, 3n.

75. RGIA f. 1287, op. 44, d. 432, l. 2.

76. TsIAM f. 54, op. 57, d. 61, ll. 1–26.

77. Nardova notes that the reform of town administration also allowed space for "constant collisions" between even different elements of town administration. See *Gorodskoe samouprav-lenie*, 168.

78. RGIA f. 1287, op. 37, d. 860, ll. 1–70b (1850–1852) (former sailors and their families).

79. The Tver' townsperson society protested the registry of 11 underaged freed serfs, but failed to move higher authorities in their favor. RGIA f. 1287, op. 37, d. 1655 (1856). In the late 1840s, the Moscow general governor asked that the right to registry without acceptance be eliminated for Moscow province, the Committee of Ministers refused his proposal. RGIA f. 1287, op. 38, d. 423, ll. 7–70b.

80. RGIA f. 1287, op. 38, d. 1675 (1879–81).

81. TsIAM f. 54, op. 57, d. 110, ll. 1–24. Something similar came to the attention of the MVD in 1896, when the Sebezh townsman A. K. Linkevich complained that his society would not release him for fear he would leave behind people they would have to take care of. See RGIA f. 44, d. 495, ll. 44–470b.

82. "O nedoimki chisliashcheisia," 4.

83. "O nedoimki v 18906," np.

84. RGIA f. 1287, op. 38, d. 112, ll. 30b, 70b (1862).

85. RGIA f. 1287, op. 38, d. 112, ll. 15–150b. This was the standard. When the Starobel'sk Town Duma complained about someone they believed should be excluded from their tax rolls they were blamed for the situation: they "committed an omission by their silence about the fact that Stoliarov did not petition for his permanent registry," despite that fact that it was their own "direct responsibility" to do so. RGIA f. 1287, op. 38, d. 835, ll. 6–60b (1868).

86. RGIA f. 1287, op. 38, d. 112, l. 16.

87. RGIA f. 1287, op. 38, d. 112., ll. 160b–17.

88. *PSZ* 2, vol. 40, no. 42643 (November 4, 1865, published December 14, 1865).

89. RGIA f. 1287, op. 38, d. 1813, ll. 1–10b.

90. The earlier law is *PSZ* 2, vol. 50, no. 55452 (December 30, 1875, published February 3, 1876). The ministries' correspondence is at RGIA f. 1287, op. 38, d. 1813, ll. 6–9, 10.

91. *PSZ* 2, vol. 53, no. 58358 (April 4, 1878).

92. LVVA f. 1394, op. 1, d. 592, unpaginated letters of 1891, 1894.

93. LVVA f. 1394, op. 1, d. 580, unpaginated report on the meeting of the Tax Commission, March 1891.

94. LVVA f. 1394, op. 1, d. 592, unpaginated letter of 1897.

95. RGIA f. 1287, op. 44, d. 432, ll. 4–50b (1894).

96. RGIA f. 1287, op. 37, d. 330, ll. 1–10b.

97. RGIA f. 1287, op. 37, d. 330, l. 10 (1846).

98. Blumenbakh particularly pointed out this fact as an example of how the current system was broken. See his *Dokladnaia zapiska*, 5.

99. P. V. Okhochinskii, *Bogodel'ni, priiuty dlia padshikh zhenshchin i deshevye kvartiry* (St. Petersburg: Vtoroe otdelenie Sobstvennoi E. I. V. Kantseliarii, 1877), 82.

100. *Sbornik svedenii po obshchestvennoi blagotvoritel'nosti*, vol. 2 (St. Petersburg: Gosudarstvennaia Tipografiia, 1883), 139.

101. Andreevskii and Ugriumov, *Gradskie bogadel'ni*, 41.

102. LVIA f. 937, op. 1, d. 1909, l. 11 (1835).

103. LVIA f. 937, op. 1, d. 3867, (1843–1844).

104. RGIA f. 1287, op. 38, d. 1674, ll. 28–290b (1883).

105. A copy was also sent to the MVD, and filed at RGIA f. 1287, op. 38, d. 1674, ll. 59–600b (1888).

106. Laws on schools include *PSZ* 2, vol. 10, no. 8419 (September 20, 1835) (the Moscow Practical Commercial Academy); vol. 11, no. 9097 (April 24, 1836), st. 8 (Gorygoretskii Agricultural School); vol. 14, no. 11971 (January 27, 1839) (St. Petersburg Higher Commercial School); vol. 23, no. 22257 (May 10, 1848) (Lazarevskii Institute of Eastern Languages).; vol. 26, no. 25269 (June 5, 1851) (School of Agriculture of the Free Economic Society); vol. 37, no. 38439 (July 3, 1862), st. 28 (St. Petersburg Practical Technological Institute); *PSZ* 3, vol. 23, no. 22819 (Aril 21, 1903) (Moscow Technical School and former Riga Polytechnical School). Laws on new professions include *PSZ* II vol. 14, no. 11934 (January 15, 1839) ("artists of the Imperial theaters"; vol. 19, no. 18290 (October 10, 1844) (service to the Russian-American Company for at least ten years); vol. 19, no. 1848 (November 28) (various kinds of chancellery work); vol. 20, no. 19085 (June 11, 1845) (military and state service); vol. 20, nos. 19227-8 (July 22, 1845) (merchants who received the Order of St. Vladimir or St. Anna); vol. 24, no. 23022 (February 16, 1849) (doctors, pharmacists, and veterinarians); vol. 34, no. 34480 (May 11, 1859), st. 8 (senior surveyors of the Ministry of State Domains); *PSZ* III, vol. 14, no. 10387 (February 28, 1894) (musicians certified by the Conservatory of the Imperial Russian Musical Society).

107. Blumenbakh, *Grazhdanskoe sostoianie*, 13.

108. Freeze, *Parish Clergy*, 385–88.

109. Frame, *School for Citizens*, 147–59,

110. Frieden, *Russian Physicians*, 210–26. Similarly, a major part of teacher's professional organization was mutual aid societies (in part because those were most easily allowed by the imperial state). See Christine Ruane, *Gender, Class, and the Professionalization of Russian City Teachers* (Pittsburgh: University of Pittsburgh Press, 1994), 96–103.

111. Korkunov, *Russkoe gosudarstvennoe pravo*, vol. 1, 275.

112. *Statisticheskie svedeniia o naselenii goroda Gatchiny v 1893 godu, sostavleny Gatchinskim dvortsovym upravleniem* (St. Petersburg: D. Semeniukov, 1894), 11, 3.

113. RGIA f. 1287, op. 37, d. 1985, ll. 3–4, 7–80b.

114. *PSZ* 2, vol. 41, no. 43848 (November 14, 1866).

115. LVVA f. 1394, op. 1, d. 593, unpaginated letters of August 10, 1891, and November 9, 1891. The phrase was "nikakaia obshchestvennaia vlast'."

116. RGIA f. 1287, op. 38, d. 2412, l. 1. The governor reported on the *starosta*'s complaint in 1888, but it is unclear exactly when the conversation or correspondence occurred. The conflict focused on two different verbs: to enter (*vstupit'*) and to be ascribed (*prichisliat'sia*).

117. RGIA f. 1287, op. 38, d. 2412, ll. 6–60b.

118. RGIA f. 1287, op. 38, d. 2412, ll. 2–20b.

119. RGIA f. 1287, op. 38, d. 2412, ll. 20b–3.

120. RGIA f. 1287, op. 38, d. 2412, l. 30b.

121. RGIA f. 1287, op. 38, d. 2412, l. 5.

122. RGIA f. 1287, op. 38, d. 2412, ll. 9–11.

123. *PSZ* vol. 31, no. 24441 (November 28), 1810.

124. RGIA f. 1287, op. 38, d. 2412, l. 190b.

125. RGIA f. 1287, op. 38, d. 2412, ll. 190b–200b.

126. RGIA f. 1287, op. 38, d. 2412, l. 230b.

127. RGIA f. 1287, op. 38, d. 2412, l. 29.

128. RGIA f. 573, op. 13, d. 14,923, l. 3.

129. RGIA f. 573, op. 13, d. 14,923, ll. 4–50b, letter from Ministry of Finance to Ministry of Internal Affairs seeking their approval of these measures, dated March 14, 1912; the Ministry of Internal Affairs agreed (l. 6, September 8, 1912); and the Ministry of Finance wrote back to the Volyn' Treasury with the decision (ll. 9–100b, October 19, 1912).

130. RGIA f. 573, op. 13, d. 14,923, ll. 11–110b, 17–170b.

131. RGIA f. 573, op. 13, d. 14,923, l. 11.

132. Bulkin, "Neskol'ko slov," 51.

133. M. P. Shchepkin, *Soslovnoe khoziaistvo Moskovskogo kupechestva* (Moscow: A. I. Mamontov i Ko., 1872), 2.

134. For example, at various point in the 1890s and into the early 1900s, the Vil'na *meshchanin* society refused to accept a number of former prisoners and exiles despite pressure from provincial authorities. LVIA f. 938, op. 10, d. 58, ll. 1–14; d. 181 continues the action into the early twentieth century.

CHAPTER 7

1. On Chekhov's ancestors and early biography, see Ronald Hingley, *A New Life of Anton Chekhov* (New York: Alfred A. Knopf, 1976), 1–33; Mikhail Chekhov, *Anton Chekhov: A Brother's Memoir*, trans. Eugene Alper (New York: Palgrave, 2010), 1–33; Rosamund Bartlett, *Chekhov: Scenes from a Life* (London: Free Press, 2004), 22–82.

2. On this statement and its significance for interpreting Chekhov, see Michael C. Finke, *Seeing Chekhov: Life and Art* (Ithaca: Cornell University Press, 2005), 6; Milton Ehre, "Introduction," *Chekhov for the Stage: The Sea Gull, Uncle Vanya, the Three Sisters, the Cherry Orchard* (Evanston: Northwestern University Press, 1992), 1; Leonid Livak, *The Jewish Persona in the European Imagination: A Case of Russian Literature* (Stanford: Stanford University Press, 2010), 275-76.

3. Hingley, *A New Life*, 13.

4. Bartlett, *Chekhov*, 41.

5. Anton Rubenstein told a similar story, in which a clerk became increasingly puzzled and insistent in his efforts to discover what exactly Rubenstein was. His initial answer of "an artist" did not satisfy the clear, for he was not a legally identifiable artist. Only when Rubenstein told him his father had been a merchant did the clerk happily write down "son of a merchant of the second guild" as an acceptable label for the already famous man. See a discussion of this in Lynn M. Sargeant, *Harmony and Discord: Music and the Transformation of Russian Cultural Life* (New York: Oxford University Press, 2011), 123.

6. Malashev also noted that his mother was descended from the *shliakhta*, but was orphaned early, and also essentially fell into serfdom. NIOR f. 178, d. 7557, ll. 1–2.

7. On the role of stewards or bailiffs, see Hoch, *Serfdom and Social Control*.

8. NIOR f. 178, d. 7557, ll. 3–5.

9. NIOR f. 178, d. 7557, l. 10.

10. Bulkin, "O moskovskikh remeslennikakh," *Russkii vestnik* 25, no. 2 (February 1860): 135.

11. NIOR f. 178, d. 7557, ll. 10–160b; 210b.

12. NIOR f. 178, d. 7557, l. 17.

13. NIOR f. 178, d. 7557, l. 36.

14. Chukmaldin, *Zapiski*, v. On the penny press and the theme of the individual made good, see Jeffrey Brooks, *When Russia Learned to Read: Literacy and Popular Literature, 1861-1917* (Princeton: Princeton University Press, 1985), 269–94.

15. Chukmaldin, *Zapiski*, viii.

16. For more on Sharapov, see Mikhail Suslov, "The Lost Chance of Conservative Modernization: S. F. Sharapov in the Economic Debates of the Late Nineteenth to the Early Twentieth Century," *Acta Slavica Iaponica* 31 (2012): 31–54.

17. Chukmaldin, *Zapiski*, 2, 60.

18. Chukmaldin, *Zapiski*, 19–21, 43.

19. Chukmaldin, *Zapiski*, 60.

20. Chukmaldin, *Zapiski*, 60–61.

21. Chukmaldin, *Zapiski*, 98.

22. Chukmaldin, *Zapiski*, 61, 66, 81.

23. Chukmaldin, *Zapiski*, 60–61.

24. Chukmaldin, *Zapiski*, 88.

25. Chukmaldin, *Zapiski*, 89.

26. Chukmaldin, *Zapiski*, 89.

27. Chukmaldin, *Zapiski*, 105–106, 121–22.

28. Chukmaldin, *Zapiski*, 163–64.

29. [Klepikov], *Avtobiografiia*, 3.

30. Stoliarov, *Zapiski*, 15.

31. [Klepikov,] *Avtobiografiia*, 3.

32. Stoliarov, *Zapiski*, 22, 29–30, 42.

33. Stoliarov, *Zapiski*, 44.

34. [Klepikov,] *Avtobiografiia*, 3.

35. [Klepikov,] *Avtobiografiia*, 3–4.

36. Stoliarov, *Zapiski*, 103.

37. Stoliarov, *Zapiski*, 104–105.

38. Stoliarov, *Zapiski*, 117.

39. Stoliarov, *Zapiski*, 163.

40. [Klepikov,] *Avtobiografiia*, 4.

41. Stoliarov, *Zapiski*, 111.

42. [Klepikov,] *Avtobiografiia*, 4–6.

43. For information on the family, see M. S. Sudovnikov, "Kupets i memuarist K. I. Klepikov," *Gertsenka: Viatskie zapiski* 9 (2005), electronic version, at www.herzenlib.ru/almanac/number/detail.php?NUMBER=number9&ELEMENT=gerzenka9_5_1, accessed July 6, 2012; and N. V. Obnorskaia, "Fenomen A. V. Chaianova cherez prizmu rodstvennykh traditsii: Pamiati Vasiliia Aleksandrovicha Chaianova (1925–2005)," at http://www.yar-genealogy.ru/alm2–24.html, accessed July 6, 2012.

44. [Klepikov,] *Avtobiografiia*, 6.

45. Stoliarov, *Zapiski*, 67.

46. Stoliarov, *Zapiski*, 122.

47. Stoliarov, *Zapiski*, 104.

48. Stoliarov, *Zapiski*, 143.

49. For example, noble status was confirmed by the process of ascription into the *rodoslovnye knigi*. See a description in Cavender, *Nests of Gentry*, 27–28.

50. *PSZ*, vol. 29, no. 22418 (January 1, 1807), st. 17. Ivanov pointed to this law as a sign of Alexander's particular attention to trade and merchants. See Ivanov, *Obozrenie prav*, 11–13.

51. Stoliarov, *Zapiski*, 106–107.

52. The other fees included 15 rubles for "town coffers"; 7 rubles, 92 kopeks for "maintenance of the Commercial Court"; and 5 rubles for "the Office of the Merchant Board, Commercial Council, Orphans and Common-Law Courts, and other expenses." TsIAM f. 3, op. 1, d. 168, l. 2.

53. TsIAM f. 5, op. 1, d. 511, l. 1200b.

54. TsGIASPb f. 222, op. 1, d. 1108, l. 281.

55. TsGIASPb f. 222, op. 1, d. 361, l. 140.

56. TsIAM f. 2, op. 1, d. 2065, ll. 1, 9, 14–140b, 18, 21–22, 350b.

57. TsGIASPb f. 222, op. 1, d. 360, l. 40.

58. TsGIASPb f. 222, op. 1, d. 507. l. 314.

59. TsIAM f. 6, op. 1, d. 12, no. 837. Similar cases in the same book include no. 1111, no. 1510, and no. 1450, in which a brother adopted his sister's two illegitimate children after her death.

60. TsGIASPb f. 222, op. 1, d. 361, l. 158.

61. TsGIASPb f. 222, op. 1, d. 361, l. 221.

62. TsGIASPb f. 222, op. 1, d. 421, l. 150.

63. "Sokrashchennaia zhizn'," 231.

64. Barkov, *Istoriia Vasiliia Dmitrievicha Barkova*.

65. TsIAM f. 2, op. 1, d. 1625, ll. 15–150b.

66. TsGIASPb f. 222, op. 1, d. 428.

67. TsIAM f. 6, op. 1, d. 12, household #653.

68. TsGIASPb f. 222, op. 1, d. 1108, l. 236.

69. Burds, *Peasant Dreams*. Such feelings were also common among the nascent worker intelligentsia, who often found themselves feeling doubly alienated: from their social equals by education and from their places of origin by work. On the latter, see Steinberg, *Proletarian Imagination*, 154–55, 178.

70. TsIAM f. 6, op. 1, d. 12, household # 935.

71. TsIAM f. 6, op. 1, d. 12, household # 1375.

72. TsGIASPb f. 222, op. 1, d. 361, l. 246.

73. Reports in *Biriuch Petrogradskkikh Gosudarstvennykh teatrov*, from http://sptl.spb.ru/biruch/index.php?view=issue&action=4&cmd=pages&id=221; http://sptl.spb.ru/biruch/index.php?view=issue&action=5&cmd=pages&id=279; and http://sptl.spb.ru/biruch/index.php?view=page&action=show&id=594; accessed August 16, 2012.

74. TsGIASPb f. 222, op. 1, d. 421, l. 212.

75. http://fgurgia.ru/showObject.do?object=166013502, accessed August 16, 2012.

76. TsGIASPb f. 222, op. 1, d. 421, l. 197.

77. A. I. Melua, "Kerblai Semen Aleksandrovich," *Entsiklopediia "Kozmonavtika,"* http://www.rtc.ru/encyk/biogr-book/10K/1264.shtml and http://www.troitskinform.ru/news/927.html, accessed August 15, 2012.

78. TsIAM f. 2, op. 1, d. 244, ll. 1, 36–37.

79. TsIAM f. 6, op. 1, d. 12, household #s 1035, 1149, 1445.

80. TsIAM f. 5, op. 1, d. 511, l. 115.

81. TsIAM f. 5, op. 1, d. 213, no. 873.

82. Cathy A. Frierson, *All Russia is Burning! A Cultural History of Fire and Arson in late Imperial Russia* (Seattle: University of Washington Press, 2002), esp. 108–28.

83. TsIAM f. 6, op. 1, d. 12, household #1699.

84. TsGIASPb f. 222, op. 1, d. 507, l. 86; d. 1108, l. 32.

85. *Otchet Odesskoi meshchanskoi upravy za 1865 god* (Odessa: P. Frantsov, 1866).

86. Laurie Bernstein, "Yellow Tickets and State-Licensed Brothels: The Tsarist Government and the Regulation of Urban Prostitution," in *Health and Society in Revolutionary Russia*, ed. Susan Gross Solomon and John F. Hutchinson (Bloomington: Indiana University Press, 1990), 45–65.

CONCLUSION

1. Gatrell, *A Whole Empire Walking*, 3, 55.

2. RGIA f. 573, op. 13, d. 15487, l. 1.

3. RGIA f. 573, op. 13, d. 15487, ll. 2–3.

4. RGIA f. 573, op. 13, d. 15487, ll. 6–60b.

5. The "Decree on the Abolition of *Sosloviia* and Civil Ranks," was released on November 11 (24), 1917, and is discussed in Sheila Fitzpatrick, "Ascribing Class: The Construction of Social Identity in Soviet Russia," *Journal of Modern History* 65, no. 4 (December 1993): 751 and elsewhere.

6. On the home front, and the ways that categorizing the population—often in ways that melded conceptions of *soslovie* with those of the nation—took on new import, see Peter Holquist, *Making War, Forging Revolution: Russia's Continuum of Crisis, 1914–21* (Cambridge, MA: Harvard University Press, 2002); and particularly Lohr, *Nationalizing the Russia Empire*.

APPENDIX

1. *Rossiiskii gosudarstvennyi arkhiv drevnikh aktov: Putevoditel'* vol. 3, part 1 (Moscow: RGADA, 1997), 38.

2. RGADA ff. 308, 691, 695, 705, 707, 712, 713, 742, 761, 764, 768, 778, 796, 807, 820, 828, 1069).

3. The relevant files are RGADA f. 778, op. 1, dd. 31, 160, 284, 285, 324, and 330.

4. TsIAM f. 397, op. 1, d. 121, "Tetrad 1795 goda dlia zapiski v Moskovskoe kupechestvo raznogo zvaniia liudei postupivshikh s kapitalom na 1796 god," numbering around 790 names of individuals who served as new heads of household. The *Notebook* includes some additional names, but in a curious document that appears to be a draft stuck in the middle of the notebook, with less description than the book as a whole. Those names have been excluded from the examination below. So too have the names of merchants from other towns who moved to Moscow.

5. TsIAM f. 2, op. 1, 3; f. 3, op. 1. These files are likely incomplete; a separate file in the archival collection lists 51 men and women who entered the society in 1851; the names in that list overlap with, but do not contain all of, the names listed in the archival registers. TsIAM f. 2, op. 3, d. 854.

6. TsIAM f. 5, op. 1, dd. 52–234, 238–41, 243–47, 250–51.

7. TsGIASPb f. 222, op. 1 holds the many records.

SELECTED BIBLIOGRAPHY

ARCHIVAL SOURCES

ARGO: Arkhiv Rossiiskogo geograficheskogo obshchestva

- f. XIV: Kazanskaia guberniia

GAIaO: Gosuarstvennyi arkhiv Iaroslavskoi oblasti

- f. 79: Iaroslavskoe gubernskoe pravlenie
- f. 100: Iaroslavskaia kazennaia palata
- f. 501: Iaroslavskaia gorodskaia duma

GARO: Gosudarstvennyi arkhiv Riazanskoi oblasti

- f. 4: Riazanskoe gubernskoe pravlenie
- f. 49: Riazanskaia gorodskaia duma

GASO: Gosudarstvennyi arkhiv Saratovskoi oblasti

- f. 2: Saratovskoe gubernskoe pravlenie
- f. 3: Saratovskaia gorodskaia duma
- f. 15: Saratovskii gorodskoi magistrat
- f. 28: Saratovskaia kazennaia palata
- f. 94: Saratovskaia meshchanskaia uprava

GATO: Gosudarstvennyi arkhiv Tverskoi oblasti

- f. 21: Tverskaia gorodskaia duma

LVIA: Lietuvos valstybes istorijos archyve

- f. 937: Vilenskaia gorodskaia duma
- f. 938: Vilenskaia gorodskaia uprava

LVVA: Latvijas Valsts Vestures Arhivs

- f. 1394: Rizhskaia podatnoe upravlenie

NIOR: Nauchno-issledovatel'skii otdel rukopisei Rossiiskoi gosudarstvennoi biblioteki

- f. 178: Muzeinoe sobranie
- f. 358: N. A. Rubakin

RGADA: Rossiiskii gosudarstvennyi arkhiv drevnykh aktov

- f. 291: Glavnyi magistrat
- f. 308: Moskovskaia ratusha i gorodovoi magistrat
- f. 691: Pereslavl'-Zalesskaia zemskaia izba, ratusha i provintsial'nyi magistrat
- f. 695: Sol'vychegodskaia zemskaia izba, ratusha i gorodovoi magistrat
- f. 705: Aleksinskaia zemskaia izba i ratusha
- f. 707: Astrakhanskaia ratusha i gubernskii magistrat
- f. 712: Vel'skaia ratusha
- f. 713: Brianskaia ratusha i gorodovoi magistrat
- f. 742: Kurskaia zemskaia izba, ratusha i gorodovoi magistrat
- f. 761: Rzhevskaia ratusha i gorodovoi magistrat
- f. 764: Rostovskaia zemskaia izba, ratusha i gorodovoi magistrat
- f. 768: Saratovskaia ratusha i gorodovoi magistrat
- f. 778: Suzdal'skaia ratusha i provintsial'nyi magistrat
- f. 796: Cheboksarskaia zemskaia izba, ratusha i gorodovoi magistrat
- f. 807: Iaroslavskaia ratusha i provintsial'nyi magistrat
- f. 820: Orlovskaia zemskaia izba, provintsial'nyi magistrate i slovesnyi sud
- f. 828: Velikoustiuzhskaia ratusha i provintsial'nyi magistrat
- f. 1069: Selenginskaia ratusha
- f. 1287: Sheremetevy, gr.

RGIA: Rossiiskii gosudarstvennyi istoricheskii arkhiv

- f. 383: Ministerstvo gosudarstvennykh imushchestv, Pervyi departament
- f. 398: Ministerstvo zemledeliia, Departament zemledeliia
- f. 472: Ministerstvo imperatorskogo dvora, Kantseliariia
- f. 515: Udel'nyi kontor
- f. 571: Ministerstvo finansov, Departament raznykh podatei i sbor
- f. 573: Ministerstvo finansov, Departament okladnykh sborov
- f. 1088: Sheremetevy, grafy
- f. 1151: Gosudarstvennyi sovet, Departament grazhdanskikh i dukhovnykh del
- f. 1286: Ministerstvo vnutrennikh del, Departament politsii ispolnitel'noi

- f. 1287: Ministerstvo vnutrennikh del, Khoziaistvennyi departament
- f. 1341: Senat, Pervyi departament
- f. 1374: Kantseliariia general-prokurora

TsGIASPb: Tsentral'nyi gosudarstvennyi arkhiv Sankt-Peterburga

- f. 222: Petrogradskaia meshchanskaia uprava
- f. 792: Petrogradskaia gorodskaia duma

TsIAM: Tsentral'nyi istoricheskii arkhiv Moskvy

- f. 2: Kupecheskoe otdelenie doma Moskovskogo gradskogo obshchestva
- f. 3: Moskovskaia kupecheskaia uprava
- f. 5: Moskovskaia meshchanskaia uprava
- f. 6: Moskovskaia remeslennaia uprava
- f. 32: Moskovskii gorodovoi magistrat
- f. 54: Moskovskoe gubernskoe pravlenie
- f. 397: Moskovskaia kupecheskaia gil'diia

PRIMARY SOURCES

Andreevskii, I. E., and P. K. Ugriumov. *Gradskie bogadel'ni v S.-Peterburge*. St. Petersburg: Shreder, 1889.

Androssov, V. P. *Statisticheskaia zapiska o Moskve*. Moscow: Semen Selivanovskii, 1832.

Arsen'ev, K. I. *Nachertanie statistiki Rossiiskogo gosudarstva*, vol. 1. St. Petersburg: Imperatorskii Vospitatel'nyi Dom, 1818.

Bakhmetev, P. "Osvobozhdenie moego ottsa ot krepostnago iga." *Trudy saratovskoi uchenoi arkhivnoi komissii* 31 (1914): 205–206.

Barkov, V. D. *Istoriia Vasiliia Dmitrievicha Barkova, potomstvennogo pochetnogo grazhdanina*. St. Petersburg: P. O. Iablonskii, 1902.

Beliaev, I. *Krest'iane na Rusi*. Moscow: Universitetskaia tipografiia, 1860.

Belliustin, I. S. *Description of the Clergy in Rural Russia: The Memoir of a Nineteenth-Century Parish Priest*. Trans. Gregory L. Freeze. Ithaca: Cornell University Press, 1985.

"Besedy s gorozhanami: o vliianii diety na chelovecheskii organizm." *Ekonom* 5, no. 117 (1843): 97–100.

Biriuch Petrogradskkikh Gosudarstvennykh teatrov. Electronic version at http://sptl.spb.ru/ biruch/index.php?view=issue&action=4&cmd=pages&id=221; http://sptl.spb.ru/biruch/ index.php?view=issue&action=5&cmd=pages&id=279; and http://sptl.spb.ru/biruch/ index.php?view=page&action=show&id=594; accessed August 16, 2012.

Blumenbakh, Evgenii G. *Grazhdanskoe sostoianie (soslovie) v Rossii, a v chastnosti v Pribaltiiskikh guberniiakh. Ego prava i obiazannosti*. Riga: Ernst Plates, 1899.

Blumenbakh, Evgenii G. *Dokladnaia zapiska i proekt reorganizatsii soslovnykh obshchestv i uchrezhdenii v Rossiiskom Gosudarstve*. Riga: V. F. Gekker, 1917.

Bobkov, F. D. "Iz zapisok byvshego krepostnogo cheloveka." In *Vospominaniia russkikh krest'ian XVIII-pervoi poloviny XIX veka*, ed. V. A. Kosheleva, 575–655. Moscow: Novoe literaturnoe obozrenie, 2006.

Bulkin. "Neskol'ko slov o Moskovskom meshchanskom obshchestve." *Russkii vestnik* 25, no. 1 (1860): 51–66.

Bulkin. "O moskovskom remeslennikakh." *Russkii vestnik* 25, no. 2 (February 1860): 133–49.

Eikhel'man, O. "Ocherki iz lektsii po russkomu gosudarstvennomu pravu." *Universitetskie izvestiia* 13, no. 6 (June 1890): Part II, 113–58.

Chekhov, Mikhail. *Anton Chekhov: A Brother's Memoir.* Trans. Eugene Alper. New York: Palgrave, 2010.

Chukmaldin, N. M. *Zapiski o moei zhizni.* Moscow: Tipo-litografiia A. V. Vasil'eva i Ko., 1902.

de Gurowski, A. *Russia as It Is.* New York: D. Appleton, 1854.

Dodonov, V. V. *Piatidesiatiletie Imperatorskogo Gatchinskogo Nikolaevskogo Sirotskogo Instituta (1837–1887).* St. Petersburg: V. S. Balashev, 1887.

Gan, I. A. *O nastoiashchem byte meshchan Saratovskoi gubernii.* St. Petersburg: Tipografiia Sht. Otd. Kor. Vnutr. Strazhi, 1860.

Gordeev, M. G. *Polveka unizhenii i bor'by.* Moscow: Trud i kniga, 1925.

Gordon, Abram Osipovich. "Po delu ob imushchestve Saratovskikh kupecheskogo i meshchanskogo soslovii." *Zapiski Senata* 97 (1888).

Goreleichenko, K. M. *Gde i kakie bol'nitsy dolzhno stroit' zemstvo? O gubernskoi zemskoi bol'nitse. Dom umalishennykh, bogadel'nia.* Ekaterinoslav: N. Ia. Pavlovskii, 1885.

Gorodovoe polozhenie s ob"iasneniiami. St. Petersburg: Tipografiia Ministerstva vnutrennikh del, 1873.

"Gorodskie sosloviia." *Nedelia* (November 21, 1899): 1543–46.

Griffiths, David, and George Munro, trans. and eds. *Catherine the Great's Charters of 1785 to the Nobility and the Towns.* Bakersfield: Charles Schlacks Jr., 1991.

Instruktsiia Kazennym palatam. Na vremia opyta edinstva kassy. St. Petersburg: V. N. Maikov, 1864.

Ivanov, Petr. *Obozrenie prav i obiazannostei Rossiiskogo kupechestva i voobshche vsego srednego sosloviia, s prisovokupleniem izlozheniia Postanovlenii, otnosiashchikhsia kak do sudebnykh mest, uchrezhdennykh dlia sosloviia sego, tak i lits izbiraemykh iz onogo k razlichnym dolzhnostiam.* Moscow: P. Kuznetsov, 1826.

"K preobrazovaniiu gorodskikh soslovnykh uchrezhdenii." *Moskovskie vedomosti* (December 1, 1899): 2.

Khavskii, P. *Sobranie zakonov o kuptsakh, meshchanakh, posadskikh i tsekhovykh, ili Gorodovoe Polozhenie so vkliucheniem zakonov predshestvuiushchikh i posleduiushchikh s 1766 po 1823 god.* St. Petersburg: Tipografiia pravitel'stvuiushchogo Senata, 1823.

[Klepikov, K. I.] *Avtobiografiia Konstantina Ignat'evicha Klepikova.* Viatka: Maisheeva, 1902.

Kratkii svod zamechanii zemskikh uchrezhdenii na proekt, sostavlennyi osoboi kommissiei pri Ministerstve finansov, o zamene podushnykh sborov pozemel'nym i podvornym nalogami. St. Petersburg: V. Bezobrazova i Komp., 1872.

Liubchetich, I. N. *Proekt organizatsii gorodskogo sosloviia i trudovykh kolonii.* Khar'kov: Pechatnoe delo, 1907.

Makarov, M. "Moskovskie meshchanskie slobody." *Moskovskie gubernskie vedomosti. Pribavlenie* (March 21, 1842): 249–52.

Materialy dlia istorii krepostnogo prava v Rossii. Berlin: Behr, 1872.

Materialy dlia istorii Pokrovskoi Bogodel'ni i Aleksandro-Mariinskogo remeslennogo uchilishcha Moskovskogo meshchanskogo obshchestva, vol. 1. Moscow: I. M. Mashistov, 1892.

Materialy dlia polnoi i sravnitel'noi statistiki Moskvy, vol. 1. Moscow: Universitetskaia tipografiia, 1841.

Materialy otnosiashchiesia do novogo obshchestvennogo ustroistva v gorodakh imperii. (Gorodovoe polozhenie 16 Iiunaia 1870 g). 2 vols. St. Petersburg: Ministerstvo vnutrennikh del, 1877.

"Meshchanskoe soslovie v Moskve (za 1845 god)," *ZhMVD* (January 1847): 71–86.

Miliukov, A. P. *Dobroe staroe vremia. Ocherk bylogo.* St. Petersburg: A. F. Bazunov, 1872.

Mysh, M. I. *Sbornik uzakonenii, pravitel'stvennykh i sudebnykh raz"iasnenii o meshchanskikh i remeslennykh upravleniiakh.* St. Petersburg: N. A. Lebedev, 1886.

Mysh, M. I. *O meshchanskikh i remeslennykh upravleniiakh. Sbornik uzakonenii, pravitel'stvennykh i sudebnykh raz"iasnenii,* 2nd ed. St. Petersburg: V. G. Avssenko, 1896.

Nastavlenie sel'skim prikazam po vysochaishemu o imperatorskoi familii Uchrezhdeniiu v udel'nykh imeniiakh uchrezhdennym. St. Petersburg: Tip. Gub. Pravleniia,1799.

Nikitenko, A. V. *Moia povest' o samom sebe.* St. Petersburg: A. S. Suvorin, 1900.

Novoe obshchestvennoe ustroistvo S. Peterburga. St. Petersburg: Ministerstvo Vnutrennykh Del, 1846.

"O litsakh, ne ob"iavivshikh kapitalov v kupechestvo." *Moskovskie gubernskie vedomosti* (March 2, 1846): 54–55.

"O Moskovskikh kuptsakh, ne ob"iavivshikh na 1841 god kapitalov i perechislennykh v meshchanstvo." *Moskovskie gubernskie vedomosti* (March 22, 1841): 84–86.

"O nedoimki, chisliashcheisia za lechenie nesostoiatel'nykh meshchan, tsekhovykh i byvshikh oruzheinikov." *Doklady Tul'skoi gubernskoi zemskoi upravy* 8 (1872): 1–8.

"O nedoimki v 18906 r. 9 ½ k., nakopivsheisia na meshchanskom obshchestva za lechenie meshchan g. Kalugi." *Doklad Kaluzhskoi gubernskoi zemskoi upravi* 20 (1885): np.

"O zamene podushnoi podati drugimi nalogami." *Materialy Gosudarstvennogo Soveta* 142 (1882).

Okhochinskii, P. V. *Bogodel'ni, priiuty dlia padshikh zhenshchin i deshevye kvartiry.* St. Petersburg: Vtoroe otdelenie Sobstvennoi E. I. V. Kantseliarii, 1877.

Otchet Kronshtadtskoi meshchanskoi upravy o prikhode, raskhode i ostatke denezhnykh summ za 1883 god. Kronshtadt: E. Barsova, 1885.

Otchet Kronshtadtskoi meshchanskoi upravy o prikhode, raskhode i ostatke denezhnykh summ za 1884 god. Kronshtadt: A. E. Barsova, 1886.

Otchet Kronshtadskoi meshchanskoi upravy o prikhode, raskhode i ostatke denezhnykh summ za 1888 god. Kronshtadt: Kronshtadtskii Vestnik, 1890.

Otchet Moskovskoi meshchanskoi upravy o summakh postupivshikh na prikhod i izraskhodovannykh v 1870 godu. Moscow: Iv. Smirnov, 1872.

Otchet o sostoianii Mariinskoi bogadel'ni s sirotskim otdeleniem kazanskogo russkogo meshchanskogo obshchestva za 1884 god. Kazan': Tipografiia Gubernskogo pravleniia, 1885.

Otchet Odesskoi meshchanskoi upravy za 1865 god. Odessa: P. Frantsov, 1866.

Palibin, M. N., ed. *Zakony o sostoianiiakh (Sv. Zak. t. IX, izd. 1899 g.) s dopolnitel-nymi uzakoneniiami, raz"iasneniiami Pravit. Senata i Sv. Sinoda, tsirkuliarami Ministerstva Vnutrennikh Del i alfavitnym ukazatelem.* St. Petersburg: N. K. Martinov, 1901.

Ploshinskii, L. O. *Gorodskoe ili srednee sostoianie russkogo naroda, v ego istoricheskom razvitii, ot nachala Rusi do noveishikh vremen.* St. Petersburg: V. P. Poliakov, 1852.

Polnoe sobranie zakonov Rossiiskoi Imperii. 45 vols. St. Petersburg: Tipografiia II Otdeleniia Sobstvennoi ego imperatorskogo Velichestva Kantseliarii, 1830.

Polnoe sobranie zakonov, 2nd collection. 55 vols. St. Petersburg: Tipografiia II Otdeleniia Sobstvennoi ego imperatorskogo velichestva kantseliarii, 1830–85.

Polnoe sobranie zakonov, 3rd collection. 33 vols. St. Petersburg: Gosudarstvennaia tipografiia, 1885-1916.

Pravila dlia popechitelei i Ekonoma Moskovskoi obshchestvennoi remeslennoi bogadel'ni. Moscow: A. A. Levenson, 1893.

Pravila o poriadke soderzhaniia Novgorodskoi gorodskoi obshchestvennoi bogadel'ni so bol'nichnim i sirotskim pri nei otdeleniiami, utverzhdennye Novgorodskoi gorodskoi dumoi na osnovanii p. 10 st. 55 Gor. Polozh. 15 Iiunia 1870 g. (t. II ch. I Sv. Zak. 1876 g. st. 2002 p. 10). Novgorod: N. I. Bogdanovskii, 1883.

"Preduvedomlenie." *Zhurnal obshchepoleznykh svedenii* 5, no. 1 (1837): 1-4.

"Preobrazovanie gorodskikh soslovnykh uchrezhdenii." *Moskovskie vedomosti* (October 30, 1899): 1–2.

Prigara, Andrei. *Opyt istorii sostoianiia gorodskikh obyvatelei v vostochnoi Rossii,* vol. 1. St. Petersburg: V. Golovin, 1868.

Proekt ustava Doma prizreniia prestarelykh i uvechnykh grazhdan i Doma prizreniia maloletnykh bednykh S.-Peterburgskogo meshchanskogo obshchestva. St. Petersburg: E. Treiman, 1875.

Rukovskii, I. P. "Istoriko-statisticheskie svedeniia o podushnykh podatiakh." In *Trudy Kommissii vysochaishe uchrezhdennoi dlia peresmotra sistemy podatei i sborov,* vol. 1, 1–216. St. Petesrburg: V. Bezobrazov i Komp., 1866.

Sal'nikov, I. "O gorodskikh obshchestvakh." *Russkii vestnik* 25, no. 2 (February 1860): Sovremennaia letopis', 227–38.

Samoilov, A. "K reorganizatsii gorodskikh soslovii." *Russkie vedomosti* (December 3, 1899): 4.

Sbornik Imperatorskogo russkogo istoricheskogo obshchestva. 148 volumes. St. Petersburg, 1867-1916.

Sbornik svedenii po obshchestvennoi blagotvoritel'nosti, vol. 2. St. Petersburg: Gosudarstvennaia Tipografiia, 1883.

Semenov, P. P., and I. E. Andreevskii. *Prikhodskie blagotvoritel'nye obshchestva.* St. Petersburg: Vtoroe otdelenie Sobstvennoi E. I. V. Kantslarii, 1875.

Semevskii, V. I. *Krest'iane v tsarstvovanie Imperatritsy Ekateriny II,* vol. 1. St. Petersburg: F. S. Sushchinskii, 1881.

Seredonin, S. M. *Istoricheskii obzor deiatel'nosti Komiteta Ministrov,* vol. 1. St. Petersburg: Gosudarstvennaia tipografiia, 1902.

Shch., A. "Nezateilivoe vospitanie. Iz zapisok A. Shch." *Atenei* 5–6 (1858): 490-503; 44-52; 120-29.

Shchepkin, M. P. *Biudzhety trekh Moskovskikh soslovii: kupecheskogo, meshchanskogo i remeslennogo.* Moscow: Grachev i Kop., 1865.

Shchepkin, M. P. *Soslovnoe khoziaistvo Moskovskogo kupechestva.* Moscow: A. I. Mamontov i Ko., 1872.

Shchepkin, M. P. *Opyty izucheniia obshchestvennogo khoziaistva i upravleniia gorodov,* vol. 1 Moscow: M. P. Shchepkin, 1882.

Shcherban', N. "Vospominaniia krepostnogo, 1800–1868." *Russkii vestnik* 130, nos. 7, 9 (July, September 1877): 320–47, 34–67.

Shipov, Nikolai. *Istoriia moei zhizni. Rasskaz byvshego krepostnogo krest'iana.* St. Petersburg: V S. Balashev, 1881.

Sokal'skii, P. *Rost srednego sosloviia v Rossii kak sledstvie ostanovki v roste gosudarstvennoi territorii.* Odessa: Slavianskaia, 1907.

"Sokrashchennaia zhizn' pokoinogo Sanktpeterburgskogo kuptsa pervoi gil'dii Aleksandra Petrovicha Berezina, pisannaia po ego vole nezadolgo do konchiny sego Bogom blagoslovennogo muzha i nakonets soglasno obrazu ego zhizni i deianii vnov' sochinennaia N. N., v pamiat' potomstva ego, po soizvoleniiu liubezneishei ego docheri i ziatia S.-Peterburgskogo vtoroi gil'dii kuptsa Petra Iakovlevicha i suprugi ego Pelagei Aleksandrovny Tufanovykh, urozhdennoi Berezinoi, v 1807 godu, Ianvaria dnia." *Russkii arkhiv* 17, no. 2 (1879): 227–35.

Statisticheskie svedeniia o naselenii goroda Gatchiny v 1893 godu, sostavleny Gatchinskim dvortsovym upravleniem. St. Petersburg: D. Semeniukov, 1894.

Stoliarov, Ivan. *Zapiski russkogo krest'ianina/Récit d'un paysan russe.* Paris: Institute d'études slaves, 1986.

Stupin, A. V. "Sobstvennoruchnye zapiski o zhizni akademika A. V. Stupina." *Shchukinskii sbornik* 3 (1904): 369–482.

Svod zakonov rossiiskoi imperii. Zakony o sostoianiiakh. St. Petersburg: II Otdeleniia Sobstvennoi ego Imperatorskogo Velichestva Kantseliarii, 1833.

Svod zakonov rossiiskoi imperii, vol. 14, *Ustavy o passportakh, o preduprezhdenii prestuplenii, o tsenzure, o soderzhashchikhsia pod strazhei, i o ssyl'nykh.* St. Petersburg: Tipografiia II otdeleniia sobstvennoi ego imperatorskogo velichestva Kantseliarii, 1857.

Travin, L. A. "Zapiski L. A. Travina." *Trudy Pskovskogo arkheologicheskogo obshchestva* 10 (1913–14): 37–129.

Ustav Doma prizreniia dlia bednykh meshchan Tsaritsynskogo meshchanskogo obshchestva, uchrezhdennogo v pamiat' trekhsotletiia Tsarstvovaniia doma Romanovykh. Tsaritsyn: V. R. Fedorova, 1913.

Ustav Doma prizreniia prestarelykh i uvechnykh grazhdan i doma prizreniia maloletnikh bednykh S.-Peterburgskogo Meshchanskogo Obshchestva. St. Petersburg: Iu. Vigandt, 1876.

Ustav Mariinskoi bogadel'ni s sirotskim otdeleniem Russkogo meshchanskogo obshchestva v g. Kazan', utverzhdennyi Gospodinom Ministrom Vnutrennikh Del, 17 Noiabria 1871 goda. Kazan': Gubernskaia tipografiia, 1871.

Ustav meshchanskoi bogadel'ni v gor. Iaroslavle. Iaroslavl': E. G. Fal'k, 1898.

Varadinov, N. *Istoriia Ministerstva Vnutrennikh del,* part II, book 2. St. Petersburg: Ministerstvo Vnutrennikh del, 1862.

Vileishis, Ia. M. *Sistematicheskii sbornik zakonov o meshchanskikh upravleniiakh s pozdneishimi raz"iasneniiami Pravitel'stvuiushchego Senata, Ministerstv i dr. uchrezhdenii.* Kherson: Khersonskoe gubernskoe pravlenie, 1914.

Voroponov, F. "Pasportnaia reforma." *Vestnik evropy* 20, no. 12 (December 1885): 845–57.

"Zapiska iz dela po voprosu o rasprostranenii sily 219 st. V t. Sv. Zak. ust. o pod. na vsekh meshchan perekhodiashchikh v kupechestvo, bez soglasiia obshchestva, s razresheniia Gg. Ministrov Finansov i Vnutrennikh Del." *Materialy Gosudarstvennyi sovet* 7 (1850): np.

SECONDARY SOURCES

Anisimov, E. V. *Podatnaia reforma Petra I: vvedenie podushnoi podati v Rossii, 1719–1728 gg.* Leningrad: Nauka, 1982.

Anisimov, E. V. "The Struggle with Fugitives during the Reform Period." Trans. Hugh F. Graham. *Soviet Studies in History* 28, no. 1 (Summer 1989): 59–77.

Avdeev, Aleksandre, Alain Blum, and Irina Troitskaia. "Peasant Marriage in Nineteenth-Century Russia." *Population-E* 59, no. 6 (2004): 721–64.

Avrutin, Eugene M. *Jews and the Imperial State: Identification Politics in Tsarist Russia.* Ithaca: Cornell University Press, 2010.

Bartlett, Roger. "Serfdom and State Power in Imperial Russia." *European History Quarterly* 33, no. 1 (2003): 29–64.

Bartlett, Rosamund. *Chekhov: Scenes from a Life.* London: Free Press, 2004.

Bater, James H. "Transience, Residential Persistence, and Mobility in Moscow and St. Petersburg." *Slavic Review* 39, no. 2 (June 1980): 239–54.

Becker, Seymour. *Nobility and Privilege in Late Imperial Russia.* DeKalb: Northern Illinois University Press, 1985.

Bernstein, Laurie. "Yellow Tickets and State-Licensed Brothels: The Tsarist Government and the Regulation of Urban Prostitution." In *Health and Society in Revolutionary Russia*, ed. Susan Gross Solomon and John F. Hutchinson, 45–65. Bloomington: Indiana University Press, 1990.

Black, Cyril E. "The Nature of Imperial Russian Society." *Slavic Review* 20, no. 4 (December 1961): 565–82.

Blum, Jerome. *Lord and Peasant in Russia from the Ninth to the Nineteenth Century.* Princeton: Princeton University Press, 1961.

Bohac, Rodney D. "The Mir and the Military Draft." *Slavic Review* 47, no 4 (Winter 1988): 652–66.

Bowman, Linda. "Russia's First Income taxes: The Effects of Modernized Taxes on Commerce and Industry, 1885–1914." *Slavic Review* 52, no. 2 (Summer 1993): 256–82.

Bradley, Joseph. *Muzhik and Muscovite: Urbanization in Late Imperial Russia.* Berkeley: University of California Press, 1985.

Bradley, Joseph. *Voluntary Associations in Tsarist Russia: Science, Patriotism, and Civil Society.* Cambridge, MA: Harvard University Press, 2009.

Breyfogle Nicholas. *Heretics and Colonizers: Forging Russia's Empire in the South Caucasus.* Ithaca: Cornell University Press, 2005.

Brooks, Jeffrey. *When Russia Learned to Read: Literacy and Popular Literature, 1861–1917.* Princeton: Princeton University Press, 1985.

Brower, Daniel. "Urbanization and Autocracy: Russian Urban Development in the First Half of the Nineteenth Century." *Russian Review* 42, no. 4 (October 1983): 377–402.

Brower, Daniel. *The Russian City between Tradition and Modernity, 1850–1900.* Berkeley: University of California Press, 1990.

Bulygin, I. A. "Osobaia kategoriia feodal'no zavisimykh krest'ian v pervoi chetverti XVIII v." In *Dvorianstvo i krepostnoi stroi Rossii XVI-XVIII vv.*, ed. N. I. Pavlenko, 190–212. Moscow: Nauka, 1975.

Burbank, Jane. *Russian Peasants Go to Court: Legal Culture in the Countryside, 1905–1917.* Bloomington: Indiana University Press, 2004.

Burbank, Jane. "An Imperial Rights Regime: Law and Citizenship in the Russian Empire." *Kritika* 7, no. 3 (Summer 2006): 397–431.

Burbank, Jane. "Thinking Like an Empire: Estate, Law, and Rights in the Early Twentieth Century." In *Russian Empire: Space, People, Power, 1700–1930*, ed. Jane Burbank and Mark von Hagen, 196–217. Bloomington: Indiana University Press, 2007.

Burds, Jeffrey. *Peasant Dreams & Market Politics: Labor Migration and the Russian Village, 1861–1905*. Pittsburgh: Univeristy of Pittsburgh Press, 1998.

Bushnell, John. "Did Serf Owners Control Serf Marriage? Orlov Serfs and Their Neighbors, 1773–1861." *Slavic Review* 52, no. 3 (Autumn 1993): 419–45.

Cavender, Mary W. *Nests of the Gentry: Family, Estate, and Local Loyalties in Provincial Russia.* Newark: University of Delaware Press, 2007.

Chernukha, V. G. *Pasport v Rossii, 1719–1917.* St. Petersburg: Liki Rossii, 2007.

Chulos, Chris J. *Converging Worlds: Religion and Community in Peasant Russia, 1861–1917.* DeKalb: Northern Illinois University Press, 2003.

Clowes, Edith W., Samuel D. Kassow, and James L. West, eds. *Between Tsar and People: Educated Society and the Quest for Public Identity in Late Imperial Russia.* Princeton: Princeton University Press, 1991.

Confino, Michael. "The *Soslovie* (Estate) Paradigm: Reflections on Some Open Questions." *Cahiers du monde russe* 49, no. 4 (2008): 681–700.

Coquin, François-Xavier. *La grande commission législative, 1767–1768. Les cahiers de doléances urbains (Province de Moscou).* Paris: Béatrice-Nauwelaerts, 1972.

de Madariaga, Isabel. *Russia in the Age of Catherine the Great.* New Haven: Yale University Press, 1981.

Dowler, Wayne. "Merchants and Politics in Russia: The Guild Reform of 1824." *Slavonic and East European Review* 65, no. 1 (January 1987): 38–52.

Druzhinin, N. P. *Meshchanskoe dvizhenie 1906–1917 gg.* Iaroslavl': Golos, 1917.

Dukes, Paul. *Catherine the Great and the Russian Nobility.* Cambridge: Cambridge University Press, 1967.

Ehre, Milton. "Introduction." In *Chekhov for the Stage: The Sea Gull, Uncle Vanya, The Three Sisters, The Cherry Orchard*, 1-16. Evanston: Northwestern University Press, 1992.

Engel, Barbara Alpern. *Between the Fields & the City: Women, Work, & Family in Russia, 1861–1914.* Cambridge: Cambridge University Press, 1996.

Eremian V. V., and M. V. Fedorov. *Mestnoe samoupravlenie v Rossii (XII-nachalo XX vv.)* Moscow: Novyi Iurist, 1998.

Etkind, Alexander. *Internal Colonization: Russia's Imperial Experience.* Cambridge: Polity, 2011.

Evtuhov, Catherine. *Portrait of a Russian Province: Economy, Society, and Civilization in Nineteenth-Century Nizhnii Novgorod.* Pittsburgh: University of Pittsburgh Press, 2011.

Field, Daniel. "The 'Great Reforms' of the 1860s." In *A Companion to Russian History*, ed. Abbott Gleason, 196–209. Maldon: Wiley-Blackwell, 2009.

Finke, Michael C. *Seeing Chekhov: Life and Art.* Ithaca: Cornell University Press, 2005.

Fitzpatrick, Sheila. "Ascribing Class: The Construction of Social Identity in Soviet Russia." *Journal of Modern History* 65, no. 4 (December 1993): 745–70.

Frank, Stephen P. "Popular Justice, Community and Culture among the Russian Peasantry, 1870–1900." *Russian Review* 46, no. 3 (July 1987): 239–65.

Franklin, Simon. "Printing and Social Control in Russia 1: Passports." *Russian History* 37 (2010): 208–37.

Freeze, Gregory L. "Social Mobility and the Russian Parish Clergy in the Eighteenth Century." *Slavic Review* 33, no. 4 (December 1974): 641–62.

Freeze, Gregory L. *The Russian Levites: Parish Clergy in the Eighteenth Century.* Cambridge, MA: Harvard University Press, 1977.

Freeze, Gregory L. *The Parish Clergy in Nineteenth-Century Russia: Crisis, Reform, Counter-Reform.* Princeton: Princeton University Press, 1983.

Freeze, Gregory L. "The Soslovie (Estate) Paradigm and Russian Social History." *American Historical Review* 91, no. 1 (February 1986): 11–36.

Frieden, Nancy Mandelker. *Russian Physicians in an Era of Reform and Revolution, 1856–1905.* Princeton: Princeton University Press, 1981.

Frierson, Cathy A. *All Russia is Burning! A Cultural History of Fire and Arson in Late Imperial Russia.* Seattle: University of Washington Press, 2002.

Gatrell, Peter. *A Whole Empire Walking: Refugees in Russia during World War I.* Bloomington: Indiana University Press, 2005.

Gaudin, Corinne. *Ruling Peasants: Village and State in Late Imperial Russia.* DeKalb: Northern Illinois University Press, 2007.

Genkin, L. B. *Pomeshchich'i krest'iane Iaroslavskoi i Kostromskoi gubernii pered reformoi i vo vremia reformy 1861 goda.* Iaroslavl': Iaroslavskii gos. pedinstitut, 1947.

Gerasimov, Ilya V. *Modernism and Public Reform in Late Imperial Russia: Rural Professionals and Self-Organization, 1905–30.* Houndmills: Palgrave Macmillan, 2009.

Gleason, Abbott. "The Terms of Russian Social History." In *Between Tsar and People: Educated Society and the Quest for Public Identity in Late Imperial Russia,* ed. Edith W. Clowes, Samuel D. Kassow, and James L. West, 15–27. Princeton: Princeton University Press, 1991.

Goncharov, Iu. M., and V. S. Chutchev. *Meshchanskoe soslovie zapadnoi sibiri vtoroi poloviny XIX-nachala XX v.* Barnaul: AzBuka, 2004.

Gorshkov, Boris. "Serfs on the Move: Peasant Seasonal Migration in Pre-Reform Russia, 1860–61." *Kritika* 1, no. 4 (Fall 2000): 627–56.

Hellie, Richard. *Enserfment and Military Change in Muscovy.* Chicago: University of Chicago Press, 1971.

Hellie, Richard. *Slavery in Russia, 1450–1725.* Chicago: University of Chicago Press, 1982.

Hellie, Richard. "The Impact of the Southern and Eastern Frontiers of Muscovy on the Ulozhenie (Law Code) of 1649 Compared with the Impact of the Western Frontier." *Russian History* 19, nos. 1–4 (1992): 99–115.

Hingley, Ronald. *A New Life of Anton Chekhov.* New York: Alfred A. Knopf, 1976.

Hittle, J. Michael. *The Service City: State and Townsmen in Russia, 1600–1800.* Cambridge, MA: Harvard University Press, 1979.

Hoch, Steven L. *Serfdom and Social Control in Russia: Petrovskoe, a Village in Tambov.* Chicago: University of Chicago Press, 1986.

Holquist, Peter. *Making War, Forging Revolution: Russia's Continuum of Crisis, 1914–21.* Cambridge, MA: Harvard University Press, 2002.

Hughes, Lindsey. *Russia in the Age of Peter the Great.* New Haven: Yale University Press, 1998.

Iakovlev, M. M. "Lobachev G. G." http://dic.academic.ru/dic.nsf/enc_music/4483/Лобачёв, accessed August 25, 2013.

Indova, E. I. "Moskovskii posad i podmoskovnye dvortsovye krest'iane v pervoi polovine XVIII v." In *Goroda feodal'noi Rossii,* 479–85. Moscow: Nauka, 1966.

Ivanova, N. A., and V. P. Zheltova. *Soslovno-klassovaia struktura Rossii v kontse XIX-nachale XX veka.* Moscow: Nauka, 2004.

Ivanova, N. A., and V. P. Zheltova. *Soslovnoe obshchestvo Rossiiskoi imperii.* Moscow: Novyi khronograf, 2010.

Johnson, Robert. *Peasant and Proletarian: The Working Class of Moscow in the Late Nineteenth Century.* New Brunswick: Rutgers University Press, 1979.

Kabuzan, V. M. *Narodonaselenie Rossii v XVIII-pervoi polovine XIX v.* Moscow: Akademiia Nauk SSSR, 1963.

Kabuzan, V. M. *Emigratsiia i reemigratsiia v Rossii v XVIII-nachale XX veka.* Moscow: Nauka, 1998.

Kamenskii, A. B. "Soslovnaia politika Ekateriny II," *Voprosy istorii* 3 (1995): 29-45.

Kamenskii, A. B. *Povsednevnost' russkikh gorodskikh obyvatelei.* Moscow: RGGU, 2006.

Kaplunovskii, A. P. "Meshchanskaia obshchina." In *Ocherki gorodskogo byta dorevoliutsionnogo Povol'zhia*, 294–415. Ul'ianovsk: Srednevolzhskii nauchnyi tsentr, 2000.

Kappeler, Andreas. *The Russian Empire.* Trans. Alfred Clayton. Harlow: Pearson, 2001.

Kassow, Samuel D. "The University Statute of 1863: A Reconsideration." In *Russia's Great Reforms, 1855–1881*, ed. Ben Eklof, John Bushnell, and Larissa Zakharova, 247–63. Bloomington: Indiana University Press, 1994.

Keep, John L. *Soldiers of the Tsar: Army and Society in Russia, 1462–1874.* Oxford: Clarendon Press, 1985.

Kenworthy, Scott Mark. *The Heart of Russia: Trinity-Sergius, Monasticism, and Society after 1825.* New York: Oxford University Press, 2010.

Kivelson, Valerie. "Muscovite 'Citizenship': Rights without Freedom." *Journal of Modern History* 74, no. 3 (September 2002): 465–89.

Kivelson, Valerie. *Cartographies of Tsardom: The Land and its Meanings in Seventeenth-Century Russia.* Ithaca: Cornell University Press, 2006.

Kliuchevskii, V. O. *Istoriia soslovii v Rossii.* In *Sochineniia v deviati tomakh*, vol. 6. Moscow: Mysl', 1989.

Kollmann, Nancy Shields. "Concepts of Society and Social Identity in Early Modern Russia." In *Religion and Culture in Early Modern Russia and Ukraine*, ed. Samuel H. Baron and Nancy Shields Kollman, 34–51. DeKalb: Northern Illinois University Press, 1997.

Kollmann, Nancy Shields. *By Honor Bound: State and Society in Early Modern Russia.* Ithaca: Cornell University Press, 1999.

Kotsonis, Yanni. *Making Peasants Backward: Agricultural Cooperatives and the Agrarian Question in Russia, 1861–1914.* New York: St. Martin's, 1999.

Kotsonis, Yanni. "'Face to Face': The State, the Individual, and the Citizen in Russian Taxation, 1863–1917." *Slavic Review* 63, no. 2 (Summer 2004): 221–46.

Kotsonis, Yanni. "'No Place to Go': Taxation and State Transformation in Late Imperial and Early Soviet Russia." *Journal of Modern History* 76, no. 3 (September 2004): 531–77.

Kozlova, N. V. *Pobegi krest'ian v Rossii v pervoi treti XVIII veka.* Moscow: Moskovskii universitet, 1983.

Kozlova, N. V. *Rossiiskoi absoliutizm i kupechestvo v XVIII veke.* Moscow: Arkheograficheskii tsentr, 1999.

Kozlova, N. V. *Liudi driakhlye, bol'nye, ubogie v Moskve XVIII veka.* Moscow: ROSSPEN, 2010.

Koznarsky, Taras. "Izmail Sreznevsky's *Zaporozhian Antiquity* as a Memory Project." *Eighteenth-Century Studies* 35, no. 1 (Fall 2001): 92–100.

Kupriianov, A. I. *Russkii gorod v pervoi polovine XIX veka: obshchestvennyi byt i kul'tura goro-zhan zapadnoi sibiri.* Moscow: AIRO-XX, 1995.

Kupriianov, A. I. *Gorodskaia kul'tura russkoi provintsii. Konets XVIII-pervaia polovina XIX veka.* Moscow: Novyi khronograf, 2007.

Kurmacheva, M. D. *Krepostnaia intelligentsiia Rossii vtoraia polovina XVIII-nachalo XIX veka.* Moscow: Nauka, 1983.

Lincoln, W. Bruce. "N. A. Miliutin and the St. Petersburg Municipal Act of 1846: A Study in Reform under Nicholas I." *Slavic Review* 33, no. 1 (March 1974): 55–68.

Lincoln, W. Bruce. Reform in Action: The Implementation of the Municipal Reform Act of 1846 in St Petersburg." *Slavonic and East European Review* 53, no. 131 (April 1975): 202–209.

Lindenmeyr, Adele. "A Russian Experiment in Voluntarism: The Municipal Guardianships of the Poor, 1894–1914." *Jahrbücher für Geschichte Osteuropas,* Neue Folge, 30, no. 3 (1982): 429–51.

Lindenmeyr, Adele. *Poverty Is Not a Vice: Charity, Society, and the State in Imperial Russia.* Princeton: Princeton University Press, 1996.

Livak, Leonid. *The Jewish Persona in the European Imagination: A Case of Russian Literature.* Stanford: Stanford University Press, 2010.

"Lobachev Vladimir Grigor'evich." http://pozhproekt.ru/enciklopediya/lobachev-vladimir-grigorevich, accessed August 25, 2013.

Lohr, Eric. *Nationalizing the Russian Empire: The Campaign against Enemy Aliens during World War I.* Cambridge, MA: Harvard University Press, 2003.

MacKay, John, trans. and ed. *Four Russian Serf Narratives.* Madison: University of Wisconsin Press, 2009.

Manchester, Laurie. *Holy Fathers, Secular Sons: Clergy, Intelligentsia, and the Modern Self in Revolutionary Russia.* DeKalb: Northern Illinois University Press, 2008.

Marrese, Michelle Lamarche. *A Woman's Kingdom: Noblewomen and the Control of Property in Russia, 1700–1861.* Ithaca: Cornell University Press, 2002.

Martin, Alexander M. *Enlightened Metropolis: Constructing Imperial Moscow, 1762–1855.* Oxford: Oxford University Press, 2013.

Melton, Edgar. "Household Economies and Communal Conflicts on a Russian Serf Estate, 1800–1817." *Journal of Social History* 26, no. 3 (Spring 1993): 569–77.

Melua, A. I. "Kerblai Semen Aleksandrovich." *Entsiklopediia "Kozmonavtika."* http://www.rtc.ru/encyk/biogr-book/10K/1264.shtml.

Mironov, B. N. *Russkii gorod v 1740–1860e gody: demograficheskoe, sotsial'noe i ekonomicheskoe razvitie.* Leningrad: Nauka, 1990.

Mironov, B. N. *Sotsial'naia istoriia Rossii perioda imperii, XVIII-nachalo XX v.: genezis lichnosti, demokraticheskoi sem'i, grazhdanskogo obshchestva i pravovogo gosudarstva.* 2 vols. St. Petersburg: D. Bulanin, 1999.

Munro, George E. *The Most Intentional City: St. Petersburg in the Reign of Catherine the Great.* Madison: Fairleigh Dickinson University Press, 2008.

Morrison, Daniel. *"Trading Peasants" and Urbanization in Eighteenth-Century Russia: The Central Industrial Region.* New York: Garland, 1987.

Nardova, V. A. *Gorodskoe samoupravlenie v Rossii v 60-kh-nachale 90-kh godov XIX v.* Leningrad: Nauka, 1984.

Obnorskaia, N. V. "Fenomen A. V. Chaianova cherez prizmu rodstvennykh traditsii: Pamiati Vasiliia Aleksandrovicha Chaianova (1925–2005)." At http://www.yar-genealogy.ru/alm2–24.html, accessed July 6, 2012.

Palat, Madhavan K. "Casting Workers as an Estate in Late Imperial Russia." *Kritika* 8, no. 2 (Spring 2007): 307–48.

Pavlova, O. K. "Soslovnoe prizrenie i blagotvoritel'nost' peterburgskogo kupechestva vo vtoroi polovine XIX-nachale XX v." In *Blagotvoritel'nost' v istorii Rossii: Novye dokumenty i issledovaniia,* ed. L. A. Bulgakova, 288–305. St. Petersburg: Nestor-Istoriia, 2008.

Pintner, Walter McKenzie. *Russian Economic Policy under Nicholas I.* Ithaca: Cornell University Press, 1967.

Pipes, Richard. *Russia under the Old Regime,* 2nd ed. London: Penguin Books, 1995.

Pomeranz, William. "'Profession or Estate'? The Case of the Russian Pre-Revolutionary *Advokatura.*" *Slavonic and East European Review* 77, no. 2 (April 1999): 240–68.

Raeff, Marc. "Preface." In *Catherine II's Charters of 1785 to the Nobility and the Towns,* trans. and ed. David Griffiths and George E. Munro, ix–xiii. Bakersfield: Charles Schlacks, 1991.

Randolph, John. *The House in the Garden: The Bakunin Family and the Romance of Russian Idealism.* Ithaca: Cornell University Press, 2007.

Ransel, David L. *A Russian Merchant's Tale: The Life and Adventures of Ivan Alekseevich Tolchenov, Based on His Diary.* Bloomington: Indiana University Press, 2009.

Rieber, Alfred. *Merchants and Entrepreneurs in Imperial Russia.* Chapel Hill: University of North Carolina Press, 1982.

Rieber, Alfred. "The Sedimentary Society." In *Between Tsar and People: Educated Society and the Quest for Public Identity in Late Imperial Russia,* ed. Edith W. Clowes, Samuel D. Kassow, and James L. West, 343–66. Princeton: Princeton University Press, 1991.

Roosevelt, Priscilla. *Life on the Russian Country Estate: A Social and Cultural History.* New Haven: Yale University Press, 1995.

Rozhkov, N. A. *Gorod i derevnia v russkoi istorii,* 2nd ed. Moscow: Skororpech, 1904.

Sargeant, Lynn. "A New Class of People: The Conservatoire and Musical Professionalization in Russia, 1861–1917." *Music & Letters* 85, no. 1 (2004): 41–61.

Sargeant, Lynn. *Harmony and Discord: Music and the Transformation of Russian Cultural Life.* New York: Oxford University Press, 2011.

Schrader, Abby M. *Languages of the Lash: Corporal Punishment and Identity in Imperial Russia.* DeKalb: Northern Illinois University Press, 2002.

Shabunin, E. A. "Obrazovanie i pravoslavie." www.orthedu.ru/kraeved/924-10.html, accessed August 25, 2013.

Smith, Alison K. "Authority in a Serf Village: Peasants, Managers, and the Role of Writing in Early Nineteenth Century Russia." *Journal of Social History* 43, no. 1 (Fall 2009): 157–73.

Smith, Alison K. "The Shifting Place of Women in Imperial Russia's Social Order." *Cahiers du Monde russe* 51, no. 2–3 (April-September 2010): 353–67.

Smith, Alison K. "'The Freedom to Choose a Way of Life:' Fugitives, Borders, and Imperial Amnesties in Russia." *Journal of Modern History* 83, no. 2 (June 2011): 243–71.

Smith, Alison K. "Freed Serfs without Free People: Manumission in Imperial Russia." *American Historical Review* 118, no. 4 (October 2013): 1029–51.

Snegirev, V. *Moskovskie slobody.* Moscow: Moskovskii rabochii, 1947.

Sokolov, A. R. *Blagotvoritel'nost' v Rossii kak mekhanizm vzaimodeistviia obshchestva i gosudarstva (nachalo XVIII-konets XIX vv.)* St. Petersburg: Liki Rossii, 2007.

Stanziani, Alessandro. "Serfs, Slaves, or Wage Earners? The Legal Status of Labour in Russia from a Comparative Perspective, from the Sixteenth to the Nineteenth Century." *Journal of Global History* 3 (2008): 183–202.

Steinberg, Mark D. *Proletarian Imagination: Self, Modernity, and the Sacred in Russia, 1910–1925.* Ithaca: Cornell University Press, 2002.

Steinwedel, Charles. "Making Social Groups, One Person at a Time: The Identification of Individuals by Estate, Religious Confession, and Ethnicity in Late Imperial Russia." In *Documenting Individual Identity: The Development of State Practices in the Modern World,* ed. Jane Caplan and John Torpey, 67–82. Princeton: Princeton University Press, 2001.

Stevens, Carol. *Soldiers on the Steppe: Army Reform and Social Change in Early Modern Russia.* DeKalb: Northern Illinois University Press, 1995.

Stites, Richard. *Serfdom, Society, and the Arts in Imperial Russia: The Pleasure and the Power.* New Haven: Yale University Press, 2005.

Sudovnikov, M. S. "Kupets i memuarist K. I. Klepikov." *Gertsenka: Viatskie zapiski* 9 (2005), electronic version, at www.herzenlib.ru/almanac/number/detail.php?NUMBER=number9 &ELEMENT=gerzenka9_5_1, accessed July 6, 2012.

Sunderland, Willard. "Peasants on the Move: State Peasant Resettlement in Imperial Russia, 1805–1830s." *Russian Review* 52, no. 4 (1993): 472–85.

Sunderland, Willard. *Taming the Wild Field: Colonization and Empire on the Russian Steppe.* Ithaca: Cornell University Press, 2004.

Suslov, Mikhail. "The Lost Chance of Conservative Modernization: S. F. Sharapov in the Economic Debates of the Late Nineteenth to the Early Twentieth Century." *Acta Slavica Iaponica* 31 (2012): 31–54.

Tolstaya, Sofia Andreevna. *My Life.* John Woodsworth and Arkadi Klioutchanski, trans. Ottawa: University of Ottawa Press, 2010.

Ulianova, Galina. "Merchant Women in Business in the Late Eighteenth and Early Nineteenth Centuries," trans. Roger Bartlett. In *Women in Eighteenth-Century Russian Culture and Society,1700-1825,* eds. Wendy Rosslyn and Alessandra Tosi, 144-67. Houndmills: Palgrave, 2007.

Vodarskii, Ia. E. *Issledovaniia po istorii russkogo goroda (fakty, obobshcheniia, aspekty).* Moscow: Institut rossiiskoi istorii RAN, 2006.

Werth, Paul W. *At the Margins of Orthodoxy: Mission, Governance, and Confessional Politics in Russia's Volga-Kama Region, 1827–1905.* Ithaca: Cornell University Press, 2002.

Werth, Paul W. "Between Particularism and Universalism: Metrical Books and Civil Status in the Russian Empire, 1800–1914," paper presented at Citizenship, Nationality, and the State in Imperial Russia and the Soviet Union Conference, Davis Center, Harvard University, 2004.

West, Sally. *I Shop in Moscow: Advertising and the Creation of Consumer Culture in Late Tsarist Russia.* DeKalb: Northern Illinois University Press, 2011.

Wirtschafter, Elise Kimerling. *From Serf to Russian Soldier.* Princeton: Princeton University Press, 1990.

Wirtschafter, Elise Kimerling. *Structures of Society: Imperial Russia's "People of Various Ranks."* DeKalb: Northern Illinois University Press, 1994.

Wirtschafter, Elise Kimerling. "Social Misfits: Veterans and Soldiers' Families in Servile Russia." *Journal of Military History* 59, no. 2 (April 1995): 215–35.

Wirtschafter, Elise Kimerling. *Social Identity in Imperial Russia*. DeKalb: Northern Illinois University Press, 1997.

Wirtschafter, Elise Kimerling. "Social Categories in Russian Imperial History." *Cahiers du monde russe* 50, no. 1 (2009): 231–50.

Worobec, Christine D. *Possessed: Women, Witches, and Demons in Imperial Russia*. DeKalb: Northern Illinois University Press, 2001.

Wortman, Richard. *The Development of a Russian Legal Consciousness*. Chicago: University of Chicago Press, 1976.

"Zabytaia 'Myslitel'naia mashina' professor A. N. Shchukareva." http://ukrainiancomputing. org/Shchukarev_r.html, accessed August 25, 2013.

Zaionchkovskii, P. A. *Voennye reform 1860-1870 godov v Rossii*. Moscow: Izdatel'stvo Moskovskogo Universiteta, 1952.

Zelnik, Reginald E. *Labor and Society in Tsarist Russia: The Factory Workers of St. Petersburg 1855–1870*. Stanford: Stanford University Press, 1971.